EMPLOYEE TRAINING AND DEVELOPMENT

Raymond A. Noe
Michigan State University

Irwin
McGraw-Hill

Boston   Burr Ridge, IL   Dubuque, IA   Madison, WI   New York   San Francisco   St. Louis
Bangkok   Bogotá   Caracas   Lisbon   London   Madrid
Mexico City   Milan   New Delhi   Seoul   Singapore   Sydney   Taipei   Toronto

This book is dedicated to the many who have helped to train and develop me along the way, including
My parents, Raymond J. and Mildred Noe
My wife, Ann, kids, Ray, Tim, and Melissa, and puppy, Rascal
The teachers who have shared their wisdom
The graduate students who have worked with me over the years

Irwin/McGraw-Hill

A Division of The McGraw-Hill Companies

EMPLOYEE TRAINING AND DEVELOPMENT

This book is printed on acid-free paper.

1 2 3 4 5 6 7 8 9 0 DOC/DOC 1 0 9 8

ISBN 0-07-059329-9

Vice president and editorial director: *Michael W. Junior*
Publisher: *Craig S. Beytien*
Senior sponsoring editor: *John E. Biernat*
Editorial assistant: *Erin Riley*
Marketing manager: *Ellen Cleary*
Project manager: *Karen Nelson*
Production associate: *Debra R. Benson*
Freelance design coordinator: *JoAnne Schopler*
Cover designer: *John Berry/Sis*
Supplement coordinator: *Marc Mattson*
Compositor: *Shepherd Incorporated*
Typeface: *10/12 Times Roman*
Printer: *R.R.Donnelley & Sons Company*

Library of Congress Cataloging-in Publication Data

Noe, Raymond A.
    Employee training and development / Raymond A. Noe
        p.   cm.
    Includes bibliographical references and index.
    ISBN 0–07–059329–9
    1. Employees--Training of.   I. Title.
    HF5549.5.T7N59   1998
658.3'124--dc21   98–3539

http://www.mhhe.com

Traditionally, training and development was not viewed as an activity that could help companies create "value" and successfully deal with competitive challenges. Today that view has changed. Companies that use innovative training and development practices are likely to report better financial performance than their competitors that do not. Training and development also helps a company to meet competitive challenges. For example, as companies attempt to expand into foreign marketplaces, their success will be determined by employees' ability to work in a new culture (the global challenge).

Customers are demanding high-quality products and services. As a result, employees must understand how to monitor and improve the quality of goods and services (a quality challenge). Many companies have decentralized operations and have employees working at home, as they travel, and at different hours. Companies are also trying to better utilize employees' talents through new work designs (such as work teams) and new technologies such as computer-assisted manufacturing processes (a high-performance work system challenge). Although many companies are interested in using high-performance work system practices including teams and computers, em-ployees may not possess the skill levels for these systems to be effective. For example, they may not have interpersonal skills to work in teams. Or they may lack math skills to use even the most basic quality control methods!

Training and development plays a key role in helping companies meet these challenges! To do so, companies need to train employees to work with persons from different cultures both in the United States and abroad. New technologies such as Web-based training and multimedia reduce the costs associated with bringing employees to a central location for training. At the same time, these training methods include the conditions necessary (practice, feedback, self-pacing, etc.) for learning to occur.

The role of training has broadened beyond training program design. Effective instructional training remains important, but training managers, human resource experts, and trainers are increasingly being asked to create systems to motivate employees to learn, create knowledge, and share that knowledge with other employees in the company.

Also, the employee–employer relationship has changed. Due to the rapidly changing business environment and competition that can quickly cause profits to shrink and skill needs to change, companies are reluctant to provide job security to employees. At the same time, as employees see downsizing take place (or experience it themselves!), they are reluctant to be fully committed to company goals and values. As a result, both employees and companies are concerned with developing future skills and managing careers. Companies want a work force that is motivated and productive, has up-to-date skills, and can quickly learn new skills needed to meet changing customer needs. Employees want to develop skills that not only are useful for their current jobs but are congruent with their personal interests and values. Employees are interested in developing skills that can help them remain employable with either their current employer or a future one. Given the increasing time demands of work, employees are also interested in maintaining balance between work and non work interests.

The chapter coverage of *Employee Training and Development* reflects the traditional as well as broadening role of training and development in organizations. Chapter 1 introduces the student to the role of training and development in companies. Chapter 2, " Strategic Training," discusses how training practices and the organization of the training function can support business goals. Because companies are interested in reducing costs, the amount of resources allocated to training is likely to be determined by how much training and development activities help the company reach business goals. Topics related to designing training programs are covered in Chapters 3 through 6. Chapter 3, "Needs Assessment," discusses how to identify when training is appropriate. Chapter 4, "Learning: Theories and Program Design," discusses the learning process and characteristics of a learning environment, while providing practical suggestions for designing training to ensure that learning occurs. Chapter 5, "Transfer of Training," emphasizes what should be done in the design of training and the work environment to ensure that training is used on the job. Chapter 6, "Training Evaluation," discusses how to evaluate training programs. Here the student is introduced to the con-

cepts of identifying cost-effective training as well as determining if training outcomes related to learning, behavior, or performance were reached. Chapters 7 and 8 cover training methods. Chapter 7, "Traditional Training Methods," discusses presentational methods (e.g., lecture), hands-on methods (e.g., on-the-job training, behavior modeling), and group methods (e.g., adventure learning). Chapter 8, "Use of New Technologies in Training," introduces the student to new technologies that are increasingly being used in training. These technology-based training methods include Web-based instruction, multimedia, and distance learning. Chapters 7 and 8 both conclude by comparing training methods on the basis of costs, benefits, and learning characteristics.

Employee development is covered in Chapter 9. This chapter introduces the student to developmental methods (assessment, relationships, job experiences, and formal courses). Topics such as 360-degree feedback and mentoring are discussed. Special issues in training and development are discussed in Chapter 10. These include cross-cultural training, diversity training, school-to-work programs, and skill-based pay. Chapters 11 and 12 deal with careers and career management. Chapter 11, "Careers and Career Management," emphasizes the changing nature of careers and the career management process. Chapter 12, "Special Challenges in Career Management," deals with special issues that trainers and managers face. These issues include skills obsolescence, plateauing, employee orientation and socialization, downsizing, outplacement, and retirement. Last, Chapter 13, "The Future of Training and Development," looks at how training and development might be different 10 or 20 years from now.

Employee Training and Development is based on my more than a dozen years of teaching training and development courses to both graduate and undergraduate students. From this experience, I realized that managers, consultants, trainers, and faculty working in a variety of disciplines (including education, psychology, business, and industrial relations) have contributed to research and practice of training and development. As a result, the book is based on research conducted in several disciplines while offering a practical perspective. The book is appropriate for students in a number of programs. It suits both undergraduate and master's-level training courses in a variety of disciplines.

Distinctive Features

There are several distinctive features of the book. First, my teaching experience taught me that students become frustrated if they do not see research and theory in practice. As a result, one distinctive feature of the book is that each chapter begins with an example of a company practice that relates to the material covered in the chapter. More examples of company practices are provided throughout the chapters.

A second distinctive feature of the book relates to the topical coverage. Some chapters relate to what I call instructional design (needs assessment, training methods, learning environment, transfer of training, and evaluation), employee development, and career management. Instructional design is still the "meat and potatoes" of training. But as the role of managers and trainers broadens, they are increasingly involved in developing employees and career management. For example, managers and trainers need to be concerned with cross-cultural training, managing diversity, outplacement, skills obsolescence, and 360-degree feedback systems—topics that fall outside the realm of instructional design.

The book begins with a discussion of strategic training. Why? Successful training efforts relate to the business goals and strategy. In successful, effective training, all aspects of training—including training objectives, methods, evaluation, and even who conducts the training—relate to the business strategy. More and more companies are demanding that the training function and training practices support business goals; otherwise training may be outsourced or face funding cuts. Although students in business schools are exposed to strategic thinking, students in psychology and education who go on to become trainers need to

understand the strategic perspective and how it relates to how the training function is organized and the type of training conducted.

Technology has not only changed the way we live and the way work is performed, but it also has influenced training practice. As a result, one chapter is devoted entirely to the use of new technologies in training such as Web-based instruction and multimedia.

The book reflects the latest "hot topics" in the training area. For example, topics such as corporate universities, competencies, continuous learning, and managing knowledge and intellectual capital are covered. Each chapter contains the most recent academic research findings and company practices.

Features Designed to Aid Learning

Employee Training and Development provides several features to aid learning:

1. Each chapter lists objectives that highlight what the student is expected to learn in that chapter.
2. In-text examples feature companies from all industries including service, manufacturing, and retail.
3. Discussion questions at the end of each chapter help students learn the concepts presented in the chapter and understand potential applications of the material.
4. Important terms and concepts used in training and development are boldfaced in each chapter. Key terms are identified at the end of each chapter. These key terms are important to help the student understand the language of training.
5. Application Assignments are useful for the students to put chapter content into practice. Most chapters include Application Assignments that require the student to use the World Wide Web.
6. Name and subject indexes at the end of the book help in finding key people and topics.

Acknowledgments

The author is only one of many important persons involved in writing a textbook. This first edition of this book would not have been possible without the energy and expertise of several persons. Editors Craig Beytein and John Biernat deserve kudos. Craig Beytein had enough confidence in my abilities as an author to ask me about this project. John Biernat provided me with the resources that I needed, gave me free reign to write the training book I wanted to write, and was always available to discuss ideas and answer questions. Erin Riley, John's assistant, did a masterful job of coordinating reviews, helping to choose the cover design, and made sure that completed manuscript made its way to the developmental editors. She performed her job with expertise despite the fact that she was newly employed. Karen Nelson, the project manager, made sure that my writing was readable and interpretable.

I take full responsibility for any errors, omissions, or misstatements of fact in this book. However, regardless of your impression of the book, it would not have been this good had it not been for the reviewers. Special thanks to the manuscript reviewers who provided me with detailed comments that helped to make the final version of the book a better product. These reviewers include

Howard J. Klein
Management Department
The Ohio State University

Ellen J. Mullen
Professional Studies in Education Development
Iowa State University

Steffanie L. Wilk
The Wharton School
Management Department
University of Pennsylvania

Marcie A. Cavanaugh
School of Industrial and Labor Relations
Cornell University

Joseph J. Martocchio
Institute of Labor and Industrial Relations
University of Illinois (Champaign)

Larry Fogli
Business and Economics Department
University of California (Berkeley)
CORE Corporation, President

B R I E F C O N T E N T S

CONTENTS

Chapter 13
The Future of Training and Development   339

1 INTRODUCTION TO EMPLOYEE TRAINING AND DEVELOPMENT

Objectives

After reading this chapter, you should be able to

1. Discuss the competitive challenges companies face and explain how training can help companies deal with these challenges.

2. Discuss various aspects of the instructional system design model.

3. Describe the amount and types of training occurring in U.S. companies.

4. Describe how much money is spent on training in U.S. companies and how the money is used.

5. Discuss the key roles and competencies required for training professionals.

6. Identify appropriate resources (e.g., journals, Web sites) for learning about training research and practice.

MIRAGE RESORTS USES TRAINING TO INCREASE ITS ODDS FOR SUCCESS

The ground rumbles and the sky explodes into orange flames as a simulated volcano erupts. The scene is the Mirage, a 3,000-guest hotel and gaming casino in Las Vegas. The name of the game here is not blackjack or craps but entertainment in countless forms. Besides the traditional slot machines and other types of gambling, the Mirage has several dolphins, which perform stunts for guests as well as for scientific study. The Mirage also is the home of the Royal White Tigers and magicians Siegfried and Roy. Mirage Resorts—which owns and operates several entertainment complexes (the Mirage, Golden Nugget, and Treasure Island)—draws

30 million visitors annually. The market for the consumer's entertainment dollar is very competitive with over 89 other casino/hotels located in Las Vegas alone, not to mention entertainment complexes in the United States and overseas, as in Lake Tahoe, Nashville, and Atlantic City and along the French Riviera. Competition in the United States has increased due to the development of casinos on Indian reservations, luring customers from cold-weather states such as Wisconsin and Minnesota to spend their gambling dollars locally rather than travel to Las Vegas.

Mirage Resorts has been very successful. Its return to investors has averaged 22 percent a year for the past 10 years, and the company has been recognized as one of America's most admired corporations. According to several trade publications, Mirage Resorts has the highest productivity among large casinos and hotels. The company's hotels have consistently maintained a 98.6 percent occupancy rate compared with 90 percent for other hotels in Las Vegas.

What is the key to this success? Mirage Resorts relies on customer service to generate repeat business. Considering that 58 percent of Treasure Island's revenue and 45 percent of the Mirage's revenue come from nongaming sources (a large proportion being room rentals), repeat visits are critical for success. Mirage Resorts believes that the key to customer service is to get employees enthusiastic about customer service.

Besides recruiting the best workers and keeping employees motivated through interesting job assignments and good working conditions, Mirage Resorts has made training a business priority. To develop its human resource practices (which include training), the company studied the human resource practices of more than 200 companies including hotels, casinos, restaurants, and manufacturing firms to determine practices that worked and those that did not—a practice known as benchmarking. As a result of this study the company places a high priority on training, spending approximately $8 million per year on it. Mirage Resorts invests in training both to improve employees' specific skills and to develop and prepare them for careers within Mirage Resorts. For example, training is used to provide employees with key skills and strategies necessary to succeed in their job and to please the customer. Blackjack dealers are taught how to shuffle cards, deal cards, pay out winnings, and recognize when cheating may be occurring. The company also maintains an extensive list of career opportunities detailing every job function and the minimum qualifications. The company provides the list not only to meet employees' career interests but to determine staffing needs for its new properties such as a $1.35 billion casino currently under construction. Mirage Resorts also invests in training designed to improve employees' nonwork lives. Courses range from wallpapering to nutrition to personal finance. Mirage believes that providing these types of courses will make employees more able to cope with nonwork life. Mirage thinks that by helping employees with their nonwork lives, they will become more committed to their jobs at Mirage Resorts.

In addition to training employees, managers receive extensive training. This training teaches the manager how to create a positive work environment for employees. For example, throughout the manager's training an emphasis is placed on explaining to employees not only what to do, but why something needs to be done. As a result of these extensive training offerings, employee relations are very positive at Mirage Resorts. ∎

Source: D. Anfuso, "Las Vegas Resort Bets on Training—and Wins," *Personnel Journal* (September 1995): 78–86; B. O'Reilly, "The Secrets of America's Most Admired Corporations: New Ideas, New Products," *Fortune* (March 3, 1997): 60–64.

Introduction

Mirage Resorts' success illustrates the key role that training can play in the effectiveness and competitiveness of U.S. businesses. **Competitiveness** refers to the company's ability to maintain and gain market share in an industry. Mirage Resorts' training practices have helped it gain a **competitive advantage** over competitors. That is, Mirage Resorts' training practices have helped the company provide service its customers value through providing employees with the knowledge and skills they need to be successful as well as motivating them to stay with the company and provide good service.

Note that training is one of several human resource management practices that can be used to increase a company's competitiveness. Other human resource management practices include recruiting employees, selecting employees, designing work, rewarding employees, and labor and employee relations. Chapter 2, "Strategic Training," details the importance placed on training in comparison to other human resource management practices. To be effective, training must play a strategic role in supporting the business.

Human resource management is one of several important functions in most companies. Other functions include accounting and finance, production and operations, research and development, and marketing. Keep in mind that although human resource management practices (such as training) can help companies gain a competitive advantage, the company needs to produce a product or provide a service that customers value. Without financial resources and physical resources (e.g., equipment) needed to produce products or provide services, a company will not survive!

The chapter begins by defining training and discussing how the training function has evolved. Next, the competitive challenges that companies face are addressed. These challenges influence the company's ability to successfully meet the needs of shareholders, the community, customers, employees, and other **stakeholders.** Stakeholders include all of the parties that have an interest in seeing that the company succeeds. The discussion of the competitive challenges highlights how training can help companies meet such challenges.

The second part of the chapter focuses on current trends in the training area. This section also introduces you to the trainer's role in a business and how the training function is organized. This section should help you understand current training practices, the types of jobs that trainers may perform, and the competencies needed to be a successful trainer (or, if you are a manager, to identify a successful trainer). The chapter concludes with an overview of the topics covered in the book.

What Is Training?

Training refers to a planned effort by a company to facilitate employees' learning of job-related competencies. These competencies include knowledge, skills, or behaviors that are critical for successful job performance. The goal of training is for employees to master the knowledge, skill, and behaviors emphasized in training programs and to apply them to their day-to-day activities. Recently it has been acknowledged that to gain a competitive advantage, training has to involve more than just basic skill development.[1] That is, to use training to gain a competitive advantage, training should be viewed broadly as a way to create intellectual capital. Intellectual capital includes basic skills (skills needed to perform one's job), advanced skills (such as how to use technology to share information with other employees), an understanding of the customer or manufacturing system, and self-motivated creativity. Intellectual capital is discussed further in Chapter 2. Keep in mind that traditionally most of the emphasis on training has been at the basic and advanced skill levels. But some estimate that soon up to 85 percent of jobs in the United States and Europe will require extensive use of knowledge. This requires employees to share knowledge and creatively use it to modify a product or serve the customer, as well as to understand the service or product development system.

Many companies have adopted this broader perspective, which is known as high-leverage training. **High-leverage training** is linked to strategic business goals and objectives, uses an instructional design process to ensure that training is effective, and compares or benchmarks the company's training programs against training programs in other companies.[2]

High-leverage training practices also help to create working conditions that encourage continuous learning. **Continuous learning** requires employees to understand the entire work system including the relationships among their jobs, their work units, and the company. (Continuous learning is similar to the idea of system understanding mentioned earlier.)[3] Employees are expected to acquire new skills and knowledge, apply them on the job, and share this information with other employees. Managers take an active role in identifying training needs and help to ensure that employees use training in their work. To facilitate the sharing of knowledge, managers may use informational maps that show where knowledge lies within the company (for example, directories that list what a person does as well as the specialized knowledge they possess) and use technology such as groupware or the Internet that allows employees in various business units to work simultaneously on problems and share information.[4] In Chapter 8 we will discuss how new technology such as the Internet and groupware are being used for training.

Republic Engineered Steels Inc., which manufactures carbon, alloy, and specialty steels, uses high-leverage training practices and continuous learning to gain a competitive advantage.[5] Republic has 10 plants in six states with its headquarters in Ohio. The company was founded in 1989, when LTV Steel Bar Division of the LTV Corporation was purchased by its employees through an employee stock ownership program initiated by the United Steelworkers of America and the company's management. Republic invests approximately $4 million a year on training programs, which is approximately 2 percent of its payroll. It provides employees with training and educational opportunities dealing with employee ownership issues as well as specific job-related skills. Topics that deal with employee ownership issues include how to read a profit and loss statement as well as differences between common and preferred stock options. There is a primer on Republic's operations. Courses are also offered in subjects such as problem-solving methods and statistical process control. All employees are trained on company time for one to six hours per week.

High-leverage training practices are one characteristic of companies considered to be **learning organizations.** A learning organization is one whose employees are continuously attempting to learn new things and apply what they have learned to improve product or service quality. Improvements do not stop when formal training is completed.[6] We will discuss learning organizations in more detail in Chapter 5.

This discussion is not meant to underestimate the importance of "traditional training" (a focus on acquisition of knowledge, skills, and abilities), but it should alert you that for many companies training involves more than a focus on acquiring skills.

Designing Effective Training

As mentioned above, high-leverage training involves use of instructional system design process to ensure that training is effective. The **instructional design process** refers to a systematic approach for developing training programs. Table 1–1 presents the six steps in this process. Step 1 is to conduct a needs assessment, which is necessary to identify if training is needed. Step 2 involves ensuring that employees have the motivation and basic skills necessary to master training content. Step 3 involves ensuring that the learning environment has the factors necessary for learning to occur. Step 4 involves ensuring that trainees apply the training content to their jobs. This involves having the trainee understand how to manage skill improvement as well as getting co-worker and manager support. Step 5 involves selecting the training methods. After a training need has been identified, the objectives of training written, and the type of learning environment identified, the next step is to select the type of training method. A wide variety of training methods to choose from includes traditional on-the-job training plus more recent developments such as virtual reality and the World Wide Web. Step 6 involves evaluation—determining whether training achieved the desired outcomes and/or financial benefits from training. As you will see, we use this process as a framework for organizing this book.

The development of a Web-based training program focusing on teaching managers skills needed to run effective business meetings provides a good example of use of the instructional design process. The first step of the process, needs assessment, involved determining that managers lacked skills for conducting effective meetings and helped to identify the type of meetings that managers were involved in. The needs assessment process involved interviewing managers and observing meetings. The needs assessment process also identified the most appropriate training method.

TABLE 1–1   Instructional Design Process

1. **Conducting Needs Assessment**
   Organizational analysis
   Person analysis
   Task analysis

2. **Ensuring Employees' Readiness for Training**
   Attitudes and motivation
   Basic skills

3. **Creating a Learning Environment**
   Identification of learning objective and training outcomes
   Meaningful material
   Practice
   Feedback
   Observation of others
   Administering and coordinating program

4. **Ensuring Transfer of Training**
   Self-management strategies
   Peer and manager support

5. **Selecting Training Methods**
   Presentational techniques
   Hands-on techniques
   Group techniques

6. **Evaluating Training Programs**
   Identification of training outcomes and evaluation design
   Cost-benefit analysis

Because the managers were geographically dispersed and had easy access to computers, and the company wanted a self-directed, self-paced program that the managers could complete during free time in their work schedule, the training designers and company management decided that Web-based training was the appropriate method. Because training was going to be conducted over the Web, the designers had to be sure that managers could access the Web and were familiar with tools for using the Web (e.g., Web browsers). This relates to determining the managers' readiness for training.

The next step was to create a positive learning environment on the Web. Designers made sure that the program objectives were clearly stated to the trainees and provided opportunities within the program for exercises and feedback. For example, trainees were asked to prepare an outline for the steps they would take to conduct an effective meeting. The designers built into the program a feedback system that indicated to the managers which of the steps they outlined were correct and which needed to be changed. The designers also built in assessment tests allowing the trainees to receive feedback through the program and to skip ahead or return to earlier material based on their scores on the tests. The assessment included a test of meeting skills that the managers completed both prior to and after completing the program. The assessment tests were stored in a data bank which the company could use to evaluate whether trainees' meeting skills improved from pretraining levels.

Why Is Training Important?

The opening vignette on Mirage Resorts illustrates how training can be used by companies to gain a competitive advantage. Typically, U.S. companies have not used training for this purpose. U.S. employers spend approximately $59 billion on formal training—only slightly more than 1 to 2 percent of their payroll.[7] Lack of investment in training is an often-cited reason why U.S. companies are losing market share to foreign competitors. For example, whereas 66 percent of German workers are involved in apprenticeship training programs, only two-tenths of 1 percent of U.S. workers are involved in similar programs.[8] On average, U.S. companies only spend about one-third as much as Japanese companies on training per year.[9] Some statistics also suggest that only 16 percent of U.S. employees have ever received any training from their employers!

    U.S. companies are starting to recognize the important role that training plays in competitiveness. For example, General Electric, U.S. Robotics, W. H. Brady, Texas Instruments, Andersen Consulting, and Federal Express all invest 3 to 5 percent of their payroll in training. Research supports the idea that investment in education and training is related to increases in productivity.[10] Training relates to competitiveness because it helps companies deal with the competitive challenges they are facing. Chapter 2, "Strategic Training," discusses how training can be used to help companies meet their business goals. Chapter 2 also discusses how the organization of the training department and the importance of training compared to other human resource management activities (such as staffing and compensation) is influenced by business strategy.

Using Training to Deal with Competitive Challenges

Companies face four competitive challenges: the quality challenge, the global challenge, the high-performance work system challenge, and the social challenge.[11] The **global challenge** involves expanding into global markets and preparing employees to work in foreign locations. The **quality challenge** involves meeting customers, service and product needs. The **social challenge** involves how to manage a diverse work force and improve employees' reading, writing, and math skills. The **high-performance work system challenge** involves integrating new technologies and work design. Each of these four challenges presents training needs, as we discuss next.

Training and the Global Challenge

Cross-cultural training is important to prepare employees and their families for overseas assignments. Cross-cultural training prepares employees and their families (1) to understand the culture and norms of the country they are being relocated to and (2) to return to the United States after their assignment. We will detail cross-cultural training in Chapter 10. Because the failure rate for expatriates (U.S. employees sent to work abroad) is higher than for European and Japanese expatriates, cross-cultural training is especially important.[12]

Additionally, U.S. companies must be willing to train foreign employees to win foreign business. Several companies bring foreign workers to the United States for training and then return them to their home country.[13] For example, Boeing brings workers from India and Poland to the United States. They return to their home country with needed knowledge in aircraft design and manufacturing.

Training and the Quality Challenge

Studies comparing U.S. competitiveness with that of other countries suggest that U.S. companies have failed to maintain industry leadership because of a decline in customers' perceptions of the quality of U.S. products. For example, U.S. factories' share of the semiconductor market has slipped from 57 to 36 percent.[14]

There is no universal definition of quality. The major differences in its various definitions relate to whether customer, product, or manufacturing process is emphasized. For example, quality expert W. Edwards Deming emphasized how well a product or service meets customer needs. Phillip Crosby's approach emphasizes how well the service or manufacturing process meets engineering standards.

The emphasis on quality is seen in the establishment of the **Malcolm Baldrige Quality Award** and the **ISO 9000** quality standards. The Baldrige award was created in 1987 by President Reagan to recognize U.S. companies' quality achievements and to publicize quality strategies.[15] To become eligible for the Baldrige, companies must complete a detailed application that consists of basic information about the firm, as well as an in-depth presentation of how it addresses specific criteria related to quality improvement. The categories and point values for the Baldrige award are found in Table 1–2. Note that the award recognizes the value of training by giving this category more possible points than all others except business results and customer satisfaction. Applications are reviewed by a board of examiners. Then applicants receive written evaluations summarizing their strengths, weaknesses, and needs for improvement.

The ISO 9000 criteria are similar to those for the Baldrige award. ISO 9000 is the name of a family of standards (ISO 9001, ISO 9002) that include 20 requirements for dealing with issues such as how to establish quality standards and document work processes. ISO 9001 is the most comprehensive standard because it covers product or service design and development, manufacturing, installation, and customer service. (ISO 9002 does not include design and devel-

TABLE 1–2   Categories and Point Values for the Malcolm Baldrige National Quality Award Examination

Leadership   **120**
The way senior executives create and sustain corporate citizenship, customer focus, clear values, and expectations and promote quality and performance excellence

Information Analysis   **75**
Management and effectiveness of the use of data and information to support customer-driven performance and market excellence

Strategic Planning   **55**
The way the company sets strategic direction, how it determines plan requirements, and how plan requirements relate to performance management

Human Resource Development and Management   **140**
Company's efforts to develop and utilize the work force and to maintain an environment conducive to full participation, continuous improvement, and personal and organizational growth

Process Management   **140**
Process design and control, including customer-focused design, product and service delivery, support services, and supply management

Business Results   **220**
Company's performance and improvement in key business areas (product, service, and supply quality, productivity, and operational effectiveness and related financial indicators)

Customer Focus and Satisfaction   **250**
Company's knowledge of the customer, customer service systems, responsiveness to customer, customer satisfaction

Total Points   **1,000**

Source: Based on Malcolm Baldrige National Quality Award 1997 Award Criteria (Gaithersburg, MD: National Institute of Standards and Technology, 1997).

opment.) These standards were developed by the International Organization for Standardization in Geneva, Switzerland.[16] To ensure high-quality products, many companies are requiring their suppliers to apply for the Baldrige Award and to achieve ISO 9000 certification. ISO 9000 has also been adopted as the national quality standard in nearly 100 countries including Austria, Switzerland, Norway, Australia, and Japan. For example, U.S. automakers hoping to win contracts from European Community customers need ISO 9000 certification.

Training can help companies meet the quality challenge by teaching employees statistical process control and other quality-related skills that they can use to build quality into a product, rather than fix the product or service after it has been delivered to the customer. **Total Quality Management (TQM)** can be defined as a cooperative form of doing business that relies on the talents and capabilities of both labor and management to continually improve quality and productivity.[17] As a result, the quality challenge has forced employers to also train employees and managers in the interpersonal skills necessary to work together to create high-quality products and services. For example, Nalco Chemical used quality training to increase its presence in the $2.9 billion wastewater management business.[18] Managers attended Phillip Crosby's quality training program; employees were trained in the same basic philosophies of quality as the managers so that they could take the same view and speak the same language as their customers. In addition, management closely reviewed how quality training related to specific aspects of each person's job. Managers made certain that employees understood why they were being trained to learn certain things and how training affected their jobs. Quality training is integrated with job training at Nalco. Salespersons learned not only to sell products to customers but also to anticipate customer problems and offer solutions. Nalco Chemical attributes its nearly 50 percent market share to quality training.

Training and the Social Challenge

Companies face several challenges as a result of social challenges related to changes in the work force—particularly the demographic and racial composition of the labor force, skill deficiencies, and changes in the employment contract and place of work. The U.S. labor force will be older and more culturally diverse than at any time in the past 40 years. By the year 2005, the median age of the labor force is expected to be approximately 40, compared with 1980's median age of 34.[19] It is also projected that by 2005 the work force will be 73 percent white, 12 percent black, 11 percent Hispanic, and 4 percent Asian and other minorities. The 20th-century work force will include the greatest proportion of women and minorities in U.S. history.[20] As Table 1–3 shows, companies can use this increased diversity to provide a competitive advantage. Training plays a key role in ensuring that employees can accept and work more effectively with each other, particularly with minorities and women. To successfully manage a diverse work force, managers and employees must be trained in a new set of skills including

1. Communicating effectively with employees from a wide variety of backgrounds.
2. Coaching and developing employees of different ages, educational backgrounds, ethnicities, physical abilities, and races.
3. Providing performance feedback that is free of values and stereotypes based on gender, ethnicity, or physical handicap.
4. Creating a work environment that allows employees of all backgrounds to be creative and innovative.[21]

TABLE 1–3   How Managing Cultural Diversity Can Provide Competitive Advantage

1. Cost argument	As organizations become more diverse, the cost of a poor job in integrating workers will increase. Those who handle this well will thus create cost advantages over those who don't.
2. Resource-acquisition argument	Companies develop reputations on favorability as prospective employers for women and ethnic minorities. Those with the best reputations for managing diversity will win the competition for the best personnel. As the labor pool shrinks and changes composition, this edge will become increasingly important.
3. Marketing argument	For multinational organizations, the insight and cultural sensitivity that members with roots in other countries bring to the marketing effort should improve these efforts in important ways. The same rationale applies to marketing to subpopulations within domestic operations.
4. Creativity argument	Diversity of perspectives and less emphasis on conformity to norms of the past (which characterize the modern approach to management of diversity) should improve the level of creativity.
5. Problem-solving argument	Heterogeneity in decisions and problem-solving groups potentially produces better decisions through a wider range of perspectives and more thorough critical analysis of issues.
6. System flexibility argument	An implication of the multicultural model for managing diversity is that the system will become less determinant, less standardized, and therefore more fluid. The increased fluidity should create greater flexibility to react to environmental changes (i.e., reactions should be faster and at less cost).

Source: T. H. Cox and S. Blake, "Managing Cultural Diversity: Implications for Organizational Competitiveness," *Academy of Management Executive* 5 (1991): 47.

Compounding the diversity of the work force are projections that the supply of individuals with the necessary education and skill will not meet the demands of jobs in the U.S. economy.[22] Most new jobs created will require higher levels of reading and writing skills. Two training problems are evident. First, new entrants to the labor market often lack appropriate skills. This means that companies will need to invest in basic skills training. Second, companies report that current employees' skill deficiencies in reading, math, and problem solving limit their ability to upgrade technology, redesign work, and improve the quality of their goods and services.[23] Also, research suggests that the skills that companies need include influence and interpersonal skills, communications skills, adaptability, personal management skills, and knowing how to learn.[24] Knowing how to learn is critical because the workplace demands that employees (1) understand their work and the way it fits into the mission of the entire organization, (2) be able to innovate to improve product and service quality, and (3) stay up to date with advances in service quality. Companies need to invest in training to improve employees' ability to learn.

The amount of work being done outside the traditional office or factory, known as **distributed work,** is increasing. Some estimates are that by year 2005 about 25 percent of the labor force will be engaged in distributed work.[25] Also, the **contingent work force**—which include part-time, temporary, and self-employed workers—is growing. This work force was estimated to include about 32 million persons in 1994, and has doubled in size over the past five years.[26] A key training issue that distributed work presents is to prepare managers and employees to coordinate their efforts so such work arrangements do not interfere with customer service or product quality. The increased use of contingent employees means that managers need to understand how to motivate employees who may actually be employed by a third party such as a temporary employee service or leasing agency.

Training and the High-Performance Work System Challenge

New technology causes changes in skill requirements and work roles and often results in redesigning work structures (e.g., using work teams).[27] For example, computer-integrated manufacturing uses robots and computers to automate the manufacturing process. The computer allows the production of different products simply by reprogramming the computer. As a result, laborer, material handler, operator/assembler, and maintenance jobs may be merged into one position. Computer-integrated manufacturing requires employees to monitor equipment and troubleshoot problems with sophisticated equipment, share information with other employees, and understand the relationships between all components of the manufacturing process.[28]

Through technology, the information needed to improve customer service and product quality becomes more accessible to employees. This means that employees are expected to take more responsibility for satisfying the customer and determining how they perform their jobs. One of the most popular methods for increasing employee responsibility and control is work teams. Work teams involve employees with various skills who interact to assemble a product or provide a service. Work teams may assume many of the activities usually reserved for managers, including selecting new team members, scheduling work, and coordinating activities with customers and other units in the company.

Improvements in microcomputers and software also have created new ways to store and find information. For example, the Internet and the World Wide Web (a user-friendly service on the Internet) allow employees to send and receive communications as well as to locate and gather resources including software, reports, still pictures, and video. The Internet also gives employees instant access to experts whom they may communicate with and "newsgroups," which are bulletin boards dedicated to areas of interest, where you can read, post, and respond to messages and articles. Internet sites also have home pages—mailboxes that identify the person or company and contain text, images, sounds, and even moving pictures! For example, the professional organization for training professionals (and an important resource for managers interested in training), the American Society for Training and Development (ASTD), has a home page on the Internet. (The address is http://www.astd.org.) From this page you can access articles that deal with specialized topics, purchase training materials, and register for the society's annual conference!

What role does training play? Employees need job-specific knowledge and basic skills to work with the equipment created with the new technology. Because technology is often used as a means to achieve product diversification and customization, employees must have the ability to listen and communicate with customers. Interpersonal skills, such as negotiation and conflict management, and problem-solving skills are more important than physical strength, coordination, and fine-motor skills—previous job requirements for many manufacturing and service jobs. Although technological advances have made it possible for employees to improve products and services, managers must give employees the power to make changes. That is, managers must learn to empower employees. **Empowerment** means giving employees responsibility and authority to make decisions regarding all aspects of product development or customer service.[29] Employees are then held accountable for products and services; in return, they share the rewards and losses of the results. For empowerment to be successful, managers must be trained how to link employees to resources within and outside the company (people, World Wide Web sites, etc.), help teams interact with teams and managers from other departments, and ensure that employees are updated on important issues and cooperate with each other. Employees must also be trained to understand how to use the Internet, World Wide Web, and other tools for communicating and gathering information.

For example, Owens-Corning Fiberglass renovated its Jackson, Tennessee, plant to utilize new glass-making technology.[30] The plant is an industry leader in fiberglass production. To meet environmental standards the plant uses a new blend of materials that do not cause air pollution. The plant also includes ergonomic devices that make it easier and safer for employees to complete a wide variety of tasks (e.g., open railroad car doors and lift heavy machinery). Self-managed work teams are used. A rigorous selection process ensures that employees have the ability to learn and get along with others. Cross-training of all team members is ongoing so team members will have the complete set of skills needed in the fiberglass-making process. **Cross-training** is training employees in all the skills needed to complete every task that the team is responsible for.

Snapshot of Training Practices

As we previously discussed, training can play a key role in helping companies gain a competitive advantage and successfully deal with competitive challenges. Before we discuss how training can be used to help companies meet their business objectives, training design, training methods, and other topics covered in the text, it is important to familiarize you with the amount and type of training that occurs in the United States. Also, you must understand what trainers do. To accomplish this, data regarding training practices (e.g., how much do companies spend on training, what type of training is occurring, who is being trained?) are presented for you. Next, we discuss the skills and competencies needed to be a trainer.

Training Facts and Figures

The snapshot of training practices we provide in this section is based on data collected from a number of different sources including surveys conducted by *Training* magazine, the American Society of Training and Develpment, and the Bureau of Labor Statistics.[31] Note that these data should be viewed as reasonable estimates of practices rather than exact facts. The generalizability of survey results of training practices to U.S. companies is somewhat limited because of potential biases in the survey methods used. For example, the *Training* survey is based on a questionnaire mailed to a scientifically determined sample (stratified random sample, to be precise), of 15,000 subscribers and nonsubscribers. The response rate was less than 11 percent. One source to consult for up-to-date news releases and training statistics is the Bureau of Labor Statistics' World Wide Web home page (visit http://www.stats.bls.gov).

Table 1–4 presents questions and answers about training practices. Of the dollars spent on training, 70 percent is for staff salaries, 7 percent for facilities and overhead, and 23 percent for expenditures related to seminars/conferences,

TABLE 1–4   Questions and Answers about Training Practices

Questions	*Answers*
What percentage of employers provide some formal training?	70%
How much do employers spend on training?	Between $50 and $60 billion
How much time do employees spend in employer-provided training?	29 hours
Which employees are most likely to receive employer-provided training?	Managers, professionals, and technical workers are more likely to receive training than laborers, machine operators, and nontechnical workers.
How do training expenditures vary by company size?	Small companies (50–99 employees) spend about one-third as much as large employers (500+ employees).
Does the amount of money spent vary by industry?	Yes. Transportation, communications, public utilities spend the most. Service, construction, and retail trades spend the least.
How much training is being outsourced (provided by outside staff such as consultants and schools)?	Most companies report they use both in-house and outside suppliers of training for all levels of employees. 50% of production worker training is done only by in-house staff; 23% of executive training is provided only by outside suppliers.

Source: Based on data reported in "Industry Report 1997," *Training* (October 1997): 37–79; L. J. Bassi and M.E. Van Buren, "The 1998 ASTD State of the Industy Report," *Training and Development* (January 1998):22-43, A. L. Gallagher, and E. Schroer, *The ASTD Training Book* (Alexandria, VA: American Society for Training and Development, 1996).

hardware, materials, and consultants. Note that although most employers provide formal training, 30 percent do not! While approximately 30 percent of managers and technical professionals receive employer-provided skill-improvement training, 16 percent or less of sales staff, clerical staff, and laborers receive any. If you broaden the definition of training to include any employment-related training (not limited to training provided by the employee's company), managers and professionals still receive over twice as much as employees in the service occupations or operators, fabricators, or laborers. Because the jobs that receive the most training require the most education, one way of interpreting this data is that educated workers are more likely to receive training. Given the greater role that line employees are beginning to play in designing and providing high-quality goods and services (recall the competitive challenges), the data suggest that companies are hurting their competitiveness by not investing more in training these employees.

Figure 1–1 shows the percentages of companies providing various types of training. The largest category—job-related skills—includes training that upgrades employees' skills or qualifies them for a job. Technical training courses account for the largest amount of training time. The second highest category, work place-related training, includes training in workplace policies that affect employees' relations or the work environment. Basic skills training occurs far less than other types of training. Although research indicates that there is a large mismatch between worker and job skill requirements, estimates indicate that many companies are not providing basic skills training. This suggests that many companies are attempting to do a better job of screening applicants for basic skills at the time of hire. The difficulty with this screening strategy is that the labor market for employees with the correct levels of basic skills is very competitive. Companies may

FIGURE 1–1

Percentages of companies providing various types of training

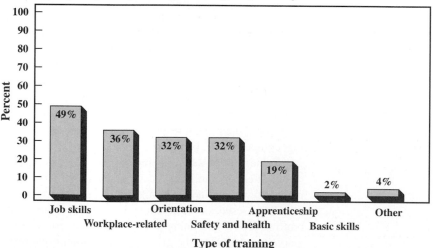

Source: Adapted from H. J. Franzis, D. E. Herz, and M. W. Harrigan, "Employer-Provided Training: Results of a New Survey," *Monthly Labor Review* (May 1995).

be forced to hire marginally qualified workers or attempt to function without appropriate levels of staffing—both are undesirable options!

The greatest training expenditures are in companies in transportation, communications, and public utilities. This is not surprising given the high level of government regulation and new technologies that have been introduced in these industries. The average total training budget for companies in these industries—approximately $610,000—is nearly two times the expenditure for companies in health or educational services, which has the lowest level of training expenditures. The low level of training expenditure in health and educational services may be the result of most employee training being provided through extensive college, university, and technical school education (e.g., medical education) employees in these industries receive prior to seeking employment.

Competencies and Positions of Training Professionals

Trainers can typically hold many jobs such as instructional designer, training administrator, or needs analyst. Each job has specific roles or functions. For example, one role of the needs analyst is to summarize data collected via interviews, observation, and even surveys to gain an understanding of training needs of a specific job or job family (a grouping of jobs). Special knowledge, skills, or behaviors—also called competencies—are needed to successfully perform each role. For example, the needs analyst must understand basic statistics and research methods to know what type of data to collect and to summarize data to determine training needs.

The most comprehensive study of training professionals has been conducted by the American Society for Training and Development (ASTD).[32] This study identified five key training roles and the important competencies required to be successful in each role. Table 1–5 shows these roles and competencies.

Note that many jobs involve training responsibilities. Specialists such as classroom instructors or instructional designers are usually primarily devoted to analysis, development, or instructional roles. Training department managers devote considerable time to the administrative and strategic role. Training managers may also still be involved in development or instructional roles, but—because of their administrative and strategic responsibilities—to a smaller extent than specialists. Human resource or personnel managers may also be required to complete many of the training roles, although their primary responsibility is in overseeing the human resources function of the company (e.g., staffing, recruiting, compensation, benefits).

Table 1–6 shows the average salaries for training professionals. Note that very rarely does anyone hold the highest-paying jobs (training manager, personnel manager) without having developed competencies in a number of training roles.

To be a successful training professional requires staying up to date on the current research and training practices. The American Society for Training and Development (ASTD), the primary professional organization for trainers, publishes

TABLE 1–5   Roles and Competencies of Trainers

Roles	*Competencies*
Analysis/Assessment Roles Researcher Needs analyst Evaluator	Industry understanding; computer competence; data analysis skill; research skill
Development Roles Program designer Materials developer Evaluator	Understanding of adult learning; skills in feedback, writing, electronic systems, and preparing objectives
Strategic Role Manager Marketer Change agent Career counselor	Career development theory; business understanding; delegation skills; training and development theory; computer competence
Instructor/Facilitator Role	Adult learning principles; skills related to coaching, feedback, electronic systems, and group processes
Administrator Role	Computer competence; skills in selecting and identifying facilities; cost-benefit analysis; project management; records management

Source: Based on P. McLagan, *Models for HRD Practice* (Alexandria, VA: American Society for Training and Development, 1989).

TABLE 1–6   Average Salaries for Training Professionals

Position	*Average Salary*
Executive level manager	$81,802
Manager of training	62,658
Specialists	
Classroom instructor	42,974
Instructional designer	47,658
Personnel manager	54,309
Managers (other than training or human resources)	63,610

Source: Adapted from R. Ganzel, "Winner Take All," *Training* (November 1997): 40–54.

Training and *Development* and *Human Resource Development Quarterly,* two good sources of current research and training practices. *Training* magazine, published by Lakewood Publications, is also a good source of information regarding training practices. More rigorous scientific studies of training practices are published in journals such as *Personnel Psychology, Journal of Applied Psychology,* and *Academy of Management Journal.*

Organization of This Book

What is training? Why is it important? What do training professionals do? How much training occurs in U.S. companies? Who is receiving training? How is the training function organized? This chapter answered these questions and offered a broad perspective of training. Chapter 2 discusses how a company's business strategy influences training practices and the organization of the training department.

The next chapters in the book address specific training issues. Chapters 3 through 8 address different aspects of the instructional system design model, the model used to guide the development of training. (See Table 1–1.) Chapter 3 deals with how to determine training needs. Chapter 4 discusses the important issue of learning—specifically, how to create an environment conducive to learning within the training session. Chapter 5 addresses transfer of training— that is, how to ensure that the training environment and the work setting are conducive to the use of knowledge and skills acquired in training. Chapter 6 introduces you to how to evaluate a training program. Chapters 7 and 8 discuss training methods. Chapter 7 looks at traditional training methods such as lecture, behavior modeling simulation, and role play. Chapter 8 examines new training methods that have developed from applications of new technology—for example, Web-based training, virtual reality, and intelligent tutoring systems.

Chapter 9 addresses the important issue of employee development. In Chapter 9, four approaches used to develop employee assessments, assignments, relationships, and courses and formal programs are discussed. Chapter 10 deals with special topics in training and development including ethics and legal issues, diversity training, cross-cultural training, and the relationship between training and other human resource management practices. Chapters 11 and 12 introduce you to such career issues as understanding what a career is, the systems companies use to manage careers, and concerns in career management such as plateauing, socialization, downsizing, and outplacement. Chapter 13, "The Future of Training and Development," discusses how the role of training in organizations may change in the future.

Students should be aware of several important features of the book. Each chapter begins with chapter objectives. These objectives (1) highlight what the student should learn from each chapter and (2) preview the topics. Next comes an opening vignette—an example of a company practice related to the chapter topics. Company examples are liberally used through each chapter to help you see how theory and research in training are put into practice. Each chapter ends with key terms, discussion questions, and application assignments. Key terms are related to important concepts emphasized in the chapter. Discussion questions and application assignments can facilitate learning through interacting with other students and actually trying to develop and conduct various training applications. Many application assignments require the use of the World Wide Web, a valuable source of information on training practices.

Key Terms

competitiveness   3
competitive advantage   3
stakeholders   3
training   3
high-leverage training   4
continuous learning   4
learning organizations   5
instructional design process   5
global challenge   7
quality challenge   7
social challenge   7

high-performance work system
  challenge   7
Malcolm Baldrige Quality
  Award   8
ISO 9000   8
Total Quality Management
  (TQM)   10
distributed work   12
contingent work force   12
empowerment   13
cross-training   13

Discussion Questions

1. Describe the four competitive challenges that companies face. How can training help companies deal with these competitive challenges?

2. What steps are included in the instructional design model? What step do you think is most important? Why?

3. How has training helped Mirage Resorts deal with competitive challenges?

4. Why do you think that managers and professionals receive more training than core employees (employees directly involved in providing service or manufacturing products)? Do you think this trend will continue? Why?

5. Which of training professionals' five roles do you believe is most difficult to learn? Which is easiest?

6. How might technology influence the importance of training professionals' roles? Can technology reduce the importance of any of the roles? Can it result in additional roles?

7. Describe the training courses that you have taken. How have they helped you? Provide recommendations for improving the courses.

Application Assignments

1. Go to the American Society for Training and Development (ASTD) home page on the World Wide Web. The address is www.astd.org. Investigate the links on the home page. One link is to *Training and Development,* the ASTD journal. Find an article related to training. Summarize the main topic of the article and identify how it relates to course topics or topics covered in this text.

2. Conduct a phone or personal interview with a manager. Ask her to describe the role that training plays in her company.

3. Conduct a phone or personal interview with a training manager. Ask him to discuss how training has changed in the past five years and how he believes it will change in the future.

Endnotes

1. J. B. Quinn, P. Anderson, and S. Finkelstein, "Leveraging Intellect," *Academy of Management Executive* 10 (1996): 7–27.

2. A. P. Carnevale, "America and the New Economy," *Training and Development Journal* (November 1990): 31–52.

3. J. M. Rosow and R. Zager, *Training the Competitive Edge* (San Francisco: Jossey-Bass, 1988).

4. L. Thornburg, "Accounting for Knowledge," *HR Magazine* (October 1994): 51–56; T. A. Stewart, "Mapping Corporate Brainpower," *Fortune* (October 30, 1995): 209.

5. Republic Engineered Steels Inc., "Office of the American Workplace, Best Practices Clearinghouse," http://www.fed.org/fed/uscompanies/labor, February 7, 1995.

6. D. Senge, "The Learning Organization Made Plain and Simple," *Training and Development Journal* (October 1991): 37–44.

7. Industry Report 1997, *Training* (October 1997): 33–76.

8. A. P. Carnevale, "Enhancing Skills in the New Economy," in *The Changing Nature of Work,* ed. A. Howard (San Francisco: Jossey-Bass, 1995): 238–51; M. McCain, "Apprenticeship Lessons from Europe," *Training and Development* (November 1994): 38–41; "Best in the World Training Practices," *Training and Development* (June 1994): 52–57.

9. *Chicago Tribune,* June 14, 1992, sec. 1, p. 18.

10. K. Kelley, "Motorola: Training for the Millennium," *Business Week,* (March 28, 1994): 158–172.

11. R. A. Noe, J. H. Hollenbeck, B. Gerhart, and P. Wright, *Human Resource Management,* 2d ed. 1997 (Burr Ridge, IL: Irwin/McGraw Hill).

12. R. L. Tung, "Expatriate Assignments: Enhancing Success and Minimizing Failure," *Academy of Management Executive* 1 (1987): 117–126.

13. G. P. Zachary, "Stalled U.S. Workers' Objections Grow as More of Their Jobs Shift Overseas," *The Wall Street Journal* (October 9, 1995): A2, A9.

14. T. A. Stewart, "The New American Century: Where Do We Stand," *Fortune* (Spring/Summer 1991): 12–23.

15. U.S. Department of Commerce, *1995 Application Guidelines: Malcolm Baldrige National Quality Award* (Gaithersburg, MD: National Institute of Science and Technology, 1995).

16. S. L. Jackson, "What You Should Know about ISO 9000," *Training* (May 1992): 48–52; Bureau of Best Practices, *Profile of ISO 9000* (Boston: Allyn & Bacon, 1992); "ISO 9000 International Standards for Quality Assurance," *Design Matters* (July 1995): http://www.best.com/ISO 9000/att/ISONet.html/.

17. J. R. Jablonski, *Implementing Total Quality Management: An Overview* (San Diego: Pfeiffer, 1991).

18. "Sales and Quality: Market Share Is Tied to Learning Skills for Both," *Total Quality* (February 1995): 5.

19. U.S. Bureau of Labor Statistics, *Employment and Earnings* (Washington, DC: U.S. Government Printing Office, January 1990); J. Jarratt and J. Coates, "Employee Development and Job Creation," in *Employees, Careers, and Job Creation,* ed. M. London (San Francisco: Jossey-Bass, 1995): 1–25; M. Cohen, *Labor Shortages as America Approaches the Twenty-First Century* (Ann Arbor: University of Michigan Press, 1995); C. Duff, " Wage-Benefit Increase Sets 14-Year Low," *The Wall Street Journal* (February 14, 1996): A2.

20. U.S. Bureau of Labor Statistics, *Occupational Outlook Handbook* (Washington, DC: U.S. Government Printing Office, May 1992).

21. M. Loden and J. B. Rosener, *Workforce America!* (Burr Ridge, IL: Business One Irwin, 1991).

22. A. P. Carnevale, L. J. Gainer, and A. S. Meltzer, *Workplace Basics: The Essential Skills That Employers Want* (San Francisco: Jossey-Bass, 1990).

23. National Association of Manufacturers/Towers Perrin Company, *Today's Dilemma: Tomorrow's Competitive Edge* (Washington DC: National Association of Manufacturers, 1991); Center for Public Resources, *Basic Skills in the U.S. Workforce* (Washington, DC: Center for Public Resources, 1983).

24. Carnevale, Gainer, and Meltzer, *Workplace Basics.*

25. P. Brotherton, "Stuff to Suit," *HR Magazine* (December 1995): 50–55.

26. J. Alley, "The Temp Biz Boom: Why It Is Good," *Fortune* (October 16, 1995): 53, 55; Jarratt and Coates, "Employee Development and Job Creation."

27. P. Choate and P. Linger, *The High-Flex Society* (New York: Knopf, 1986); P. B. Doeringer, *Turbulence in the American Workplace* (New York: Oxford University Press, 1991).

28. K. A. Miller, *Retraining the American Workforce* (Reading, MA: Addison-Wesley, 1989).

29. T. J. Atchison, "The Employment Relationship: Untied or Re-Tied," *Academy of Management Executive* 5 (1991): 52–62.

30. F. Bleakley, "How an Outdated Plant Was Made New," *The Wall Street Journal* (November 10, 1994): B1, B11.

31. L. J. Bassi and M.E. Van Buren, "The 1998 ASTD State of the Industy Report," *Training and Development* (January 1998):22-43, A. L. Gallagher, and E. Schroer, The ASTD Training Data Book, (Alexandria, VA: American Society for Training and Development, 1996); Bureau of Labor Statistics, "BLS Reports on the Amount of Employer-Provided Formal Training," press release (July 10, 1996); "1997 Industry Report," Training 33 (October 1997): 37–79; H. J. Frazis, D. E. Herz, and M. W. Harrigan, "Employer-Provided Training: Results from a New Survey," Monthly Labor Review 5 (May 1995): 3–17.

32. W. J. Rothwell, "Selecting and Developing the Professional HRD Staff," in *The ASTD Training and Development Handbook,* 4th ed., ed. R. L. Craig (New York: McGraw-Hill, 1996): 48–76; P. A. McLagan, *The Research Report: Models for HRD Practice* (Alexandria, VA: American Society of Training and Development, 1989).

2 STRATEGIC TRAINING

Objectives

After reading this chapter, you should be able to

1. Discuss how business strategy influences the type and amount of training in a company.

2. Explain how the role of training has changed.

3. Explain how changes in work roles influence training.

4. Discuss how a company's staffing and human resource planning strategies influence training.

5. Explain the training needs created by concentration, internal growth, external growth, and disinvestment business strategies.

6. Discuss the advantages and disadvantages of organizing the training function according to the faculty, customer, matrix, and corporate university models.

7. Discuss the characteristics of the virtual training organization and how it can contribute to the company's business strategy.

TRAINING'S CHANGING ROLE AT IBM

The education division of IBM once spent $2 billion on training each year. The education function employed more than 7,000 persons. IBM was recognized as having one of the top training functions in the United States. Forty hours of yearly training was mandatory for all managers to ensure that they adhered to the "IBM way" of managing. In the late 1970s and early 1980s (before the boom in the personal computer and birth of smaller players such as Dell Computer and Gateway) IBM was the dominant firm in the computer industry. During this time, IBM's business strategy could be characterized as a blend of an internal growth and concentration strategy. IBM was focused on selling existing products related to its mainframe and midsize computers. IBM also marketed computer service contracts to companies that purchased its products. IBM was most interested in developing new products (such as printers) to complement existing products. The corporate culture was characterized by process and protocol, with a well-defined hierarchy of control. The company was well known for its no-layoff policy and history of taking care of its employees through career development, training, and excellent fringe benefits (i.e., a paternalistic culture).

Then the late 1980s and early 1990s brought improvements in technology (resulting in increased speed and power of personal computers and reduced need for large and midsize mainframe computers, which represented a large source of revenues for IBM) plus increased competition in the computer industry both in the United States and abroad. IBM experienced severe financial difficulties. To survive IBM had to change the paternalistic culture and get rid of segments of its business that were no longer profitable. The value of every business unit (including the educational unit) was carefully evaluated. As a re-

sult, IBM changed its business strategy to focus more on growing through acquiring companies while disinvesting the company of divisions that were not profitable or becoming obsolete because of new technology.

Based on this strategy, IBM spun off the education division into two subsidiaries: Skill Dynamics and Workforce Solutions. These subsidiaries are now expected to operate as profit centers. That is, they are expected to report profit and losses just as the other IBM divisions, which focus on specific products such as midrange computers and magnetic storage devices. These two companies must now actively market their services to other IBM business units, which can also contract with outside consultants to provide training products and services. In addition, Skill Dynamics and Workforce Solutions are free to market their training products and services to any outside company. There is no subsidy from the corporation—if they cannot sell services, they will go out of business. ■

Source: D. Kirkpatrick, "Breaking Up IBM," *Fortune* (July 27, 1992): 44–48.

Introduction

As the chapter opening shows, IBM's training function was radically affected by business conditions and a change in business strategy. To contribute to a company's success, training activities should help a company achieve its business strategy. A **business strategy** can be considered to be a plan that integrates the company's goal, policies, and actions.[1] The strategy influences how the company uses physical capital (e.g., plants and equipment), financial capital (e.g., assets and cash reserves), and human capital (employees). For example, at Amoco Oil, the human resource function uses financial and operating information to determine the human resource needs and develop appropriate plans to recruit, develop, motivate, and retain employees.[2]

Business strategy has a major impact on the type and amount of training that occurs and whether resources (money, trainers' time, and program development) should be devoted to training. Also, strategy influences the type, level, and mix of skills needed in the company. Strategy has a particularly strong influence on determining

1. The amount of training devoted to current or future job skills.
2. The extent to which training is customized for the particular needs of an employee or developed based on the needs of a team, unit, or division.
3. Whether training is restricted to specific groups of employees (such as persons identified as having managerial talent) or open to all employees.
4. Whether training is planned and systematically administered, provided only when problems occur, or spontaneously as a reaction to what competitors are doing.
5. The importance placed on training compared to other human resource management practices such as selection and compensation.[3]

Before we discuss the different types of business strategies and the role of training to help the company achieve each strategy, it is important to understand internal and external factors that influence the role that training plays in a company. The chapter begins by discussing several internal and external factors that influence how training relates to the business strategy. One internal factor is how the work roles of employees, managers, and executives are defined. Another internal factor is organizational characteristics. These include the degree to which business units are integrated, staffing and human resource planning strategy, degree of unionization, and manager, trainer, and employee involvement in training. External factors include the company's global presence and current business conditions.

Next we discuss specific strategic types and their implications for training. We also discuss how expectations regarding the role of training in the organization influence how training may be used to achieve strategic objectives. Traditionally, training has been used as a means to develop specific knowledge and skills. But as managers and trainers recognize the potential contribution of training to business goals, the role of training has broadened to include creating and sharing knowledge. The chapter ends with a description of several different ways of organizing the training function, emphasizing that two models for organizing the function—the virtual training organization and the corporate university model—are gaining in popularity as companies use training to help meet business goals.

The Work Roles of Employees, Managers, and Executives

Employees' Work Roles

Traditionally, the employee's role was to perform tasks and administer services according to the manager's directions. Employees were discouraged from becoming involved in improving the quality of the product or services. This was considered the responsibility of engineers and other specialists in the company's quality control unit. However, with the movement toward high-performance work systems using the team concept, employees today are performing many management roles (e.g., hiring, scheduling work, interacting with customers and vendors). For example, the team concept is used at Eaton's Belmond, Iowa, plant, which manufactures engine valves for automobiles and trucks.[4] Different groups or "cells" of employees work on separate aspects of the manufacturing process. Each of three different cells has its own responsibilities. All cell members know how to run the other operations within the cell. They rotate responsibilities every two hours. Each cell has a leader responsible for many of the duties usually done by the supervisor (e.g., completing requisition slips for new parts and purchase orders, reading blueprints for new orders, scheduling).

For teams to be effective, several conditions must exist. First, the members must understand and agree with the team goals and objectives. Second, team members must understand and accept their roles. The roles may include advising, promoting, organizing budgets and schedules, and developing new ideas.[5] For example, team members need to agree on who will be responsible for gathering and sharing information with other team members (adviser role). Third, team members need to agree on the procedures for accomplishing work. Last, team members need to have strong relationship skills (e.g., communication and conflict resolution skills).

For businesses using teams to manufacture goods and provide services, training is very important for ensuring that the teams are successful. Team members need training in interpersonal, problem-solving, and team skills (e.g., how to resolve conflicts, make decisions, and give feedback) so they can function as a team. Many times when teams are used, employees are also responsible for evaluating the quality of services or products. They need to be trained to use data to make decisions. This involves training in statistical process control techniques. For example, team members may need to understand the type of information they can gain about a manufacturing process by computing a mean and standard deviation of the number of defects that occurred in a one-hour period. As we discussed in Chapter 1, team members also often receive training in skills needed for all positions on the team (i.e., cross-training), not just for the particular job they are doing. To encourage cross-training, companies may adopt skill-based pay systems, which base an employee's pay rate on the number of skills in which he is competent rather than the skills he is using for his current job. Skill-based pay systems are discussed in Chapter 10.

Managers' Work Roles

Research suggests that managers in traditional work environments are expected to do the following:[6]

- *Manage individual performance.* Motivate employees to change performance, provide performance feedback, and monitor training activities.

- *Develop employees.* Explain work assignments and provide technical expertise.
- *Plan and allocate resources.* Translate strategic plans into work assignments and establish target dates for projects.
- *Coordinate interdependent groups.* Persuade other units to provide products or resources needed by the work group, and understand the goals and plans of other units.
- *Manage group performance.* Define areas of responsibility, meet with other managers to discuss effects of changes in the work unit on their groups, facilitate change, and implement business strategy.
- *Monitor the business environment.* Develop and maintain relationships with clients and customers, and participate in task forces to identify new business opportunities.
- *Represent one's work unit.* Develop relationships with other managers, communicate the needs of the work group to other units, and provide information on work group status to other groups.

Regardless of their level in the company (e.g., senior management), all managers are expected to serve as a spokesperson to other work units, managers, and vendors (i.e., represent the work unit). Of course, the amount of time managers devote to some of these roles is affected by their level. Line managers spend more time managing individual performance and developing employees than midlevel managers or executives do. The most important roles for midlevel managers and executives are planning and allocating resources, coordinating interdependent groups, and managing group performance (especially managing change). Executives also spend time monitoring the business environment by analyzing market trends, developing relationships with clients, and overseeing sales and marketing activities.

The roles and duties of managers in companies that use high-performance work systems (such as teams) are shown in Table 2–1. The managers' role is to create the conditions necessary to ensure team success. These include managing alignment, coordination, decision processes, continuous learning, creativity, and maintaining trust.[7]

To manage successfully in a team environment, managers need to be trained in "people skills," including negotiation, sensitivity, coaching, conflict resolution, and communication skills. A lack of people skills has been shown to be related to managers' failure to advance in their careers.[8]

Executives' Work Roles

Executive typically refers to the chairperson of the board, the chief operating officers, the vice presidents, and the heads of business units and divisions. Executives are responsible for creating a context for company change, building employees' commitment and sense of ownership, and achieving a balance between the company's current performance and innovation.

TABLE 2–1   The Roles and Duties of Managers in Companies That Use High-Performance Work Practices

Roles	Key Duties
Managing alignment	Clarify team goals and company goals.
	Help employees manage their objectives.
	Scan organization environment for useful information for the team.
Coordinating activities	Ensure that team is meeting internal and external customer needs.
	Ensure that team meets its quantity and quality objectives.
	Help team resolve problems with other teams.
	Ensure uniformity in interpretation of policies and procedures.
Facilitating decision-making process	Facilitate team decision making.
	Help team use effective decision-making processes (deal with conflict, statistical process control).
Encouraging continuous learning	Help team identify training needs.
	Help team become effective at on-the-job training.
	Create environment that encourages learning.
Creating and maintaining trust	Ensure that each team member is responsible for his or her work load and customers.
	Treat all team members with respect.
	Listen and respond honestly to team ideas.

Organizational Characteristics That Influence Training

The amount and type of training as well as the organization of the training function are influenced by the organization's degree of integration of business units; its global presence; its business conditions; its staffing strategy; its human resource planning; its extent of unionization; and manager, employee, and human resource staff involvement in training and development.[9]

Integration of Business Units

The degree to which a company's units or businesses are integrated affects the kind of training that takes place. In a highly integrated business, employees need to understand other units, services, and products in the company. Training likely includes rotating employees between jobs in different businesses so they can gain an understanding of the whole business.

Global Presence

As we noted in Chapter 1, the development of global product and service markets is an important challenge for U.S. companies. For companies with global operations, training is used to prepare employees for temporary or long-term overseas assignments. Also, because employees are geographically dispersed outside the United States, companies need to determine whether training will be conducted and coordinated from a central U.S. facility (such as Motorola University located near the company's headquarters in Schaumburg, Illinois) or will be the responsibility of satellite installations located near overseas facilities.

Business Conditions

Business conditions create specific human resource requirements.[10] For companies in an unstable business environment—one characterized by mergers, acquisitions, or disinvestment of businesses—training may be abandoned, left to the discretion of managers, or become more short-term (such as only offering training courses to correct skill deficiencies rather than preparing staff for new assignments). These programs emphasize the development of skills and characteristics (e.g., how to deal with change) needed regardless of the structure the company takes. Training may not even occur as a result of a planned effort. Employees who remain with a company following a merger, acquisition, or disinvestment usually find that their job now has different responsibilities requiring new skills. For employees in companies experiencing growth—that is, an increased demand for their product and services—there may be many new opportunities for lateral job moves and promotions resulting from the expansion of sales, marketing, and manufacturing operations or from the start-up of new business units. These employees are usually excited about participating in development activities because new positions often offer higher salaries and more challenging tasks.

During periods when companies are trying to revitalize and redirect their business, earnings are often flat. As a result, fewer incentives for participation in training—such as promotions and salary increases—may be available. In many cases, companies downsize their work forces as a way of cutting costs. Training activities under these conditions focus on ensuring that employees are available to fill the positions vacated by retirement or turnover. Training also involves helping employees avoid skill obsolescence. (Strategies to help employees avoid skill obsolescence are discussed in Chapter 12.)

The Importance of Training Compared to Other Human Resource Management Practices

Human resource management (HRM) practices consist of the management activities related to investments (time, effort, and money) in staffing (determining how many employees are needed, and recruiting and selecting employees), performance management, training, and compensation and benefits. The type of training and resources devoted to training are influenced by the strategy adopted for two human resource management practices: staffing and human resource planning.

Staffing Strategy

Staffing strategy refers to the company's decisions regarding where to find employees, how to select them, and the mix of employee skills and statuses (temporary, full-time, etc.). For example, one staffing decision a company has to make is how much to rely on the internal labor market (within the company) or external labor market (outside the company) to fill vacancies. Two aspects of a company's staffing strategy influence training: the criteria used to make promotion and assignment decisions (assignment flow) and the places where the company prefers to obtain the human resources to fill open positions (supply flow).[11]

Companies vary on the extent to which they make promotion and job assignment decisions based on individual performance or on group or business-unit performance. They also vary on the extent to which their staffing needs are met by relying on current employees (internal labor market) or on employees from competitors and recent entrants into the labor market, such as college graduates (external labor market). Figure 2–1 displays the two dimensions of staffing strategy. The interaction between assignment and supply flow results in four distinct types of companies: fortresses, baseball teams, clubs, and academies. Each company type places a different emphasis on training activities. For example, some companies (such as medical research companies) emphasize innovation and creativity. These types of companies are labeled baseball teams. Because it may be difficult to train skills related to innovation and creativity, they tend to handle staffing needs by luring employees away from competitors or by hiring graduating students with specialized skills.

As the chapter opening highlights, the restructuring of IBM demonstrates how training practices can be affected by business strategy. IBM—historically the dominant firm in the computer industry—had positioned itself as an "academy" because of its large investment in employee training and development as well as its exclusive reliance on the internal labor market for its staffing needs.[12] However, IBM decentralized its human resource management function, creating two separate companies: Workforce Solutions and Skill Solutions. IBM has moved from an academy-type staffing strategy to a baseball team strategy, recruiting talent from the external labor market and decreasing its emphasis on developing internal talent.

Human Resource Planning

Human resource planning includes the identification, analysis, forecasting, and planning of changes needed in the human resources area to help the company meet changing business conditions.[13] Human resource planning allows the company to anticipate the movement of human resources in the company because of turnover, transfers, retirements, or promotions. Human resource plans can help identify where employees with certain types of skills are needed in the company. Training can be used to prepare employees for increased responsibili-

FIGURE 2–1

Implications of staffing strategy for training

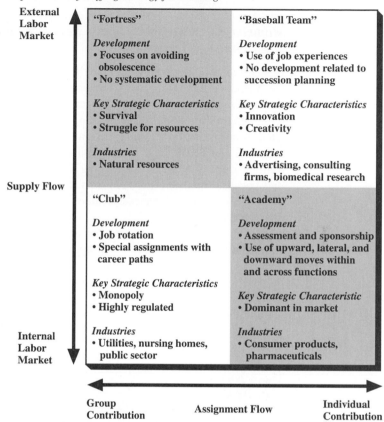

Source: Adapted from J. A. Sonnenfeld and M. A. Peiperi, "Staffing Policy as a Strategic Response: A Typology of Career Systems," *Academy of Management Review* 13 (1988): 588–600.

ties in their current job, promotions, lateral moves, transfers, and downward job opportunities that are predicted by the human resource plan.

Extent of Unionization

Unions' interest in training has resulted in joint union–management programs designed to help employees prepare for new jobs. When companies begin retraining and productivity-improvement efforts without involving unions, the efforts are likely to fail. The unions may see the programs as just another attempt to make employees work harder without sharing the productivity gains. Joint union–management programs (detailed in Chapter 10) ensure that all parties (unions, management, employees) understand the development goals and are committed to making the changes necessary for the company to make profits and for employees to both keep their jobs and share in any increased profits.

Manager, Employee, and Human Resource Staff Involvement in Training and Development

How often and how well a company's training program is used is affected by the degree to which managers, employees, and specialized development staff are involved in the process. If managers are not involved in the training process (e.g., determining training needs, being used as trainers), training may be unrelated to business needs. Managers may also not be committed to ensuring that training is effective (e.g., giving trainees feedback on the job). As a result, training's potential impact on helping the company reach its goals may be limited because managers may feel that training is a "necessary evil" forced on them by the training department, rather than a means of helping them to accomplish business goals.

If line managers are aware of what development activity can achieve, such as reducing the time it takes to fill open positions, they will be more willing to become involved in it. They will also become more involved in the training process if they are rewarded for participating. At Xerox, performance evaluations are directly related to pay increases.[14] Managers' performance appraisals include their actions to train and develop women and minorities (e.g., moving women and minorities into pivotal jobs that provide them the experience needed to become senior managers).

An emerging trend is that employees must initiate the training process.[15] The greater a company's acceptance of a continuous learning philosophy, the more development planning is expected. Companies will support training and development activities (such as tuition reimbursement, supporting courses, seminars, and workshops) but give employees the responsibility for planning their development. Training and development planning involves identifying needs, choosing the expected outcome (e.g., behavior change, greater knowledge), identifying the actions that should be taken, deciding how progress toward goal attainment will be measured, and creating a timetable for improvement. To identify strengths and weaknesses and training needs, employees need to analyze what they want to do, what they can do, how others perceive them, and what others expect of them. A need can result from gaps between current capabilities, interests, and the type of work or position the employee wants in the future. The needs assessment process is discussed in greater detail in Chapter 3.

The Changing Role of Training

Figure 2–2 shows the changing role of training. Training is moving from a primary focus on teaching employees specific skills to a broader focus on creating and sharing knowledge.[16]

FIGURE 2–2

The broadening of training's role

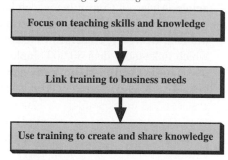

Source: Based on J. J. Martocchio and T. T. Baldwin, "The Evolution of Strategic Organizational Training: New Objectives and a Research Agenda," *Research in Personnel and Human Resource Management* vol. 15, ed. G. R. Ferris (Greenwich, CT: JAI Press, 1997): 1–46.

Focus on Teaching Skills and Knowledge.   Traditionally, training was viewed as a means to teach employees specific skills and behaviors. This role of training will continue into the future. This view of training suggests that business conditions are predictable, they can be controlled by the company, and the company can control and predict the knowledge and skills that employees will need in the future.

Link Training to Business Needs.   As the competitive challenges discussed in Chapter 1 indicate, unpredictability in the external environment in which companies operate is likely to continue. This means that because problems cannot be predicted in advance, training needs to be delivered on an as-needed basis to help employees deal with specific business problems as they occur. Several training methods (e.g., action learning) have been developed to teach employees skills while they focus on specific business problems. These methods are detailed in Chapters 7 and 8. In addition, in this role training activities are developed and based on business needs and are directly related to them.

Use Training to Create and Share Knowledge.   Many companies believe that to gain a competitive advantage the key is to develop intellectual capital. **Intellectual capital** includes cognitive knowledge (know what), advanced skills (know how), system understanding and creativity (know why), and self-motivated creativity (care why).[17] Traditionally, training departments have focused their resources on cognitive and advanced skills. But the real value of training may be in having employees understand the manufacturing or service process and the interrelationships between departments and divisions (system understanding) as well as motivating them to be innovative and deliver high-quality products and services (care why). Particularly for companies in service industries such as software development, medical care, communications, and education, system understanding and self-motivated creativity are critical. Training is viewed as part of a larger system to create and share knowledge. For example, Andersen Consulting is well known for devoting time and money to train its employees. Andersen invests between 3 and 5 percent of its payroll dollars in training. However, Andersen Consulting also has a knowledge sharing database which links more than 80,000 employees in 36 countries. This information system can be used to share training content, find information about potential clients, or post work problems on an electronic bulletin board.

Training Needs in Different Strategies

Table 2–2 describes four business strategies—concentration, internal growth, external growth, and disinvestment—and highlights the implications of each for training practices.[18] Each strategy differs based on the goal of the business. A **concentration strategy** focuses on increasing market share, reducing costs, or creating and maintaining a market niche for products and services. Southwest Airlines has a concentration strategy. It focuses on providing short-haul, low-fare, high-frequency air transportation. It utilizes one type of aircraft (the Boeing 737), has no reserved seating, and serves no meals. This has enabled Southwest to keep costs low and revenues high. An **internal growth strategy** focuses on new market and product development, innovation, and joint ventures. For example, the merger between two publishing companies, McGraw-Hill and Richard D. Irwin, created one company with strengths in the U.S. and international college textbook markets. An **external growth strategy** emphasizes acquiring vendors and suppliers or buying businesses that allows the company to expand into new markets. For example, General Electric, a manufacturer of lighting products and jet engines, acquired the National Broadcast Corporation (NBC), a television and communications company. A **disinvestment strategy** emphasizes liquidation and divestiture of businesses. For example, General Mills recently sold its restaurant businesses.

Preliminary research suggests a link between business strategy and amount and type of training.[19] As shown in Table 2–2, training issues vary greatly from one strategy to another. For example, divesting companies need to train employees in job-search skills and focus on cross-training remaining employees who may find themselves in jobs with expanding responsibilities. Companies focusing on a market niche (a concentration strategy), need to emphasize skill currency and development of their existing work force.

It is important to identify the prevailing business strategy to ensure that the company is allocating enough of its budget to training activities, that employees are receiving training on relevant topics, and that employees are receiving the right amount of training.[20] How might a manager or trainer identify the company's business strategy? The company's mission and goals may be useful for understanding the strategy. The **mission** is the company's reason for existing. It may specify the customers served, the needs satisfied, or the value received by the customer. It may be accompanied by a statement of the company's mission

TABLE 2–2 Implications of Business Strategy for Training

Strategy	Emphasis	How Achieved	Key Issues	Training Implications
Concentration	• Increase market share • Reduce operating costs • Create or maintain market niche	• Improve product quality • Improve productivity or innovate technical processes • Customize products or services	• Skill currency • Development of existing work force	• Team building • Cross-training • Specialized programs • Interpersonal skill training • On-the-job training
Internal growth	• Market development • Product development • Innovation • Joint ventures	• Market existing products/add distribution channels • Expand global market • Modify existing products • Create new or different products • Expand through joint ownership	• Create new jobs and tasks • Innovation	• Support or promote high-quality communication of product value • Cultural training • Help in development of organizational culture that values creative thinking and analysis • Technical competence in jobs • Manager training in feedback and communication • Conflict negotiation skills
External growth (acquisition)	• Horizontal integration • Vertical integration • Concentric diversification	• Acquire firms operating at same stage in product market chain (new market access) • Acquire business that can supply or buy products • Acquire firms that have nothing in common with acquiring firm	• Integration • Redundancy • Restructuring	• Determining capabilities of employees in acquired firms • Integrating training systems • Methods and procedures of combined firms • Team building
Disinvestment	• Retrenchment • Turnaround • Divestiture • Liquidation	• Reduce costs • Reduce assets • Generate revenue • Redefine goals • Sell off all assets	• Efficiency	• Motivation, goal setting, time management, stress management, cross-training • Leadership training • Interpersonal communications • Outplacement assistance • Job-search skills training

and values. **Goals** are what the company hopes to achieve in the medium–to–long-term future. The overarching goal of most profit-making companies in the United States is to maximize shareholder wealth. But companies have other goals as well. Take, for example, Allied-Signal, which manufactures and sells aerospace and automotive products, chemicals, fibers, plastics, and other materials. Allied-Signal's goals are to keep customer satisfaction a top priority, use learning to improve skills and enhance the company's future, and achieve financial targets by focusing on growth and productivity. In a letter to the shareholders, CEO Larry Bossidy acknowledges the strategic role of training in Allied-Signal. He recognizes that most of the company's recent improvements in productivity, speed, and quality are related to new skills acquired by employees through training. The company has intensified its commitment to using training as a means to achieve business goals by building a corporate learning center near corporate headquarters in New Jersey.

A good example of how a training function can contribute to business strategy is evident in the changes made by SunU, the training and development organization of Sun Microsystems, a manufacturer of computer workstations and workstation software.[21] SunU realigned its training philosophy and the types of training conducted to be more linked to the strategy of Sun Microsystems. Sun Microsystems was in a constantly evolving business due to new technologies, products, and product markets (an internal growth strategy). SunU found that its customers wanted training services that could be developed quickly, could train many people, and would not involve classroom training. Because of the internal growth strategy, Sun Microsystems was also interested in maintaining and improving the knowledge and competence of its current work force.

Table 2–3 presents the questions that SunU used to determine how to better contribute to the business strategy. These questions are part of what is known as a SWOT analysis (strengths, weaknesses, opportunities, and threats). The **SWOT analysis** involves identifying the company's operating environment (e.g., product markets, new technologies) to identify opportunities and threats as well as an internal analysis of the company's strengths and weaknesses including people, technology, and financial resources. Note that the questions SunU asked not only deal with the delivery of training, but attempt to understand internal customer needs and potential business needs as determined by Sun Microsystems' business strategy.

As a result of the need to better align the training function with the needs generated by the business strategy, SunU took several steps. First, SunU developed a new approach to determining the knowledge and skills that the employees needed to meet business goals. SunU identified several basic competencies (such as customer relations). A team of trainers at SunU constantly reviews these competencies and discusses them with key senior managers. For example, in the customer service competency, vice presidents and directors of sales and marketing are interviewed to identify training needs. As a result of this process SunU learned more about the business needs and was able to develop relevant training. To help deliver training quickly to a large number of trainees without relying on the classroom, SunU developed videoconferencing programs that

TABLE 2–3   SunU's Analysis to Align Training with Business Strategy

Customers
Who are our customers and how do we work for them?

Organization
What is the nature of practices required to complete our mission?

Products and Services
How do we ensure that our products and services meet strategic
requirements?

Research and Development
How do we stay current in the training and learning fields and use our
knowledge in these areas?

Business Systems
What are the processes, products, tools, and procedures required to achieve
our goals?

Continuous Learning
How do we recognize that learning at Sun Microsystems is continuous,
is conscious, and comes from many sources?

Results
How do we obtain results according to our customers' standards?

Source: Based on P. A. Smith, "Reinventing SunU," *Training and Development* (July 1994): 23–27.

allow training to be delivered simultaneously to several sites without requiring
trainees to travel to a central location. To help maintain and improve the knowledge and abilities of its employees, SunU developed a desktop library that enables all employees to access CD-ROMs containing up-to-date information on
technologies and products as well as profiles on customers and competitors.

Models of Organizing the Training Department

Next we discuss five models of organizing the training department: the faculty
model, customer model, matrix model, corporate university model, and virtual
model.[22] This review of these structures should help you to understand that the organization of the training department has important consequences for how the training department (and trainers employed in the department) contributes (or fails to
contribute) to the business strategy. Keep in mind that—particularly with large, decentralized companies—there may be multiple separate training functions, each organized using a different model. The virtual training organization and the corporate
university model are the models that companies are moving to in order to ensure

that training is used to help the company achieve its business objectives. These models are also being adopted as companies begin to value intellectual capital and view training as part of a learning system designed to create and share knowledge.

Faculty Model

Training departments organized by the **faculty model** look a lot like the structure of a college. Figure 2–3 shows the faculty model. The training department is headed by a director with a staff of experts who have specialized knowledge of a particular topic or skill area. These experts develop, administer, and update training programs. For example, sales trainers are responsible for sales skills training (cultivating clients, negotiating a sale, closing a sale), and computer experts provide training on topics such as using e-mail and the World Wide Web as well as software design language.

The faculty model has several strengths. First, training staff are clearly experts in the area they train in. Second, the training department's plans are easily determined by staff expertise. The content and timing of programs are determined primarily by when they are available and the expertise of the trainers. Organizing by the faculty model also has several disadvantages. Companies that use the faculty model may create a training function that has expertise that does not meet the needs of the organization. Trainers in a faculty model may also be unaware of business problems or unwilling to adapt materials to fit a business need. This can result in demotivated trainees who fail to learn because course content lacks meaningfulness for them—that is, it does not relate to problems or needs of the business. Programs and courses that may be needed may not be offered because trainers are not experts in certain areas. Skill and knowledge emphasized in programs may not match the needs of the company. To overcome these disadvantages of the faculty model, managers need to frequently survey training's customers to ensure that course offerings are meeting their needs. Ex-

FIGURE 2–3

The faculty model

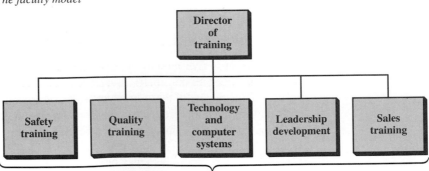

Training specialty areas

pert trainers also need to ensure that they adapt course materials so that they are meaningful for participants.

Customer Model

Training departments organized according to the **customer model** are responsible for the training needs of one division or function of the company. For example, trainers might be responsible for programs related to information systems, marketing, or operations. Figure 2–4 shows the customer model. This model overcomes a major problem of the faculty model. Training programs are developed more in line with the particular needs of a business group rather than on the expertise of the training staff. Trainers in this model are expected to be aware of business needs and to update courses and content to reflect them. If needs change such that training is no longer available from a source inside the company, the trainers may use outside experts (e.g., consultants). Materials provided by a training staff organized by this model are likely to be meaningful to trainees.

There are several disadvantages of this model. First, trainers have to spend considerable time learning the business function before they can be useful trainers. Second, a large number of programs covering similar topics may be developed by customers. These programs may also vary greatly in effectiveness. It may be difficult for the training director to oversee each function to ensure that (1) a common instructional design process is used or (2) the company's quality philosophy is consistently emphasized in each program. For example, quality training may be developed separately for marketing and for operations employees. This type of structure is likely to be unattractive to trainers who consider presentation and teaching to be their primary job function. In the customer model, trainers are likely to be employees from the functional area (e.g., manufacturing engineers) who have great functional expertise but lack training in instructional design and learning theory. As a result, courses may be meaningful but poor from a design perspective (e.g., have inadequate feedback and practice opportunities).

FIGURE 2–4

The customer model

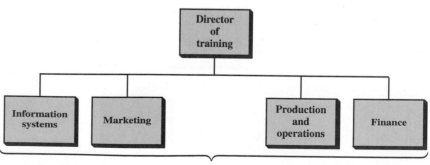

Matrix Model

The **matrix model** involves trainers reporting to both a manager in the training department and a manager in a particular function. Figure 2–5 shows the matrix model. The trainer has the responsibility of being both a training expert and a functional expert. For example as Figure 2–5 shows sales trainers report to both the director of training and the marketing manager. One advantage of the matrix model is that it helps ensure that training is linked to needs of the business. Another advantage is that the trainer gains expertise in understanding a specific business function. Because the trainer is also responsible to the training director, it is likely that the trainer will stay professionally current (e.g., up to date on new training delivery mechanisms such as the Internet). A major disadvantage of the matrix model is that the trainer likely will have more time demands and conflicts because she reports to two managers: a functional manager and a training director.

Corporate University Model (Corporate Training Universities)

An emerging model for organizing training is the corporate university model in Figure 2–6. The **corporate university model** differs from the other models in that the client group includes not only employees and managers but also stakeholders outside the company including community colleges, universities, high schools, and grade schools. Training functions organized by the university model tend to offer a wider range of programs and courses than functions organized by the other models. Important culture and values also tend to be emphasized more

FIGURE 2–5

The matrix model

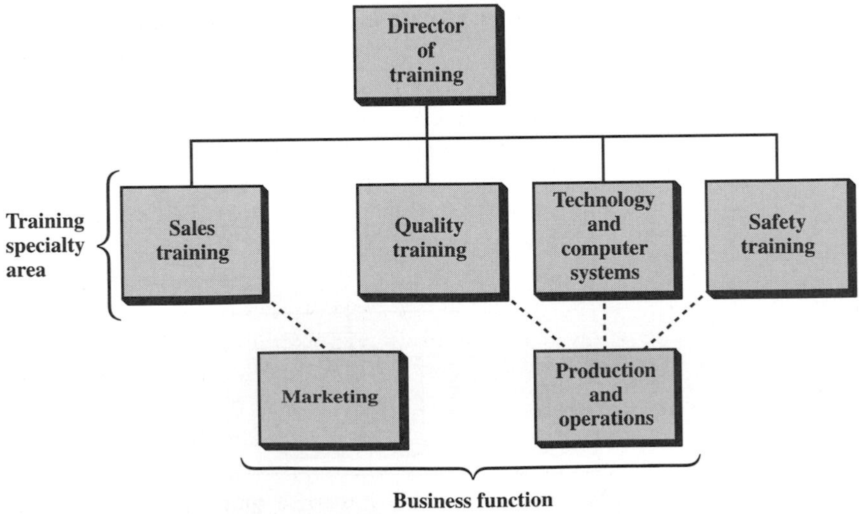

Business function

FIGURE 2–6

The corporate university model

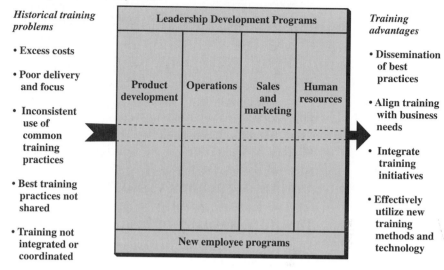

Historical training problems

- **Excess costs**

- **Poor delivery and focus**

- **Inconsistent use of common training practices**

- **Best training practices not shared**

- **Training not integrated or coordinated**

Leadership Development Programs

| Product development | Operations | Sales and marketing | Human resources |

New employee programs

Training advantages

- **Dissemination of best practices**

- **Align training with business needs**

- **Integrate training initiatives**

- **Effectively utilize new training methods and technology**

often in the training curriculum of corporate universities than the other models. The university model centralizes training to make sure that "best training practices" that may be used in one unit of the company are disseminated across the company. Also, the corporate university enables the company to control costs by developing consistent training practices and policies.

Motorola University is an excellent example of the university model.[23] In the late 1970s, international competition in the electronics and telecommunications industries was strong. As a result, Bob Galvin, who was chief executive officer at the time, believed that Motorola could gain a competitive advantage via employees with more specialized knowledge and skills than their competitors. Based on his beliefs and vision, Motorola University was created in 1989. Motorola University includes 110 full-time and 300 part-time staff. Curriculum is arranged by function: engineering, manufacturing, sales, and marketing. Each curriculum includes three sets of skills: relational skills, technical skills, and business skills. Motorola University takes responsibility for teaching relational skills (customer satisfaction, effective meetings, negotiations, etc.). However, the curriculum for technical and business skills (basic math, electronics, accounting, etc.) is developed in partnership with community colleges and technical schools. One example of Motorola's expanded client base for training activities is its partnership with Northwestern University. Motorola and Northwestern jointly developed a quality course for the second year of Northwestern's MBA program.

To ensure that the training conducted at Motorola University is helping to meet business needs, there are several regional training centers located close to Motorola facilities. Trainers at these sites provide training to local facilities as well as identify new training programs or improvements in programs that need to be made to help the facilities deal with their unique training needs.

Motorola attributes its success to a common culture that emphasizes risk taking and teamwork. Also, to reach the quality goals the company has established, every employee (including workers responsible for product assembly such as cellular phones) must understand algebra and be able to read engineering requirements. As a result, the training curriculum includes remedial reading and math courses plus courses on risk taking and teamwork.

Motorola University continues to play a key role in the company's success. Motorola is the largest provider of wireless communications equipment in the world, and its semiconductor business leads the world in most markets it serves. Motorola is number one in the world in cellular telephones, paging, and two-way radios. Because of expanding global business opportunities, Motorola has recently developed a Motorola University for Europe, Middle East, and Africa.[24]

Virtual Model (Virtual Training Organizations)

Many organizations such as Corning, Apple, and MCI are organizing their training function so that they can respond to client needs quickly and provide high-quality services.[25] **Virtual training organizations** operate according to three principles. First, employees (not the company) have primary responsibility for learning. Second, the most effective learning takes place on the job, not in the classroom. Third, for training to translate into improved job performance, the manager–employee relationship (not employee–trainer relationship) is critical. That is, for employees to use training content on the job, they are responsible for learning course content and understanding how content may be applied to their work. Managers are responsible for (1) holding employees accountable to use training on the job and (2) removing obstacles that may interfere with their doing so.

A virtual training organization (VTO) is characterized by five competencies: strategic direction, product design, structural versatility, product delivery, and accountability for result. Strategic direction includes a clearly described goal and direction to the department, as well as a customer focus that includes customizing training to meet customer needs and continuously improving programs. A virtual training organization views not only trainees as customers, but also managers who make decisions to send employees to training and senior-level managers who allocate money for training. Table 2–4 contrasts a virtual training organization with a traditional training department. Compared to a traditional training department, a virtual training organization is customer-focused. It takes more responsibility for learning and evaluating training effectiveness, provides customized training solutions based on customer needs, and determines when and how to deliver training based on customer needs. The most noticeable difference between a VTO and a traditional training department is its structure. The traditional training organization tends to operate with a fixed staff of trainers and administrators who perform very specific functions such as instructional design. The number of trainers in VTOs varies according to the demand for

TABLE 2–4   Comparison between a Virtual Training Organization and a Traditional Training Department

A Traditional Training Department	*A Virtual Training Organization*
Strategic Direction	
Leaves objectives unstated or vague	Broadly disseminates a clearly articulated mission
Assumes that class participants are its only customers	Recognizes that its customer base is segmented
Limits offerings to predetermined courses	Provides customized solutions to its clients' needs
Continues to supply products that are no longer useful	Understands product life cycles
Organizes its offerings by courses	Organizes its offerings by competencies
Tries to mandate training	Competes for internal customers
Product Design	
Uses rigid and cumbersome design methodologies	Uses benchmarking and other innovative design strategies to develop products quickly
Views suppliers as warehouses of materials	Involves suppliers strategically
Structural Versatility	
Employs trainers who serve primarily as facilitators and classroom instructors	Employs professionals who serve as product managers and internal consultants
Operates with a fixed number of staff	Leverages resources from many areas
Relies solely on training staff to determine the department's offerings	Involves line managers in determining direction and content
Product Delivery	
Distributes a list of courses	Offers a menu of learning options
Offers courses on a fixed schedule at fixed locations	Delivers training at the work site
Accountability for Results	
Believes that the corporation manages employee development	Believes individual employees must take responsibility for their personal growth
Ends its involvement with participants when courses end	Provides follow-up on the job to ensure that learning takes place
Considers the instructor the key player in supporting learning	Considers the manager the key player in supporting learning
Relies on course critiques as its primary source of feedback	Evaluates the strategic effects of training and its bottom-line results
Vaguely describes training outcomes	Guarantees that training will improve performance

Source: S. S. McIntosh, "Envisioning Virtual Training Organization," *Training and Development* (May 1995): 47.

products and services. The trainers not only have specialized competencies (e.g., instructional design) but can also serve as internal consultants and provide a wide range of services (e.g., needs assessment, content improvement, customization of programs, results measurement).

Because many companies are recognizing training's critical role in meeting competitive challenges, there is an increasing trend for the training function, regardless of company size, to be organized as a virtual training organization and also for companies to develop a separate corporate university. For example, Gates Bar-B-Q, a restaurant chain in Kansas City, Missouri, has created Rib Tech, the College of Barbecue Knowledge.[26] Although the company only has 300 employees, the owner has invested in training because it has helped him solve a major problem facing businesses with multiple locations: maintaining consistent quality. The college offers seven basic courses in such topics as sandwich cutting. All employees must attend classes to maintain their current position, and training attendance is considered in determining promotions. Advanced classes include how to cook ribs (covering such topics as the right combination of hickory and oak in a barbecue pit) and the best way to season meat. The College of Barbecue Knowledge is responsible for the consistency in food, service, and staff appearance found across the chain of restaurants. Because of this consistency, the chain is a Kansas City landmark, lines often form outside the restaurant, it ships barbecue sauce nationwide, and it operates its own catering service.

Summary

For training to help a company gain a competitive advantage, it must help the company reach business goals and objectives. This chapter emphasized how changes in work roles, organizational factors, and the role of training influence the amount and type of training as well as the organization of the training functions. The chapter discussed how different strategies (concentration, internal growth, external growth, and disinvestment) influence the goals of the business and create different training needs. The chapter concludes with a discussion of different models of the training function. As training is expected to make a greater contribution to achievement of business strategies and goals, the virtual training organization and corporate university models will become more prevalent.

Key Terms

business strategy   24
human resource management (HRM)
   practices   29
staffing strategy   30
human resource planning   30
intellectual capital   33

concentration strategy   34
internal growth strategy   34
external growth strategy   34
disinvestment strategy   34
mission   34
goals   36

Discussion Questions

1. How would you expect the training activities of a company that is dominant in its product market to differ from those of a company that emphasizes research and development?

2. What do you think is the most important organizational characteristic that influences training? Why?

3. Which model or combination of models is best for organizing the training function? Why?

4. Chesebrough-Pond's, a producer of health and beauty aids, decided several years ago to expand its product lines by repackaging Vaseline Petroleum Jelly in pocket-size squeeze tubes called Vaseline Lip Therapy. The company decided to place a strategic emphasis on developing markets for this product. The company knew from market research studies that its petroleum jelly customers were already using the product in its original container to prevent chapped lips. Company managers reasoned that their market could be expanded significantly if the product were repackaged to fit conveniently in consumers' pockets and purses. Identify the business strategy. What training needs result from this strategy? What are the training implications of this decision for (1) manufacturing and (2) the sales force?

5. How might organizing the training function as a virtual training organization contribute to a Total Quality Management philosophy?

6. Compare and contrast the corporate university model with the faculty model. How are they similar? How do they differ?

7. What is intellectual capital? How is intellectual capital influencing the changing role of the training from skill and knowledge acquisition to creating and sharing knowledge?

8. How could SWOT analysis be used to align training activities with business strategies and goals?

9. What are the training implications of the increased use of teams to manufacture products or provide services?

Application Assignments

1. Using Motorola University's Web site (www.mot.com/MU/), answer these questions:
   a. What is the mission of Motorola University?
   b. What learning services does it provide?

2. Find a company's annual report by using the World Wide Web or visiting a library. Using the annual report, do the following:
   a. Identify the company's mission, values, and goals.
   b. Find any information provided in the report regarding the company's training practices and how they relate to the goals and strategies. Be prepared to give a brief presentation to the class on your research.

Endnotes

1. J. Quinn, *Strategies for Change: Logical Incrementalism* (Homewood, IL: Richard D. Irwin, 1980).
2. D. Ullrich and A. Yeung, "A Shared Mindset," *HR Magazine* (March 1989): 38–45.
3. R. S. Schuler and S. F. Jackson, "Linking Competitive Strategies with Human Resource Management Practices," *Academy of Management Executive* 1 (1987): 207–219.
4. M. Berg, "Eaton's Self-Managed Workteams" (Plan B paper submitted in partial fulfillment of the requirements for the MAIR degree, Industrial Relations Center, University of Minnesota, 1992).
5. D. F. Van Eynde, "High Impact Team Building Made Easy," *HR Horizons* (Spring 1992): 37–41; ed. J. R. Hackman, *Groups That Work and Those That Don't: Creating Conditions for Effective Teamwork* (San Francisco: Jossey-Bass, 1990); D. McCann and C. Margerison, "Managing High-Performance Teams," *Training and Development Journal* (November 1989): 53–60.
6. A. I. Kraut, P. R. Pedigo, D. D. McKenna, and M. D. Dunnette, "The Role of the Manager: What's Really Important in Different Managerial Jobs," *Academy of Management Executive* 4 (1988): 36–48; F. Luthans, "Successful vs. Effective Real Managers," *Academy of Management Executive* 2 (1988): 127–132; H. Mintzberg, *The Nature of Managerial Work* (New York: Harper & Row, 1973); S. W. Floyd and B. Wooldridge, "Dinosaurs or Dynamos? Recognizing Middle Management's Strategic Role," *Academy of Management Executive* 8 (1994): 47–57.
7. B. Gerber, "From Manager into Coach," *Training* (February 1992): 25–31; C. Carr, "Managing Self-Managed Workers," *Training and Development Journal* (September 1991): 37–42.
8. P. Kizilos, "Fixing Fatal Flaws," *Training* (September 1991): 66–70; F. S. Hall, "Dysfunctional Managers: The Next Human Resource Challenge," *Organizational Dynamics* (August 1991): 48–57.
9. R. J. Campbell, "HR Development Strategies," in *Developing Human Resources,* ed. K. N. Wexley (Washington, DC: BNA Books, 1991): 5-1–5-34; J. K. Berry, "Linking Management Development to Business Strategy," *Training and Development Journal* (August 1990): 20–22.
10. M. London, "Organizational Support for Employees' Career Motivation: A Guide to Human Resource Strategies in Changing Business Conditions," *Human Resource Planning* 11, no. 1 (1988): 23–32.
11. J. A. Sonnenfeld and M. A. Peiperl, "Staffing Policy as a Strategic Response: A Typology of Career Systems," *Academy of Management Review* 13 (1988): 588–600.
12. D. Kirkpatrick, "Breaking Up IBM," *Fortune* (July 27, 1992): 44–58.

13. V. R. Ceriello and C. Freeman, *Human Resource Management Systems: Strategies, Tactics, and Techniques* (Lexington, MA: Lexington Books, 1991).

14. V. Sessa, "Managing Diversity at the Xerox Corporation: Balanced Workforce Goals and Caucus Groups," in *Diversity in the Workplace: Human Resource Initiatives,* ed. S. E. Jackson & Associates (New York: Guilford Press, 1992): 37–64.

15. D. T. Jaffe and C. D. Scott, "Career Development for Empowerment in a Changing Work World," in *New Directions in Career Planning and the Workplace,* ed. J. M. Kummerow (Palo Alto, CA: Consulting Psychologist Press, 1991): 33–60; L. Summers, "A Logical Approach to Development Planning," *Training and Development* 48 (1994): 22–31; D. B. Peterson and M. D. Hicks, *Development First* (Minneapolis, MN: Personnel Decisions, Inc., 1995).

16. T. T. Baldwin, C. Danielson, and W. Wiggenhorn, "The Evolution of Learning Strategies in Organizations: From Employee Development to Business Redefinition," *Academy of Management Executive* 11: 47–58; J. J. Martocchio and T. T. Baldwin, "The Evolution of Strategic Organizational Training," in *Research in Personnel and Human Resource Management* 15, ed. G. R. Ferris (Greenwich, CT: JAI Press, 1997): 1–46.

17. J. B. Quinn, P. Andersen, and S. Finkelstein, "Leveraging Intellect," *Academy of Management Executive* 10 (1996): 7–39.

18. A. P. Carnevale, L. J. Gainer, and J. Villet, *Training in America* (San Francisco: Jossey-Bass, 1990); L. J. Gainer, "Making the Competitive Connection: Strategic Management and Training," *Training and Development* (September 1989): s1–s30.

19. S. Raghuram and R. D. Arvey, "Business Strategy Links with Staffing and Training Practices," *Human Resource Planning* 17 (1994): 55–73.

20. Carnevale, Gainer, and Villet, *Training in America.*

21. P. A. Smith, "Reinventing SunU," *Training and Development* (July 1994): 23–27.

22. M. London, *Managing the Training Enterprise* (San Francisco: Jossey-Bass, 1994); D. Laird, *Approaches to Training and Development,* 2d ed. (Boston: Addison-Wesley, 1985).

23. W. Wiggenhorn, "Motorola U: When Training Becomes an Education," *Harvard Business Review* (July–August 1990): 71–83.

24. From Motorola home page on the World Wide Web at http://www.mot.com, February 18, 1997. "Motorola University Europe, Middle East, and Africa presents 'Empire of the mind.'" From the World Wide Web, go to .http://www.mot.com/MU/opportunities/Q496EMEA.html, February 18, 1997.

25. S. S. McIntosh, "Envisioning Virtual Training Organization," *Training and Development* (May 1995): 46–49.

26. K. S. Breaux, "In Ribs 101, Star Pupils Win Promotions," *Wall Street Journal* (September 10, 1996): B1–B2.

3   NEEDS ASSESSMENT

Objectives

After reading this chapter, you should be able to

1. Discuss the role of organization analysis, person analysis, and task analysis in needs assessment.

2. Identify different methods used in needs assessment and identify the advantages and disadvantages of each method.

3. Discuss the concerns of upper-level and midlevel managers and trainers in needs assessment.

4. Explain how person characteristics, input, output, consequences, and feedback influence performance and learning.

5. Create conditions to ensure that employees are receptive to training.

6. Discuss the steps involved in conducting a task analysis.

7. Analyze task analysis data to determine the tasks in which people need to be trained.

8. Explain competency models and the process used to develop them.

TRAINING ENGINEERS TO BECOME TRAINERS

The management team at Texas Instruments faced a serious problem: how to train engineering experts to become trainers for new engineers. The problem was that while the engineers had technical expertise, there was a large disparity in their level of instructional expertise. Some engineers had taught courses at local colleges; others had no experience. When inexperienced instructors were taught by experienced ones, both students and instructors were frustrated. The solution was to conduct an assessment of the engineers' training needs.

A team of training and development specialists was charged with conducting the needs assessment. They started with an organization analysis. This involved (1) gathering information on the department mission, (2) identifying current and previous courses, seminars, and experiences used to develop staff, and (3) determining the roles of the training staff. They shared the information they gathered with top-level managers. The top-level managers were supportive in terms of both providing money and encouraging subordinates to participate in the project.

The specialist team next conducted a task analysis. They identified tasks that needed to be performed through reviewing documentation as well as conducting a survey, observation, and interviews. Written documentation—such as competency studies and project checklists—as well as meetings with staff were used to identify relevant tasks. The result was a task list organized into five job function areas. This task list was used to develop a survey that asked staff to rate each task's importance and their interest in more training. The team also conducted classroom observations of new and experienced instructors to identify strengths and weaknesses of the instructors' presentations. Last, the team held personal interviews with both instructors and noninstructors to validate the information gathered through written documentation and surveys.

The needs assessment resulted in understanding the instructors' strengths as well as differences between experienced and inexperienced instructors, and led to recommendations of areas for training. The needs assessment helped Texas Instruments identify with confidence what types of training were needed to improve the engineers' instructional skills. ∎

Source: J. L. Wircenski, R. L. Sullivan, and P. Moore, "Assessing Training Needs at Texas Instruments," *Training and Development* (April 1989).

Introduction

The Texas Instruments example highlights that before you choose a training method, it is important to identify whether training is necessary. As discussed in Chapter 1, the first step in the instructional design process is to conduct a needs assessment. **Needs assessment** refers to the process used to determine if training is necessary.

Figure 3–1 shows the causes and outcomes resulting from needs assessment. As we see, there are many different "pressure points" that suggest that training is necessary. These pressure points include performance problems, new technology, internal or external customer requests for training, job redesign, new legislation, changes in customer preferences, new products, or employees' lack of basic skills. Note that these pressure points do not guarantee that training is the correct solution. Consider, for example, a delivery truck driver whose job is to deliver anesthetic gases to medical facilities. The driver mistakenly hooks up the supply line of a mild anesthetic to the supply line of a hospital's oxygen system, contaminating the hospital's oxygen supply. Why did the driver make this mistake, which is a clearly a performance problem? The driver may have made this mistake because of a lack of knowledge about the appropriate line hookup for the anesthetic, anger over a requested salary increase that his manager re-

FIGURE 3–1

The needs assessment process

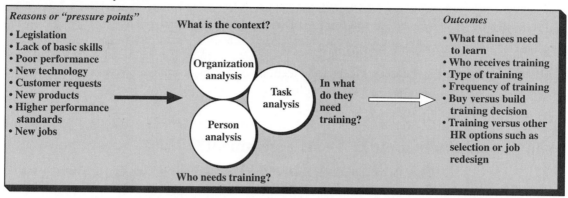

cently denied, or mislabeled valves for connecting the gas supply. Only the lack of knowledge can be addressed by training. The other pressure points require addressing issues related to the consequence of good performance (pay system) or the design of the work environment.

Needs assessment typically involves organizational analysis, person analysis, and task analysis.[1] Organizational analysis involves considering the context in which training will occur. That is, **organizational analysis** involves determining the appropriateness of training, given the company's business strategy, its resources available for training, and support by managers and peers for training activities. You are already familiar with one aspect of organizational analysis. Chapter 2 discussed the role of the company's business strategy in determining the frequency and type of training.

Person analysis helps to identify who needs training. **Person analysis** involves (1) determining whether performance deficiencies result from a lack of knowledge, skill, ability (a training issue) or from a motivational or work-design problem, (2) identifying who needs training, and (3) determining employees' readiness for training. **Task analysis** includes identifying the important tasks and knowledge, skill, and behaviors that need to be emphasized in training for employees to complete their tasks.

In practice, organizational analysis, person analysis, and task analysis are usually not conducted in any specific order. However, because organizational analysis is concerned with identifying whether training fits with the company's strategic objectives and whether the company wants to devote time and money to training, it is usually conducted first. Person analysis and task analysis are often conducted at the same time because it is often difficult to determine whether performance deficiencies are a training problem without understanding the tasks and the work environment.

What outcomes result from a needs assessment? As shown in Figure 3–1, the needs assessment process results in information related to who needs training and what trainees need to learn, including the tasks in which they need to be trained plus knowledge, skill, behavior, or other job requirements. Needs assessment helps to determine whether the company will purchase training from a vendor or consultant or else develop training using internal resources. Determining exactly what trainees need to learn is critical for the next step in the instructional design process: identifying learning outcomes and objectives. Chapter 4 explores identifying learning outcomes, learning objectives, and creating a training environment so that learning occurs.

Who Should Participate in Needs Assessment?

Since the goal of needs assessment is to determine if a training need exists, who it exists for, and what tasks need to be trained, it is important to include managers, trainers, and employees in the needs assessment process. Traditionally, only trainers were concerned with the needs assessment process. But, as Chapter 2 showed, as training increasingly becomes used to help the company achieve its strategic goals, both upper- and top-level managers are involved in the needs assessment process.

Table 3–1 shows the questions that upper-level managers, midlevel managers, and trainers are interested in answering for organization analysis, person analysis, and task analysis. Upper-level managers include directors, chief execu-

TABLE 3–1   Key Concerns of Upper- and Midlevel Managers and Trainers in Needs Assessment

	Upper-Level Managers	*Midlevel Managers*	*Trainers*
Organizational analysis	Is training important to achieve our business objectives? How does training support our business strategy?	Do I want to spend money on training? How much?	Do I have the budget to buy training services? Will managers support training?
Person analysis	What functions or business units need training?	Who should be trained? Managers? Professionals? Core employees?	How will I identify which employees need training?
Task analysis	Does the company have the people with the knowledge, skills, and ability needed to compete in the marketplace?	For what jobs can training make the biggest difference in product quality or customer service?	What tasks should be trained? What knowledge, skills, ability, or other characteristics are necessary?

tive officers (CEOs), and vice presidents. Upper-level managers view the needs assessment process from the broader company perspective. They do not focus on specific jobs. Upper-level managers are involved in the needs assessment process to identify the role of training in relation to other human resource practices in the company (e.g., selection, compensation). That is, upper-level managers help to determine if training is related to the company's business strategy—and, if so, what type of training. Upper-level managers are also involved in identifying what business functions or units need training (person analysis) and in determining if the company has the knowledge, skills, and abilities in the work force that are necessary to meet its strategy and be competitive in the marketplace. Mid-level managers are more concerned with how training may affect the attainment of financial goals for the units they supervise. As a result, for midlevel managers organizational analysis focuses on identifying (1) how much of their budgets they want to devote to training, (2) the types of employees who should receive training (e.g., engineers, or core employees who are directly involved in producing goods or providing services), and (3) for what jobs training can make a difference in terms of improving products or customer service.

As we discussed in Chapter 2, trainers need to consider if training is aligned with the business strategy. However, trainers are primarily interested in needs assessment to provide them with information that they need to administer, develop, and support training programs. This includes determining if training should be purchased or developed in-house, identifying the tasks that need to be trained, and determining top- and midlevel managers' interest and support for training.

While upper-level managers are usually involved to determine if training meets the company's strategy and then to provide appropriate financial resources, upper-level managers are not usually involved in identifying which employees need training, the tasks for which trained is needed, and the knowledge, skills, abilities, and other characteristics needed to complete those tasks. This is the role of subject matter experts (SMEs). **Subject matter experts (SMEs)** are employees, managers, technical experts, trainers, and even customers or suppliers who are knowledgeable in regards to (1) training issues including tasks to be performed, (2) knowledge, skills, and abilities required for successful task performance, (3) necessary equipment, and (4) conditions under which the tasks have to be performed. There is no rule regarding how many types of employees should be represented in the group conducting the needs assessment. Still, it is important to get a sample of job incumbents involved in the process because they tend to be most knowledgeable about the job and can be a great hindrance to the training process if they do not feel they have had input into the needs assessment.

Methods Used in Needs Assessment

Several methods are used to conduct needs assessment, including observing employees performing the job, reading technical manuals and other documentation, interviewing SMEs, and asking SMEs to complete questionnaires designed to identify tasks and knowledge, skills, abilities, and other characteristics required for a job. Table 3–2 presents advantages and disadvantages of each method. As the opening vignette showed, Texas Instruments used all four methods. Boeing uses a process borrowed from the field of artificial intelligence. Experts are observed and interviewed to identify their thinking processes for solving problems, dealing with uncertainty, and minimizing risks. The expert practices that are uncovered are then included in the training curriculum.[2]

For newly created jobs, trainers often do not have job incumbents to rely on for this information. Rather, technical diagrams, simulations, and equipment designers can provide information regarding the training requirements, tasks, and conditions under which the job is performed.

Because no one method is superior to the others, multiple methods are usually used. The methods vary in the type of information as well as the level of detail of the information. Questionnaires have the advantage of being able to collect information from a large number of persons. Also, questionnaires allow many employees to participate in the needs assessment process. However, when using questionnaires it is difficult to collect detailed information regarding training needs. Face-to-face and telephone interviews are time consuming. However,

TABLE 3–2   Advantages and Disadvantages of Needs Assessment Techniques

Technique	Advantages	Disadvantages
Observation	• Generates data relevant to work environment • Minimizes interruption of work	• Needs skilled observer • Employees' behavior may be affected by being observed
Questionnaires	• Inexpensive • Can collect data from a large number of persons • Data easily summarized	• Requires time • Possible low return rates, inappropriate responses • Lacks detail
Read technical manuals and records	• Good source of information on procedure • Objective • Good source of task information for new jobs and jobs in the process of being created	• You may be unable to understand technical language • Materials may be obsolete
Interview subject matter experts	• Good at uncovering details of training needs, as well as causes and solutions of problems	• Time-consuming • Difficult to analyze • Needs skilled interviewer

Source: Based on S. V. Steadham, "Learning to Select a Needs Assessment Strategy," *Training & Development Journal* (January 1980): 56–61, and R. J. Mirabile, "Everything You Wanted to Know about Competency Modeling," *Training & Development* (August 1997): 74.

more detailed information regarding training needs can be collected. For example, the author is currently involved in a needs assessment project for the educational services division of a financial services company. The company wants to determine the training needs of 3,000 employees including managers, non-managers, and regional trainers in the needs assessment process. The company has five regional sites geographically dispersed across the United States (e.g., Midwest region, West region).

One of the potential training needs identified by the corporate training staff is that employees are unable to use new technologies to access training programs such as the Internet. Questionnaires administered to all 3,000 employees to help determine their training needs will include questions related to skills in using new technology. Because there are too many skills and tasks related to the use of technology to include all of them on the questionnaire (e.g., how to use the personal computer operating system, web-browsers, CD-ROM, spreadsheets), several general questions will be included, for instance, "To what extent do you believe you need training to use new technologies that the company is implementing at your workplace?". Phone interviews will then be conducted with a small sample of the employees to gather more detailed information regarding specific skill needs.

With the increasing emphasis on Total Quality Management, many companies are often also using information about other companies' training practices (a process known as benchmarking) to help determine the appropriate type, level, and frequency of training.[3] For example, Chevron, Federal Express, GTE, Xerox, and several other companies are members of the American Society for Training and Development (ASTD) benchmarking forum. A common survey instrument is completed by each company. The survey includes questions on training costs, staff size, administration, design, program development, and delivery. The information is summarized and shared with the participating companies.

The Needs Assessment Process

Here we examine the three elements of needs assessment: organizational analysis, person analysis, and task analysis.

Organizational Analysis

Three factors need to be considered before choosing training as the solution to any pressure point: the company's strategic direction, managers' and peers' support for training activities, and the training resources available.

Company's Strategic Direction.   How the company's business strategy influenced training was discussed in Chapter 2. The strategic role of training influences the frequency and type of training, and how the training function is organized in the company. In companies in which training is expected to contribute to the achievement of business strategies and goals, the amount of money allocated to training and the frequency of training will likely be higher than in companies in which training is done haphazardly or not with strategic intent in mind. For example, companies who have adopted high performance work systems (e.g., teams) are likely to have greater training budgets and conduct more training than companies who have traditional work systems. The business strategy also influences the type of training. For example, as noted in Chapter 2, companies who have adopted a disinvestment strategy are more likely to focus on outplacement assistance and job search skills training than companies with other strategic initiatives. Last, the greater the strategic role of training the more likely the company will organize the training function using the virtual training organization or corporate university models. Both of these models emphasize that training is used to help solve business problems.

Support of Managers and Peers for Training Activities.   A number of studies have found that peer and manager support for training is critical. The key factors for success are a positive attitude among peers and managers about participation in training activities, managers' and peers' willingness to provide information to trainees about how they can more effectively use knowledge, skill, or behaviors learned in training on the job, and opportunities for trainees to use training content in their jobs.[4] If peers' and managers' attitudes and behaviors are not supportive, employees are not likely to apply training content to their jobs.

Training Resources.   It is necessary to identify whether the company has the budget, time, and expertise for training. For example, if the company is installing computer-based manufacturing equipment in one of its plants, it has three possible strategies for dealing with the need to have computer-literate employees. First, the company can decide that given its staff expertise and budget, it can use internal consultants to train all affected employees. Second, the company may decide that it is more cost-effective to identify employees who are computer-literate by using tests and work samples. Employees who fail the test or perform below standards on the work sample can be reassigned to other jobs. Choosing this strategy suggests that the company has decided to devote resources to selection and placement rather than training. Third, because it lacks time or expertise, the company may decide to purchase training from a consultant.

If a company decides to purchase a training program from a consultant or vendor rather than build the program in-house, it is important to choose a provider who will provide a high-quality product. Training providers may include individual consultants, consulting firms, or academic institutions. Many companies identify vendors and consultants who can provide training services by using requests for proposals.[5] A **request for proposal (RFP)** is a document that outlines for potential vendors and consultants the type of service the company is seeking, the type and number of references needed, the number of employees who need to be trained, funding for the project, the follow-up process used to determine level of satisfaction and service, expected date of completion of the project, and the date when proposals must be received by the company. The request for proposal may be mailed to potential consultants and vendors or posted on the company's Web site. The request for proposal is valuable because

---

TABLE 3–3   Questions to Ask Vendors and Consultants

How much and what type of experience does your company have in designing and delivering training?

What are the qualifications and experiences of your staff?

Can you provide demonstrations or examples of training programs you have developed?

Would you provide references of clients for whom you worked?

What evidence do you have that your programs work?

Source: Based on R. Zemke and J. Armstrong, "Evaluating Multimedia Developers," *Training* (November 1996): 33–38.

it provides a standard set of criteria against which all consultants will be evaluated. The RFP also helps eliminate the need to evaluate outside vendors who cannot provide the needed services.

Usually the RFP helps to identify several vendors who meet the criteria. The next step is to choose the preferred provider. Table 3–3 provides examples of questions to ask vendors. Managers and trainers should check the vendor's reputation by contacting prior clients and professional organizations (such as the American Society for Training and Development). The consultant's experience should be evaluated. (For example, in what industry has the vendor worked?) Managers should carefully consider the services, materials, and fees outlined in the consulting contract. For example, it is not uncommon for training materials, manuals, and handouts to remain the property of the consultant. If the company wishes to use these materials for training at a later date, it would have to pay additional fees to the consultant.

When using a consultant or other outside vendor to provide training services, it is also important to consider the extent to which the training program will be customized based on the company's needs or whether the consultant is going to provide training services based on a generic framework that it applies to many different organizations. For example, Towers Perrin, a well-known, successful New York consulting firm, told several clients that it would study their companies in detail and provide a customized diversity training program to fit their needs. However, six companies (including Nissan USA, Thompson Consumer Electronics, and Harris Bank) were given the same 18 recommendations (e.g., separate the concept of affirmative action from that of managing diversity)![6]

How long should you expect it would take a vendor or consultant to develop a training program? The answer is "It depends."[7] Some consultants estimate that development time ranges from 10 to 20 hours for each hour of instruction. Highly technical content requiring more frequent meeting with subject matter experts can add an additional 50 percent more time. For training programs using new technology (such as a CD-ROM) development time can range from 300 to 1,000 hours per hour of program time depending on how much animation, graphics, video, and audio is included, how much new content needs to be developed, the number of practice exercises and type of feedback to be provided to trainees, and the amount of "branches" to different instructional sequences. Chapter 8 details the use of new technologies in training.

Person Analysis

As we mentioned earlier in the chapter, person analysis helps to identify employees who need training. This involves identifying if current performance or expected performance indicates a need for training. The need for training may result from the pressure points in Figure 3–1, including performance problems, changes in the job, or use of new technology. Next we discuss a process showing how to analyze employees' performance to assess whether training is appropriate. This analysis involves determining employees' readiness for training. **Readiness for training** refers to whether (1) employees have the personal characteristics (ability, attitudes, beliefs, and motivation) necessary to learn program content and apply it on the job and (2) the work environment will facilitate learning and not interfere with performance.

A major pressure point for training is poor or substandard performance. Poor performance is indicated by customer complaints, low performance ratings, or on-the-job incidents such as accidents and unsafe behavior. Another potential indicator of the need for training is if the job changes such that current levels of performance need to be improved or employees must be able to complete new tasks.

Figure 3–2 shows the factors that influence employees' performance. These factors include person characteristics, input, output, consequences, and feedback.[8] **Person characteristics** refer to the employees' knowledge, skill, ability, and attitudes. **Input** relates to the instructions that tell employees what, how, and when to perform. Input also refers to the resources that the employees are given to help them perform. These resources may include equipment, time, or budget. **Output** refers to the job's performance standards. **Consequences** refer to the type of incentives that employees receive for performing well. **Feedback** refers to the information that employees receive while they are performing.

Person characteristics, input, output, consequences, and feedback also influence motivation to learn. **Motivation to learn** is trainees' desire to learn the content of training programs.[9] Consider how your motivation to learn may be influenced by personal characteristics and the environment. You may have no problem understanding and comprehending the contents of this textbook. But your learning may be inhibited because of your attitude toward the course. That is, perhaps you don't believe the course will be important for your career. Maybe you're taking the course only because it fits your schedule or is required in your degree program. Learning may also be inhibited by the environment. For example, maybe you want to learn, but your study environment prevents you from doing so. Every time you are prepared to read and review your notes and the textbook, your roommates could be having a party. Even if you don't join them, the music may be so loud that you can't concentrate!

FIGURE 3–2

Factors that influence employee performance and learning

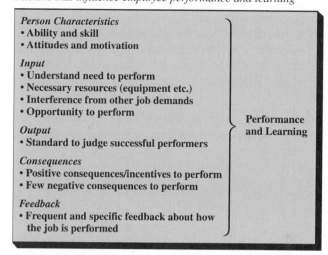

Source: G. Rummler, "In Search of the Holy Performance Grail," *Training and Development* (April 1996): 26–31.

Marriott International Inc., the hotel and restaurant chain, found that personal characteristics were having a significant influence on the success rate of the company's welfare-to-work program.[10] This program involved training welfare recipients for jobs in the company's hotels and restaurants (these types of programs are discussed in greater detail in Chapter 9). Many trainees were unable to complete the training program because of poor attendance resulting from unreliable child care, drug problems, or abusive husbands or boyfriends. As a result, Marriott has instituted tight standards for selecting welfare recipients into the training program. These standards include requiring trainees to have child care, transportation, and housing arrangements. Also, Marriott plans to add an additional drug test during training. Currently, trainees are only tested for drugs at the beginning of training.

A number of research studies have shown that motivation to learn is related to knowledge gained, behavior change, or skill acquisition resulting from training.[11] Besides considering person characteristics, input, output, consequences, and feedback in determining if training is the best solution to a performance problem, managers should also consider these factors prior to sending employees to a training program. These factors relate to the employees' motivation to learn. Here we describe each of these factors and its relationship to performance and learning.

Person Characteristics.   **Basic skills** refer to skills that are necessary for employees to successfully perform on the job and learn the content of training programs. Basic skills include cognitive ability and reading and writing skills. For

---

TABLE 3–4   Steps in Performing a Literacy Audit

Step 1:   Observe employees to determine the basic skills they need to be successful in their job. Note the materials the employee uses on the job, the tasks performed, and the reading, writing, and computations completed by the employee.

Step 2:   Collect all materials that are written and read on the job and identify computations that must be performed to determine the necessary level of basic skill proficiency. Materials include bills, memos, and forms such as inventory lists and requisition sheets.

Step 3:   Interview employees to determine the basic skills they believe are needed to do the job. Consider the basic skill requirements of the job yourself.

Step 4:   Determine whether employees have the basic skills needed to successfully perform the job. Combine the information gathered by observing and interviewing employees and evaluating materials they use on their jobs. Write a description of each job in terms of reading, writing, and computation skills needed to perform successfully.

Step 5:   Develop or buy tests that ask questions relating specifically to the employees' job. Ask employees to complete the tests.

Step 6:   Compare test results with the description of the basic skills required for the job (from step 5). If the level of employees' reading, writing, and computation skills does not match the basic skills required by the job, then a basic skills problem exists.

Source: U.S. Department of Education, U.S. Department of Labor. *The Bottom Line: Basic Skills in the Workplace* (Washington, DC: 1988): 14–15.

example, one assumption that your professor is making in this course is that you have the necessary reading level to comprehend this textbook and the other course materials such as overhead transparencies, videos, or readings. If you lacked the necessary reading level, you likely would not learn much about training in this course. As Chapter 1 mentioned, recent forecasts of skill levels of the U.S. work force indicate that managers will likely have to work with employees who lack basic skills. A literacy audit can be used to determine employees' basic skill levels. Table 3–4 shows the activities involved in conducting a literacy audit.

Cognitive Ability.   Research shows that cognitive ability influences learning and job performance. **Cognitive ability** includes three dimensions: verbal comprehension, quantitative ability, and reasoning ability.[12] Verbal comprehension refers to the person's capacity to understand and use written and spoken language. Quantitative ability refers to how fast and accurately a person can solve math problems. Reasoning ability refers to the person's capacity to invent solutions to problems. Research shows that cognitive ability is related to successful performance in all jobs.[13] The importance of cognitive ability for job success increases as the job becomes more complex.

For example, a supermarket cashier needs low to moderate levels of all three dimensions of cognitive ability to successfully perform her job. An emergency room physician needs higher levels of verbal comprehension, quantitative ability, and reasoning ability than the cashier. The supermarket cashier needs to understand basic math operations (addition, subtraction, etc.) to give customers the correct amount of change. The cashier also needs to invent solutions to problems. (For example, how does the cashier deal with items that are not priced that the customer wants to purchase?) The cashier also needs to be able to understand and communicate with customers (verbal comprehension). The physician also needs quantitative ability, but at a higher level. For example, when dealing with an infant experiencing seizures in an emergency situation, the physician needs to be able to calculate the correct dosage of medicine (based on an adult dosage) to stop the seizures after considering the child's weight. The physician has to be able to quickly diagnose the situation and determine what actions (blood tests, X-rays, respiratory therapy) are necessary. The physician also needs to communicate clearly to the patient (or its parents) the treatment and recovery process.

Cognitive ability influences job performance and ability to learn in training programs. If trainees lack the cognitive ability level necessary to perform job tasks, they will not perform well. Also, trainees' level of cognitive ability can influence performance if they can learn in training programs.[14] Trainees with low levels of cognitive ability are more likely to fail to complete training or (at the end of training) receive lower grades on tests to measure how much they have learned.

To identify employees without the cognitive ability to succeed on the job or in training programs, companies use paper-and-pencil cognitive ability tests. Determining a job's cognitive ability requirement is part of the task analysis process discussed later in this chapter.

Reading Ability.   Lack of the appropriate reading level can impede performance and learning in training programs. Material used in training should be evaluated to ensure that its reading level does not exceed that required by the job. **Readability** refers to the difficulty level of written materials.[15] A readability assessment usually involves analysis of sentence length and word difficulty.

If trainees' reading level does not match the level needed for the training materials, four options are available. First, determine whether it is feasible to use video or on-the-job training, which involves learning by watching and practicing rather than by reading. Second, employees without the necessary reading level could be identified through reading tests and reassigned to other positions more congruent with their skill levels. Third, again using reading tests, identify employees who lack the necessary reading skills and provide them with remedial training. Fourth, determine whether the job can be redesigned to accommodate employees' reading levels. The fourth option is certainly most costly and least practical. Therefore, alternative training methods need to be considered or you can elect a nontraining option. Nontraining options include selecting employees for jobs and training opportunities on the basis of reading, computation, writing, and other basic skill requirements.

Many companies are finding that employees lack the basic skills needed to successfully complete training programs. For example, a training program for 1,800 hourly employees at Georgia-Pacific (a paper manufacturer) was ineffective.[16] Employees reported that they understood training content but once they left training and returned to their jobs, they couldn't successfully perform maintenance tasks. In trying to determine the cause of the failed training, employees' basic skills were tested. Tests revealed that many employees had difficulty reading and writing. As a result, they were unable to understand the materials used in training. This translated into reduced learning and poor job performance.

To help ensure that employees have the necessary basic skills needed to succeed in training, Georgia-Pacific developed a basic skills assessment and training program. The first step involved assessment (or measurement) of employees' basic skills. A test of reading and math skills was given to employees. People who scored at or above a ninth grade reading level were eligible to attend training programs. Those with literacy levels below ninth grade were counseled to attend basic skills training. Because Georgia-Pacific's primary concern was how to convince employees to attend training, the company had to establish trust with the employees. In general, employees who lack basic skills are embarrassed to admit they have difficulty and are afraid that their lack of literacy will cost them their jobs. To alleviate these fears, employees received confidential counseling about their test results, they were not required to start basic skills training immediately after the assessment, and the company did not put information regarding test results (pass or fail) in employees' personnel files.

A local community college supplied the basic skills training. Classes were set up close to Georgia-Pacific's plants so employees could attend classes before or after their work shifts. There was no charge for the classes. Now the work force has the necessary basic skills. To ensure that new employees do not lack basic skills, Georgia-Pacific has changed its hiring qualifications. The company does not accept applications from anyone who hasn't completed a specific 18-month schedule of courses at the community college.

Another approach to improving basic skills is incorporating basic skills instruction into training programs. An example is the electronics technician training program developed by the Ford Foundation.[17] Before the start of the program, students are given information about electronic technician jobs. Students are told they will learn how to think about operating, maintaining, and repairing electrical equipment that they are familiar with such as flashlights, curling irons, and lamps. These appliances were selected because they are useful for introducing basic electronic concepts and procedures.

Trainees are given a book that covers the basic literacy skills needed to read training and job-related material in electronics. The book's exercises and worksheets help the trainee master "reading-to-do" and "reading-to-learn" skills that have been identified as required in the majority of jobs.[18] Reading-to-do involves searching for and reading information in manuals, books, or charts (e.g., looking up information such as repair specifications in a technical manual or scanning tables and graphs to locate information). Reading-to-learn involves reading information to apply it in the future, such as reading instructions on how to use a piece of equipment (e.g., paraphrasing and summarizing information).

Besides learning reading skills related to electronics, trainees study how electronics is used in flashlights and table lamps. The textbook introduces students to math concepts and their applications, including scientific notation needed to understand waves that appear on an oscilloscope. This training program has prepared competent electronic technicians for entry-level positions.

Self-Efficacy.   **Self-efficacy** is the employee's belief that she can successfully perform her job or learn the content of the training program. The job environment can be threatening to many employees who may not have been successful performers in the past. For example, as you will see in Chapter 10, people who are hired from a welfare-to-work program—a program designed to help get work for employees on welfare—may lack self-efficacy. The training environment can also be threatening to employees who have not received training or formal education for some length of time, lack education, or are not experienced in the training program's subject matter. For example, training employees to use equipment for computer-based manufacturing may represent a potential threat, especially if employees are intimidated by new technology and do not have the confidence in their ability to master the skills needed to use a computer. Research has demonstrated that self-efficacy is related to performance in training programs.[19] Employees' self-efficacy level can be increased by

1. Letting employees know that the purpose of training is to try to improve performance rather than to identify areas in which employees are incompetent.
2. Providing as much information as possible about the training program and purpose of training prior to the actual training.
3. Showing employees the training success of their peers who are now in similar jobs.
4. Providing employees with feedback that learning is under their control and they have the ability and the responsibility to overcome any learning difficulties they experience in the program.

Awareness of Training Needs, Career Interests, and Goals.   To be motivated to learn in training programs, employees must be aware of their skill strengths and weaknesses and of the link between the training program and improvement of their weaknesses.[20] Managers should make sure that employees understand why they are asked to attend training programs, and they should communicate the link between training and improvement of skill weaknesses or knowledge deficiencies. This can be accomplished by sharing performance feedback with the employee, holding career development discussions, or having the employee complete a self-evaluation of his skill strengths and weaknesses as well as career interests and goals.

If possible, employees need to be given a choice of what programs to attend and must understand how actual training assignments are made to maximize motivation to learn. Several recent studies have suggested that giving trainees a choice regarding which programs to attend and then honoring those choices maximizes motivation to learn. Giving employees choices but not necessarily honoring them can undermine motivation to learn.[21]

Input.   Employees' perceptions of two characteristics of the work environment—situational constraints and social support—are determinants of performance and motivation to learn. **Situational constraints** include lack of proper tools and equipment, materials and supplies, budgetary support, and time. **Social support** refers to managers' and peers' willingness to provide feedback and reinforcement.[22] If employees have the knowledge, skills, attitudes, and behavior needed to perform but do not have the proper tools and equipment needed their performance will be inadequate.

To ensure that the work environment enhances trainees' motivation to learn,

1. Provide materials, time, job-related information, and other work aids necessary for employees to use new skills or behavior before participating in training programs.
2. Speak positively about the company's training programs to employees.
3. Let employees know they are doing a good job when they are using training content in their work.
4. Encourage work-group members to involve each other in trying to use new skills on the job by soliciting feedback and sharing training experiences and situations in which training content was helpful.
5. Provide employees with time and opportunities to practice and apply new skills or behaviors to their work.

Output.   On-the-job, poor or substandard performance can occur because employees do not know at what level they are expected to perform. For example, they may not be aware of quality standards related to speed or degree of personalization of service that are expected. Employees may have the knowledge, skill, and attitudes necessary to perform, but they fail to perform because they are not aware of the performance standards. Lack of awareness of the performance standards is a communications problem, but it is not a problem that training can "fix."

Understanding the need to perform is important for learning. Trainees need to understand what specifically they are expected to learn in the training program. In training programs, to insure that trainees master training content at the appropriate level, trainees also need to understand the level of proficiency that is expected of them. For example, for tasks, level of proficiency relates to how well they are to perform a task. For knowledge, level of proficiency may relate to a score on a written test. The standards or level of performance are part of the learning objectives (discussed in Chapter 4).

Consequences.   If employees do not believe that rewards or incentives for performance are adequate, they will be unlikely to meet performance standards even if they have the necessary knowledge, behavior, skill, or attitudes. Also work group norms may encourage employees not to meet performance standards. Norms are accepted standards of behavior for work-group members. For example, during labor contract negotiations baggage handlers for Northwest Airlines worked slowly loading and unloading baggage from airplanes. As a result, many passenger departures and arrivals were delayed. The baggage handlers had the knowledge, skills, and behaviors necessary to unload the planes but they worked slowly because they were trying to send a message to management that the airlines could not perform effectively if their contract demands were not met.

Consequences also affect learning in training programs. Employees' motivation to learn can be enhanced by communicating to them the potential job-related, personal, and career benefits they may receive as a result of attending training and learning the content of the training program. These benefits may include learning a more efficient way to perform a process or procedure, establishing contacts with other employees in the company (also known as networking), or increasing their opportunity to pursue other jobs in the company. It is important that the communication from the manager about potential benefits be realistic. Unmet expectations about training programs can hinder motivation to learn.[23]

Feedback.   Performance problems can result when employees do not receive feedback regarding the extent to which they are meeting performance standards. Training may not be the best solution to this type of problem if employees know what they are supposed to do (output), but do not understand how close their performance is to the standard. Employees need to be given specific, detailed feedback of effective and ineffective performance. For employees to perform to standard, feedback needs to be given to employees frequently, not just during a yearly performance evaluation.

In Chapter 4 the role of feedback in learning is discussed in detail. Keep in mind that feedback is critical for shaping trainees behaviors and skills.

Determining If Training Is the Best Solution.   As this chapter has said, to determine if training is needed, for any performance problem you need to analyze characteristics of the performer, input, output, consequences, and feedback. How might this be done? Based on the model in Figure 3–2, you should ask several questions to determine if training is the likely solution to a performance problem.[24] Assess whether

1. The performance problem is important and has the potential to cost the company a significant amount of money from lost productivity or customers.
2. Employees do not know how to perform effectively. Perhaps they received little or no previous training or the training was ineffective. (This problem is a characteristic of the person.)

3. Employees cannot demonstrate the correct knowledge or behavior. Employees were trained but they infrequently or never used the training content (knowledge, skills, etc.) on the job. (This is an input problem.)

4. Performance expectations are clear (input) and there are no obstacles to performance such as faulty tools or equipment.

5. There are positive consequences for good performance, while poor performance is not rewarded. For example, if employees are dissatisfied with their compensation, their peers or a union may encourage them to slow down their pace of work. (This involves consequences.)

6. Employees receive timely, relevant, accurate, constructive, and specific feedback about their performance (a feedback issue).

7. Other solutions such as job redesign or transferring employees to other jobs are too expensive or unrealistic.

If employees lack the knowledge and skill to perform and the other factors are satisfactory, training is needed. If employees have the knowledge and skill to perform but input, output, consequences, or feedback are inadequate, training may not be the best solution. For example, if poor performance results from faulty equipment, training cannot solve this problem but repairing the equipment will! If poor performance results from lack of feedback, then employees may not need training, but their managers may need training on how to give performance feedback!

Task Analysis

Task analysis results in a description of work activities, including tasks performed by the employee and the knowledge, skills, and abilities required to complete the tasks. Before understanding the steps in a task analysis, you must understand its terminology. A **job** is a specific position requiring the completion of certain tasks. (The tasks in Figure 3–3 are part of the electrical maintenance worker's job.) A **task** is a statement of an employee's work activity in a specific job. Figure 3–3 shows several tasks for the electrical maintenance worker job. These tasks include replacing light bulbs, electrical outlets, and light switches. To complete tasks, employees must have specific levels of knowledge, skill, ability, and other considerations (KSAOs). **Knowledge** includes facts or procedures (e.g., the chemical properties of gold). **Skill** indicates competency in performing a task (e.g., negotiation skill, a skill in getting another person to agree to take a certain course of action). **Ability** includes the physical and mental capacities to perform a task (e.g., spatial ability, the ability to see the relationship between objects in physical space). **Other** refers to the conditions under which tasks are performed. These conditions include identifying the equipment and environment that the employee works in (e.g., the need to wear an oxygen mask, work in extremely hot conditions), time constraints for a task (e.g., deadlines), safety considerations, or performance standards.

FIGURE 3–3

Sample items from task analysis questionnaires for the electrical maintenance job

Job: Electrical Maintenance Worker

Task #s	Task Description	Task Performance Ratings		
		Frequency of performance	Importance	Difficulty
199-264	Replace a light bulb	0 1 2 3 4 5	0 1 2 3 4 5	0 1 2 3 4 5
199-265	Replace an electrical outlet	0 1 2 3 4 5	0 1 2 3 4 5	0 1 2 3 4 5
199-266	Install a light fixture	0 1 2 3 4 5	0 1 2 3 4 5	0 1 2 3 4 5
199-267	Replace a light switch	0 1 2 3 4 5	0 1 2 3 4 5	0 1 2 3 4 5
199-268	Install a new circuit breaker	0 1 2 3 4 5	0 1 2 3 4 5	0 1 2 3 4 5
		Frequency of performance 0=never 5=often	**Importance** 1=negligible 5=extremely high	**Difficulty** 1=easiest 5=most difficult

Source: E. F. Holton III and C. Bailey, "Top to Bottom Curriculum Redesign," *Training & Development* (March 1995): 40–44.

Task analysis should be undertaken only after you have determined from the organizational analysis that the company wants to devote time and money for training. Why? As you will see shortly, task analysis is a time-consuming, tedious process that involves a large time commitment to gather and summarize data from many different persons in the company including managers, job incumbents, and trainers.

Steps in a Task Analysis.   A task analysis involves four steps:[25]

1. Select the job(s) to be analyzed.

2. Develop a preliminary list of tasks performed on the job by (1) interviewing and observing expert employees and their managers and (2) talking with others who have performed a task analysis.

3. Validate or confirm the preliminary list of tasks. This involves having a group of subject matter experts (job incumbents, managers, etc.) answer in a meeting or on a written survey several questions regarding the tasks. The types of questions that may be asked include the following: How frequently is the task performed? How much time is spent performing each task? How important or critical is the task for successful performance of the job? How difficult is the task to learn? Is performance of the task expected of entry-level employees?

Table 3–5 presents a sample task analysis questionnaire. This information is used to determine which tasks will be focused on in the training program. The person or committee conducting the needs assessment must decide the level of ratings across dimensions that will determine that a task should be included in the training

TABLE 3–5   Sample Task Statement Questionnaire

Name   Date

Position

Please rate each of the task statements according to three factors: the *importance* of the task for effective performance, how *frequently* the task is performed, and the degree of *difficulty* required to become effective in the task. Use the following scales in making your ratings.

Importance

4 = Task is critical for effective performance.

3 = Task is important but not critical
    for effective performance.

2 = Task is of some importance
    for effective performance.

1 = Task is of no importance
    for task performance.

0 = Task is not performed.

Frequency

4 = Task is performed once a day.

3 = Task is performed once a week.

2 = Task is performed once every few months.

1 = Task is performed once or twice a year.

0 = Task is not performed.

Difficulty

4 = Effective performance of the task requires extensive prior experience and/or training
    (12–18 months or longer).

3 = Effective performance of the task requires minimal prior experience and training
    (6–12 months).

2 = Effective performance of the task requires a brief period of prior training and experience
    (1–6 months).

1 = Effective performance of the task does not require specific prior training and/or experience.

0 = This task is not performed.

Task	*Importance*	*Frequency*	*Difficulty*
1. Ensuring maintenance on equipment, tools, and safety controls			
2. Monitoring employee performance			
3. Scheduling employees			
4. Using statistical software on the computer			
5. Monitoring changes made in processes using statistical methods			

TABLE 3–6   Key Points to Remember When Conducting a Task Analysis

A task analysis should identify both what employees are actually doing and what they should be doing on the job.

Task analysis begins by breaking the job into duties and tasks.

Use more than two methods for collecting task information to increase the validity of the analysis.

For task analysis to be useful, information needs to be collected from subject matter experts (SMEs). SMEs include job incumbents, managers, and employees familiar with the job.

In deciding how to evaluate tasks, the focus should be on tasks necessary to accomplish the company's goals and objectives. These may not be the tasks that are the most difficult or take the most time.

Source: Adapted from A. P. Carnevale, L. J. Gainer, and A. S. Meltzer, *Workplace Basics Training Manual* (San Francisco: Jossey-Bass, 1990).

program. Tasks that are important, frequently performed, and of moderate-to-high level of difficulty should be trained. Tasks that are not important and infrequently performed will not be trained. It is difficult for managers and trainers to decide if tasks that are important, performed infrequently, and requiring minimal difficulty should be included in training. Managers and trainers must determine whether or not important tasks, regardless of how frequently they are performed, or their level of difficulty, will be included in training.

4. Once the tasks are identified, it is important to identify the knowledge, skills, or abilities necessary to successfully perform each task. This information can be collected using interviews and questionnaires. Recall this chapter's discussion of how ability influences learning. Information concerning basic skill and cognitive ability requirements is critical for determining if certain levels of knowledge, skills, and abilities will be prerequisites for entrance to the training program (or job) or if supplementary training in underlying skills is needed. For training purposes, information concerning how difficult it is to learn the knowledge, skill, or ability is important—as is whether the knowledge, skill, or ability is expected to be acquired by the employee before taking the job.[26]

Table 3–6 summarizes key points to remember regarding task analysis.

Example of a Task Analysis.   Each of the four steps of a task analysis can be seen in this example from a utility company. Trainers were given the job of developing a training system in six months.[27] The purpose of the program was to identify tasks and knowledge, skills, abilities, and other considerations that would serve as the basis for training program objectives and lesson plans.

The first phase of the project involved identifying potential tasks for each job in the utility's electrical maintenance area. Procedures, equipment lists, and information provided by subject matter experts (SMEs) were used to generate the tasks. SMEs included managers, instructors, and senior technicians. The tasks were incorporated into a questionnaire administered to all technicians in the electrician maintenance department. The questionnaire included 550 tasks. Figure 3–3 shows sample items from the questionnaire for the electrical maintenance job. Technicians were asked to rate each task on importance, difficulty, and frequency of performance. The rating scale for frequency included zero. A zero rating indicated that the technician rating the task had never performed the task. Technicians who rated a task zero were asked not to evaluate the task's difficulty and importance.

Customized software was used to analyze the ratings collected via the questionnaire. The primary requirement used to determine whether a task required training was its importance rating. A task rated "very important" was identified as one requiring training regardless of its frequency or difficulty. If a task was rated moderately important but difficult, it also was designated for training. Tasks rated unimportant, not difficult, and done infrequently were not designated for training.

The list of tasks designated for training were reviewed by the SMEs to determine if they accurately described job tasks. The result was a list of 487 tasks. For each of the 487 tasks, two SMEs identified the necessary knowledge, skills, abilities, and other factors required for performance. This included information on working conditions, cues that initiate the task's start and end, performance standards, safety considerations, and necessary tools and equipment. All data were reviewed by plant technicians and members of the training department. More than 14,000 knowledge, skill, ability, and other considerations were clustered into common areas. An identification code was assigned to each group that linked groups to task and knowledge, skill, ability, and other factors. These groups were then combined into clusters. The clusters represented qualification areas. That is, the task clusters related to linked tasks that the employees must be certified in to perform the job. The clusters were used to identify training lesson plans and course objectives. Trainers also reviewed the clusters to identify prerequisite skills for each cluster.

Competency Models

Traditionally, as you have just seen, needs assessment has involved identifying knowledge, skills, abilities, and tasks. However, a current trend in training is for needs assessment to focus on competencies. A **competency** refers to areas of personal capability that enable employees to successfully perform their jobs by achieving outcomes or successfully performing tasks.[28] A competency can be knowledge, skills, attitudes, values, or personal characteristics. A **competency model** identifies the competencies necessary for each job as well as the knowledge, skills, behavior, and personality characteristics underlying each competency.[29] Table 3–7 shows a competency model for a systems engineer. The left side of the table lists technical competencies within the technical cluster (systems architecture, data migration, documentation). The right side shows behaviors that might be used to determine a systems engineer level of proficiency for each competency.

TABLE 3–7   Example of Competencies and a Competency Model

Technical Cluster	*Proficiency Ratings*
Systems Architecture Ability to design complex software applications, establish protocols, and create prototypes.	**0**—Is not able to perform basic tasks. **1**—Understands basic principles; can perform tasks with assistance or direction. **2**—Performs routine tasks with reliable results; works with minimal supervision. **3**—Performs complex and multiple tasks; can coach or teach others. **4**—Considered an expert in this task; can describe, teach, and lead others.
Data Migration Ability to establish the necessary platform requirements to efficiently and completely coordinate data transfer.	**0**—Is not able to perform basic tasks. **1**—Understands basic principles; can perform tasks with assistance or direction. **2**—Performs routine tasks with reliable results; works with minimal supervision. **3**—Performs complex and multiple tasks; can coach or teach others. **4**—Considered an expert in this task; can describe, teach, and lead others.
Documentation Ability to prepare comprehensive and complete documentation including specifications, flow diagrams, process control, and budgets.	**0**—Is not able to perform basic tasks. **1**—Understands basic principles; can perform tasks with assistance or direction. **2**—Performs routine tasks with reliable results; works with minimal supervision. **3**—Performs complex and multiple tasks; can coach or teach others. **4**—Considered an expert in this task; can describe, teach, and lead others.

Source: R.J. Mirabile, "Everything You Wanted to Know about Competency Modeling," *Training & Development* (August 1997): 73–77

How are competencies identified and competency models developed? First, the job or position to be analyzed needs to be identified. Second, any changes in the business strategy need to be identified. The implications of business strategy for training were discussed in Chapter 2. Changes in the business strategy might cause new competencies to be needed or old competencies to be altered. Third, effective and ineffective performers need to be identified. Fourth, the competencies responsible for effective and ineffective performance need to be identified. There are several approaches for identifying competencies. These include analyzing one or several "star" performers, surveying persons who are familiar with the job (subject matter experts), and developing competencies based on benchmark data of good performers in other companies.[30] Fifth, the model needs to be validated. That is, you must determine if the competencies included in the model truly are related to effective performance. In Table 3–7's example of the technical competencies for the system engineer, it is important to verify that (1) the three competencies shown are needed to be successful in the job and (2) the level of proficiency of the competency is appropriate.

Competency models are used for identifying training needs as well as for development. That is, a competency model can be used to identify what employees need to be trained in for the job. Competency models can also be used in development planning for employees who aspire to a position. By comparing their current personal competencies to those required for a job, employees can identify competencies that need development and choose actions to develop those competencies. These actions may include courses, job experiences, and other types of development. (Development methods are detailed in Chapter 9.)

Summary

The first step in a successful training effort is to determine that a training need exists through a process known as needs assessment. Needs assessment involves three steps: organizational analysis, person analysis, and task analysis. Various methods—including observation, interviews, and surveys or questionnaires—are used to conduct a needs assessment. Each has advantages and disadvantages. Organizational analysis involves determining (1) the extent to which training is congruent with the company's business strategy and resources and (2) if peers and managers are likely to provide the support needed for trainees to use training content in the work setting.

Person analysis focuses on identifying if there is evidence that training is the solution, who needs training, and if employees have the prerequisite skills, attitudes, and beliefs needed to ensure they master the content of training programs. Because performance problems are one of the major reasons companies consider training employees, it is important to consider how personal characteristics, input, output, consequences, and feedback relate to performance and learning. This means that managers and trainers need to be concerned about employees' basic skill levels, attitudes, and the work environment in determining if performance problems can be solved using training.

Training is likely the best solution to a performance problem if employees don't know how to perform. If employees have not received feedback about their performance, they lack the equipment needed to perform the job, the consequences for good performance are negative, or they are unaware of an expected standard for performance, then training is not likely to be the best solution.

To maximize employees' motivation to learn in training programs, managers and trainers need to understand these factors prior to sending employees to training. For example, lack of basic skills or reading skills can inhibit both job performance and learning.

A task analysis involves identifying the task and knowledge, skills, and abilities that will be trained. The chapter concludes by discussing a new approach to needs assessment, competency modeling.

Key Terms

needs assessment   50
organizational analysis   51
person analysis   51
task analysis   51
subject matter experts (SMEs)   53
request for proposal (RFP)   56
readiness for training   58
person characteristics   58
input   58
output   58
consequences   58
feedback   58
motivation to learn   58
basic skills   59

cognitive ability   60
readability   61
self-efficacy   63
situational constraints   64
social support   64
job   66
task   66
knowledge   66
skill   66
ability   66
other   66
competency   70
competency model   70

Discussion Questions

1. Which of the factors that influence performance and learning do you think is most important? Which is least important?

2. If you had to conduct a needs assessment for a new job at a new plant, describe the method you would use.

3. Why should upper-level managers be included in the needs assessment process?

4. Explain how you would determine if employees had the reading level necessary to succeed in a training program.

5. What conditions would suggest that a company should buy a training program from an outside vendor? Which would suggest that the firm should develop the program itself?

6. Assume you have to prepare older employees with little computer experience to attend a training course on how to use the World Wide Web. How will you ensure they have high levels of readiness for training?

7. Review the accompanying sample tasks and task ratings for the electronic technician's job. What tasks do you believe should be emphasized in the training program? Why?

Task	Importance	Frequency	Learning Difficulty
1. Replaces components	1	2	1
2. Repairs equipment	2	5	5
3. Interprets instrument readings	1	4	5
4. Uses small tools	2	5	1

Explanation of Ratings:
Frequency: 1 = very infrequently to 5 = very frequently.
Importance: 1 = very important to 5 = very unimportant.
Learning difficulty: 1 = easy to 5 = very difficult.

8. How is competency modeling similar to traditional needs assessment? How does it differ?

Application Assignments

1. Develop a competency model for a job held by a friend, spouse, or roommate (someone other than yourself). Use the process discussed in this chapter to develop your model. Note the most difficult part of developing the model. How could the model be used?

2. The Department of Social Services represents a large portion of your county's budget and total number of employees. The job of eligibility technician is responsible for all client contact, policy interpretation, and financial decisions related to several forms of public aid (e.g, food stamps, aid to families with dependent children). Eligibility technicians must read a large number of memos and announcements of new and revised policies and procedures. Eligibility technicians were complaining they had difficulty reading and responding to this correspondence. The county decided to send the employees to a speed reading program costing $250 per person. The county has 200 eligibility technicians.

   Preliminary evaluation of the speed reading program was that trainees liked it. Two months after the training was conducted, the technicians told their managers that they were not using the speed reading course in their jobs, but were using it in leisure reading at home. When their managers asked why they weren't using it on the job, the typical response was "I never read those memos and policy announcements anyway."

   A. Evaluate the needs assessment process used to determine that speed reading was necessary. What was good about it? Where was it faulty?

   B. How would you have conducted the needs assessment? Be realistic.

Endnotes

1. I. L. Goldstein, E. P. Braverman, and H. Goldstein, "Needs Assessment," in *Developing Human Resources,* ed. K. N. Wexley, (Washington, DC: Bureau of National Affairs, 1991): 5–35 to 5–75.

2. L. Overmyer-Day and G. Benson, "Training Success Stories," *Training and Development* (June 1996): 24–29.

3. L. E. Day, "Benchmarking Training," *Training and Development* (November 1995): 27–30.

4. J. Z. Rouillier and I. L. Goldstein, "Determinants of the Climate for Transfer of Training" (presented at Society of Industrial/Organizational Psychology meeting, St. Louis, MO, 1991); J. S. Russell, J. R. Terborg, and M. L. Powers, "Organizational Performance and Organizational Level Training and Support," *Personnel Psychology* 38 (1985): 849–63; H. Baumgartel, G. J. Sullivan, and L. E. Dunn, "How Organizational Climate and Personality Affect the Pay-off from Advanced Management Training Sessions," *Kansas Business Review* 5 (1978): 1–10.

5. B. Gerber, "How to Buy Training Programs," *Training* (June 1989): 59–68.

6. D. A. Blackmon, "Consultants' Advice on Diversity Was Anything but Diverse," *Wall Street Journal* (March 11, 1997): A1, A16.

7. R. Zemke and J. Armstrong, "How Long Does It Take? (The Sequel)," *Training* (May 1997): 69–79.

8. G. Rummler, "In Search of the Holy Performance Grail," *Training and Development* (April 1996): 26–31; D. G. Langdon, "Selecting Interventions," *Performance Improvement* 36 (1997): 11–15.

9. R. A. Noe, "Trainee Attributes and Attitudes: Neglected Influences on Training Effectiveness," *Academy of Management Review* 11 (1986): 736–49.

10. D. Milibank, "Marriott Tightens Job Program Screening," *Wall Street Journal* (July 15, 1997): A1, A12.

11. T. T. Baldwin, R. T. Magjuka, and B. T. Loher, "The Perils of Participation: Effects of Choice on Trainee Motivation and Learning," *Personnel Psychology* 44 (1991): 51–66; S. I. Tannenbaum, J. E. Mathieu, E. Salas, and J. A. Cannon-Bowers, "Meeting Trainees' Expectations: The Influence of Training Fulfillment on the Development of Commitment, Self-Efficacy, and Motivation," *Journal of Applied Psychology* 76 (1991): 759–69.

12. J. Nunally, *Psychometric Theory* (New York: McGraw-Hill, 1978).

13. L. Gottsfredson, "The g Factor in Employment," *Journal of Vocational Behavior* 19 (1986): 293–96.

14. M. J. Ree and J. A. Earles, "Predicting Training Success: Not Much More than g," *Personnel Psychology* 44 (1991): 321–32.

15. D. R. Torrence and J. A. Torrence, "Training in the Face of Illiteracy," *Training and Development Journal* (August 1987): 44–49.

16. M. Davis, "Getting Workers Back to the Basics," *Training and Development* (October 1997): 14–15.

17. J. M. Rosow and R. Zager, *Training: The Competitive Edge* (San Francisco: Jossey-Bass, 1988), Chapter 7 ("Designing Training Programs to Train Functional Illiterates for New Technology").

18. A. P. Carnevale, L. J. Gainer, and A. S. Meltzer, *Workplace Basics Training Manual, 1990* (San Francisco: Jossey-Bass, 1990).

19. M. E. Gist, C. Schwoerer, and B. Rosen, "Effects of Alternative Training Methods on Self-Efficacy and Performance in Computer Software Training," *Journal of Applied Psychology* 74 (1990): 884–91; J. Martocchio and J. Dulebohn, "Performance Feedback Effects in Training: The Role of Perceived Controllability,"*Personnel Psychology* 47 (1994): 357–73; J. Martocchio, "Ability Conceptions and Learning," *Journal of Applied Psychology* 79 (1994): 819–25.

20. R. A. Noe and N. Schmitt, "The Influence of Trainee Attitudes on Training Effectiveness: Test of a Model," *Personnel Psychology* 39 (1986): 497–523.

21. M. A. Quinones, "Pretraining Context Effects: Training Assignments as Feedback," *Journal of Applied Psychology* 80 (1995): 226–38; T. T. Baldwin, R. J. Magjuka, and B. T. Loher, "The Perils of Participation: Effects of Choice of Training on Trainees Motivation and Learning," *Personnel Psychology* 44 (1991): 51–65.

22. L. H. Peters, E. J. O'Connor, and J. R. Eulberg, "Situational Constraints: Sources, Consequences, and Future Considerations," in *Research in Personnel and Human Resource Management,* ed. K. M. Rowland and G. R. Ferris (Greenwich, CT: JAI Press, 1985), 3: 79–114; E. J. O'Connor, L. H. Peters, A. Pooyan, J. Weekley, B. Frank, and B. Erenkranz, "Situational Constraints Effects on Performance, Affective Reactions, and Turnover: A Field Replication and Extension," *Journal of Applied Psychology* 69 (1984): 663–72; D. J. Cohen, "What Motivates Trainees?" *Training and Development Journal* (November 1990): 91–93; Russell, Terborg, and Power, "Organizational Performance and Organizational Level Training and Support."

23. W. D. Hicks and R. J. Klimoski, "Entry into Training Programs and Its Effects on Training Outcomes: A Field Experiment," *Academy of Management Journal* 30 (1987): 542–52.

24. R. F. Mager and P. Pipe, *Analyzing Performance Problems: Or You Really Oughta Wanna,* 2d ed. (Belmont, CA: Pittman Learning, 1984); Carnevale, Gainer, and Meltzer, *Workplace Basics Training Manual;* G. Rummler, "In Search of the Holy Performance Grail."

25. C. E. Schneier, J. P. Guthrie, and J. D. Olian, "A Practical Approach to Conducting and Using Training Needs Assessment," *Public Personnel Management* (Summer 1988): 191–205.

26. I. Goldstein, "Training in Organizations," in *Handbook of Industrial/Organizational Psychology,* 2d ed., ed. M. D. Dunnette and L. M. Hough (Palo Alto, CA: Consulting Psychologists Press, 1991), 2: 507–619.

27. E. F. Holton III and C. Bailey, "Top-to-Bottom Curriculum Redesign," *Training and Development* (March 1995): 40–44.

28. A. Reynolds, *The Trainer's Dictionary: HRD Terms, Abbreviations, and Acronyms,* (HRD Press, 1993).

29. M. Dalton, "Are Competency Models a Waste?" *Training and Development* (October 1997): 46–49.

30. J. Kochanski, "Competency-Based Management," *Training and Development* (October 1997): 41–44.

4   LEARNING: THEORIES AND PROGRAM DESIGN

Objectives

After reading this chapter, you should be able to

1. Discuss the five types of learner outcomes.

2. Explain the implications of learning theory for instructional design.

3. Incorporate adult learning theory into the design of a training program.

4. Describe how learners receive, process, store, retrieve, and act upon information.

5. Discuss the internal conditions (within the learner) and external conditions (learning environment) necessary for the trainee to learn each type of capability.

6. Be able to choose and prepare a training site.

7. Explain the four components of program design: course parameters, objectives, lesson overview, and detailed lesson plan.

FOOD FOR THOUGHT

In the rolling hills of the Hudson River Valley, a 90-minute drive from New York City, is the world's finest training facility for chefs. The Culinary Institute of America (CIA) has approximately 2000 full-time students in its degree programs. CIA graduates are chefs in some of the best restaurants in the world such as the Mansion on Turtle Creek in Dallas, Texas. CIA graduates also work in prestigious private dining rooms (like the White House) and direct food service operations for large hotel chains such as the Marriott, Hyatt, Radisson, and Hilton. Besides offering degree programs, the CIA also hosts more than 6,000 trainees from a wide variety of companies that have food service operations.

Whether an instructor is teaching meat-cutting or sautéing techniques, the programs' learning environments are basically the same. A lecture is followed by demonstration and several hours of guided hands-on practice. The trainee then receives feedback from the instructor. The trainer moves from a show-and-tell approach to become a coach over the course of the training session. Videos are produced for every class that a student will take. They can be viewed from residence halls or can be seen at the video learning center where students can review the tapes at their own pace; the students control what they see.

CIA programs deal not only with cognitive learning but with physical and emotional learning. In addition to cook-ing and baking courses, students are required to study psychology, total quality management, languages, marketing, communications, restaurant management, and team supervision. Physical fitness and stress management are required parts of the curriculum. Why? Running a commercial kitchen involves long hours and high levels of stress—it is very physically demanding.

Thanks to the learning environment created at CIA, the institute is recognized as the world leader in gastronomic training as it provides a foundation of basic knowledge for chefs from around the world. ■

Source: Based on R. Zemke, "Cooking Up World-Class Training," *Training* 34 (1997): 52–58.

Introduction

Training at the Culinary Institute of America is designed to teach aspiring chefs how to prepare food (knowledge) as well as develop the necessary motor skills (e.g., chopping onions). These are types of learning outcomes. CIA's training programs also illustrate several conditions necessary for learning to occur: opportunities for trainees to learn by observing an expert, practicing, and receiving feedback.

As CIA training illustrates, for learning to occur it is important to identify *what* is to be learned—that is, identify the learning outcomes. As a student you are probably most familiar with one type of learning outcome: intellectual skills. However, training programs often focus on other outcomes such as motor skills (e.g., climbing) and attitudes. Understanding learning outcomes is crucial because they influence the characteristics of the training environment that are necessary for learning to occur. These characteristics include using materials in training that are meaningful to the trainees, providing opportunities to practice, and receiving feedback. For example, if trainees are to master motor skills such as chopping onions, they must have opportunities to practice chopping onions and receive feedback about their cutting skills.

Also, the design of the training program is important for learning to occur. This includes creating the program schedule, providing a physically comfortable training environment, and arranging the seating in the training environment to facilitate interaction between trainees and between trainer and trainees.

This chapter begins by defining learning and acquainting you with the different learning outcomes. Next, we discuss various theories of learning and their implications for creating a learning environment designed to help the trainee learn the desired outcomes. The last section of the chapter looks at practical issues in training program design including selecting and preparing a training site and developing lesson plans.

What Is Learning? What Is Learned?

Learning is a relatively permanent change in human capabilities that is not a result of growth processes.[1] These capabilities are related to specific learning outcomes, as Table 4–1 shows.

Verbal information includes names or labels, facts, and bodies of knowledge. Verbal information includes specialized knowledge that employees need in their jobs. For example, a manager must know the names of different types of equipment as well as the body of knowledge related to Total Quality Management.

Intellectual skills include concepts and rules. These concepts and rules are critical to solve problems, serve customers, and create products. For example, a manager must know the steps in the performance appraisal process (e.g., gather data, summarize data, prepare for appraisal interview with employee) in order to conduct an employee appraisal.

Motor skills include coordination of physical movements. For example, a telephone repair person must have the coordination and dexterity necessary to climb ladders and telephone poles.

Attitudes are a combination of beliefs and feelings that predispose a person to behave a certain way. Attitudes include a cognitive component (beliefs), an affective component (feeling), and an intentional component (the way a person

TABLE 4–1   Learning Outcomes

Type of Learning Outcome	Description of Capability	Example
Verbal information	State, tell, or describe previously stored information	State three reasons for following company safety procedures
Intellectual skills	Apply generalizable concepts and rules to solve problems and generate novel products	Design and code a computer program that meets customer requirements
Motor skills	Execute a physical action with precision and timing	Shoot a gun and consistently hit a small moving target
Attitudes	Choose a personal course of action	Choose to respond to all incoming mail within 24 hours
Cognitive strategies	Manage one's own thinking and learning processes	Selectively use three different strategies to diagnose engine malfunctions

Source: R. Gagne and K. Medsker, *The Conditions of Learning,* (New York: Harcourt-Brace, 1996).

intends to behave in regard to the subject of the attitude). Important work-related attitudes include job satisfaction, commitment to the organization, and job involvement. Suppose you say that an employee has a "positive attitude" toward her work. This means the person likes her job (the affective component). She may like her job because it is challenging and provides an opportunity to meet people (the cognitive component). Because she likes her job, she intends to stay with the company and do her best at work (the intentional component). Training programs may be used to develop or change attitudes because they have been shown to be related to physical and mental withdrawal from work, turnover, and behaviors that impact the well-being of the company (e.g., helping new employees).

Cognitive strategies regulate the processes of learning. They relate to the learner's decision regarding what information to attend to (i.e., pay attention to), how to remember, and how to solve problems. For example, a physicist recalls the colors of the light spectrum through remembering the name "Roy G. Biv" (red, orange, yellow, green, blue, indigo, violet).

As we will see in this chapter, each learning outcome requires a different set of conditions for learning to occur. Before we investigate the learning process in detail, we should consider the theories that help to explain how people learn.

Learning Theories

Several theories relate to how we learn. Each theory relates to different aspects of the learning process. Many of the theories also relate to trainees' motivation to learn, which we discussed in Chapter 3.

Reinforcement Theory

Reinforcement theory emphasizes that people are motivated to perform or avoid certain behaviors because of past outcomes that have resulted from those behaviors.[2] There are several processes in reinforcement theory. Positive reinforcement is a pleasurable outcome resulting from a behavior. Negative reinforcement is the removal of an unpleasant outcome. The process of withdrawing positive or negative reinforcers to eliminate a behavior is known as extinction. Punishment is presenting an unpleasant outcome after a behavior, leading to a decrease in that behavior.

From a training perspective, reinforcement theory suggests that for learners to acquire knowledge, change behavior, or modify skills, the trainer needs to identify what outcomes the learner finds most positive (and negative). Trainers then need to link these outcomes to learners acquiring knowledge, skills, or changing behaviors. As we mentioned in Chapter 3, there are several types of benefits that learners can obtain from participating in training programs. The benefits may include learning an easier or more interesting way to perform their job (job-related), meeting other employees who can serve as resources when problems occur (personal), or increasing opportunities to consider new positions in the company (career-related). According to reinforcement theory, trainers can

TABLE 4–2   **Schedules of Reinforcement**

Type of Schedule	Description	Effectiveness
Ratio Schedules		
Fixed-ratio schedule	Reinforcement whenever target behavior has taken place a given number of times	Rapid learning; frequent instances of target behavior; rapid extinction
Continuous reinforcement	Reinforcement after each occurrence of target behavior	Same direction of behavior as with fixed-ratio schedules but more extreme
Variable-ratio schedule	Reinforcement after several occurrences of target behavior: number of occurrences before reinforcement may differ each time	Target behavior less susceptible to extinction than with fixed-ratio schedules
Interval Schedules		
Fixed-interval schedule	Reinforcement at a given time interval after performance of target behavior	Lower performance of target behavior than with ratio schedules; lower effectiveness if time interval is long
Variable-interval schedule	Reinforcement occurring periodically after performance of target behavior; time intervals may differ each time	Target behavior less susceptible to extinction than with fixed-interval schedules; lower performance of target behavior than with ratio schedules

Source: P. Wright, and R. A. Noe, *Management of Organizations* (Burr Ridge, IL: Irwin/McGraw-Hill, 1996).

withhold or provide these benefits to learners who master program content. The effectiveness of learning depends on the pattern or schedule for providing these reinforcers or benefits. Schedules of reinforcement are shown in Table 4–2.

Behavior modification is a training method that is primarily based on reinforcement theory. For example, a training program in a bakery focused on eliminating unsafe behaviors such as climbing over conveyor belts (rather than walking around them) and sticking hands into equipment to dislodge jammed materials without turning off the equipment.[3] Employees were shown slides depicting safe and unsafe work behaviors. After viewing the slides, employees were shown a graph of the number of times safe behaviors were observed during past weeks. Employees were encouraged to increase the number of safe behaviors they demonstrated on the job. They were given several reasons for doing so: for their own protection, to decrease costs for the company, and to help their plant get out of last place in the safety rankings of the company's plants. Immediately after the training, safety reminders were posted in employees' work areas. Also, after training, data showing the number of safe behaviors performed by employees continued to be collected and displayed on the graph in the work area. Employees' supervisors were also instructed to recognize the workers whenever they saw them perform a safe work behavior. In this example, the data of safe behavior posted in the work areas and supervisors' recognition of safe work behavior represent positive reinforcers.

Social Learning Theory

Social learning theory emphasizes that people learn by observing other persons (models) whom they believe are credible and knowledgeable.[4] Social learning theory also recognizes that behavior that is reinforced or rewarded tends to be repeated. The models' behavior or skill that is rewarded is adopted by the observer. According to social learning theory, learning new skills or behavior comes from (1) directly experiencing the consequences of using behavior or skills or (2) the process of observing others and seeing the consequences of their behavior.[5]

According to social learning theory, learning also is influenced by a person's self-efficacy. **Self-efficacy** is a person's judgment about whether she can successfully learn knowledge and skills. Chapter 3 emphasizes self-efficacy as an important factor to consider in the person analysis phase of needs assessment. Why? Self-efficacy is one determinant of readiness to learn. A trainee with high self-efficacy will put forth effort to learn in a training program and is most likely to persist in learning even if an environment is not conducive to learning (e.g., noisy training room). In contrast, a person with low self-efficacy will doubt he can master the content of a training program and is more likely to withdraw both psychologically and/or physically (daydream or fail to attend the program). This is because these persons believe that they are unable to learn. Regardless of their effort level, they will be unable to learn.

A person's self-efficacy can be increased using several methods: verbal persuasion, logical verification, observation of others (modeling), and past accomplishments.[6] **Verbal persuasion** means offering words of encouragement to convince others they can learn. **Logical verification** involves perceiving a relationship between a new task and a task already mastered. Trainers and managers can remind employees when they encounter learning difficulties that they have been successful at learning similar things. **Modeling** involves having employees who already have mastered the learning outcomes demonstrate them for trainees. As a result, employees are likely to be motivated by the confidence and success of their successful peers. **Past accomplishments** refers to allowing employees to build a history of successful accomplishments. Managers can place employees in situations where they are likely to succeed and provide training so that employees know what to do and how to do it.

Social learning theory suggests four processes involved in learning: attention, retention, motor reproduction, and motivational processes. (See Figure 4–1.)

Attention suggests that persons cannot learn by observation unless they are aware of the important aspects of a model's performance. Attention is influenced by characteristics of the model and the learner. Learners must be aware of the skills or behavior they are supposed to observe. The model must be clearly

FIGURE 4–1

Processes of social learning theory

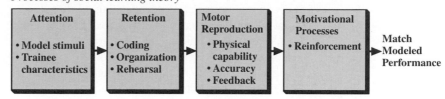

Source: Based on A. Bandura, *Social Foundations of Thoughts and Actions* (Englewood Cliffs, NJ: Prentice-Hall, 1986).

identified and credible. The learner must have the physical capability (sensory capability) to observe the model. Also, if the learner has successfully learned other skills or behavior by observing the model, he is more likely to attend to the model.

Learners must remember the behaviors or skills that they observe. This is the role of retention. Learners have to code the observed behavior and skills in memory in an organized manner so they can recall them for the appropriate situation. Behaviors or skills can be coded as visual images (symbols) or verbal statements.

Motor reproduction involves trying out the observed behaviors to see if they result in the same reinforcement that the model received. The ability to reproduce the behaviors or skills depends on the extent to which the learner can recall the skills or behavior. The learner must also have the physical capability to perform the behavior or exhibit the skill. For example, a firefighter can learn the behaviors necessary to carry a person away from a dangerous situation, but may be unable to demonstrate the behavior because he lacks upper body strength. Note that performance of behavior is usually not perfect on the first attempt. Learners must have the opportunity to practice and receive feedback to modify their behavior to be similar to the model's behavior.

Learners are more likely to adopt a modeled behavior if it results in positive outcomes. Social learning theory emphasizes that behaviors that are reinforced (a motivational process) will be repeated in the future. For example, a major source of conflict and stress for managers often relates to the performance appraisal interview. A manager may learn behaviors that allow the employee to be more participative in a performance appraisal interview (e.g., give the employee the opportunity to voice her concerns) through observing successful managers. If the manager uses this behavior in the performance appraisal interview and the behavior is rewarded by employees (e.g., they say "I really felt the feedback meeting was better than any one we have ever had") or the new behavior leads to reduced conflicts with employees (e.g., negative reinforcement), the manager will more likely use this behavior the next time she has to conduct an appraisal interview.

As we will see in Chapters 7 and 8's discussion of training methods, social learning theory is the primary basis for behavior modeling training and has influenced the development of multimedia training programs. For example, in the training program called "Getting Your Ideas Across," trainees are first presented with the five key behaviors for getting your ideas across: (1) state the point and purpose of the message, (2) present points to aid understanding, (3) check the audience for reactions and understanding, (4) handle reactions from the audience to what was presented, and (5) summarize the main point. The trainer provides a rationale for each key behavior. Next, trainees view a video of a business meeting in which a manager is having difficulty getting subordinates to accept his ideas regarding how to manage an impending office move. The manager, who is the model, is ineffective in getting his ideas across to his subordinates. As a result, the video shows that the subordinates are dissatisfied with the manager and his ideas. The video is turned off and the trainer leads the trainees in a discussion of what the manager did wrong in trying to get his ideas across. Trainees again view the video. But this time the manager, in the same situation, is shown using the key behaviors. As a result subordinates react quite positively to their boss (the model). Following this video segment, the trainer leads a discussion of how the model used the key behaviors to successfully get his ideas across.

After observing the model and discussing the key behaviors, trainees are paired with another trainee for practice. Each group is given a situation and message to communicate. The trainees take turns trying to get their ideas across to each other using the key behaviors. Each trainee is expected to provide feedback to each other regarding their use of the key behaviors. The trainer also observes and provides feedback to each group. Before leaving training, the trainees are given a pocket-size card with the key behaviors, which they take back with them to the job. Also, they complete a planning guide in which they describe a situation where they want to use the key behaviors and how they plan to use them.

Goal Setting Theory

Goal setting theory assumes behavior results from a person's conscious goals and intentions.[7] Goals influence behavior by directing energy and attention, sustaining effort over time and motivating the person to develop strategies for goal attainment.[8] Research suggests that specific challenging goals result in better performance than vague, unchallenging goals.[9] Goals have been shown to lead to high performance only if people are committed to the goal. Employees are less likely to be committed to a goal if they believe it is too difficult.

An example of how goal setting theory influences training methods is seen in a program designed to improve pizza deliverers' driving practices.[10] The majority of pizza deliverers are young (age 18 to 24), inexperienced drivers, who are compensated based on the number of pizzas they can deliver. This created a situation where deliverers are rewarded for fast but unsafe driving practices—for example, not wearing a safety belt, failing to use turn signals, and not coming to complete stops at intersections. These unsafe practices have resulted in a high driving accident rate.

Prior to goal setting, pizza deliverers were observed by their managers leaving the store for and arriving from deliveries. The managers observed the number of complete stops at intersections over a one-week period. In the training session, managers and trainers presented the deliverers with a series of questions for discussion. Here are examples: In what situations should you come to a complete stop? What are the reasons for coming to a complete stop? What are the reasons for not coming to a complete stop?

After the discussion, pizza deliverers were asked to agree on the need to come to a complete stop at intersections. Following their reaching agreement, the managers shared the data they collected regarding the number of complete stops at intersections they had observed the previous week. (Complete stops were made 55 percent of the time.) The trainer asked the pizza deliverers to set a goal for complete stopping over the next month. They decided on a goal of 75 percent complete stops.

After the goal setting session, managers at each store continued observing their drivers complete intersection stops. The following month in the work area, a poster showed the percentages of complete stops for every four-day period. The current percentage of total complete stops was also displayed.

Goal setting theory also is used in training program design. Goal setting theory suggests that learning can be facilitated by providing trainees with specific challenging goals and objectives. Specifically, the influence of goal setting theory can be seen in the development of training lesson plans. As you will see later in the chapter, these lesson plans begin with specific goals providing information regarding the expected action that the learner will demonstrate, conditions under which learning will occur, and the level of performance that will be judged acceptable.

Need Theories

Need theories help to explain the value that a person places on certain outcomes. A **need** is a deficiency that a person is experiencing at any point in time. A need motivates a person to behave in a manner to satisfy the deficiency. Maslow and Alderfer's need theories focused on physiological needs, relatedness needs (needs to interact with other persons), and growth needs (self-esteem, self-actualization).[11] Both Maslow and Alderfer believed that persons start by trying to satisfy needs at the lowest level, then progressing up the hierarchy as lower-level needs are satisfied. That is, if physiological needs are not met, a person's behavior will focus first on satisfying these needs before relatedness or growth needs receive attention. The major difference between Alderfer's and Maslow's hierarchies of needs is that Alderfer allows the possibility that if higher-level needs are not satisfied, employees will refocus on lower-level needs.

McClelland's need theory focused primarily on needs for achievement, affiliation, and power.[12] According to McClelland, these needs can be learned. Need for achievement relates to a concern for attaining and maintaining self-set standards of excellence. Need for affiliation involves concern for building and maintaining relationships with other people and for being accepted by others. The need for power is a concern for obtaining responsibility, influence, and reputation.

Need theories suggest that to motivate learning, trainers should identify trainees' needs and communicate how training program content relates to fulfilling these needs. Also, if certain basic needs of trainees (e.g., physiological and safety needs) are not met, they are unlikely to be motivated to learn. For example, consider a word processing training class for secretaries in a downsizing company. It is doubtful that even the best designed training class will result in learning if employees believe their job security is threatened (unmet need for security) by the company's downsizing strategy. Also, it is unlikely the secretaries will be motivated to learn if they believe that word processing skills emphasized in the program cannot help them keep their current employment or increase their chances that they can find another job inside or outside the company.

Another implication of need theory relates to providing employees with a choice of training programs to attend. As Chapter 3 mentioned, giving employees a choice of which training course to attend can increase their motivation to learn. This occurs because trainees are able to choose programs that best match their needs.

Expectancy Theory

Expectancy theory suggests that a person's behavior is based on three factors: expectancy, instrumentality, and valence.[13] Beliefs about the link between trying to perform a behavior and actually performing well are called **expectancies.** Expectancy is similar to self-efficacy. In expectancy theory, a belief that performing a given behavior (e.g., attending a training program) is associated with a particular outcome (e.g., being able to better perform your job) is called **instrumentality. Valence** is the value that a person places on an outcome (e.g., how important it is to perform better on the job).

According to expectancy theory, various choices of behavior are evaluated according to their expectancy, instrumentality, and valence. Figure 4–2 shows how behavior is determined based on finding the mathematical product of expectancy, instrumentality, and valence. People choose the behavior with the highest value.

From a training perspective, expectancy theory suggests that learning is most likely to occur when employees believe they can learn the content of the

FIGURE 4–2

Expectancy theory of motivation

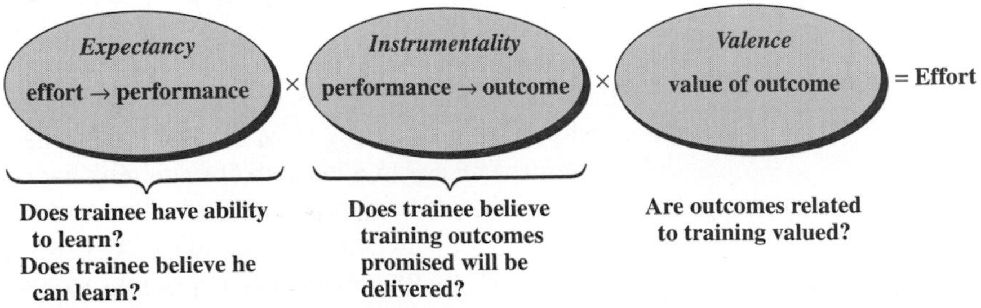

Expectancy		Instrumentality		Valence	
effort → performance	×	performance → outcome	×	value of outcome	= **Effort**
Does trainee have ability to learn? **Does trainee believe he can learn?**		**Does trainee believe training outcomes promised will be delivered?**		**Are outcomes related to training valued?**	

program (expectancy), learning is linked to outcomes such as better job performance, a salary increase, or peer recognition (instrumentality), and employees value these outcomes.

Adult Learning Theory

Adult learning theory was developed out of a need for a specific theory of how adults learn. Most educational theories as well as formal educational institutions were developed exclusively to educate children and youth. Pedagogy, the art and science of teaching children, dominated educational theory. Pedagogy gives the instructor major responsibility for making decisions about learning content, method, and evaluation. Students are generally seen as (1) being passive recipients of directions and content, and (2) bringing few experiences that may serve as resources to the learning environment.[14]

Educational psychologists, recognizing the limitations of formal education theories, developed **andragogy,** the theory of adult learning. Malcolm Knowles is most frequently associated with adult learning theory. This model is based on several assumptions:

1. Adults have the need to know why they are learning something.
2. Adults have a need to be self-directed.
3. Adults bring more work-related experiences into the learning situation.
4. Adults enter into a learning experience with a problem-centered approach to learning.
5. Adults are motivated to learn by both extrinsic and intrinsic motivators.[15]

Adult learning theory is especially important to consider in developing training programs because the audience for many such programs tends to be adults, most of whom have not spent a majority of their time in a formal education setting. Table 4–3 shows implications of adult learning theory for learning.

TABLE 4–3   Implications of Adult Learning Theory for Training

Design Issue	Implications
Self-concept	Mutual planning and collaboration in instruction
Experience	Use learner experience as basis for examples and applications
Readiness	Develop instruction based on the learner's interests and competencies
Time perspective	Immediate application of content
Orientation to learning	Problem-centered instead of subject-centered

Source: Based on M. Knowles, *The Adult Learner,* 4th ed. (Houston, TX: Gulf Publishing, 1990).

Note that a common theme in these applications is mutuality. That is, the learner and the trainer are both involved in creating the learning experience and making sure that learning occurs.

Information Processing Theory

Compared to other learning theories, information processing theories give more emphasis to the internal processes that occur when training content is learned and retained. Figure 4–3 shows a model of information processing. Information processing theories propose that information or messages taken in by the learner undergo several transformations in the human brain.[16] Information processing begins when a message or stimuli (which could be sound, smell, touch, or pictures) from the environment is received by receptors (ears, nose, skin, eyes). The message is registered in the senses and stored in short-term memory. The message is then transformed or coded for storage in long-term memory. A search process occurs in memory during which time a response to the message or stimulus is organized. The response generated relates to one of the five learning outcomes: verbal information, cognitive skills, motor skills, intellectual skills, or attitudes. The final link in the model is feedback from the environment. This feedback provides the learner with an evaluation of the response given. This information can come from another person or the learner's own observation of the results of his action. If the evaluation of the response is positive, this provides reinforcement that the behavior is desirable to be stored in long-term memory for use in similar situations.

Besides emphasizing the internal processes needed to capture, store, retrieve, and respond to messages, the information processing model highlights how external events influence learning. These events include:[17]

1. Changes in the intensity or frequency of the stimulus that affect attention.
2. Informing the learner of the objectives to establish an expectation.
3. Enhancing perceptual features of the material (stimulus) draws the attention of the learner to certain features.

FIGURE 4–3

A model of human information processing

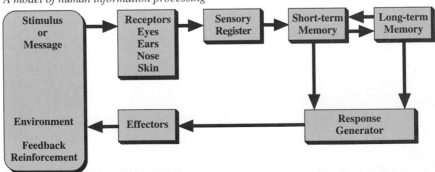

Source: Adapted from R. Gayne, "Learning Processes and Instruction, *Training Research Journal* 1 (1995/96) 17–28.

4. Verbal instructions, pictures, diagrams, and maps suggest ways to code the training content so that it can be stored in memory.

5. Meaningful learning context (examples, problems) creates cues that facilitate coding.

6. Demonstration or verbal instructions help organize the learner's response as well as facilitate the selection of the correct response.

The Learning Process

Now that we have reviewed learning theories, we are ready to answer two questions: How do people learn? What are the implications of the learning process for instruction?

Figure 4–4 shows the learning processes. These processes include expectancy, perception, working storage, semantic encoding, long-term storage, retrieval, generalizing, and gratification.[18] **Expectancy** refers to the mental state that the learner brings to the instructional process. This includes the factors that we discussed as being part of readiness for training (motivation to learn, basic skills) as well as an understanding of the purpose of the instruction and the likely benefits that may result from learning and using the learned capabilities on the job. **Perception** refers to the ability to organize the message from the environment so that it can be processed and acted upon. Both **working storage** and **semantic encoding** relate to short-term memory. In working storage, rehearsal and repetition of information occur, allowing material to be coded for memory.

Working storage is limited by the amount of material that can be processed at any one time. Research suggests that not more than five messages can be prepared for storage at any one time. Semantic encoding refers to the actual coding process of incoming messages. After messages have been attended to, rehearsed, and coded, they are ready for storage in long-term memory.

To use learned material (e.g., cognitive skills, verbal information) it must be retrieved. **Retrieval** involves identifying learned material in long-term memory and using it to influence performance. An important part of the learning process is not only being able to reproduce exactly what was learned, but being able to adapt the learning to use in similar but not identical situations. This is known as **generalizing.** Finally, **gratifying** refers to the feedback that the learner receives as a result of using learning content. Feedback is necessary to allow the learner to adapt responses to be more appropriate. Feedback also provides information about the incentives or reinforcers that may result from performance.

Implications of the Learning Process for Instruction

Instruction refers to the characteristics of the environment in which learning is to occur.[19] The right side of Figure 4–4 shows the relationship between the learning process and the form of instruction. Below we detail the implications of the learning process for the design of instruction.

FIGURE 4–4

The relationship between learning processes instructional events and forms of instruction

Processes of Learning	External Instructional Events	Forms of Instruction
1. Expectancy	1. Informing the learner of the lesson objective	1a. Demonstrate the expected performance. 1b. Indicate the kind of verbal question to be answered.
2. Perception	2. Presenting stimuli with distinctive features	2a. Emphasize the features of the subject to be perceived. 2b. Use formatting and figures in text to emphasize features.
3. Working storage	3. Limiting the amount to be learned	3a. Chunk lengthier material. 3b. Provide a visual image of material to be learned. 3c. Provide practice and overlearning to aid the attainment of automaticity.
4. Semantic encoding	4. Providing learning guidance	4a. Provide verbal cues to proper combining sequence. 4b. Provide verbal links to a larger meaningful context. 4c. Use diagrams and models to show relationships among concepts.
5. Long-term storage	5. Elaborating the amount to be learned	5a. Vary the context and setting for presentation and recall of material. 5b. Relate newly learned material to previously learned information. 5c. Provide a variety of contexts and situations during practice.
6. Retrieval	6. Providing cues that are used in recall	6a. Suggest cues that elicit the recall of material. 6b. Use familiar sounds or rhymes as cues.
7. Generalizing	7. Enhancing retention and learning transfer	7a. Design the learning situation to share elements with the situation of use. 7b. Provide verbal links to additional complexes of information.
8. Gratifying	8. Providing feedback about performance correctness	8a. Provide feedback on degree of accuracy and timing of performance. 8b. Confirm whether original expectancies were met.

Source: R. Gagne, "Learning Processes and Instruction," *Training Research Journal* 1 (1995/96): 17–28.

Employees Need to Know Why They Should Learn.   Employees learn best when they understand the objective of the training program. The **objective** refers to the purpose and expected outcome of training activities. There may be objectives for each training session as well as overall objectives for the program. Training objectives based on the training needs analysis help employees understand why they need training. Objectives are also useful for identifying the types of training outcomes that should be measured to evaluate a training program's effectiveness.

A training objective has three components:[20]

1. A statement of what the employee is expected to do (performance).
2. A statement of the quality or level of performance that is acceptable (criterion).
3. A statement of the conditions under which the trainee is expected to perform the desired outcome (conditions).

For example, a training objective for a customer-service training program for retail salespersons might be "After training, the employee will be able to express concern [performance] to all irate customers by a brief (fewer than 10 words) apology, only after the customer has stopped talking [criteria] and no matter how upset the customer is [conditions]."

Good training objectives provide a clear idea of what the trainees are expected to do at the end of training. Standards of satisfactory performance (e.g., speed, time constraints, products, reactions) that can be measured or evaluated should be included. Any resources (equipment, tools) that the trainees need to perform the action or behavior specified in the objective need to be described. The conditions under which performance of the objective is expected to occur also need to be described. These conditions can relate to the physical work setting (e.g., at night), mental stresses (e.g., an angry customer), or equipment failure (e.g., malfunctioning landing gear on an airplane).

Employees Need to Use Their Own Experiences as a Basis for Learning. Employees are more likely to learn when the training is linked to their current job experiences and tasks—that is, when it is meaningful to them.[21] To enhance the meaningfulness of training content, the message should be presented using concepts, terms, and examples familiar to trainees. For example, in a retail salesperson customer-service program, the meaningfulness of the material will be increased by using scenarios of unhappy customers actually encountered by salespersons in stores. Recent research indicates that besides linking training to current job experiences, learning can be enhanced by providing trainees with the opportunity to choose their practice strategy and other characteristics of the learning environment.[22]

Employees Need to Have Opportunities to Practice.   **Practice** involves having the employee demonstrate the learned capability (e.g., cognitive strategy, verbal information) emphasized in the training objectives under the conditions and performance standards specified by the objective. For practice to be effective, it needs to actively involve the trainee, include overlearning (repeated practice), take the appropriate amount of time, and include the appropriate unit of learning (amount of material). Practice also needs to be relevant to the training objectives.

Learning will not occur if employees practice only by talking about what they are expected to do. For example, using the objective for the customer-service course previously discussed, practice would involve having trainees participate in role playing with unhappy customers (customers upset with poor service, poor merchandise, or exchange policies). Trainees need to continue to practice even if they have been able to perform the objective several times **(overlearning).** Overlearning helps the trainee become more comfortable using new knowledge and skills and increases the length of time the trainee will retain the knowledge, skill, or behavior.

Trainers need to be sure that instruction does not exceed employees' short-term and long-term memory capacities. As we noted earlier, research suggests that no more than four to five items can be attended to at one time. If a lengthy procedure or process is to be taught, instruction needs to be delivered in shorter sessions or chunks in order not to exceed memory limits.[23] Visual images are another way to reduce demands on memory. Finally, automatizing (making performance of a task so automatic that it requires little thought or attention to be performed) is another way to reduce memory demands. For example, it would be difficult for a jet engine mechanic to perform some of the later parts of a maintenance procedure unless the earlier steps (such as removing the cover of the turbines) have been automatized. The more automization of a procedure that occurs, the more memory is freed up to concentrate on other learning and thinking. Automatization occurs through overlearning, that is, learners are provided with extra learning opportunities even after they have demonstrated that they can perform adequately.

It is also important to consider whether to have only one practice session or to use distributed (multiple) practice sessions. Distributed practice sessions have been shown to result in more efficient learning of skills than continuous practice.[24] With factual information, the less meaningful the material and the greater its length or difficulty, the better distributed practice sessions are for learning.

A final issue related to practice is how much of the training should be practiced at one time. One option is that all tasks or objectives should be practiced at the same time (whole practice). Another option is that an objective or task should be practiced individually as soon as each is introduced in the training program (part practice). It is probably best to employ both whole and part practice in a training session. Trainees should have the opportunity to practice individual skills or behaviors. If the skills or behaviors introduced in training are related to one another, the trainee should demonstrate all of them in a practice session after they are practiced individually.

For example, one objective of the customer-service training for retail salespersons is learning how to deal with an unhappy customer. Salespersons are likely to have to learn three key behaviors: (1) greeting disgruntled customers, (2) understanding their complaints, and then (3) identifying and taking appropriate action. Practice sessions should be held for each of the three behaviors (part practice). Then another practice session should be held so that trainees can practice all three skills together (whole practice). If trainees were only given the opportunity to practice the behaviors individually, it is unlikely that they would be able to deal with an unhappy customer.

For practice to be relevant to the training objectives, several conditions must be met.[25] Practice must involve the actions emphasized in the training objectives, be completed under the conditions specified in the training objectives, help trainees perform to meet the criteria or standard that was set, provide some means to evaluate the extent to which trainees' performance meets the standards, and allow trainees to correct their mistakes.

Practice must be related to the training objectives. The trainer should identify what trainees will be doing when practicing the objectives (performance), the criteria for attainment of the objective, and the conditions under which they may perform. These conditions should be present in the practice session. Next, the trainer needs to consider the adequacy of the trainees' performance. That is, how will trainees know whether their performance meets performance standards? Will they see a model of desired performance? Will they be provided with a checklist or description of desired performance? Can the trainees decide if their performance meets standards, or will the trainer or a piece of equipment compare their performance with standards?

The trainer must also decide, if trainees' performance does not meet standards, if they will understand what is wrong and how to fix it. That is, trainers need to consider if trainees can diagnose their performance and take corrective action or if they will need help from the trainer or a fellow trainee.

Employees Need Feedback.   **Feedback** is information about how well people are meeting the training objectives. To be effective, feedback should focus on specific behaviors and be provided as soon as possible after the trainees' behavior.[26] Also, positive trainee behavior should be verbally praised or reinforced. Videotape is a powerful tool for giving feedback. Trainers should view the videotape with trainees, provide specific information about how behaviors need to be modified, and praise trainee behaviors that meet objectives.

Employees Learn by Observing and Interacting with Others.   As we mentioned earlier in the chapter, according to social learning theory, people learn by observing and imitating the actions of models. For the model to be effective, the desired behaviors or skills need to be clearly specified, and the model should have characteristics (such as age or position) similar to the target audience.[27] After observing the model, trainees should have the opportunity to reproduce the skills or behavior shown by the model in practice sessions.

Communities of practice refer to groups of employees who work together, learn from each other, and develop a common understanding of how to get work accomplished.[28] The idea of communities of practice suggests that learning occurs on the job as a result of social interaction. Every company has naturally occurring communities of practice that develop as a result of relationships that employees develop to accomplish work. For example, Xerox needed to train service representatives as a result of merging three separate service departments into a single unit. Xerox trained the service reps by bringing them together in shared work spaces where they were in constant contact with each other. In this environment, the service representatives taught each other how to do their jobs and practiced their skills on customer calls. One representative described the experience as involving continuous learning through sharing information with other reps and hearing how other reps dealt with different types of service calls.

Employees Need the Training Program to Be Properly Coordinated and Arranged.   Training coordination is one of several aspects of training administration. **Training administration** refers to coordinating activities before, during, and after the program.[29] Training administration involves

1. Communicating courses and programs to employees.
2. Enrolling employees in courses and programs.
3. Preparing and processing any pretraining materials such as readings or tests.
4. Preparing materials that will be used in instruction (e.g., copies of overheads, cases).
5. Arranging for the training facility and room.
6. Testing equipment that will be used in instruction.
7. Having backup equipment (e.g., paper copy of slides, an extra overhead projector bulb) should equipment fail.
8. Providing support during instruction.
9. Distributing evaluation materials (e.g., tests, reaction measures, surveys).
10. Facilitating communications between trainer and trainees during and after training (e.g., coordinating exchange of e-mail addresses).
11. Recording course completion in the trainees' training records or personnel files.

Good coordination ensures that trainees are not distracted by events (such as an uncomfortable room or poorly organized materials) that could interfere with learning. Activities before the program include communicating to trainees the purpose of the program, the place it will be held, the name of a person to contact if they have questions, and any preprogram work they are supposed to complete. Books, speakers, handouts, and videotapes need to be prepared. Any necessary arrangements to secure rooms and equipment (such as VCRs) should be made. The physical arrangement of the training room should complement the training technique. For example, it would be difficult for a team-building session to be effective if the seats could not be moved for group activities. If visual aids will be used, all trainees should be able to see them. Make sure that the room is physically comfortable with adequate lighting and ventilation. Trainees should be informed of starting and finishing times, break times, and location of bathrooms. Minimize distractions such as phone messages. If trainees will be asked to evaluate the program or take tests to determine what they have learned, allot time for this activity at the end of the program. Following the program, any credits or recording of the names of trainees who completed the program should be done. Handouts and other training materials should be stored or returned to the consultant. The end of the program is also a good time to consider how the program could be improved if it will be offered again. We will discuss practical issues in selecting and preparing a training site and designing a program later in the chapter.

Instructional Emphasis for Learning Outcomes

The discussion of the implications of the learning process for instruction provided general principles regarding how to facilitate learning. However, you should understand the relationship between these general principles and the learning process. As we said earlier in the discussion of learning outcomes, different internal and external conditions are necessary for learning each outcome. **Internal conditions** refer to processes within the learner that must be present for learning to occur. These processes include how information is registered, stored in memory, and recalled. **External conditions** refer to processes in the learning environment that facilitate learning. These conditions include the physical learning environment, as well as opportunities to practice, and to receive feedback and reinforcement. The external conditions should directly influence the design or form of instruction. Table 4–4 shows what is needed during instruction at each step of the learning process. For example, during the process of committing training content to memory, verbal cues, verbal links to a meaningful context, and diagrams and models are necessary. If training content is not coded (or incorrectly coded), learning will be inhibited.

Considerations in Designing Effective Training Programs

Earlier in the chapter we discussed implications of learning theory for instruction. The importance of objectives, meaningful material, properly coordinated and arranged training, and opportunities for practice and feedback were emphasized. How do trainers ensure that these conditions are present in training programs? The last section of the chapter discusses the practical steps in designing effective training programs, courses, and lessons. This includes selecting and preparing the training site and program design.

Selecting and Preparing the Training Site

The **training site** refers to the room where training will be conducted. A good training site

1. Is comfortable and accessible.
2. Is quiet, private, and free from interruptions.

TABLE 4-4   Internal and External Conditions Necessary for Learning Outcomes

Learning Outcome	Internal Conditions	External Conditions
Verbal Information Labels, facts, and propositions	Previously learned knowledge and verbal information Strategies for coding information into memory	Repeated practice Meaningful chunks Advance organizers Recall cues
Intellectual Skills Knowing how		Link between new and previously learned knowledge
Cognitive Strategies Process of thinking and learning	Recall prerequisites, similar tasks, and strategies	Verbal description of strategy Strategy demonstration Practice with feedback Variety of tasks that provide opportunity to apply strategy
Attitudes Choice of personal action	Mastery of prerequisites Identification with model Cognitive dissonance	Demonstration by a model Positive learning environment Strong message from credible source Reinforcement
Motor Skills Muscular actions	Recall of part skills Coordination program	Practice Demonstration Gradual decrease of external feedback

Source: Based on R. M. Gagne and K. L. Medsker, *The Conditions of Learning* (Fort Worth, TX: Harcourt-Brace College Publishers, 1996).

3. Has sufficient space for trainees to move easily around in, offers enough room for trainees to have adequate work space, and has good visibility for trainees to see each other, the trainer, and any visual displays or examples that will be used in training (e.g., videos, product samples, charts, slides).[30]

Details to Be Considered in the Training Room.   Table 4–5 presents characteristics of the meeting room that a trainer, program designer, or manager should use to evaluate a training site. Keep in mind that many times trainers do not have the luxury of choosing the "perfect" training site. Rather, they use their evaluation of the training site to familiarize themselves with the site's strengths and weaknesses in order to adjust the training program and/or physical arrangements of the site (e.g., rearrange the trainer's position so it is closer to electrical outlets needed to run a VCR).

TABLE 4–5   Details to Consider when Evaluating a Training Room

Noise. Check for noise from heating and air conditioning systems, from adjacent rooms and corridors, and from outside the building.

Colors. Pastel hues such as oranges, greens, blues, and yellows are warm colors. Variations of white are cold and sterile. Blacks and brown shades will close in psychologically and become fatiguing.

Room structure. Use rooms that are somewhat square in shape. Long, narrow rooms make it difficult for trainees to see, hear, and identify with the discussion.

Lighting. Main source of lighting should be fluorescent lights. Incandescent lighting should be spread throughout the room and used with dimmers when projection is required.

Wall and floor covering. Carpeting should be placed in the meeting area. Solid colors are preferable because they are not distracting. Only meeting-related materials should be on the meeting room walls.

Meeting room chairs. Chairs should have wheels, swivels, and backs that provide support for the lower lumbar region.

Glare. Check and eliminate glare from metal surfaces, TV monitors, and mirrors.

Ceiling. Ten-foot-high ceilings are preferable.

Electrical outlets. Outlets should be available every six feet around the room. A telephone jack should be next to the outlets. Outlets for the trainer should be available.

Acoustics. Check the bounce or absorption of sound from the walls, ceiling, floor, and furniture. Try voice checks with three or four different people, monitoring voice clarity and level.

Source: Based on C. L. Finkel, "Meeting Facilities," in *The ASTD Training and Development Handbook,* 3d. ed., ed. R. L. Craig (New York: McGraw-Hill, 1996): 978–89.

Because of technology's impact on the delivery of training programs, many training sites include instructor- and trainee-controlled equipment. For example, at Microsoft's customer briefing center in Chicago, Illinois, 16 different computer platforms, ranging from laptops to mainframe systems, are available to use for training. Two seminar rooms include videoconferencing technology, which allows training sessions to be transmitted from Microsoft's corporate headquarters in Redmond, Washington, to Chicago. The Chicago site can link up to any of 25 Microsoft locations or a combination of 11 sites at once. Presenters have access to a videocassette recorder, compact disc player, cassette decks, and document camera. The seminar rooms have touchscreen systems controlling both the audiovisual equipment and the room environment.[31]

Seating Arrangements.   Seating arrangements at the training site should be based on an understanding of the desired type of trainee interaction and trainee–trainer interaction.[32] Figure 4–5 shows several types of seating arrangements.

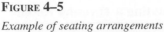

FIGURE 4–5

Example of seating arrangements

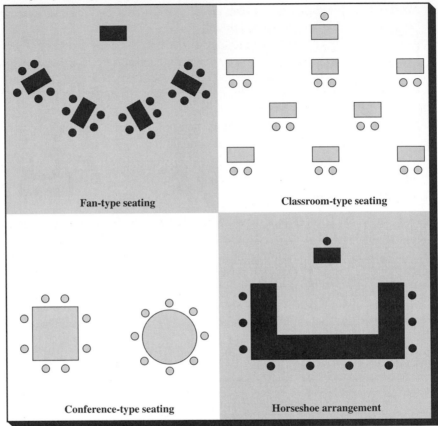

Source: Based on F. H. Margolis and C. R. Bell, *Managing the Learning Process* (Minneapolis, MN: Lakewood Publications, 1984).

Fan-type seating is conducive to allowing trainees to see from any point in the room, trainees can easily switch from listening to a presentation to practicing in groups, and trainees can communicate easily with everyone in the room. Fan-type seating is effective for training that includes trainees working in groups and teams to analyze problems and synthesize information.

If the training primarily involves knowledge acquisition, with lecture and audiovisual presentation, being the primary training method used, traditional classroom-type seating is appropriate. Traditional classroom instruction allows for trainee interaction with the trainer, but makes it difficult for trainees to work in teams (particularly if the seats are not movable to other locations in the room).

If training emphasizes total-group discussion with limited presentation and no small-group interaction, a conference-type arrangement may be most effective. If the training requires both presentation and total-group instruction, the horseshoe arrangement will be useful.

Program Design

As mentioned earlier in the chapter, for learning to occur in training programs requires meaningful material, clear objectives, and opportunities for practice and feedback. However, even if a training program contains all of these conditions, it still may not result in learning for several reasons. Proper equipment and materials may not be available during the session, trainers may be rushed to present content and fail to allow adequate time for practice, or the actual activities that occur in the training session may not relate to the learning objectives. **Program design** refers to the organization and coordination of the training program. A training program may include one or several courses. Each course may contain one or more lessons. Program design includes considering the purpose of the program as well as designing specific lessons within the program. Effective program design includes course parameters, objectives, a lesson plan overview, and a detailed lesson plan.[33]

Next we discuss each feature of effective program design. We then offer an example based on a training program developed to increase managers' effectiveness in conducting performance appraisal feedback interviews. Performance appraisal feedback sessions are meetings between managers and subordinates during which the strengths and weaknesses of an employee's performance are discussed. Improvement goals are usually agreed upon. Based on a needs assessment, one company discovered that managers were uncomfortable conducting performance appraisal feedback sessions. In this company, managers often were very authoritarian in the sessions. That is, they tended to tell employees what aspects of their job performance needed to be improved, rather than allowing the employees to participate in the session or working with them to identify and solve performance problems.

Course Parameters.   The **course parameters** refer to general information about the training program including the course title, description of the audience, statement of purpose, goals of the course, location, time, prerequisites, and name of the trainer. The course parameters are based on the information obtained from the needs assessment discussed in Chapter 3.

Table 4–6 presents the course parameters for the performance appraisal feedback course. The course was designed for managers. The purpose of the course was to prepare managers to conduct effective performance appraisal feedback sessions with their subordinates.

Objectives.   Earlier in the chapter, we discussed characteristics of good objectives. Within a training program, there are usually different types of objectives. **Program objectives** are broad summary statements of the purpose of the program. **Course objectives** or **lesson objectives** relate to goals of the course or the lesson. These objectives are more specific than the program objectives in terms of the expected behaviors, the content, the conditions, and the standards.

For the performance appraisal feedback training program, objectives included "Describe the eight steps in the problem solving approach without error"

TABLE 4–6   Course Parameters

Course title: Conducting Effective Performance Feedback Sessions

Target audience: Managers

Purpose: To prepare managers to conduct effective performance feedback sessions with their direct reports

Goals: Managers will be able to conduct a performance feedback session using the problem solving approach.

Total time: 1 day

Number of participants per session: 20–25

Locations: Various

Prerequisites: None

Instructor: Ann Noe

---

and "Demonstrate the eight steps in the problem solving approach in a role play exercise without error." The eight steps included explain the purpose of the meeting, ask the employee to describe what he has done that deserves recognition, ask the employee to describe what he should stop doing, start doing, or do differently, ask the employee for areas in which you can provide assistance, give him your opinion of his performance, ask for and listen to the employee's concerns about your evaluation, agree on steps to be taken by each of you, and agree to a follow-up date.[34]

The Detailed Lesson Plan.   Lesson plans can be designed for programs lasting a day, a week, or several hours. If training takes place over several days, a separate lesson plan is prepared for each day.

The **detailed lesson plan** translates the content and sequence of training activities into a guide that is used by the trainer to help deliver the training. That is, lesson plans include the sequence of activities that will be conducted in the training session as well as identifying the administrative details. Table 4–7 shows a lesson plan. The lesson plan provides a table of contents for the training activity. This helps to ensure that training activities are consistent regardless of the trainer. Lesson plans also help to ensure that both the trainee and trainer are aware of the course and program objectives. Most training departments have written lesson plans which are stored in notebooks or in electronic databases. Because lesson plans are documented, they can be shared with trainees and customers of the training department (i.e., managers who pay for training services) to provide them with detailed information of program activities and objectives.

The lesson plan includes the course title, learning objective, topics to be covered, target audience, time of session, instructor activity (what the instructor will do during the session), learner activity (e.g., listen, practice, ask question), and any prerequisites.[35] Because the lesson objective involves having trainees

TABLE 4–7   **Sample of a Detailed Lesson Plan**

Course title: Conducting an Effective Performance Feedback Session

Lesson title: Using the problem solving style in the feedback interview

Lesson length: Full day

Learning objectives:

1. Describe the eight key behaviors used in the problem solving style of giving appraisal feedback without error.

2. Demonstrate the eight key behaviors in an appraisal feedback role play without error.

Target audience: Managers

Prerequisites

Trainee: None

Instructor: Familiarity with the tell-and-sell, tell-and-listen, and problem solving approaches used in performance appraisal feedback interviews

Room arrangement: Fan-type

Materials and equipment needed: VCR, overhead projector, pens, transparencies, VCR tape "performance appraisal interviews," role play exercises

Evaluation and assignments: Role play; read article "Conducting Effective Appraisal Interviews"

Comment: Article needs to be distributed two weeks prior to session.

Lesson Outline	Instructor Activity	Trainee Activity	Time
Introduction	Presentation	Listening	8–8:50 A.M.
View videos of 3 styles		Watching	8:50–10 A.M.
Break			10–10:20 A.M.
Discussion of strengths and weaknesses of each style	Facilitator	Participation	10:20–11:30 A.M.
Lunch			11:30 A.M.–1 P.M.
Presentation of eight key behaviors of problem solving style	Presentation	Listening	1–2 P.M.
Role plays	Watch exercise	Practice using key behaviors	2–3 P.M.
Wrap-up	Answer questions	Questions	3–3:15 P.M.

successfully demonstrate the key behaviors, meeting this objective requires that trainees both understand the key behaviors and practice using them. The example shows that the instructor is involved in presenting key behaviors to the trainees, facilitating discussion, and overseeing role play exercises. The trainees are involved in both passive learning (listening) and active learning (discussion, role play exercises) in the session.

The prerequisites include (1) arrangement of the training site, equipment, and materials needed, (2) instructor preparation, and (3) trainee prerequisites. In the example, the trainer needs a VCR to show a video of performance appraisal feedback styles. The trainer also needs an overhead projector to record points made by the trainees during the planned discussion of the strengths and weaknesses of the appraisal styles presented on the video. The room needs to be fan-shaped so trainees can see the trainer and each other. Also, the fan arrangement is good for role-playing exercises that involve trainees working in groups of two or three.

Trainee prerequisites refer to any preparation, basic skills, or knowledge that the trainee needs prior to participating in the program. Trainee prerequisites may include basic math and reading skills, completion of prior training sessions, or successful completion of tests or certificate or degree programs. Instructor prerequisites indicate what the instructor needs to do to prepare for the session (e.g., rent equipment, review previous day's training session). Lesson plans also may cover how the lesson will be evaluated and any assignments that the trainees need to complete. In the example, trainees are required to read an article on effective performance appraisal feedback interviews. The instructor needs to be familiar with the eight key behaviors for conducting problem-solving appraisal feedback interviews.

Lesson Plan Overview. The **lesson plan overview** matches major activities of the training program and specific times or time intervals.[36] Table 4–8 provides an example of a lesson plan overview for the performance appraisal feedback training.

Completing a lesson plan overview helps the trainer determine the amount of time that needs to be allocated for each topic covered in the program. The lesson plan overview is also useful in determining when trainers are needed during a program, time demands on trainees, program breaks for snacks, lunch, and dinner, and opportunities for practice and feedback. For the performance appraisal feedback, the lesson plan shows that approximately half of the training time is devoted to active learning by the trainees (discussion, role plays, question-and-answer session).

TABLE 4–8   Sample Lesson Overview

8–8:50 A.M.	Introduction
8:50–10 A.M.	Watch videos of three styles of appraisal feedback
10–10:20 A.M.	Break
10:20–11:30 A.M.	Discussion of strengths and weaknesses of each style
11:30–1 P.M.	Lunch
1–2 P.M.	Presentation and video of eight key behaviors of problem solving approach
2–3 P.M.	Role plays
3–3:15 P.M.	Wrap-up (questions and answers)

Summary

Learning must occur for training to be effective. This chapter began by defining learning and identifying the capabilities that can be learned: verbal information, intellectual skills, motor skills, attitudes, and cognitive strategies. To understand how these capabilities can be learned, we discussed several theories of learning: reinforcement theory, social learning theory, goal setting theory, need theories, expectancy theory, adult learning theory, and information processing theory. Next, we investigated the learning process and the implications of how people learn for designing instruction. The learning process emphasized that internal processes (expectancy, storage, and retrieval) as well as external processes (gratifying) influence learning. The chapter then discussed the relationship between the implications of the learning process and design of instruction. Important design elements include providing the learner with an understanding of why she should learn, meaningful content, practice opportunities, feedback, a model, a coordinated program, and a good physical learning environment. The chapter concluded by discussing how to select and prepare a training site and effective program design. Effective program design includes developing course parameters, objectives, a lesson plan overview, and a detailed lesson plan.

Key Terms

learning   79
verbal information   79
intellectual skills   79
motor skills   79
attitudes   79
cognitive strategies   80
reinforcement theory   80
social learning theory   82
self-efficacy   82
verbal persuasion   82
logical verification   82
modeling   82
past accomplishments   82
goal setting theory   84
need   85
expectancies   86
instrumentality   86
valence   86
andragogy   87
expectancy   89
perception   89
working storage   89

semantic encoding   89
retrieval   89
generalizing   89
gratifying   89
instruction   89
objective   90
practice   91
overlearning   92
feedback   93
communities of practice   93
training administration   94
internal conditions   95
external conditions   95
training site   95
program design   99
course parameters   99
program objectives   99
course objectives (lesson objectives)   99
detailed lesson plan   100
lesson plan overview   102

Discussion Questions

1. Compare and contrast any two of the following learning theories: expectancy theory, social learning theory, reinforcement theory, information processing theory.

2. What learning condition do you think is most necessary for learning to occur? Which is least critical? Why?

3. How do instructional objectives help learning to occur?

4. Assume you were training an employee to diagnose and repair a loose wire in an electrical socket. After demonstrating the procedure to follow, you let the trainee show you how to do it. The trainee correctly demonstrates the process and repairs the connection on the first attempt! Has learning occurred? Justify your answer.

5. Your boss says, "Why do I need to tell you what type of learning capability I'm interested in? I just want a training program to teach employees how to give good customer service!" Explain to the boss how "good customer service" can be translated into different learning outcomes.

6. How does practice aid in the learning process?

7. What learning conditions are necessary for short- and long-term retention of training content to occur?

8. Under what circumstances might a traditional seating arrangement be superior to a fan-type seating arrangement?

9. Detailed lesson plans have important information for trainers. List the different types of information found in a detailed lesson plan. Also, indicate the importance of each type of information for learning.

Application Assignments

1. Using any source possible (magazines, journals, personal conversation with a trainer), find a description of a training program. Consider the learning process and the implications of the learning process for instruction discussed in the chapter. Evaluate the degree to which the program facilitates learning. Provide suggestions for improving the program.

2. You are training director of a hotel chain, Noe Suites. Noe Suites hotels have 100 to 150 rooms, a small indoor pool, and restaurant at each location. Hotels are strategically located near exit ramps of major highways in college towns such as East Lansing, Michigan, and Columbus, Ohio. You received the following e-mail message from the vice president of operations:

   To: You, Training Director

   From: Vice President of Operations, Noe Suites

   As you are probably aware, one of the most important aspects of quality service is known as "recovery"—that is, the employee's ability to respond effectively to customer complaints. There are three possible outcomes to a customer complaint: The customer complains and is satisfied by the response, the customer complains and is dissatisfied with the response, and the customer does not complain but remains dissatisfied. Many dissatisfied customers do not complain because they want to avoid confrontation, there is no convenient way to complain, or they do not believe that complaining will do much good.

I have decided that to improve our level of customer service, we need to train our hotel staff in the "recovery" aspect of customer service. My decision is based on the results of recent focus groups we held with customers. One theme that emerged from these focus groups was that we had some weaknesses in the recovery area. For example, last month in one of the restaurants, a waiter dropped the last available piece of blueberry pie on a customer as he was serving her. The waiter did not know how to correct the problem other than offer an apology.

I have decided to hire two well-known consultants in the service industry to discuss recovery as well as to provide an overview of different aspects of quality customer service. These consultants have worked in service industries as well as manufacturing industries.

I have scheduled the consultants to deliver a presentation in three training sessions. Each session will last three hours. There will be one session for each shift of employees (day, afternoon, and midnight shifts).

The sessions will consist of a presentation and question-and-answer session. The presentation will last one and a half hours and the question-and-answer session approximately 45 minutes. There will be a half-hour break.

My expectations are that following this training, the service staff will be able to successfully recover from service problems.

Because you are an expert on training, I want your feedback on the training session. Specifically, I am interested in your opinion regarding whether our employees will learn about service recovery from attending this program. Will they be able to recover from service problems in their interactions with customers? What recommendations do you have for improving the program?

3. Identify what is wrong with each of the following training objectives. Then rewrite it.

   a. To be aware of the safety rules for operating the ribbon-cutting machine in three minutes.

   b. Given a personal computer, a table, and chair, enter the data into a Microsoft Excel spreadsheet.

   c. Use the World Wide Web to learn about training practices.

   d. Given a street address in the city of Okemos, Michigan, be able to drive the ambulance from the station to the address in less than 10 minutes.

4. Go to www.funderstanding.com. This web site has information about learning in both company and school (K-12) environments. Click on the "About Learning" icon. Click on the "How Learning Should be Designed" hyperlink. Several learning theories are listed. A definition and basic elements of each theory are provided. Choose any one of the learning theories shown. Be prepared in class to define the theory, describe its basic elements, and discuss how it could be used in the design of a training program.

Endnotes

1. R. M. Gagne and K. L. Medsker, *The Conditions of Learning,* (Fort Worth, TX: Harcourt-Brace, 1996).
2. B. F. Skinner, *Science and Human Behavior* (New York: Macmillan).
3. J. Komaki, K. D. Barwick, and L. R. Scott, "A Behavioral Approach to Occupational Safety: Pinpointing and Reinforcing Safe Performance in a Food Manufacturing Plant," *Journal of Applied Psychology* 63, (1978): 434–45.
4. A. Bandura, *Social Foundations of Thought and Action* (Englewood Cliffs, NJ: Prentice-Hall, 1986); A. Bandura, "Self-Efficacy Mechanisms in Human Behavior," *American Psychologist* 37 (1982): 122–47.
5. Bandura, *Social Foundations of Thought and Action.*
6. M. E. Gist and T. R. Mitchell, "Self-Efficacy: A Theoretical Analysis of Its Determinants and Malleability," *Academy of Management Review* 17 (1992): 183–221.
7. E. A. Locke and G. D. Latham, *A Theory of Goal Setting and Task Performance* (Englewood Cliffs, NJ: Prentice Hall, 1990).
8. Locke and Latham, *A Theory of Goal Setting and Task Performance.*
9. E. A. Locke, K. N. Shaw, L. M. Saari, and G. P. Latham, "Goal Setting and Task Performance," *Psychological Bulletin* 90 (1981): 125–52.
10. T. D. Ludwig and E. S. Geller, " Assigned versus Participative Goal Setting and Response Generalization: Managing Injury Control among Professional Pizza Drivers," *Journal of Applied Psychology* 82 (1997): 253–61.
11. A. H. Maslow, "A Theory of Human Motivation," *Psychological Reports* 50 (1943): 370–96; C. P. Alderfer, "An Empirical Test of a New Theory of Human Needs," *Organizational Behavior and Human Performance* 4 (1969): 142–75.
12. D. McClelland, "Managing Motivation to Expand Human Freedom," *American Psychologist* 33 (1978): 201–10.
13. V. H. Vroom, *Work and Motivation* (New York: John Wiley, 1964).
14. M. S. Knowles, "Adult Learning," in *The ASTD Training and Development Handbook,* ed. R. L. Craig (New York: McGraw-Hill): 253–65.
15. M. Knowles, *The Adult Learner,* 4th ed. (Houston: Gulf Publishing, 1990).
16. Gagne and Medsker, *The Conditions of Learning;* W. C. Howell and N. J. Cooke, "Training the Human Information Processor: A Review of Cognitive Models," in *Training and Development in Organizations,* ed. I. L. Goldstein and Associates (San Francisco: Jossey-Bass, 1991): 121–82.
17. R. M. Gagne, "Learning Processes and Instruction," *Training Research Journal* 1 (1995/96): 17–28.
18. Ibid.
19. Ibid.
20. B. Mager, *Preparing Instructional Objectives,* 2d ed. (Belmont, CA: Lake Publishing, 1984); B. J. Smith and B. L. Delahaye, *How to Be an Effective Trainer,* 2d ed. (New York: John Wiley and Sons, 1987).
21. K. A. Smith-Jentsch, F. G. Jentsch, S. C. Payne, and E. Salas, "Can Pre-training Experiences Explain Individual Differences in Learning?" *Journal of Applied Psychology* 81 (1996): 110–16.
22. J. K. Ford, D. A. Weissbein, S. M. Guly, and E. Salas, "Relationship of Goal Orientation, Metacognitive Activity and Practice Strategies with Learning Outcomes and Transfer" *Journal of Applied Psychology,* in press.

23. J. C. Naylor and G. D. Briggs, "The Effects of Task Complexity and Task Organization on the Relative Efficiency of Part and Whole Training Methods," *Journal of Experimental Psychology* 65 (1963): 217–24.

24. W. McGehee and P. W. Thayer, *Training in Business and Industry* (New York: Wiley, 1961).

25. R. M. Mager, *Making Instruction Work* (Belmont, CA: David Lake, 1988).

26. Gagne and Medsker, *The Conditions of Learning.*

27. P. J. Decker and B. R. Nathan, *Behavior Modeling Training: Principles and Applications* (New York: Praeger, 1985).

28. D. Stamps, "Communities of Practice," *Training* (February 1997): 35–42.

29. Smith and Delahaye, *How to Be an Effective Trainer.* M. Van Wart, N. J. Cayer, and S. Cook, *Handbook of Training and Development for the Public Sector,* (San Francisco: Jossey-Bass, 1993)

30. Ibid.

31. "Top Training Facilities," *Training* (March 1995): special section.

32. L. Nadler and Z. Nadler, *Designing Training Programs,* 2d ed. (Houston: Gulf Publishing Company, 1994); T. W. Goad, "Building Presentations: A Top-Down Approach," in *Effective Training Delivery* (Minneapolis: Lakewood Publishing, 1989): 21–24; F. H. Margolis and C. R. Bell, *Managing the Learning Process,* (Minneapolis: Lakewood, 1984).

33. Van Wart, Cayer, and Cook, *Handbook of Training and Development for the Public Sector.*

34. G. P. Latham and K. N. Wexley, *Increasing Productivity through Performance Appraisal,* 2d ed. (Reading, MA: Addison-Wesley, 1994).

35. Van Wart, Cayer, and Cook, *Handbook of Training and Development for the Public Sector.*

36. Ibid.

5 TRANSFER OF TRAINING

Objectives

After reading this chapter, you should be able to

1. Diagnose and solve a transfer of training problem.

2. Create a work environment that will facilitate transfer of training.

3. Explain to a manager how he can ensure that transfer of training occurs.

4. Discuss the implications of identical elements, stimulus generalization, and cognitive theories for transfer of training.

5. Develop a self-management module for a training program.

6. Discuss the technologies that can be used to support transfer of training.

7. Discuss the key features of the learning organization.

TRANSFER OF TRAINING MEANS THE DIFFERENCE BETWEEN LIFE AND DEATH

The Baltimore Police Department needed to teach police sergeants the skills needed to handle hostage-barricade situations in which lives are at stake. These situations include negotiating with a troubled husband holding his wife and/or children hostage, a fired employee returning to the company waving a gun and threatening to kill the manager and co-workers, or bank robbers who have taken hostages and promise to kill one each hour until their demands are met. The first hour of a hostage situation is critical. The sergeant must quickly organize resources to achieve a successful end to the situation with minimal or no injuries.

To train police sergeants to prepare for such situations, the department decided to use a training simulation. A simulation was chosen because it provides a model of reality, a mock-up of a real situation without the danger. Multiple scenarios can be incorporated into the simulation, allowing the sergeants to practice the exact skills they will need when faced with a hostage crisis.

The simulation begins by having the trainee briefed on the hostage situation. Then she is directed to take charge of resolving the incident in the presence of an instructor who has personally been involved in similar real-life incidents. Each trainee supervises one difficult and one easy scenario. The simulation is designed to emphasize the importance of clear thinking and decision making in a situation in which time is critical. It is essential that the trainees take actions according to a set of priorities. These priorities place the greatest value on minimizing the risks to the hostages and isolating suspects before

communicating with them. The simulation scenarios include elements of many actual hostage incidents such as forced entry, taking persons against their will, the presence of a weapon, and threats. As trainees work in the simulation, their actions are evaluated by the instructor. The instructor provides feedback to the trainees in writing after they complete the simulation or the instructor can correct mistakes as they happen.

The simulation has been an effective training tool. For example, one sergeant who found himself in a bank robbery hostage situation was able to exert leadership skills quickly, take the suspect into custody, and resolve the situation without injuries. ■

Source: Based on J. F. Reintzell, "When Training Saves Lives," *Training and Development* 51, (1997): 41–42.

Introduction

The simulation used by the Baltimore Police Department ensured that transfer of training occurred. That is, the sergeants used the skills learned in the simulation in an actual hostage situation. For training programs to be successful, trainees must effectively and continually apply the learned capabilities gained in training to their jobs.[1] This is known as **transfer of training.** Several factors influence transfer of training: trainee characteristics, training design, and the work environment.[2]

Figure 5–1 presents a model of the transfer process. As the model shows, transfer of training includes both the generalization of training to the job and the maintenance of learned material. **Generalization** refers to a trainee's ability to apply learned capabilities (verbal knowledge, motor skills, etc.) to on-the-job work problems and situations that are similar but not completely identical to those problems and situations encountered in the learning environment. Generalization is illustrated in the chapter opening. Evidence of generalization was provided by the Baltimore police sergeant who successfully dealt with a bank-hostage situation by using the skills emphasized in the simulation. The Baltimore police department is also concerned with maintenance. **Maintenance** refers to the process of continuing to use newly acquired capabilities over time. At the conclusion of the simulation, officers may be able to demonstrate how to successfully free hostages. However, the incidence of hostage situations is fairly low compared to other tasks that police officers perform (e.g., issuing traffic citations, investigating burglaries). As a result, the police department is concerned

FIGURE 5–1

A model of the transfer process

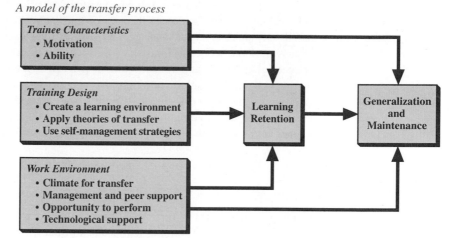

Source: Adapted from T. T. Baldwin and J. K. Ford, "Transfer of Training: A Review and Directions for Future Research," *Personnel Psychology* 41 (1988): 63–103.

 that officers may forget what they learned in training and therefore have difficulties in hostage situations. To ensure that officers have opportunities to practice these infrequently used but important skills, the training department will occasionally schedule mock hostage situations.

For generalization and maintenance to occur, capabilities must be learned and retained. Training design, trainee characteristics, and the work environment influence learning, retention, maintenance, and generalization. **Training design** refers to the characteristics of the learning environment. In Chapter 4 we covered important features of the learning environment—including meaningful material, opportunities to practice, feedback, learning objectives, and program organization—and physical features of the training site. Another factor that influences learning and retention is **trainee characteristics.** Trainee characteristics include ability and motivation that affect learning. The influence of trainee characteristics on learning was discussed in Chapters 3 and 4. If trainees lack the basic skills needed to master learned capabilities (e.g., cognitive ability, reading skills), are not motivated to learn, and do not believe that they can master the learned capabilities (low self-efficacy), it is doubtful the learning and transfer of training will occur. The third factor that influences the learning, retention, and transfer is the work environment. The **work environment** includes factors on the job that influence transfer of training including managers' support, peer support, technology support, the climate for transfer, and the opportunity to use newly acquired capabilities on the job.

This chapter will focus on identifying additional factors besides the learning environment and trainee characteristics already discussed that influence transfer of training. This chapter includes a detailed discussion of the role of transfer of training theories and the work environment in transfer of training.

The chapter is organized based on the model shown in Figure 5–1. The chapter begins with a discussion of training design issues related to transfer of training. This includes (1) application of theories of transfer of training to training design and (2) an emphasis on self-management as part of the training program. Next, we discuss how the work environment influences the transfer of training process. Trainees', managers', and trainers' roles in ensuring that transfer of training occurs are emphasized. Through discussion of learning organizations you will gain a perspective on how the work climate can influence transfer of training. The chapter also points out that holding trainees accountable for using and sharing information learned in training with their colleagues can enhance transfer of training.

Training Design

Training design refers to factors built into the training program to increase the chances that transfer of training will occur. In Chapter 4 we discussed the important factors needed for learning to occur (objective, practice, feedback, meaningful material, etc.). For transfer of training to occur we need to apply transfer of training theories and principles of self-management.

Applications of Transfer of Training Theory

There are three theories of transfer of training that have implications for training design (the learning environment). These theories include the theory of identical elements, stimulus generalization, and cognitive theory.[3] Table 5–1 shows each theory's primary emphasis and the conditions under which it is most appropriate to consider.

Theory of Identical Elements.   The **theory of identical elements** proposes that transfer of training occurs when what is being learned in the training session is identical to what the trainee has to perform on the job.[4] Transfer will be maximized to the degree that the tasks, materials, equipment, and other characteristics of the learning environment are similar to those encountered in the work environment.

The use of identical elements theory is shown in the chapter opening. The training simulation mirrored exactly the circumstances of actual hostage situations that the police officers encountered. Also, a checklist of activities and behaviors that the sergeants were provided with in training was the exact checklist used in hostage situations that occurred on-the-street.

Another application of the theory of identical elements is found in the use of simulators for training airline pilots. Pilots are trained in a simulator, which looks exactly like the cockpit of a jet aircraft. All aspects of the cockpit in the simulator (e.g., gauges, dials, lights) are the same as in a real aircraft. In psychological terms, the learning environment has complete fidelity with the work environment. If skills in flying, take-off, landing, and dealing with emergency situ-

---

TABLE 5–1   Transfer of Training Theories

Theory	*Emphasis*	*Appropriate Conditions*
Identical elements	Training environment is identical to work environment.	Work environment features are predictable and stable. *Example:* training to use equipment.
Stimulus generalization	General principles are applicable to many different work situations.	Work environment is unpredictable and highly variable. *Example:* training in interpersonal skills.
Cognitive theory	Meaningful material and coding schemes enhance storage and recall of training content.	All types of training and environments.

---

ations are learned in the simulator, they will be transferred to the work setting (commercial aircraft).

The identical elements approach has also been used to develop instruments designed to measure the similarity of jobs.[5] Job similarity can be used as one measure of the extent to which training in the knowledge and skills required for one job prepares an employee to perform a different job.

The theory of identical elements is used in the development of many training programs, particularly those that deal with the use of equipment or involve specific procedures that must be learned. Identical elements theory is particularly relevant to make sure that "near transfer" occurs. **Near transfer** refers to trainees' ability to apply learned capabilities exactly to the work situation. An important issue to consider in designing training programs based on identical elements is the relationship between the actions, behavior, or knowledge emphasized in the program and performance. That is, do behaviors or skills emphasized in the program contribute to or interfere with effective task performance? For example, in police officer training, new hires (cadets) practice shooting targets. During practice sessions, cadets fire a round of shells, empty the cartridges into their hands, and dispose of the empty cartridges into the nearest garbage can. This process is repeated several times. After graduation from the police academy, one new officer was involved in a shooting. He fired his gun, emptied the cartridges into his hand, and proceeded to look for a garbage can for the empty cartridges. As a result, he was seen by the gunman, shot, and killed!

Identical elements theory does not help us to understand how to encourage transfer where the learning environment and the training environment are not necessarily identical. This may be the case particularly for interpersonal skills training. For example, a person's behavior in a conflict situation is not easily predictable. Therefore, trainees must learn general principles of conflict resolution that they can apply to a wide variety of situations as the circumstances dictate (e.g., an irate customer versus a customer who lacks product knowledge).

Stimulus Generalization Approach.   The **stimulus generalization approach** suggests that the way to understand the transfer of training issue is to construct training so that the most important features or general principles are emphasized. It is also important to identify the range of work situations in which these general principles can be applied. The stimulus generalization approach emphasizes "far transfer." **Far transfer** refers to the trainee's ability to apply learned capabilities to the work environment, even though the work environment (equipment, problems, tasks) is not identical to that of the training session.

The stimulus generalization approach can be seen in the design of managerial skill training programs, known as behavior modeling training, which are based on social learning theory. Recall from our earlier discussion of social learning theory that modeling, practice, feedback, and reinforcement play key roles in learning. One step in developing behavior modeling programs is to identify key behaviors that are needed to be successful in a situation. The model demonstrates these key behaviors on a video and trainees have opportunities to practice the behaviors. In behavior modeling training, the key behaviors are believed to be applicable to a wide variety of situations. In fact, the practice sessions in behavior modeling training require the trainee to use the behaviors in a variety of situations that are not identical.

Cognitive Theory of Transfer.   The cognitive theory of transfer is based on the information processing model of learning discussed in Chapter 4. Recall that the storage and retrieval of information are key aspects of this model of learning. According to the **cognitive theory of transfer,** the likelihood of transfer depends on the trainee's ability to retrieve learned capabilities. This theory suggests that the likelihood of transfer is enhanced by providing the trainee with meaningful material that enhances the chances that she will link what she encounters in the work environment to the learned capability. Also, important is providing the trainee with schemes for coding learned capabilities in memory so that they are easily retrievable.

The influence of cognitive theory is seen in training design by encouraging trainees, as part of the program, to consider potential applications of the training content to their jobs. Many training programs include having trainees identify a work problem or situation and discuss the potential application of training content. Application assignments increase the likelihood that trainees will recall the training content and apply it to the work setting when they encounter the appropriate cues (problems, situations) in the environment. The use of application assignments in training helps the trainee understand the link between the learned capability and real-world application, which makes it easier to recall the capability when needed.

Self-Management Strategies

Self-management refers to a person's attempt to control certain aspects of decision making and behavior. Training programs should prepare employees to self-manage their use of new skills and behaviors on the job. Self-management involves

1. Determining the degree of support and negative consequences in the work setting for using newly acquired capabilities.
2. Setting goals for using learned capabilities.
3. Applying learned capabilities to the job.
4. Monitoring use of learned capabilities on the job.
5. Self-reinforcement.[6]

Research suggests that trainees exposed to self-management strategies exhibit higher levels of transfer of behavior and skills than trainees who are not provided with self-management strategies.[7]

Self-management is important because the trainee is likely to encounter several obstacles in the work environment that inhibit transfer of training. Table 5–2 shows these obstacles. They include (1) lack of support from peers and managers and (2) factors related to the work itself (e.g., time pressure). Given the restructuring, downsizing, and cost cutting occurring in many companies, these obstacles are often a reality for trainees.

For example, new technologies allow employees to gain access to resources and product demonstrations using the World Wide Web or personal computers equipped with CD-ROM drives. But while employees are being trained to use these resources using state-of-the-art technology, they often become frustrated because comparable technology is not available to them at their work site. Employees' computers may lack sufficient memory or links to the World Wide Web for them to use what they have learned.

These obstacles inhibit transfer because they cause lapses. **Lapses** refer to the trainee using previously learned, less effective capabilities instead of trying to apply the capability emphasized in the training program. Lapses into old behavior

---

TABLE 5–2   Examples of Obstacles in the Work Environment That Inhibit Transfer

Obstacle	*Description of Influence*
Work-related factor (lack of time, budget, inappropriate equipment, few opportunities to use new skills)	Trainee has difficulty using new capabilities.
Lack of peer support	Peers urge trainee to rely on old behaviors and skills.
Lack of management support	Managers do not reinforce training or provide opportunities to use new capabilities.

Source: Based on R. D. Marx, "Self-Managed Skill Retention," *Training and Development Journal* (January 1986): 54–57.

and skill patterns are common. One key for the trainee is to avoid a consistent pattern of slipping back or using old, ineffective learned capabilities (e.g., knowledge, skills, behaviors, strategies). Also, trainees should understand that lapses are common and be prepared to cope with them. Trainees who are unprepared for lapses may give up trying to use new capabilities—especially trainees with low self-efficacy and self-confidence.

One way to prepare trainees to deal with these obstacles is to provide instruction in self-management techniques at the end of the training program. Table 5–3 shows an example of self-management instruction. The module begins with a discussion of lapses emphasizing that lapses are not evidence of personal inadequacy; rather they result from habits of usage of knowledge and skill that have developed over time. Lapses provide information necessary for improvement. They help identify the circumstances that will have the most negative influence on transfer of training. Next, a specific behavior, skill, or strategy is targeted for transfer. Then, obstacles that inhibit transfer of training are identified; these can include both work environment characteristics and personal characteristics (such as low self-efficacy). Trainees are then provided with an overview of coping skills or strategies that they can use to deal with these obstacles. These skills and strategies include time management, creating a personal support network (persons to talk with about how to transfer skills to the work setting), and self-monitoring to identify

---

TABLE 5–3   Sample Content of Self-Management Module

1. Discuss lapses.
  • Note evidence of inadequacy.
  • Provide direction for improvement.

2. Identify skills targeted for transfer.

3. Identify personal or environment factors contributing to lapse.
  • Low self-efficacy.
  • Time pressure.
  • Lack of manager or peer support.

4. Discuss coping skills and strategies.
  • Time management.
  • Setting priorities.
  • Self-monitoring.
  • Self-rewards.
  • Creating a personal support network.

5. Identify when lapses are likely.
  • Situations.
  • Actions to deal with lapses.

6. Discuss resources to ensure transfer of skills.
  • Manager.
  • Trainer.
  • Other trainees.

Source: Adapted from R. D. Marx, "Relapse Prevention for Managerial Training: A Model for Maintenance of Behavior Change," *Academy of Management Review* 7 (1982): 433–41; R. D. Marx, "Improving Management Development through Relapse Prevention Strategies," *Journal of Management Development* 5, (1986): 27–40; M. L. Broad and J. W. Newstrom, *Transfer of Training* (Reading, MA: Addison-Wesley, 1992).

successes in transferring skills to the job. Next, to deal with lapses you need an awareness of where the situations are most likely to occur. The final part of the module deals with the use of resources to aid transfer of training. These resources may include communications with the trainer or fellow trainees via e-mail as well as discussions with their boss.

For example, a manager may have attended a training program designed to increase her leadership skills. After a discussion of lapses, the manager identifies a target skill. Let's say the target skill is participative decision making—that is, discussing problems and potential solutions with subordinates before making decisions that will affect the work group. Next, the manager identifies factors that may contribute to a lapse. One factor may be a manager's lack of confidence in being able to deal with subordinates who disagree with her view. Potential coping strategies that the manager identifies may include (1) scheduling time on the calendar to meet with subordinates (time management), (2) communicating to the boss the transfer goal and asking for help (create a support group), and (3) taking an assertiveness training course. In what situation may the manager be especially likely to experience a lapse? The manager identifies that she may be most likely to lapse back into an autocratic style when faced with a short time frame for making a decision (time pressure being an obstacle). The manager recognizes that it may be inappropriate to try to gain consensus for a decision when time constraints are severe and subordinates lack expertise. In the last step of the module, the manager suggests that she will (1) meet with her mentor to review her progress, (2) talk with other managers about how they effectively use participative decision making, and (3) resolve to communicate with other managers who attended the training session with her. The manager also commits to monitoring her use of participative decision making, noting successes and failures in a diary.

Work Environment Characteristics Influencing Transfer of Training

As Figure 5–1 shows, there are several work environment characteristics that influence transfer of training. These include the climate for transfer, managerial and peer support, opportunity to perform, and technological support. The chapter concludes by discussing learning organizations—a multifaceted approach for encouraging learning and transfer of training.

Climate for Transfer

One way to think about the work environment's influence on transfer of training is to consider the overall climate for transfer. **Climate for transfer** refers to trainees' perceptions about a wide variety of characteristics of the work environment that facilitate or inhibit use of trained skills or behavior. These characteristics include manager and peer support, opportunity to use skills, and the

TABLE 5–4   Characteristics of a Positive Climate for Transfer

Characteristic	*Example*
Supervisors and co-workers encourage and set goals for trainees to use new skills and behaviors acquired in training.	Newly trained managers discuss how to apply their training on the job with their supervisors and other managers.
Task cues: Characteristics of a trainee's job prompt or remind him to use new skills and behaviors acquired in training.	The job of a newly trained manager is designed in such a way as to allow him or her to use the skills taught in training.
Feedback consequences: Supervisors support the application of new skills and behaviors acquired in training.	Supervisors notice newly trained managers who use their training.
Lack of punishment: Trainees are not openly discouraged from using new skills and behaviors acquired in training.	When newly trained managers fail to use their training, they are not reprimanded.
Extrinsic reinforcement consequences: Trainees receive extrinsic rewards for using new skills and behaviors acquired in training.	Newly trained managers who successfully use their training will receive a salary increase.
Intrinsic reinforcement consequences: Trainees receive intrinsic rewards for using new skills and behaviors acquired in training.	Supervisors and other managers appreciate newly trained managers who perform their job as taught in training.

Source: Adapted from J. B. Tracey, S. I. Tannenbaum, and M. J. Kavanagh, "Applying Trained Skills on the Job: The Importance of the Work Environment," *Journal of Applied Psychology* 80 (1995): 235–52.

consequences for using learned capabilities.[8] Table 5–4 shows characteristics of a positive climate for transfer of training. Research has shown that transfer of training climate is significantly related to positive changes in managers' administrative and interpersonal behaviors following training.

Manager Support

Manager support refers to the degree to which trainees' managers (1) emphasize the importance of attending training programs and (2) stress the application of training content to the job. For example, trainers at the California Housing Partnership train project managers of rental housing on how to schedule complex tasks. Unfortunately, many trainees do not implement the scheduling system because when they return to their community agencies, their managers are not convinced that the scheduling system is worthwhile to use.[9]

Managers can provide different levels of support for training activities, as we see in Figure 5–2.[10] The greater the level of support, the more likely that transfer of training will occur. The basic level of support that a manager can provide is acceptance allowing trainees to attend training. The greatest level of sup-

FIGURE 5–2

Levels of management support for training

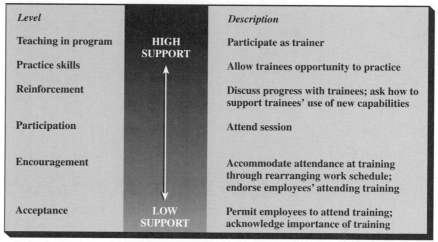

Level		Description
Teaching in program	**HIGH SUPPORT**	Participate as trainer
Practice skills		Allow trainees opportunity to practice
Reinforcement		Discuss progress with trainees; ask how to support trainees' use of new capabilities
Participation		Attend session
Encouragement		Accommodate attendance at training through rearranging work schedule; endorse employees' attending training
Acceptance	**LOW SUPPORT**	Permit employees to attend training; acknowledge importance of training

port is to participate in training as an instructor (teaching in the program). Managers who serve as instructors are more likely to provide many of the lower-level support functions such as reinforcing use of newly learned capabilities, discussing progress with trainees, and providing opportunities to practice. To maximize transfer of training, trainers need to achieve the highest level of support possible. Managers can also facilitate transfer through reinforcement (use of action plans). An **action plan** is a written document that includes the steps that the trainee and manager will take to ensure that training transfers to the job. (See Figure 5–3.) The action plan identifies (1) specific projects or problems that the trainees will work on and (2) equipment or other resources that the manager will provide to help the trainee. The action plan includes a schedule of specific dates and times when the manager and trainee agree to meet to discuss the progress being made in using learned capabilities on the job.

Table 5–5 presents a checklist that can be used to determine the level of manager support for training. The more statements that managers agree with, the greater their level of support for the training program. There are several ways to gain managers' support for training.[11] First, managers need to be briefed on the purpose of the program and its relationship to business objectives and the business strategy. The schedule of topics and a checklist of what managers should do following training so that transfer occurs should be distributed. Second, trainees should be encouraged to bring work problems and situations they face on the job to the training session. These can be used as practice exercises or input into action plans. Trainees should jointly identify the problems and situations with their manager. Third, information collected regarding the benefits of the course from past participants should be shared with managers. Fourth, trainers can assign trainees to complete action plans with their managers. Fifth, if possible, use

FIGURE 5–3

Sample action plan

Training Topic: _____
Objective:

Training Topic: _____
Objective:

Activities used to accomplish objective
Additional courses, seminars, workshops:

_____
_____
_____
_____

Self-instruction (books, articles, Web-based instruction):

_____
_____
_____
_____
_____

On-the-job activities (projects, problems, assignments, committee work):

_____
_____
_____
_____
_____

Other:

_____
_____
_____

Support

Manager	*Peer*	
		Feedback
		Resources
		Other

Progress date checks: _____ _____ _____

---

managers as trainers. That is, train the managers first, and then give them responsibility to train their subordinates.

At a minimum, special sessions should be scheduled with managers to explain the purpose of the training and set expectations that they will encourage attendance at the training session, provide practice opportunities, reinforce use of training, and follow up with trainees to determine the progress in using newly acquired capabilities.

TABLE 5–5   Checklist for Determining Level of Manager Support for Training

	Agree	Disagree
I have a good sense of what the class is about.		
I know how the training matches what I need for employees to do.		
There are tangible ways that the training will help employees.		
There are tangible ways that the training will help our unit.		
I can see why the organization is interested in providing the training.		
In performance appraisals, I can evaluate employees on what they learn in the class.		
I know enough about the training to support employees when they return to work.		
We have the tools and technologies that will be discussed in the class.		
I'm glad employees are attending the class.		
I've discussed the topic and the class with the employees who will participate.		
They know that I care about what will be taught in the class.		

Source: A. Rossett, "That Was a Great Class, but . . . ," *Training and Development* (July 1997): 21.

Peer Support

Transfer of training can also be enhanced by creating a support network among the trainees.[12] A **support network** is a group of two or more trainees who agree to meet and discuss their progress in using learned capabilities on the job. This could involve face-to-face meetings or communications via electronic mail. Trainees could share successful experiences in using training content on the job. They can also discuss how they obtained resources needed to use training content or how they coped with a work environment that interfered with use of training content.

Trainers might also use a newsletter to show how trainees are dealing with transfer of training issues. Distributed to all trainees, the newsletter might feature interviews with trainees who were successful in using new skills. Trainers may also provide trainees with a mentor—a more experienced employee who previously attended the same training program. The mentor may be a peer. The mentor can provide advice and support related to transfer of training issues (e.g., how to find opportunities to use the learned capabilities).

Opportunity to Use Learned Capabilities

Opportunity to use learned capabilities (**opportunity to perform**) refers to the extent to which the trainee is provided with or actively seeks experience with newly learned knowledge, skill, and behaviors from the training program. Opportunity to perform is influenced by both the work environment and trainee motivation. One way trainees have the opportunity to use learned capabilities is through assigned work experiences (e.g., problems, tasks) that require their use. The trainees' manager usually plays a key role in determining work assignments. Opportunity to perform is also influenced by the degree to which trainees take personal responsibility to actively seek out assignments that allow them to use newly acquired capabilities.

Opportunity to perform includes breadth, activity level, and task type.[13] *Breadth* includes the number of trained tasks performed on the job. *Activity level* is the number of times or the frequency with which trained tasks are performed on the job. *Task type* refers to the difficulty or criticality of the trained tasks that are actually performed on the job. Trainees who are given opportunities to use training content on the job are more likely to maintain learned capabilities than trainees given few opportunities.[14]

Opportunity to perform can be measured by asking former trainees to indicate (1) whether they perform a task, (2) how many times they perform the task, and (3) the extent to which they perform difficult and challenging tasks. Individuals who report low levels of opportunity to perform may be prime candidates for "refresher courses" (courses designed to let trainees practice and review training content). Refresher courses are necessary because these persons have likely experienced a decay in learned capabilities since they haven't had opportunities to perform. Low levels of opportunity to perform may also indicate that the work environment is interfering with using new skills. For example, the manager may not support training activities or give the employee the opportunity to perform tasks using skills emphasized in training. Finally, low levels of opportunity to perform may indicate that training content is not important for the employee's job.

Technological Support

Electronic performance support systems (EPSS) are computer applications that can provide, as requested, skills training, information access, and expert advice.[15] EPSS systems may be used to enhance transfer of training by providing the trainee with an electronic information source that they can refer to on an as-needed basis as they attempt to apply learned capabilities on the job. EPSS use in training is discussed in detail in Chapter 8, "Use of New Technologies in Training."

For example, Atlanta-based poultry processor Cagle's Inc. uses EPSS for employees who maintain the chicken-processing machines.[16] Because the machines that measure and cut chickens are constantly increasing in sophistication, it is impossible to continually train technicians so that they know the equipment's details. However, technicians are trained on the basic procedures they need to know to maintain these types of machines. When the machines encounter a problem, the technicians rely on what they have learned in training as well as the EPSS system, which provides more detailed instructions about the repairs. The EPSS system also tells technicians the availability of parts and where in inventory to find replacement parts. The EPSS system consists of a postage-stamp size computer monitor attached to a visor that magnifies the screen. The monitor is attached to a three-pound computer about half the size of a portable compact disc player. Attached to the visor is a microphone that the technician uses to give verbal commands to the computer. The EPSS helps employees diagnose and fix the machines very quickly. This is important given that the plant processes more than 100,000 chickens a day and chicken is a perishable food product!

Trainers can also monitor trainees' use of EPSS. This provides the trainer with valuable information about the transfer of training problems that trainees are encountering. These problems might relate to the training design (e.g., lack of understanding of process or procedure) or work environment (e.g., trainees not having or being able to find resources or equipment needed to complete an assignment).

Creating a Positive Work Environment for Transfer: The Learning Organization

To ensure that trainees have the opportunity to perform, managers and peers support training activities, trainees are motivated to learn, and the work environment is favorable for learning, many companies are attempting to become learning organizations. A **learning organization** is a company that has an enhanced capacity to learn, adapt, and change.[17] Training processes are carefully scrutinized and aligned with company goals. In a learning organization, training is seen as one part of a system designed to create intellectual capital. Recall from Chapter 1 that intellectual capital includes not only learning basic capabilities needed to perform the current jobs, but also stimulating creativity and innovation plus motivating employees to acquire and apply knowledge.

The essential features of a learning organization appear in Table 5–6. Note that the learning organization emphasizes that learning occurs not only at the individual-employee level (as we traditionally think of learning), but also at the group and organizational levels. The learning organization emphasizes system-level learning. **System-level learning** refers to the company's ability to preserve what is learned over time. That is, despite the fact that employees (and even divisions) of the company no longer exist, their knowledge is still available. Two features of Table 5–6's learning organization relate directly to system-level learning. Continuous learning and knowledge generation encourage employees to share information with each other. How might this occur? There are several ways to create and share knowledge:[18]

1. Use technology and software such as LOTUS Notes and e-mail, or create a company Intranet that allows people to store information and share it with others.
2. Publish directories that list what employees do, how they can be contacted, and the type of knowledge they have.

TABLE 5–6   Key Features of a Learning Organization

Feature	Description
Continuous learning	Employees share learning with each other and use job as a basis for applying and creating knowledge.
Knowledge generation and sharing	Systems are developed for creating, capturing, and sharing knowledge.
Critical systematic thinking	Employees are encouraged to think in new ways, see relationships and feedback loops, and test assumptions.
Learning culture	Learning is rewarded, promoted, and supported by manager and company objectives.
Encouragement of flexibility and experimentation	Employees are free to take risks, innovate, explore new ideas, try new processes, and develop new products and services.
Valuing of employees	System and environment focus on ensuring the development and well-being of every employee.

Source: Adapted from M. A. Gephart, V. J. Marsick, M. E. Van Buren, and M. S. Spiro, "Learning Organizations Come Alive," *Training and Development* 50 (1996): 34–45.

3. Develop informational maps that identify where specific knowledge is stored in the company.

4. Create a chief information officer position for cataloging and facilitating the exchange of information in the company.

5. Require employees to give presentations to other employees about what they have learned from training programs they have attended.

6. Allow employees to take time off from work (e.g., sabbaticals) to acquire knowledge or study problems.

7. Create an on-line library of learning resources such as journals, technical manuals, training opportunities, and seminars.

For example, Arthur Andersen has created a knowledge system that allows consultants to form relationships with people working on similar projects.[19] The consultants are organized into communities of practice based on their competencies. The knowledge system allows the consultants to store and access information about clients, processes, and technical information. Through sharing information the consultants can develop new applications themselves and help other consultants at Andersen learn from their experiences.

Companies that are striving to become learning organizations also usually change the structure of the organization. The restructuring can involve organizing work by teams instead of an assembly line process, creating smaller business units or profit centers that are required to capture and share knowledge and make decisions as needed to improve customer service or product quality. For example, the *Calgary Herald* newspaper used teams of senior managers plus sales and editorial representatives to protect and expand its advertising revenue from home builders.[20] A competing paper in Calgary had launched an aggressive campaign to take some of this revenue away from the *Herald.* The traditional response would have been to look at the problem from strictly an advertising perspective (e.g., increase advertising sales pressure). Instead, using ideas from the multifunctional teams (e.g., a drawing among readership for a $250,000 home), revenues increased and readership of the *Herald*'s "Homes" section increased. A beneficial side benefit was that reporters and sales people realized they could work together without compromising the values of their discipline.

Summary

Learning is an important aspect of any training program. But equally important is getting trainees to use learned capabilities on the job (transfer of training). This chapter discussed how trainee characteristics, trainee design features, and the work environment influence transfer of training. From a design standpoint, the chapter emphasized that it is important to consider identical elements, stimulus generalization, and cognitive theories related to transfer of training in program design. Trainees may need self-management skills to cope with a work environment that is not always conducive to transfer of training. The climate for transfer, manager and peer support, technology support, and opportunity to perform are features of the work environment that influence transfer of training. Transfer of training is an important issue to companies that consider themselves to be learning organizations. Many companies are attempting to become learning organizations to ensure that individual, team, and organizational structures create, nurture, and share knowledge.

Key Terms

transfer of training   110
generalization   110
maintenance   110
training design   111
trainee characteristics   111
work environment   111
theory of identical elements   112
near transfer   113
stimulus generalization
  approach   114
far transfer   114
cognitive theory of transfer   114

self-management   115
lapses   115
climate for transfer   117
manager support   118
action plan   119
support network   121
opportunity to perform   122
electronic performance support system
  (EPSS)   122
learning organization   123
system-level learning   123

Discussion Questions

1. Consider three time periods (pretraining, during training, and after training) and three parties involved in transfer of training (manager, trainer, trainee). Construct a matrix showing what each party can do to facilitate transfer of training at each time period.

2. Distinguish between the following: (1) maintenance and generalization and (2) learning and transfer.

3. What could be done to increase the likelihood of transfer of training occurring if the work environment conditions are unfavorable and cannot be changed?

4. Discuss how trainees can support each other so that transfer of training occurs.

5. What is the most important feature of the learning organization? Which is least important? Why?

6. What technologies might be useful for ensuring transfer of training? Briefly describe each technology and how it could be used.

7. How might you motivate managers to play a more active role in ensuring that transfer of training occurs?

8. Is training transfer an important issue in the companies where you have worked? How is transfer evaluated in those companies?

9. Discuss the major emphasis of identical elements, stimulus generalization, and cognitive theories of transfer.

Application Assignments

1. Develop a questionnaire to measure the degree to which the work environment supports transfer of training. Include the questions and the rating scales you would use. Use the checklist in Table 5–5 as an example.

2. Design an action planning sheet that a manager and employee could use to facilitate transfer of training. Justify each category included in the action plan.

3. Develop specific recommendations that the instructor could use to make this class a learning organization.

4. This assignment relates to Application Assignment #2 in Chapter 4.

   You received the following e-mail from the vice president of operations:

   Thanks for your recommendations regarding how to make the "Improving Service Quality Program" a success. To improve hotel staff ability to respond effectively to customer complaints, that is "recovery," we have incorporated many of your ideas into the program, including

   1. Having trainees bring an example of a customer problem to class.
   2. Giving trainees the opportunity to practice dealing with irate customers.

3. Providing trainees with feedback during role plays.

4. Have trainers identify and communicate objectives of the program to trainees.

5. Have trainers communicate to the trainees specific key behaviors related to customer service.

I am now concerned about how to make sure our training investments pay off. That is, I am really interested in the effective, continuous application of the skills and knowledge gained in training to employees' jobs.

What recommendations do you have?

Endnotes

1. M. L. Broad and J. W. Newstrom, *Transfer of Training* (Reading, MA: Addison-Wesley, 1992).

2. T. T. Baldwin and J. K. Ford, "Transfer of Training: A Review and Directions for Future Research," *Personnel Psychology* 41 (1988): 63–105.

3. J. M. Royer, "Theories of the Transfer of Learning," *Educational Psychologist* 14 (1979): 53–69.

4. E. L. Thorndike and R. S. Woodworth, "The Influence of Improvement of One Mental Function upon the Efficiency of Other Functions," *Psychological Review* 8 (1901): 247–61.

5. J. A. Sparrow, "The Measurement of Job Profile Similarity for the Prediction of Transfer of Learning," *Journal of Occupational Psychology* 62 (1989): 337–41.

6. C. A. Frayne and J. M. Geringer, "Self-Management Training for Joint Venture General Managers," *Human Resource Planning* 15 (1993): 69–85.

7. A. Tziner, R. R. Haccoun, and A. Kadish, "Personal and Situational Characteristics Influencing the Effectiveness of Transfer of Training Strategies," *Journal of Occupational Psychology* 64 (1991): 167–77; R. A. Noe, J. A. Sears, and A. M. Fullenkamp, "Release Training: Does it Influence Trainees' Post-Training Behavior and Cognitive Strategies?" *Journal of Business and Psychology* 4, 317–28; M. E. Gist, C. K. Stevens, and A. G. Bavetta, "Effects of Self-Efficacy and Post-Training Intervention on the Acquisition and Maintenance of Complete Interpersonal Skills," *Personal Psychology* 44, 837–61.

8. J. B. Tracey, S. I. Tannenbaum, and M. J. Kavanaugh, "Applying Trained Skills on the Job: The Importance of the Work Environment," *Journal of Applied Psychology* 80 (1995): 239–52; P. E. Tesluk, J. L. Farr, J. E. Mathieu, and R. J. Vance, "Generalization of Employee Involvement Training to the Job Setting: Individual and Situational Effects," *Personnel Psychology* 48 (1995): 607–32; J. K. Ford, M. A. Quinones, D. J. Sego, and J. S. Sorra, "Factors Affecting the Opportunity to Perform Trained Tasks on the Job," *Personnel Psychology* 45 (1992): 511–27.

9. A. Rossett, "That Was a Great Class, but . . . ," *Training and Development* (July 1997): 19–24.

10. J. M. Cusimano, "Managers as Facilitators," *Training and Development* 50 (1996): 31–33.

11. S. B. Parry, "Ten Ways to Get Management Buy-In," *Training and Development* (September 1997): 21–22; Broad and Newstrom, *Transfer of Training*.

12. C. M. Petrini, ed., "Bringing It Back to Work," *Training and Development Journal* (December 1990): 15–21.

13. Ford, Quinones, Sego, and Sorra, "Factors Affecting the Opportunity to Perform Trained Tasks on the Job."

14. Ibid., 511–27; M.A. Quinones, J.K. Ford, D.J. Sego, and E.M. Smith, "The Effects of Individual and Transfer Environment Characteristics on the Opportunity to Perform Trained Tasks," *Training Research Journal* 1 (1995/96): 29–48.

15. G. Stevens and E. Stevens, "The Truth about EPSS," *Training and Development* 50 (1996): 59–61.

16. "In Your Face EPSs," *Training* (April 1996): 101–2.

17. M. A. Gephart, V. J. Marsick, M. E. Van Buren, and M. S. Spiro, "Learning Organizations Come Alive," *Training and Development* 50 (1996): 35–45; C. M. Solomon, "HR Facilitates the Learning Organization Concept," *Personnel Journal* (November 1994): 56–66.
    T. A. Stewart, "Getting Real about Brainpower," *Fortune,* (November 27, 1995): 201–3; L. Thornburg, "Accounting for Knowledge," *HR Magazine* (October 1994): 51–56.

18. Gephart, Marsick, Van Buren, and Spiro, "Learning Organizations Come Alive."

19. J. B. Quinn, P. Anderson, and S. Finkelstein, "Leveraging Intellect," *Academy of Management Executive* 10 (1996): 7–27.

20. T. Gilbert, "Creating a Learning Newspaper," in *The Fifth Discipline Fieldbook,* eds. P. M. Senge, C. Roberts, R. B. Ross, B. J. Smith, and A. Kleiner (New York: Currency-Doubleday 1994): 474–78.

6 TRAINING EVALUATION

Objectives

After reading this chapter, you should be able to

1. Explain why evaluation is important.
2. Identify and choose outcomes to evaluate a training program.
3. Discuss the process used to plan and implement a good training evaluation.
4. Discuss the strengths and weaknesses of different evaluation designs.
5. Choose the appropriate evaluation design based on the characteristics of the company and the importance and purpose of the training.
6. Conduct a cost-benefit analysis for a training program.

FILLING PRESCRIPTIONS: NO ROOM FOR ERROR

Pharmacy technicians wait on customers, take refill information over the phone from doctors, and provide customers with information regarding generic drugs in place of brand-name drugs when the two are identical (which costs the customer less money). At Walgreen Company, a training course for new technicians was developed to replace on-the-job training they received from the pharmacists who hired them. This course involved 20 hours of classroom training and 20 hours of supervision on the job. Since the company has several thousand stores, large amounts of money and time were being invested in the training. As a result, the company decided to evaluate the program.

The evaluation consisted of comparing technicians who had completed the program with some who had not. Surveys asking questions about new employees' performance were sent to the pharmacists who supervised the technicians. Some questions related to speed of entering patient and drug data into the store computer and how often the technician offered customers generic drug substitutes. In comparing the two groups, the results showed that formally trained technicians were more efficient and wasted less of the pharma-cist's time than those who received tra-ditional on-the-job training. Sales in pharmacies with formally trained tech-nicians exceeded sales in pharmacies with on-the-job–trained technicians by an average of $9,500 each year. ∎

Source: B. Gerber, "Does Your Training Make a Difference? Prove It!" *Training* (March 1995): 27–34.

Introduction

As the opening vignette illustrates, Walgreen Company wanted to determine if the time, money, and effort devoted to training technicians actually made a dif-ference. That is, it was interested in assessing the effectiveness of the training program. **Training effectiveness** refers to the benefits that the company and the trainees receive from training. Benefits for trainees may include learning new skills or behavior. Benefits for the company may include increased sales and more satisfied customers. A training evaluation includes measuring specific out-comes or criteria to determine the benefits of the program. **Training outcomes or criteria** refer to measures that the trainer and the company use to evaluate training programs. To determine the effectiveness of the program, Walgreen had to conduct an evaluation. **Training evaluation** refers to the process of collecting the outcomes needed to determine if training is effective. In Walgreen's case, outcomes included information on store sales and pharmacists' observations of technicians' behavior. Walgreen also had to determine the process it would use to collect information to give the highest level of confidence possible that it could draw conclusions regarding the effectiveness of the training program based on the information collected. This process relates to choosing the evalua-tion design. The **evaluation design** refers to from whom, what, when, and how information needed for determining the effectiveness of the training program will be collected.

This chapter will help you understand why and how to evaluate training programs. The chapter begins by discussing the types of outcomes used in train-ing program evaluation. The next section of the chapter discusses issues related to choosing an evaluation design. An overview of the types of designs is pre-sented. The practical factors that influence the type of design chosen for an eval-uation are discussed. The chapter concludes by reviewing the process involved in conducting an evaluation.

Reasons for Evaluating Training

Companies are investing millions of dollars in training programs to help gain a competitive advantage. Firms with high-leverage training practices not only in-vest large sums of money into developing and administering training programs but also evaluate training programs. Training evaluation involves both formative and summative evaluation.[1] **Formative evaluation** refers to evaluation conducted to improve the training process. That is, formative evaluation helps to ensure that (1) the training program is well organized and runs smoothly and (2) trainees learn and are satisfied with the program. Formative evaluation provides information about how to make the program better. Formative evaluation usually involves collecting qualitative data about the program. Qualitative data includes opinions, beliefs, and feelings about the program. This information is collected using questionnaires or interviews with potential trainees and/or managers who are purchasing or paying for trainees to attend the program. To conduct a formative evaluation, employees and managers are asked to actually participate in the program or preview its contents.

Pilot testing refers to the process of previewing the training program with potential trainees and managers, or other customers (persons who are paying for the development of the program). For example, a group of potential trainees and their managers may be asked to preview or pilot test a Web-based training program. As they complete the program, trainees and managers may be asked to provide their opinions regarding whether graphics, videos, or music used in the program contribute to (or interfere with) learning. They may also be asked how easy it is to understand how to move through the program, complete the exercises, and evaluate the quality of feedback they receive from completing the exercises. The information gained from this preview is used by program developers to improve the program before it is made available to all employees.

Summative evaluation refers to evaluation conducted to determine the extent to which trainees have changed as a result of participating in the training program. That is, have trainees acquired knowledge, skills, attitudes, behavior, or other outcomes identified in the training objectives? Summative evaluation may also include measuring the monetary benefits (also known as return on investment) the company receives from the program. Summative evaluation usually involves collecting quantitative (numerical) data using tests, ratings of behavior, or objective measures of performance such as volume of sales, accidents, or patents.

From the discussion of summative and formative evaluation, it is probably apparent to you why a training program should be evaluated:

1. To identify the program's strengths and weaknesses. This includes determining if the program is meeting the learning objectives, the quality of the learning environment, and if transfer of training to the job is occurring.
2. To assess whether the content, organization, and administration of the program including the schedule, accommodations, trainers, and materials contribute to learning and the use of training content on the job.
3. To identify which trainees benefited most or least from the program.
4. To gather data to assist in marketing programs through collecting information from participants about whether they would recommend

the program to others, why they attended the program, and their level of satisfaction with the program. To determine the financial benefits and costs of the program.

5. To compare the costs and benefits of training versus non training investments (such as work redesign or a better employee selection system).

6. To compare the costs and benefits of different training programs to choose the best program.

Overview of the Evaluation Process

Before we discuss each aspect of training evaluation in detail, it is important to understand the evaluation process. Figure 6–1 summarizes the evaluation process. The previous discussion of formative and summative evaluation suggests that training evaluation involves scrutinizing the program both before and after the program is completed. Figure 6–1 emphasizes that training evaluation be considered by managers and trainers before training has actually occurred. The evaluation process should begin with determining training needs (as discussed in Chapter 3). Needs assessment helps identify what knowledge, skills, behavior, or other learned capabilities are needed. Once the learned capabilities are identified, the next step in the process is to identify specific, measurable training objectives to guide the pro-

FIGURE 6–1

The evaluation process

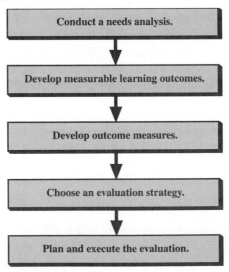

Source: Based on D. A. Grove and C. Ostroff, "Program Evaluation," in *Developing Human Resources,* ed. K. N. Wexley (Washington, DC: Bureau of National Affairs, 1991): 5-185 to 5-220.

gram. We discussed the characteristics of good objectives in Chapter 4. The more specific and measurable these objectives are, the easier it is to identify relevant outcomes for the evaluation. Based on the learning objectives, outcome measures are designed to assess the extent to which learning and transfer should be developed. Once the outcomes are identified, the next step is to determine an evaluation strategy. Factors such as expertise, how quickly the information is needed, change potential, and the organizational culture should be considered in choosing a design. Planning and executing the evaluation involves previewing the program (formative evaluation) as well as collecting training outcomes according to the evaluation design. The results of the evaluation are used to modify, market, or gain additional support for the program. Next we examine each aspect of the evaluation process starting with the development of outcome measures.

Outcomes Used in Evaluating Training Programs

To evaluate a training program, it is necessary to identify how you will determine if the program is effective. As mentioned earlier in the chapter, this involves identifying training outcomes or criteria.

Table 6–1 shows D. L. Kirkpatrick's four-level framework for categorizing training outcomes.[2] Both level 1 and level 2 criteria (reactions and learning) are collected before trainees return to their job. Level 3 and level 4 criteria (behavior and results) measure the degree to which trainees are using training content on the job. That is, level 3 and level 4 criteria are used to determine transfer of training.

Both training practitioners and academic researchers have argued that more comprehensive models of training criteria are needed.[3] That is, there are additional training outcomes that are useful for evaluating training programs. These outcomes include attitudes, motivation, and return on investment. As a result, training outcomes are classified into five categories: cognitive outcomes, skill-based outcomes, affective outcomes, results, and return on investment.[4] Table 6–2 shows examples of these outcomes and how they are measured.

TABLE 6–1   Kirkpatrick's Four-Level Framework of Evaluation Criteria

Level	Criteria	Focus
1	Reactions	Trainee satisfaction
2	Learning	Acquisition of knowledge, skills, attitudes, behavior
3	Behavior	Improvement of behavior on the job
4	Results	Business results achieved by trainees

TABLE 6–2   **Outcomes Used in Evaluating Training Programs**

Outcome	Example	How Measured
Cognitive outcomes	• Safety rules • Electrical principles • Steps in appraisal interview	• Pencil-and-paper tests • Work sample
Skill-based outcomes	• Use a jigsaw • Listening skills • Coaching skills • Land an airplane	• Observation • Work sample • Ratings
Affective outcomes	• Satisfaction with training • Beliefs regarding other cultures	• Interviews • Focus groups • Attitude surveys
Results	• Absenteeism • Accidents • Patents	• Observation • Track data from information system or performance records
Return on investment	• Dollars	• Identify and compare costs and benefits of the program

Cognitive Outcomes.   **Cognitive outcomes** are used to determine the degree to which trainees are familiar with principles, facts, techniques, procedures, or processes emphasized in the training program. Cognitive outcomes—which include the level 2 (learning) criteria from Kirpatrick's framework—measure what knowledge trainees learned in the program. Typically, paper-and-pencil tests are used to assess cognitive outcomes. Table 6–3 provides an example of items from a pencil-and-paper test used to measure trainees' knowledge of decision-making skills.

Skill-Based Outcomes.   **Skill-based outcomes** are used to assess the level of technical or motor skills and behaviors. Skill-based outcomes include acquisition or learning of skills (skill learning) and use of skills on the job (skill transfer). The extent to which trainees have learned skills can be evaluated by observing their performance in work samples such as simulators. Skill transfer is usually determined by observation. For example, a resident medical student may perform surgery while the surgeon carefully observes, giving advice and assistance as needed. Peers and managers may also be asked to rate trainees' behav-

---

TABLE 6–3   Sample Test Items Used to Measure Learning

For each question, check all that apply.

1. If my boss returned a piece of work to me and asked me to make changes on it, I would:

____ Prove to my boss that the work didn't need to be changed.

____ Do what the boss says, but show where changes are needed.

____ Make the changes without talking to my boss.

____ Request a transfer from the department.

2. If I were setting up a new process in my office, I would:

____ Do it on my own without asking for help.

____ Ask my boss for suggestions.

____ Ask the people who work for me for suggestions.

____ Discuss it with friends outside the company.

Source: Based on A. P. Carnevale, L. J. Gainer, and A. S. Meltzer, *Workplace Basics Training Manual* (San Francisco: Jossey-Bass, 1990): 8.12.

ior or skills based on their observations. Table 6–4 shows a sample rating form. This form was used as part of an evaluation of a training program developed to improve school principals' management skills. Skill-based outcomes relate to Kirkpatrick's level 2 (learning) and level 3 (behavior).

Affective Outcomes.   **Affective outcomes** include attitudes and motivation. One type of affective outcome is trainees' reactions toward the training program. **Reaction outcomes** refer to trainees' perceptions of the program including the facilities, trainers, and content. (Reaction outcomes are often referred to as a measure of "creature comfort.") Table 6–5 shows a sample reaction measure. This information is typically collected at the program's conclusion. Reactions are useful for identifying what trainees thought was successful and inhibited learning.

Reaction outcomes are typically collected via a questionnaire completed by trainees. It usually asks questions like the following: "How satisfied are you with the training program?" "Did the session meet your personal expectations?" "How comfortable did you find the classroom?" Keep in mind that while reactions provide useful information, they usually only weakly relate to learning or transfer of training.

Other affective outcomes that might be collected in an evaluation include tolerance for diversity, motivation to learn, safety attitudes, and customer service orientation. Affective outcomes can be measured using surveys. The specific attitude of interest depends on the program objectives. For example, attitudes toward equal employment opportunity laws might be an appropriate outcome to use to evaluate a diversity training program.

TABLE 6–4   Sample Rating Form Used to Measure Behavior

Rating task: Consider your opportunities over the past three months to observe and interact with the principal/assistant principal you are rating. Read the definition and behaviors associated with the skill. Then complete your ratings using the following scale:

Always	Usually	Sometimes	Seldom	Never
1	2	3	4	5

I. *Sensitivity:* Ability to perceive the needs, concerns, and personal problems of others; tact in dealing with persons from different backgrounds; skill in resolving conflict; ability to deal effectively with people concerning emotional needs; knowing what information to communicate to whom.

To what extent in the past three months has the principal or assistant principal:

____ 1. Elicited perceptions, feelings, and concerns of others.

____ 2. Expressed verbal and nonverbal recognition of the feelings, needs, and concerns of others.

____ 3. Took actions that anticipated the emotional effects of specific behaviors.

____ 4. Accurately reflected the point of view of others by restating it, applying it, or encouraging feedback.

____ 5. Communicated all information to others that they needed to perform their job.

____ 6. Diverted unnecessary conflict with others in problem situations.

II. *Decisiveness:* Ability to recognize when a decision is required and act quickly. (Disregard the quality of the decision.)

To what extent in the past three months has this individual:

____ 7. Recognized when a decision was required by determining the results if the decision was made or not made.

____ 8. Determined whether a short- or long-term solution was most appropriate to various situations encountered in the school.

____ 9. Considered decision alternatives.

____ 10. Made a timely decision based on available data.

____ 11. Stuck to decisions once they were made, resisting pressures from others.

TABLE 6–5   Sample Reaction Measure

Rate each of the following characteristics of the training program by
   checking your response.

	Excellent	Good	Fair	Poor
Learning atmosphere				
Program organization				
Trainer knowledge				
Room conditions				
Quality of presentation				
Facilities				
Overall rating of the program				
What would have made the program more effective?				

_____

_____

Results.   **Results** are used to determine the training program's payoff for the company. Examples of results outcomes include reduced costs related to employee turnover or accidents, increased production, and improvements in product quality or customer service. For example, to evaluate a program designed to teach delivery van drivers safe driving practices, Federal Express tracked drivers' accidents and injuries over a 90-day period after they had completed the training program.[5]

Return on Investment.   **Return on investment (ROI)** refers to comparing the training's monetary benefits with the cost of the training. Training costs include direct and indirect costs.[6] **Direct costs** include salaries and benefits for all employees involved in training, including trainees, instructors, consultants, and employees who design the program; program material and supplies; equipment or classroom rentals or purchases; and travel costs. **Indirect costs** are not related directly to the design, development, or delivery of the training program. They include general office supplies, facilities, equipment, and related expenses; travel and expenses not directly billed to one program; training department management and staff salaries not related to any one program; and administrative and staff support salaries. **Benefits** refer to what of value the company gains from the training program.

   Later in the chapter we will show a detailed example of how to determine the costs, benefits, and return on investment from a training program.

How Do You Know If Your Outcomes Are Good?

An important issue in choosing outcomes is to determine if they are good. That is, are these outcomes the best ones to measure to determine if the training program is effective? Good training outcomes need to be relevant, reliable, discriminate, and practical.[7]

Relevance

Criteria relevance refers to the extent to which training outcomes are related to the learned capabilities emphasized in the training program. The learned capabilities required to succeed in the training program should be the same as those required to be successful on the job. We want the outcomes collected in training to be as similar as possible to what trainees learned in the program. One way to ensure that the outcomes collected are relevant is to choose outcomes based on the learning objectives for the program. Recall that the learning objectives show the expected action, conditions under which the trainee is to perform, and the level or standard of performance.

Figure 6–2 shows two ways that training outcomes may lack relevance. **Criteria contamination** refers to the extent that training outcomes measure inappropriate capabilities or are affected by extraneous conditions. For example, if managers' evaluations of job performance are used as a training outcome, trainees may receive higher ratings of job performance simply because the managers know they attended the training program, believe the program is valuable, and therefore give high ratings to ensure that the training looks like it positively affects performance. Criteria may also be contaminated if the conditions under which the outcomes measures are collected vary from the learning environment. That is, trainees may be asked to perform their learned capabilities using equipment, time constraints, or physical working conditions that are not similar to those in the learning environment.

FIGURE 6–2

Criterion deficiency, relevance, and contamination

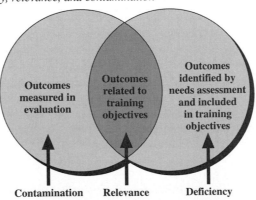

For example, trainees may be asked to demonstrate spreadsheet skills using a newer version of spreadsheet software than they used in the training program. This likely will result in no changes in their spreadsheet skills from pretraining levels. In this case, poor-quality training is not the cause for the lack of change in their spreadsheet skills. Trainees may have learned the necessary spreadsheet skills, but the environment for the evaluation differs substantially from the learning environment, so no change in their skill levels is observed.

Criteria may also be deficient. **Criterion deficiency** refers to the failure to measure training outcomes that were emphasized in the training objectives. For example, the objectives of the spreadsheet skills training program emphasize both understanding the commands available on the spreadsheet (e.g., compute) and using the spreadsheet to calculate statistics using a data set. An evaluation design that uses only learning outcomes such as a test of knowledge of the purpose of key strokes is deficient. It is deficient because the evaluation does not measure outcomes that were included in the training objectives (e.g., use spreadsheet to compute the mean and standard deviation of a set of data).

Consider our previous discussions of learning (Chapter 4) and transfer of training (Chapter 5). Remember that for training to be successful, learning *and* transfer of training must occur. Figure 6–3 shows the multiple objectives of training programs and their implication for choosing evaluation outcomes. Training programs usually have objectives related to both learning and transfer. That is, they want trainees to acquire knowledge and cognitive skill and also to demonstrate the use of the knowledge or strategy in their on-the-job behavior.

FIGURE 6–3

Training program objectives and their implications for evaluation

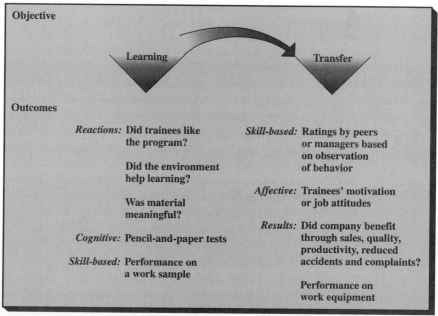

As a result, to ensure an adequate training evaluation, it is important to collect outcomes measures related to both learning and transfer.

Reliability

Reliability refers to the degree to which outcomes can be measured consistently over time. For example, a trainer gives restaurant employees a written test measuring knowledge of safety standards to evaluate a safety training program they attended. The test is given before (pretraining) and after (posttraining) employees attend the program. A reliable test is one that includes items for which the meaning or interpretation of these items by the trainees does not change over time. A reliable test allows the trainer to have confidence that any improvements in posttraining test scores from pretraining levels result from learning that occurred in the training program, not from test characteristics (e.g., items are more understandable the second time) or the test environment (e.g., trainees performed better on the posttraining test because the classroom was more comfortable and quieter).

Discrimination

Discrimination refers to the degree to which trainees' performance on the outcome actually reflect true differences in performance. For example, if we were interested in measuring electricians' knowledge of electrical principles using a paper-and-pencil test, we would want the test to be able to detect true differences in trainees' knowledge of electrical principles. That is, we would want the test to discriminate on the basis of trainees' knowledge of electrical principles. (People who score higher have better understanding of principles of electricity than those who score lower on the test.)

Practicality

Practicality refers to the ease with which the outcomes measures can be collected. One reason that companies give for not including learning, performance, and behavior outcomes in their evaluation of training programs is that collecting them is too burdensome. (It takes too much time and energy, which detracts from the business.) For example, in evaluating a sales training program, it may be impractical to ask customers to rate the salesperson's behavior because this would place too much of a time commitment on the customer (and probably damage future sales relationships).

Evaluation Practices

Figure 6–4 shows outcomes used in training evaluation practices. Surveys of companies' evaluation practices indicate that reactions (an affective outcome) and cognitive outcomes are the most frequently used outcomes in training evaluation.[8] Re-

FIGURE 6–4

Training evaluation practices

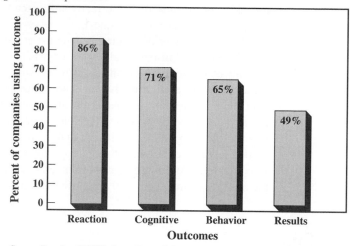

Source: Based on "1996 Industry Report," *Training* 33 (1996): 63.
Note: Percentages represent, in all industries, companies with 100 or more employees that
use these outcomes in training evaluation.

sults outcomes are used by less than 50 percent of the companies that conduct
evaluations. Keep in mind that while most companies are conducting training
evaluations, some surveys indicate that 20 percent of all companies are not!

It is important to recognize the limitations of using only reaction and cognitive outcomes. While they are useful for determining if conditions conducive to
learning exist in the training program and the extent to which trainees have mastered the content of the program, reaction and cognitive outcomes provide no indication of transfer of training—that is, the extent to which skills or attitudes
have changed on the job, knowledge has been applied to work problems, or
training has influenced company effectiveness.

Note that outcome measures are independent of each other. That is, it is
tempting to assume that satisfied trainees learn more and will apply their knowledge and skill to the job, resulting in behavior change and positive results for the
company. However, research indicates that the relationships between reaction,
cognitive, behavior, and results outcomes are small.[9]

Which training outcomes measure is best? The answer depends on the training objectives. For example, if the instructional objectives identified business-
related outcomes such as increased customer service or product quality, then results outcomes should be included in the evaluation. As Figure 6–3 shows, both
reaction and cognitive outcomes may affect learning. Reaction outcomes provide information regarding the extent to which the trainer, facilities, or learning
environment may have hindered learning. Cognitive outcomes directly measure
the extent to which trainees have mastered training content. Reaction and cognitive outcomes do not help determine the extent to which trainees actually use the
training content in their jobs. To the extent possible, evaluation should include

skill-based, affective, or results outcomes to determine the extent to which transfer of training has occurred—that is, training has influenced a change in behavior, skill, or attitude or has directly influenced objective measures related to company effectiveness (e.g., sales).

Positive transfer of training is demonstrated when learning occurs and positive changes in skill-based, affective, or results outcomes are also observed. No transfer of training is demonstrated if learning occurs but no changes are observed in skill-based, affective, or learning outcomes. Negative transfer is evident when learning occurs but skills, affective outcomes, or results are less than at pretraining levels. Results of evaluation studies that find no transfer or negative transfer suggest that the trainer and the manager need to investigate whether a good learning environment (e.g., opportunities for feedback and practice) was provided in the training program, trainees were motivated and able to learn, and the needs assessment correctly identified training needs.

Evaluation Designs

The design of the training evaluation determines the confidence that can be placed in the results. No training evaluation can be absolutely certain that the results of the evaluation are completely true. What the evaluator strives for is to use the most rigorous design possible (given the circumstances under which the evaluation occurs) to rule out alternative explanations for the results.

We will begin our discussion of evaluation designs by identifying these "alternative explanations" that the evaluator should attempt to control for. Next, we will compare various evaluation designs. Finally, we will end this section by discussing practical circumstances that the trainer needs to consider in selecting an evaluation design.

Threats to Validity: Alternative Explanations for Evaluation Results

Table 6–6 presents threats to validity of an evaluation. **Threats to validity** refer to a factor that will lead one to question either (1) the believability of the study results or (2) the extent to which the evaluation results are generalizable to other groups of trainees and situations.[10] The believability of study results refers to **internal validity.** The internal threats to validity relate to characteristics of the company (history), the outcome measures (instrumentation, testing), and the persons in the evaluation study (maturation, regression toward the mean, mortality, initial group differences). These characteristics can cause the evaluation study to reach the wrong conclusions about training effectiveness. An evaluation study needs internal validity to have confidence that the results of the evaluation (particularly if they are positive) are due to the training program and not to another factor. For example, consider a group of managers who have attended a communication skills training program. At the same time as they attend the program, it is announced that the company will be restructured. After the program, the man-

TABLE 6–6   **Threats to Validity**

Threats to Internal Validity	_Description_
Company	
History	Event occurs, producing changes in training outcomes.
Persons	
Maturation	Changes in training outcomes resulting from trainee's physical growth or emotional state.
Mortality	Study participants leave company.
Initial group differences	Training group differs from comparison group on individual differences that influence outcomes (knowledge, skills, ability, behavior).
Outcome Measures	
Testing	Trainees are sensitized to perform well on posttest measures.
Instrumentation	Trainee interpretation of outcomes changes over course of evaluation.
Regression toward the mean	High- and low-scoring trainees move toward middle or average on posttraining measure.
Threats to External Validity	_Description_
Reaction to pretest	Use of test before training causes trainee to pay attention to material on test.
Reaction to evaluation	Being evaluated causes trainee to try harder in training program.
Interaction of selection and training	Characteristics of trainee influence program effectiveness.
Interaction of methods	Results of trainees who received different methods can only be generalized to trainees who receive same training in the same order.

Source: Based on T. D. Cook, D. T. Campbell, and L. Peracchio, "Quasi-Experimentation," in _Handbook of Industrial and Organizational Psychology,_ 2d ed., Vol. 1, eds. M. D. Dunnette and L. M. Hough (Palo Alto, CA: Consulting Psychologists Press, 1990): 491–576.

agers may become better communicators simply because they are scared that otherwise they will lose their jobs. Perhaps no learning actually occurred in the training program!

Trainers are also interested in the generalizability of the study results to other groups and situations (i.e., they are interested in the **external validity** of the study). As shown in Table 6–6, threats to external validity relate to how study participants react to being included in the study and the effects of multiple types of training. Because evaluation usually does not involve all employees who have completed a program (or who may take training in the future), trainers want to be able to say that the training program will be effective in the future with similar groups.

Methods to Control for Threats to Validity.   Because trainers often want to use evaluation study results as a basis for changing training programs or demonstrating that training does work (as a means to gain additional funding for training from those who control the training budget), it is important to minimize the threats to validity. There are three ways to minimize threats to validity: the use of pretest and posttest in evaluation designs, comparison groups, and random assignment.

Pre- and Posttests.   One way to improve the internal validity of the study results is to first establish a baseline or **pretraining measure** of the outcome. Another measure of the outcomes can be taken after training. This is referred to as a **posttraining measure.** A comparison of the posttraining and pretraining measure can give an indication of the degree to which trainees have changed as a result of training.

Use of Comparison Groups.   Besides pre- and posttraining measures of the outcomes, internal validity can be improved by using a control or comparison group. A **comparison group** refers to a group of employees who participate in the evaluation study but do not attend the training program. The comparison group has personal characteristics (e.g., gender, education, age, tenure, skill level) as similar to the trainees as possible. Use of a comparison group in training evaluation helps to rule out the possibility that changes found in the outcome measures are due to factors other than training. Use of a comparison group helps to control for the effects of history, testing, instrumentation, and maturation because both the comparison and training group are treated similarly, receive the same measures, and have the same amount of time to develop.

For example, consider an evaluation of a safety training program. Safe behaviors are measured before and after safety training for both trainees and a comparison group. If the level of safe behavior improves for the training group from pretraining levels, but remains relatively the same for the comparison group at both pre- and posttraining, we can reasonably conclude that the training (not some other factor such as the attention given to both the trainees and comparison group by asking them to participate in the study) was responsible for the observed differences in safe behaviors.

Random Assignment.   **Random assignment** refers to assigning employees to the training and comparison group on the basis of chance. That is, employees are assigned to the training program without consideration of individual differences (ability, motivation) or prior experiences. Random assignment helps to ensure that trainees are similar in individual differences such as age, gender, ability, and motivation. Because it is often impossible to identify and measure all of the individual characteristics that might influence the outcome measures, random assignment ensures that these characteristics are equally distributed in the comparison group and the training group. Random assignment helps to reduce the effects of employees dropping out of the study (mortality) and differences between the training group and comparison group in ability, knowledge, skill, or other personal characteristics.

Keep in mind that random assignment is often impractical. Companies want employees assigned to training who need training. Also, they are unwilling to provide a comparison group. One solution to this problem is to identify the factors on which the training and comparison groups differ and control for these factors in the analysis of the data (a statistical procedure known as analysis of covariance). Another method is to determine trainees' characteristics after they are assigned and ensure that the comparison group includes employees with similar characteristics.

Types of Evaluation Designs

A number of different designs can be used to evaluate training programs.[11] Table 6–7 compares each design on the basis of who is involved (trainees, comparison group) and when measures are collected (pretraining, posttraining). As shown in Table 6–7, research designs vary based on whether they include pre- and posttraining measurement of outcomes and a comparison group. In general, designs that use pretraining and posttraining measures of outcomes and include

TABLE 6–7   Comparison of Evaluation Designs

		Measures	
Design	*Groups*	*Pretraining*	*Posttraining*
Posttest-only	Trainees	No	Yes
Pretest posttest	Trainees	Yes	Yes
Posttest-only Comparison group	Trainees Comparison	No	Yes
Pretest posttest Comparison group	Trainees Comparison	Yes	Yes
Time series	Trainees	Yes	Yes, several
Solomon Four-group	Trainees A	Yes	Yes
	Trainees B	No	Yes
	Comparison A	Yes	Yes
	Comparison B	No	Yes

a comparison group reduce the risk that alternative factors (other than the training itself) are responsible for the results of the evaluation. This increases the trainer's confidence in using the results to make decisions. Of course, the trade-off is that evaluation using these designs is more difficult to conduct than evaluations not using pretraining and posttraining measures or comparison groups.

Posttest Only.   The **posttest-only** design refers to an evaluation design in which only posttraining outcomes are collected. This design can be strengthened by adding a comparison group (which helps to rule out alternative explanations for changes). The posttest-only design is appropriate when trainees (and the comparison group, if one is used) can be expected to have similar levels of knowledge, behavior, or results outcomes (e.g., same number of sales, equal awareness of how to close a sale) prior to training.

Pretest/Posttest.   The **pretest/posttest** refers to an evaluation design in which both pretraining and posttraining outcomes measures are collected. There is no comparison group. The lack of a comparison group makes it difficult to rule out the effects of business conditions or other factors as explanations for changes. This design is often used by companies that want to evaluate a training program but are uncomfortable with excluding certain employees or that only intend to train a small group of employees.

Pretest/Posttest with Comparison Group.   The **pretest/posttest with comparison group** refers to an evaluation design that includes trainees and a comparison group. Outcome measures are collected from both groups pre- and post-training. If improvement is greater for the training group than the comparison group, this provides evidence that training is responsible for the change. This type of design controls for most of the threats to validity.

Table 6–8 presents an example of a pretest/posttest comparison group design. This evaluation involved determining the relationship between three conditions or treatments and learning, satisfaction, and use of computer skills.[12] The three conditions or treatments (types of computer training) were behavior modeling, self-paced studying, and lecturing. A comparison group was also included in the study. Behavior modeling involved watching a video showing a model performing key behavior necessary to complete a task. In this case the task was procedures on the computer. (We discuss behavior modeling in detail in Chapter 7.)

Forty trainees were included in each condition. Measures of learning included a test consisting of 11 items designed to measure information that trainees needed to know to operate the computer system (e.g., "does formatting destroy all data on the disk?"). Also, trainees' comprehension of computer procedures (procedural comprehension) was measured by presenting trainees with scenarios on the computer screens and asking them what would appear next on the screen. Use of computer skills (skill-based learning outcome) was measured by asking trainees to complete six computer tasks (e.g., changing directories). Satisfaction with the program (reaction) was measured by six items (e.g., "I would recommend this program to others").

TABLE 6–8   Example of a Pretest Posttest Comparison Group Design

	Pretraining	Training	Posttraining Time 1	Posttraining Time 2
Lecture	Yes	Yes	Yes	Yes
Self-paced	Yes	Yes	Yes	Yes
Behavior modeling	Yes	Yes	Yes	Yes
No training (comparison)	Yes	No	Yes	Yes

Source: Based on S. J. Simon and J. M. Werner, "Computer Training through Behavior Modeling, Self-Paced and Instructional Approaches: A Field Experiment," *Journal of Applied Psychology* 81 (1996): 648–59.

As shown in Table 6–8, measures of learning and skills were collected from the trainees prior to attending the program (pretraining). Measures of learning and skills were also collected immediately after training (posttraining time 1) and four weeks after training (posttraining time 2). The satisfaction measure was collected immediately following training.

The posttraining time 2 measures collected in this study help to determine the extent to which training transfer and retention of the information and skills occurred. That is, immediately following training, we may find the trainees appeared to learn and acquire skills related to computer training. Collection of the posttraining measures four weeks after training provides information about trainees' level of retention of the skills and knowledge.

Statistical procedures known as analysis of variance and analysis of covariance were used to test for differences between pretraining measures and posttraining measures for each condition. Also, differences between each of the training conditions and the comparison group were analyzed. These procedures test to determine if differences between the groups are large enough to conclude with a high degree of confidence that training was responsible for the observed differences (rather than chance fluctuations in trainees' scores on the measures).

Time Series.   **Time series** refers to an evaluation design in which training outcomes are collected at periodic intervals pre- and posttraining. (In the other evaluation designs discussed, training outcomes are collected only once before and after training.) A comparison group can also be used with a time series design. One advantage of the time series design is that it allows an analysis of the stability of training outcomes over time. This type of design is frequently used to evaluate training programs that focus on improving readily observable outcomes such as accident rates, productivity, or absenteeism that vary over time.

Table 6–9 presents an example of a time series design. This design was used to evaluate how much a training program improved the number of safe work behaviors in a food manufacturing plant.[13] This plant was experiencing an accident

TABLE 6–9   **Example of a Time Series Design**

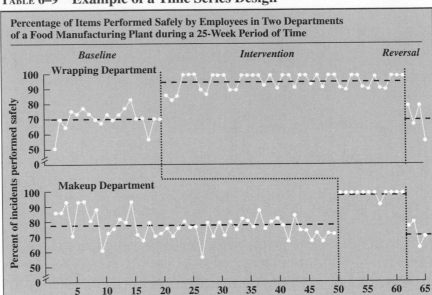

Source: "A Behavioral Approach to Occupational Safety: Pinpointing Safe Performance in a Food Manufacturing Plant" by J. Komaki, K. D. Badwick, and L. R. Scott, 1978, *Journal of Applied Psychology,* 63. Copyright 1978 by the American Psychological Association. Adapted by permission.

rate similar to that of the mining industry, the most dangerous area of work. Employees were engaging in unsafe behaviors such as putting their hands into conveyors to unjam them (resulting in crushed limbs).

To improve safety, a training program was developed to teach employees safe behavior, provide them with incentives for safe behaviors, and encourage them to monitor their own behavior.

To evaluate the program, the design included a comparison group (the Makeup Department) and a trained group (the Wrapping Department). The Makeup department is responsible for measuring and mixing ingredients, preparing the dough, placing the dough into the oven and removing it when it is cooked, and packaging the finished product. The Wrapping Department is responsible for bagging, sealing, and labeling the packaging and stacking it on skids for shipping. Outcomes included observations of safe work behaviors. These observations were taken over a 25-week period.

The baseline shows the percentage of safe acts prior to introduction of the safety training program. Training directed at increasing the number of safe behaviors was introduced after approximately five weeks (20 observation sessions) in the Wrapping Department and 10 weeks (50 observation sessions) in the Makeup Department. As shown, the number of safe acts observed varied across the observation period for both groups. However, the number of safe behaviors

---

TABLE 6–10   Example of a Solomon Four-Group Design

	Pretest	*Training*	*Posttest*
Group 1	Yes	IL-based	Yes
Group 2	Yes	Traditional	Yes
Group 3	No	IL-based	Yes
Group 4	No	Traditional	Yes

Source: Based on R. D. Bretz and R. E. Thompsett, "Comparing Traditional and Integrative Learning Methods in Organizational Training Programs," *Journal of Applied Psychology* 77 (1992): 941–51.

increased after the training program was conducted for the trained group (Wrapping Department). The level of safe acts remained stable across the observation period. (See the Intervention period.) When the Makeup Department received training (at 10 weeks or after 50 observations) a similar increase in the percentage of safe behaviors was observed.

Solomon Four-Group.   The **Solomon four-group** design combines the pretest/posttest comparison group, and the posttest-only control group design. In the Solomon four-group design, a training group and a comparison group are measured on the outcomes both before and after training. Another training group and control group are measured only after training. This design controls for most threats to internal and external validity.

An application of the Solomon four-group design is shown in Table 6–10. This design was used to compare the effects of integrative-learning–(IL) based training with traditional (lecture-based) training of manufacturing resource planning. Manufacturing resource planning is a method for effectively planning, coordinating, and integrating the use of all resources of a manufacturing company.[14] The IL-based training differed from the traditional training in several ways. IL-based training sessions began with a series of activities intended to create a relaxed, positive environment for learning. The students were asked what manufacturing resource planning meant to them, and attempts were made to reaffirm their beliefs and unite the trainees around a common understanding of manufacturing resource planning. Students presented training material and participated in group discussions, games, stories, and poetry related to the manufacturing processes.

Because the company was interested in the effects of IL related to traditional training, groups who received traditional training were used as the comparison group (rather than groups who received no training).

A test of manufacturing resource planning (knowledge test) and a reaction measure were used as outcomes. The study found that participants in the IL-based learning groups learned slightly less than participants in the traditional training groups. IL-group participants had much more positive reactions than those in the traditional training program.

Considerations in Choosing an Evaluation Design

There is no one appropriate evaluation design. An evaluation design should be chosen based on your evaluation of the factors shown in Table 6–11. There are several reasons why no evaluation or a less rigorous evaluation design may be appropriate than a more rigorous design including a comparison group, involving random assigned and requiring pre- and posttraining measures. Managers and trainers may be unwilling to devote the time and effort necessary to collect training outcomes. Second, managers or trainers may lack the expertise to conduct an evaluation study. Third, a company may view training as an investment from which it expects to receive little or no return. You should consider a more rigorous evaluation design (pretest/posttest with comparison group) if[15]

1. The evaluation results can be used to change the program.
2. The training program is ongoing and has the potential to affect many employees (and customers).
3. The training program involves multiple classes and a large number of trainees.
4. Cost justification for training is based on numerical indicators. (Here the company has a strong orientation toward evaluation.)
5. You or others have the expertise (or the budget to purchase expertise from outside the company) to design and evaluate the data collected from an evaluation study.

TABLE 6–11   Factors That Influence the Type of Evaluation Design

Factor	How Factor Influences Type of Evaluation Design
Change potential	Can program be modified?
Importance	Does ineffective training affect customer service, product development, or relationships between employees?
Scale	How many trainees are involved?
Purpose of training	Is training conducted for learning, results, or both?
Organization culture	Is demonstrating results part of company norms and expectations?
Expertise	Can a complex study be analyzed?
Cost	Is evaluation too expensive?
Time frame	When do we need the information?

Source: Based on S. I. Tannenbaum and S. B. Woods, "Determining a Strategy for Evaluating Training: Operating within Organizational Constraints," *Human Resource Planning* 15 (1992): 63–81.

6. The cost of the training creates a need to show that it works.

7. There is sufficient time for conducting an evaluation. Here, information regarding training effectiveness is not needed immediately.

8. There is interest in measuring change (in knowledge, behavior, skill, etc.) from pretraining levels or comparing two or more different programs.

For example, if you are interested in determining how much employees' communications skills have changed as a result of a training program, a pretest/posttest comparison group design is necessary. Trainees should be randomly assigned to training and no-training conditions. These evaluation design features give you a high degree of confidence that any communication skill change is the result of participating in the training program.[16] This type of evaluation design is also necessary if you are asked to compare the effectiveness of two training programs.

Evaluation designs without pretest or comparison groups are most appropriate in situations where you are interested in identifying if a specific level of performance has been achieved. (For example, are employees who participated in training able to adequately communicate their ideas?) In this situation, you are not interested in determining how much change has occurred. Rather, you are interested in whether the trainees achieved a certain proficiency level.

Arthur Andersen's evaluation strategy for a training course delivered to the company's tax professionals shows how company norms regarding evaluation and the purpose of training influence the type of evaluation design chosen.[17] Arthur Andersen views training as an effective method for developing human resources. Training is expected to provide a good return on investment. Arthur Andersen used a combination of affective, cognitive, behavior, and results criteria to evaluate a five-week course designed to prepare tax professionals to understand state and local tax law. The course involved two weeks of self-study and three weeks of classroom work. A pretest/posttest comparison design was used. Before they took the course, trainees were tested to determine their knowledge of state and local tax laws and they completed a survey designed to assess their self-confidence in preparing accurate tax returns. The evaluators also identified the trainees' (accountants') billable hours related to calculating state and local tax returns and the revenue generated by the activity. After the course, evaluators again identified billable hours and surveyed trainees' self-confidence. The results of the evaluation indicated that the accountants were spending more time doing state and local tax work than before training. Also, the trained accountants produced more revenue doing state and local tax work than accountants who had not yet received the training (comparison group). There was also a significant improvement in the accountants' confidence following training and they were more willing to promote their expertise in state and local tax preparation. Finally, after 15 months, the revenue gained by the company more than offset the cost of training. On average, the increase in revenue for the trained tax accountants was more than 10 percent.

Determining Return on Investment

Earlier in the chapter we discussed return on investment (ROI) as an important training outcome. Here we discuss how to calculate ROI. ROI results from a cost-benefit analysis. **Cost-benefit analysis** in this situation is the process of determining the economic benefits of a training program using accounting methods. Determining the economic benefits of training involves determining training costs and benefits. Training cost information is important for several reasons:[18]

1. To understand total expenditures for training, including direct and indirect costs.
2. To compare the costs of alternative training programs.
3. To evaluate the proportion of money spent on training development, administration, and evaluation as well as to compare monies spent on training for different groups of employees (exempt versus nonexempt, for example).
4. To control costs.

Determining Costs

One method for comparing costs of alternative training programs is the resource requirements model.[19] The resource requirements model compares equipment, facilities, personnel, and materials costs across different stages of the training process (training design, implementation, needs assessment, development, and evaluation). Use of the resource requirements model can help determine overall differences in costs between training programs. Also, costs incurred at different stages of the training process can be compared across programs.

Accounting can also be used to calculate costs.[20] Seven categories related to the cost sources are calculated. These costs include those related to program development or purchase, instructional materials for trainers and trainees, equipment and hardware, facilities, travel and lodging, and salary of trainer and support staff as well as the cost of lost productivity while trainees attend the program (or cost of temporary employees who replace the trainees while they are at training). This method also identifies when the costs are incurred. One-time costs include those related to needs assessment and program development. Costs per offering relate to training site rental fees, trainer salaries, and other costs that are realized every time the program is offered. Costs per trainee include meals, materials, and lost productivity or expenses incurred to replace the trainees while they attend training.

Determining Benefits

To identify the potential benefits of training, the company must review the original reasons that the training was conducted. For example, training may have been conducted to reduce production costs or overtime costs or to increase the amount of repeat business. A number of methods may be helpful in identifying the benefits of training:

1. Technical, academic, and practitioner literature summarizes the benefits that have been shown to relate to a specific training program.
2. Pilot training programs assess the benefits from a small group of trainees before a company commits more resources.
3. Observance of successful job performers can help a company determine what successful job performers do differently from unsuccessful job performers.[21]

Example of a Cost-Benefit Analysis

A cost-benefit analysis is best explained by an example.[22] A wood plant produced panels contractors used as building materials. The plant employed 300 workers, 48 supervisors, seven shift superintendents, and a plant manager. The business had three problems. First, 2 percent of the wood panels produced each day were rejected because of poor quality. Second, the production area was experiencing poor housekeeping, such as improperly stacked finished panels that would fall on employees. Third, the number of preventable accidents was higher than the industry average. To correct these problems, supervisors were trained in (1) performance management and interpersonal skills related to quality problems and poor work habits of employees and (2) rewarding employees for performance improvement. The supervisors, shift superintendents, and plant manager attended training. Training was conducted in a hotel close to the plant. The training program was purchased from a consultant and used videotape. Also, the instructor for the program was a consultant. Table 6–12 shows each type of cost and how they were determined.

The benefits of the training were identified by considering the objectives of the training program and the type of outcomes the program was to influence. These outcomes included the quality of panels, housekeeping, and accident rate. Table 6–13 shows how the benefits of the program were calculated.

Once the cost and benefits of the program are determined, ROI is calculated by dividing return or benefits by costs. In our example, ROI was 6.7. That is, every dollar invested in the program returned approximately seven dollars in benefits. How do you determine if the ROI is acceptable? One way is for managers and trainers to agree on what level of ROI is acceptable. Another method is to use the ROI that other companies obtain from similar types of training. Table 6–14 provides examples of ROI obtained from several types of training programs.

In our example, the outcomes were very measurable. That is, it was easy to see changes in quality, count accident rates, and observe housekeeping behavior. For training programs that focus on "soft" outcomes (e.g., attitudes, interpersonal

TABLE 6–12 Determining Costs for a Cost-Benefit Analysis

Direct Costs	
Instructor	$ 0
In-house instructor (12 days @ $125 per day)	1,500
Fringe benefits (25% of salary)	375
Travel expenses	0
Materials ($60 × 56 trainees)	3,360
Classroom space and audiovisual equipment (12 days @ $50 per day)	600
Refreshments ($4 per day × 3 days × 56 trainees)	672
Total direct costs	6,507
Indirect Costs	
Training management	0
Clerical and administrative salaries	750
Fringe benefits (25% of salary)	187
Postage, shipping, and telephone	0
Pre- and posttraining learning materials ($4 × 56 trainees)	224
Total indirect costs	1,161
Development costs	
Fee for program purchase	3,600
Instructor training	1,400
Registration fee	975
Travel and lodging	625
Salary	156
Benefits (25% of salary)	6,756
Total development costs	
Overhead costs	
General organizational support, top management time	1,443
(10% of direct, indirect, and development costs)	1,443
Total overhead costs	
Compensation for Trainees	
Trainees' salaries and benefits (based on time away from job)	16,969
Total training costs	32,836
Cost per trainee	587

skills), it may be more difficult to estimate the value. In the case of soft outcomes, trainees, managers, or human resources may be able to provide reasonable estimates of value.[23] For example, to calculate ROI for a training program designed to cut absenteeism, trainees and their supervisors were asked to estimate the cost of an absence. The values were averaged to obtain an estimate.

TABLE 6–13   Determining Benefits for a Cost-Benefit Analysis

Operational Results Area	How Measured	Results before Training	Results after Training	Differences (+ or −)	Expressed in Dollars
Quality of panels	Percent rejected	2 percent rejected— 1,440 panels per day	1.5 percent rejected— 1,080 panels per day	.5 percent— 360 panels	$720 per day, $172,800 per year
Housekeeping	Visual inspection using 20-item checklist	10 defects (average)	2 defects (average)	8 defects	Not measurable in $
Preventable accidents	Number of accidents	24 per year	16 per year	8 per year	$48,000 per year
	Direct cost of accidents	$144,000 per year	$96,000 per year	$48,000 per year	

$$ROI = \frac{Return}{Investment} = \frac{Operational\ results}{Training\ costs} = \frac{\$220{,}800}{\$32{,}836} = 6.7$$

Total savings: $220,800

Source: Adapted from D. G. Robinson and J. Robinson, "Training for Impact," *Training & Development Journal* (August 1989): 30–42.

Other Methods for Cost-Benefit Analysis

It is important to recognize that other more sophisticated methods are available for determining the dollar value of training. For example, utility analysis assesses the dollar value of training based on estimates of the difference in job performance between trained and untrained employees, the number of individuals trained, the length of time a training program is expected to influence performance, and the variability in job performance in the untrained group of employees.[24] These methods require the use of a pretest/posttest design with a comparison group. Other types of economic analysis evaluate training as it benefits the firm or the government using direct and indirect training costs, government incentives paid for training, wage increases received by trainees as a result of completion of training, tax rates, and discount rates.[25]

TABLE 6–14   Example of Return on Investment

Industry	Training Program	ROI
Bottling company	Workshops on managers' roles	15:1
Large commercial bank	Sales training	21:1
Electric and gas utility	Behavior modification	5:1
Oil company	Customer service	4.8:1
Health maintenance organization	Team training	13.7:1

Source: Based on J. J. Philips, "ROI: The Search for Best Practices," *Training and Development* (February 1996): 45.

Summary

Evaluation provides information used to determine training effectiveness. Evaluation involves identifying the appropriate outcomes to measure. The outcomes used in evaluating training programs include trainees' satisfaction with the training program, learning of knowledge or skills, use of knowledge and skills on the job, and results such as sales, productivity, or accidents. Evaluation may also involve comparing the costs of training to the benefits received (return on investment). It is important that the outcomes used in training evaluation help to determine the degree to which the program resulted in both learning and transfer of training. Evaluation also involves choosing the appropriate design to maximize the confidence that can be placed in the results. The design chosen is based on a careful analysis of how to minimize threats to internal and external validity as well as the purpose, expertise, and other company and training characteristics. The types of designs used for evaluation vary on the basis of whether they include pre- and posttraining measures of outcomes and a training and a comparison group. The chapter concludes by noting that a good evaluation requires thinking about the evaluation in advance of conducting the training program. Information from the needs assessment and specific and measurable learning objectives can help identify measurable outcomes that should be included in the evaluation design.

Key Terms

training effectiveness   130
training outcomes (criteria)   130
training evaluation   130
evaluation design   130

formative evaluation   131
pilot testing   131
summative evaluation   131
cognitive outcomes   134

Discussion Questions

1. What can be done to motivate companies to evaluate training programs?

2. What do threats to validity have to do with training evaluation? Identify internal and external threats to validity. Are internal and external threats similar? Explain.

3. What are the strengths and weaknesses of each of the following designs: posttest-only, pretest/posttest comparison group, Pretest/posttest only?

4. What are results outcomes? Why do you think that most organizations don't use results outcomes for evaluating their training programs?

5. In the chapter we discussed several factors that influence the choice of evaluation design. Which of these factors would have the greatest influence on your choice of an evaluation design? Which would have the smallest influence? Explain your choices.

6. How might you estimate the benefits from a training program designed to teach employees how to use the World Wide Web to monitor stock prices?

7. A group of managers ($N = 25$) participated in the problem-solving module of a leadership development program two weeks ago. The module consisted of two days focused on the correct process to use in problem solving. Each manager supervises 15 to 20 employees. The company is willing to change the program and there is an increasing emphasis in the company to show that training expenses are justifiable. You are asked to evaluate this program. Your boss would like the results of the evaluation no later than six weeks from now. Discuss the outcomes you would collect and the design you would use. How might your answer change if the managers have not yet attended the program?

Application Assignments

1. Consider this course as a training program. In teams of up to five students, identify (1) the types of outcomes you would recommend to use in evaluating this course and (2) the evaluation design you would use. Justify your choice of a design based on minimizing threats to validity and practical considerations.

2. Domino's Pizza was interested in determining whether or not a new employee could learn how to make a pizza using a computer/based training method (CD-ROM). The CD-ROM application addresses the proper procedure for "massaging" a dough ball and stretching it to fit a 12-inch pizza pan. Domino's quality standards emphasize the roundness of the pizza, an even border, and uniform thickness of the dough. Traditionally, on-the-job training is used to teach new employees how to stretch pizza dough to fit the pizza pan.

   Questions

   A. What outcomes or criteria should Domino's Pizza measure to determine if CD-ROM training is an effective method for teaching new employees how to stretch pizza dough to fit a 12-inch pan? Who would be involved in the evaluation?

   B. Describe the evaluation design you would recommend that Domino's Pizza use to determine if CD-ROM training is more effective than on-the-job training.

Endnotes

1. M. Van Wart, N. J. Cayer, and S. Cook, *Handbook of Training and Development for the Public Sector,* (San Francisco: Jossey-Bass, 1993).

2. D. L. Kirkpatrick, "Evaluation," in *The ASTD Training and Development Handbook,* 2d ed., ed. R. L. Craig (New York: McGraw-Hill, 1996): 294–312.

3. K. Kraiger, J. K. Ford, and E. Salas, "Application of Cognitive, Skill-Based, and Affective Theories of Learning Outcomes to New Methods of Training Evaluation," *Journal of Applied Psychology* 78 (1993): 311–28; J. J. Phillips, "ROI: The Search for Best Practices," *Training and Development* (February 1996): 42–47; G. M. Alliger, S. I. Tannenbaum, W. Bennet, Jr., H. Traver, and A. Shortland, "A Meta-analysis of the Relations Among Training Criteria," *Personnel Psychology* 50 (1997): 341–55.

4. Kraiger, Ford, and Salas, "Application of Cognitive, Skill-Based, and Affective Theories"; J. J. Phillips, "ROI: The Search for Best Practices"; D. L. Kirkpatrick, "Evaluation of Training," in *Training and Development Handbook,* 2d ed., ed. R. L. Craig (New York: McGraw-Hill, 1976): 18-1 to 18-27.

5. J. J. Phillips, "Was It the Training?" *Training and Development* (March 1996): 28–32.

6. Phillips, "ROI: The Search for Best Practices."

7. D. A. Grove and C. Ostroff, "Program Evaluation," in *Developing Human Resources,* ed. K. N. Wexley (Washington, DC: Bureau of National Affairs, 1991): 5-185 to 5-220.

8. H. J. Frazis, D. E. Herz, and M. W. Horrigan, "Employer-Provided Training: Results from a New Survey," *Monthly Labor Review* 118 (1995): 3–17.

9. G. M Alliger and E. A. Janak, "Kirkpatrick's Levels of Training Criteria: Thirty Years Later," *Personnel Psychology* (Summer 1989): 331–42.

10. T. D. Cook, D. T. Campbell, and L. Peracchio, "Quasi Experimentation," in *Handbook of Industrial and Organizational Psychology,* 2d ed., Vol. 1, eds. M. D. Dunnette and L. M. Hough (Palo Alto, CA: Consulting Psychologists Press, 1990): 491–576.

11. Ibid.; J. J. Phillips, *Handbook of Training Evaluation and Measurement Methods,* 2d ed., (Houston, TX: Gulf Publishing, 1991).

12. S. J. Simon and J. M. Werner, "Computer Training through Behavior Modeling, Self-Paced and Instructional Approaches: A Field Experiment," *Journal of Applied Psychology* 81 (1996): 648–59.

13. J. Komaki, K. D. Bardwick, and L. R. Scott, "A Behavioral Approach to Occupational Safety: Pinpointing and Reinforcing Safe Performance in a Food Manufacturing Plant," *Journal of Applied Psychology* 63 (1978): 434–45.

14. R. D. Bretz and R. E. Thompsett, "Comparing Traditional and Integrative Learning Methods in Organizational Training Programs," *Journal of Applied Psychology* 77 (1992): 941–51.

15. S. I. Tannenbaum and S. B. Woods, "Determining a Strategy for Evaluating Training: Operating within Organizational Constraints," *Human Resource Planning* 15 (1992): 63–81; R. D. Arvey, S. E. Maxwell, and E. Salas, "The Relative Power of Training Evaluation Designs under Different Cost Configurations," *Journal of Applied Psychology* 77 (1992): 155–60.

16. P. R. Sackett and E. J. Mullen, "Beyond Formal Experimental Design: Toward an Expanded View of the Training Evaluation Process," *Personnel Psychology* 46 (1993): 613–27.

17. B. Gerber, "Does Your Training Make a Difference? Prove It?" *Training* (March 1995): 27–34.

18. A. P. Carnevale and E. R. Schulz, "Return on Investment: Accounting for Training," *Training and Development Journal,* (July 1990): S1–S32.

19. Ibid.; G. Kearsley, *Costs, Benefits, and Productivity in Training Systems* (Boston: Addison-Wesley, 1982).

20. S. D. Parry, "Measuring Training's ROI," *Training and Development* (May 1996): 72–77.

21. D. G. Robinson and J. Robinson, "Training for Impact," *Training and Development Journal,* (August 1989): 30–42.

22. Ibid.

23. J. J. Phillips, "How Much Is the Training Worth?" *Training and Development* (April 1996): 20–24.

24. J. E. Matheiu and R. L. Leonard, "Applying Utility Analysis to a Training Program in Supervisory Skills: A Time-Based Approach," *Academy of Management Journal* 30 (1987): 316–35; F. L. Schmidt, J. E. Hunter, and K. Pearlman, "Assessing the Economic Impact of Personnel Programs on Work-Force Productivity," *Personnel Psychology* 35 (1982): 333–47; J. W. Boudreau, "Economic Considerations in Estimating the Utility of Human Resource Productivity Programs," *Personnel Psychology* 36 (1983): 551–76.

25. U. E. Gattiker, "Firm and Taxpayer Returns from Training of Semiskilled Employees," *Academy of Management Journal* 38 (1995): 1151–73.

7 TRADITIONAL TRAINING METHODS

Objectives

After reading this chapter, you should be able to

1. Discuss the strengths and weaknesses of presentational, hands-on, and group building training methods.

2. Provide recommendations for effective on-the-job training.

3. Develop a case study.

4. Develop a self-directed learning module.

5. Discuss the key components of behavior modeling training.

6. Explain the conditions necessary for adventure learning to be effective.

7. Discuss what team training should focus on to improve team performance.

TRAINING METHODS THAT "STICK" IN THE READY-MIX BUSINESS

At 5:30 AM the drivers prepare to deliver the first of many loads of concrete. In the concrete business, a perishable product needs to be delivered on a timely basis to construction sites. Morse Bros., located in Tangent, Oregon, is one of only a few ready-mix firms in the Northwest that provide regular training for their drivers. Drivers play a key role in determining the success of the business. For example, the company's fleet of 73 mixer trucks can burn more than 2,000 gallons of fuel in an eight-hour day due to excessive idling. Fully loaded, a ready-mix truck weighs up to 35 tons. Ready-mix trucks are often called upon to navigate uneven terrain at construction sites. As a result, drivers must understand how to avoid rollovers that can damage lives and equipment and the tedious task of having to remove hardened concrete with a jackhammer. Ready-mix drivers often know little about the concrete

161

mixture they are carrying. Morse Bros. trains drivers about the product they carry so they can tell customers how putting certain additives in the concrete mixture might suit their needs.

What method does Morse Bros. use to train its drivers? Morse Bros. produces training videos which are presented by mentor-drivers. The mentor-driver's job is to select the weekly video, schedule viewing sessions, keep attendance records, and guide a wrap-up discussion following each video. The mentor-drivers are trained to call attention to key learning points covered in the video and relate the topic to issues the drivers deal with on the job. Because training sessions are scheduled early in the morning at the beginning of the drivers' shift, time is limited. Videos seldom run more than 10 minutes. For example, one called *Another Pair of Eyes* trains drivers to observe test procedures used by testing agencies at job sites. Samples are tested several times a month. A sample that fails can leave the company liable for demolition and removal of the concrete structure. Morse Bros. provides training on test procedures because

samples often fail a test due to contamination (e.g., dirt) that gets into the test cylinder. Another video emphasizes cold-weather precautions: Drain all tanks and hoses at the end of the day, park the drum in neutral. At each training session, drivers are asked to answer several questions related to the content of the program. At the end of a session, drivers and the mentor-driver discuss anything that might be interfering with the quality of the product or timeliness of delivery. Mentor-drivers then share this information with company managers.

The training program has been recognized by other companies inside and outside of the concrete industry. Several ready-mix companies have contracted with Morse Bros. to help set up mentor-driver programs at their plants. Morse Bros. sells its training videos to other companies through the National Ready Mix Association. Several videos have won awards from organizations that honor excellence in video productions. ■

Source: T. Skylar, "When Training Collides with a 35-Ton Truck," *Training* (March 1996): 32–38.

Introduction

Morse Bros. uses videos and on-the-job training to prepare its drivers to deliver concrete safely and effectively to job sites. This example illustrates that even inexpensive and easy-to-use training methods such as video and on-the-job training can have a positive impact on a business. Besides video and on-the-job training, a number of different training methods are used to help employees acquire new knowledge, skills, and behaviors. Figure 7–1 presents the most popular training methods based on a survey of companies conducted by Lakewood Publications, publishers of *Training* magazine. The survey results suggest that lectures and videotapes are the most frequently used training methods. Other frequently used methods include case studies and role plays. Companies are also beginning to use new technologies for training. As Figure 7–1 shows, computer-based training using a CD-ROM is the most frequently used new technology.

FIGURE 7–1

Overview of use of instructional methods

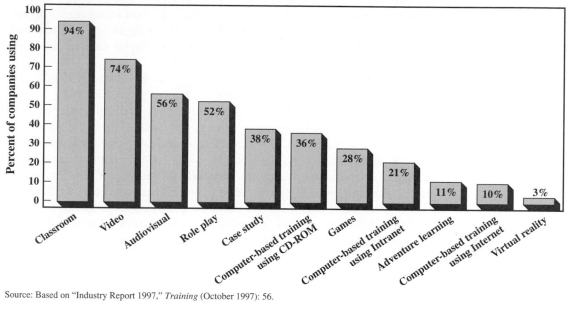

Source: Based on "Industry Report 1997," *Training* (October 1997): 56.

In this chapter we focus on more traditional training methods. These methods are "traditional" in the sense that they do not require new technology (e.g., the Internet) for delivery. In Chapter 8 we discuss new training methods such as the World Wide Web, distance learning, and virtual reality resulting from recent technological advances.

We organize training methods into three broad categories: presentation methods, hands-on methods, and group building methods.[1] For each training method we provide a description of the method, a discussion of advantages and disadvantages, and tips for the trainer in designing or choosing the method. The chapter concludes by comparing methods based on several characteristics including the learning outcome(s) influenced, the extent to which the method facilitates learning and transfer, cost, and effectiveness.

Presentation Methods

Presentation methods refer to methods in which trainees are passive recipients of information. This information may include facts or information, processes, and problem-solving methods. Presentation methods include lectures and audiovisual techniques.

Lecture

A **lecture** involves the trainer communicating through spoken words what she wants the trainees to learn. The communication of learned capabilities is primarily one-way—from the trainer to the audience. As Figure 7–1 shows, lecture remains a popular training method despite new technologies such as interactive video and computer-assisted instruction.

A lecture is one of the least expensive, least time-consuming ways to present a large amount of information efficiently in an organized manner.[2] The lecture format is also useful because it is easily employed with large groups of trainees. Besides being the primary means to communicate large amounts of information, lectures are also used to support other training methods such as behavior modeling and technology-based techniques. For example, a lecture may be used to communicate information regarding the purpose of the training program, conceptual models, or key behaviors to trainees prior to their receiving training that is more interactive and customized to their specific needs.

Table 7–1 describes several variations of the standard lecture method. All have advantages and disadvantages.[3] Team teaching brings more expertise and alternative perspectives to the training session. Team teaching does require more time on the part of trainers to not only prepare their particular session but also coordinate with other trainers. This is especially necessary when there is a great deal of integration between topics. Panels are especially good for showing trainees different viewpoints in a debate. A potential disadvantage of a panel is that trainees who are relatively naive about a topic may have difficulty understanding the important points. Guest speakers can motivate learning by bringing to the trainees relevant examples and applications. For guest speakers to be effective, the trainer needs to set expectations with the

---

TABLE 7–1   Variations of the Lecture Method

Method	Description
Standard lecture	Trainer talks while trainees listen and absorb information.
Team teaching	Two or more trainers present different topics or alternative views of the same topic.
Guest speakers	Speaker visits the session for a predetermined time period. Primary instruction is conducted by the guest or speaker.
Panels	Two or more speakers present information and ask questions.
Student presentations	Groups of trainees present topics to the class.

speaker regarding how his presentation should relate to the course content. Student presentations may increase the material's meaningfulness and trainees' attentiveness, but it can inhibit learning if the trainees do not have presentational skills.

There are several disadvantages to the lecture method. Lectures tend to lack participant involvement, feedback, and meaningful connection to the work environment—all of which inhibit learning and transfer of training. Lectures appeal to few of the trainees' senses since they focus primarily on hearing information. Lectures also make it difficult for the trainer to judge quickly and efficiently the learners' level of understanding. To overcome these problems, the lecture is often supplemented with question-and-answer periods, discussion, or case studies. These techniques allow the trainer to build into the lecture more active participation, job-related examples, and exercises, which facilitates learning and transfer of training.

Audiovisual Techniques

Audiovisual instruction includes overheads, slides, and video. As Figure 7–1 shows, video is one of the most popular instructional method.[4] It has been used for improving communications skills, interviewing skills, and customer-service skills and for illustrating how procedures (e.g., welding) should be followed. Video is, however, rarely used alone. It is usually used in conjunction with lectures to show trainees real-life experiences and examples. For example, excerpts from the movie *Hoosiers* are often used to complement a lecture on the topic of leadership. In the movie, Gene Hackman plays a basketball coach in a rural Indiana high school. The coach successfully molds the team member's skills and develops their confidence. The team wins the Indiana state high school basketball championship against a larger school with better facilities and more talented players. Video is also a major component of behavior modeling and, naturally, interactive video instruction.

The use of video in training has a number of advantages. First, the trainer can review, slow down, or speed up the lesson, which gives him flexibility in customizing the session depending on trainees' expertise. Second, trainees can be exposed to equipment, problems, and events that cannot be easily demonstrated, such as equipment malfunctions, angry customers, or emergencies. Third, trainees are provided with consistent instruction. Program content is not affected by the interests and goals of a particular trainer. Fourth, videotaping trainees allows them to see and hear their own performance without the interpretation of the trainer. As a result, trainees cannot attribute poor performance to the bias of external evaluators such as the trainer or peers.

Most problems in video result from the creative approach used.[5] These problems include too much content for the trainee to learn, poor dialogue between the actors (which hinders the credibility and clarity of the message), overuse of humor or music, and drama that makes it confusing for the trainee to understand the important learning points emphasized in the video.

Hands-on Methods

Hands-on methods refer to training methods that require the trainee to be actively involved in learning. These methods include on-the-job training, simulations, case studies, business games, role plays, and behavior modeling. These methods are ideal for developing specific skills, understanding how skills and behaviors can be transferred to the job, experiencing all aspects of completing a task, or dealing with interpersonal issues that arise on the job.

On-the-Job Training (OJT)

Companies spend between $90 and $180 billion annually on informal on-the-job training compared with $30 billion on formal off-the-job training.[6] **On-the-job training (OJT)** refers to new or inexperienced employees learning through observing peers or managers performing the job and trying to imitate their behavior. OJT can be useful for training newly hired employees, upgrading experienced employees' skills when new technology is introduced, cross-training employees within a department or work unit, and orienting transferred or promoted employees to their new jobs.

OJT takes various forms, including apprenticeships and self-directed learning programs. (Both are discussed later in this chapter.) OJT is an attractive training method because, compared to other methods, it needs less investment in time or money for materials, trainers' salary, or instructional design. Managers or peers who are job knowledge experts are used as instructors. As a result, it may be tempting to let them conduct the training as they believe it should be done.

There are several disadvantages to this unstructured approach to OJT.[7] Managers and peers may not use the same process to complete a task. They may pass on bad habits as well as useful skills. Also, they may not understand that demonstration, practice, and feedback are important conditions for effective on-the-job training. Unstructured OJT can result in poorly trained employees, employees who use ineffective or dangerous methods to produce a product or provide a service, and products or service quality that varies in quality.

OJT must be structured to be effective. Table 7–2 shows the principles of structured OJT. Because OJT involves learning by observing others, successful OJT is based on the principles emphasized by social learning theory. These include the use of a credible trainer, a manager or peer who models the behavior or skill, communication of specific key behaviors, practice, feedback, and reinforcement. For example, at Rochester Gas & Electric in Rochester, New York, radiation and chemistry instructors teach experienced employees how to conduct OJT.[8] While teaching these employees how to demonstrate software to new employees, the trainer may ask the employees to watch other OJT instructors as they train new recruits so they can learn new teaching techniques. Regardless of the specific type, effective OJT programs include

1. A policy statement that describes the purpose of OJT and emphasizes the company's support for it.

TABLE 7–2 Principles of On-the-Job Training

Preparing for Instruction

1. Break down the job into important steps.
2. Prepare the necessary equipment, materials, and supplies.
3. Decide how much time you will devote to OJT and when you expect the employee to be competent in skill areas.

Actual Instruction

1. Tell the trainee the objective of the task and ask her to watch you demonstrate it.
2. Show the trainee how to do it without saying anything.
3. Explain the key points or behaviors. (Write out the key points for the trainee, if possible.)

4. Show the trainee how to do it again.
5. Have the trainee do one or more single parts of the task and praise him for correct reproduction (optional).
6. Have the trainee do the entire task and praise him for correct reproduction.
7. If mistakes are made, have the trainee practice until accurate reproduction is achieved.
8. Praise the trainee for his success in learning the task.

Source: Based on W. J. Rothwell and H. C. Kazanas, "Planned OJT Is Productive OJT," *Training and Development Journal* (October 1990): 53–55; P. J. Decker and B. R. Nathan, *Behavior Modeling Training* (New York: Praeger Scientific, 1985).

2. A clear specification of who is accountable for conducting OJT. If managers conduct OJT, this is mentioned in their job descriptions and is part of their performance evaluation.
3. A thorough review of OJT practices (program content, types of jobs, length of program, cost savings) at other companies in similar industries.
4. Training of managers and peers in the principles of structured OJT. (See Table 7–2.)
5. Availability of lesson plans, checklists, procedure manuals, training manuals, learning contracts, and progress report forms for use by employees who conduct OJT.
6. Evaluation of employees' levels of basic skills (reading, computation, writing) before OJT.[9]

For example, Borden's Inc.'s North American Pasta Division's OJT program has many of these characteristics.[10] Not all managers and peers are used as trainers. Borden's invests in trainer selection, training, and rewards to ensure OJT's effectiveness. Employees and managers interested in being instructors are required to apply for the position. Those chosen as instructors are required to complete a demanding train-the-trainer course. The course involves classroom training as well as time on the manufacturing floor to learn how to operate machinery such as pasta machines and correctly teach other employees to use the equipment. Borden's also builds accountability into the OJT program. Trainees are responsible for completing a checklist that requires them to verify that the trainer helped them learn the skills needed to operate the equipment and used effective instructional techniques.

Self-Directed Learning

Self-directed learning involves having employees take responsibility for all aspects of learning—when it is conducted and who will be involved.[11] Trainees master predetermined training content at their own pace without an instructor. Trainers may serve as facilitators. That is, trainers are available to evaluate learning or answer questions for the trainee. The trainer does not control or disseminate instruction. The learning process is controlled by the trainee.

For example, at Corning Glass, new engineering graduates participate in an OJT program called SMART (self-managed, awareness, responsibility, and technical competence).[12] Each employee is responsible for seeking the answers to a set of questions (e.g., "Under what conditions would a statistician be involved in the design of engineering experiments?") by visiting plants and research facilities and meeting with technical engineering experts and managers. After employees complete the questions, they are evaluated by a committee of peers who have already completed the SMART program. Evaluations have shown that the program cuts employees' start-up time in their new jobs from six weeks to three. It is effective for a number of reasons. It encourages new employees' active involvement in learning and allows flexibility in finding time for training. A peer-review evaluation component motivates employees to complete the questions correctly. And, as a result of participating in the program, employees make contacts throughout the company and gain a better understanding of the technical and personal resources available within the company.

There are several advantages and disadvantages of self-directed learning.[13] It allows trainees to learn at their own pace and receive feedback about the learning performance. For the company, self-directed learning requires fewer trainers, reduces costs associated with travel and meeting rooms, and makes multiple-site training more realistic. Self-directed learning provides consistent training content that captures the knowledge of experts. Self-directed learning also makes it easier for shift employees to gain access to training materials. For example, Four Seasons hotels faced the challenge of opening a new hotel in Bali, Indonesia.[14] It needed to teach English skills to 580 employees, none of whom spoke English or understood Western cuisine or customs. Four Seasons created a self-directed learning center enabling employees to teach themselves English. The center emphasizes communications, not simply just learning to speak English. As a result of this emphasis, the center features video recorders, training, modules, books, and magazines. Monetary incentives were provided for employees to move from the lowest to the highest level of English skills. Besides English, the center also teaches Japanese (the language of 20 percent of the hotel visitors) and provides training for foreign managers in Bahasa Indonesian, the native language of Indonesia.

A major disadvantage of self-directed learning is that trainees must be willing and comfortable learning on their own. That is, trainees must be motivated to learn. From the company perspective, self-directed learning results in higher development costs, and development time is longer than with other types of training programs.

Several steps are necessary to develop effective self-directed learning:[15]

1. Conducting a job analysis to identify the tasks that must be covered.

2. Writing trainee-centered learning objectives directly related to the tasks. Because the objectives take the place of the instructor, they must indicate what information is important, what actions the trainee should take, and what the trainee should master.

3. Developing the content for the learning package. This involves developing scripts (for video) or text screens (for computer-based training). The content should be based on the trainee-centered learning objectives. Another consideration in developing the content is the media (e.g., paper, video, computer, World Wide Web site) that will be used to communicate the content.

4. Breaking the content into smaller pieces ("chunks"). The chunks should always begin with the objectives that will be covered and include a method for trainees to evaluate their learning. Practice exercises should also appear in each chunk.

5. Developing an evaluation package. This should include evaluation of the trainee and evaluation of the self-directed learning package. Trainee evaluation should be based on the objectives (a process known as criterion referencing). That is, questions should be developed that are written directly from the objectives and can be answered directly from the materials. Evaluation of the self-directed learning package should involve determining ease of use, how up-to-date the material is, if the package is being used as intended, and whether trainees are mastering the objectives.

Self-directed learning is likely to become more common in the future as companies seek to train staff flexibly, take advantage of technology, and encourage employees to be proactive in their learning rather than driven by the employer.

Apprenticeship

Apprenticeship is a work-study training method with both on-the-job and classroom training.[16] To qualify as a registered apprenticeship program under state or federal guidelines, at least 144 hours of classroom instruction and 2,000 hours, or one year, of on-the-job experience are required.[17] Apprenticeships can be sponsored by individual companies or by groups of companies cooperating with a union. The majority of apprenticeship programs are in the skilled trades such as plumbing, carpentry, electrical work, and bricklaying.

Table 7–3 shows an example of an apprenticeship program for a machinist. The hours and weeks that must be devoted to completing specific skill units are clearly defined. OJT involves assisting a certified tradesperson (a journeyman) at the work site. The on-the-job training portion of the apprenticeship follows the guidelines for effective on-the-job training.[18] Modeling, practice, feedback, and evaluation are involved. First, the employer verifies that the trainee has the required knowledge of the operation or process. Next, the trainer, who is usually a more experienced, licensed employee demonstrates each step of the process, emphasizing safety issues and key steps. The senior employee provides the apprentice with the opportunity to perform the process until all are satisfied that he can perform it properly and safely.

A major advantage of apprenticeship programs is that learners can earn pay while they learn. This is important because programs can last several years. Learners' wages usually increase automatically as their skills improve. Also, apprenticeships are usually effective learning experiences because they involve learning why and how a task is performed in classroom instruction provided by local trade schools, high schools, or community colleges. Apprenticeships also usually result in full-time employment for trainees when the program is completed. In Minneapolis, Minnesota, E. J. Ajax and Sons and a local technical college run an apprenticeship program to teach the process of making metal hinges.[19] Program graduates get jobs paying $10 an hour with the company.

One disadvantage of many apprenticeship programs is that minorities' and women's access to these programs has been restricted.[20] Another disadvantage is that there is no guarantee that jobs will be available when the program is completed. Finally, apprenticeship programs prepare trainees who are well trained in one craft or occupation. Due to the changing nature of jobs (thanks to new technology and use of cross-functional teams), many employers may be reluctant to employ workers from apprenticeship programs. Employers may believe that because apprentices are narrowly trained in one occupation or with one company, program graduates may only have company-specific skills and may be unable to acquire new skills or adapt their skills to changes in the workplace.

Apprenticeship programs are a more important part of education in training in countries such as Germany and Denmark than in the United States.[21] For example, the German apprenticeship experience is similar to that in the United States in that it combines classroom-based and on-the-job training. But the apprenticeship system is more linked with the education and training systems in Germany. The German apprenticeship system has been highlighted as a model for providing young people with the skills and credentials needed for an occupation. The system relies on the belief that students who do not attend college should be encouraged to learn an occupation. Two-thirds of secondary school graduates participate in apprenticeship programs. The German system identifies more than 300 occupations, each with its own set of standards and curriculum. Government, business, labor, and education are all involved at all stages of the process of managing and implementing apprenticeships.

TABLE 7–3   **Example of a Machinist Apprenticeship**

Hours	Weeks	Unit
240	6.0	Bench work
360	9.0	Drill press
240	6.0	Heat treat
200	5.0	Elementary layout
680	17.0	Turret lathe (conventional and numerical control)
800	20.0	Engine lathe
320	8.0	Tool grind
640	16.0	Advanced layout
960	24.0	Milling machine
280	7.0	Profile milling
160	4.0	Surface grinding
240	6.0	External grinding
280	7.0	Internal grinding
200	5.0	Thread grinding
520	13.0	Horizontal boring mills
240	6.0	Jig bore/jig grinder
160	4.0	Vertical boring
600	15.0	Numerical control milling
240	6.0	Computer numerical control
640	16.0	Related training
8,000	200.0	TOTAL

Probationary: **The following hours are included in the totals above, but must be completed in the first 1,000 hours of apprenticeship:**

Hours	Weeks	Unit
80	2.0	Drill press (probation)
280	7.0	Lathe work (probation)
360	9.0	Milling machine (probation)
40	1.0	Elementary layout (probation)
80	2.0	Related training (probation)
840	21.0	TOTAL

Source: A. H. Howard III, "Apprenticeship," in *The ASTD Training and Development Handbook,* 4th ed., ed. R. L. Craig (New York: McGraw-Hill, 1996): 808.

The German apprenticeship model has recently had its problems.[22] German businesses such as Siemens and Daimler Benz have been experiencing high wage and welfare costs so they are creating most new jobs outside the country. These firms want flexible workers who will upgrade their skills, rather than employees from the apprenticeship program who are well trained in just one trade or occupation. As a result, the availability of apprenticeships for trainees has declined.

Simulations

A **simulation** is a training method that represents a real-life situation, with trainees' decisions resulting in outcomes that mirror what would happen if they were on the job. Simulations, which allow trainees to see the impact of their decisions in an artificial, risk-free environment, are used to teach production and process skills as well as management and interpersonal skills.

Simulators replicate the physical equipment that employees use on the job. For example, at Motorola's Programmable Automation Literacy Lab, employees who may never have worked with a computer or robot learn to operate it.[23] Before entering the lab, employees are given a two-hour introduction to factory automation, which introduces new concepts, vocabulary, and computer-assisted manufacturing. The simulator allows trainees to become familiar with the equipment by designing a product (a personalized memo holder). Also, trainees do not have to be afraid of the impact of wrong decisions; errors are not as costly as they would be if the trainees were using the equipment on an actual production line. Success in completing simple exercises using the robot and computer increase their confidence so that they can work successfully in an automated manufacturing environment.

Simulations are also used to develop managerial skills. Looking Glass© is a simulation designed to develop both teamwork and individual management skills.[24] In this program, participants are assigned different roles in a glass company. On the basis of memos and correspondence, each participant interacts with other members of the management team over the course of six hours. Participants' behavior and interactions in solving the problems described in correspondence are recorded and evaluated. At the conclusion of the simulation, participants are given feedback regarding their performance.

A key aspect of simulators is the degree to which they have fidelity to the equipment and situation that the trainee will encounter on the job. That is, simulators need to have identical elements to those found in the work environment. The simulator needs to respond exactly like the equipment would under the conditions and response given by the trainee. For this reason simulators are expensive to develop and need constant updating as new information about the work environment is obtained. For example, American Airlines Flight 965 crashed into the mountains near Cali, Colombia, after one of the pilots entered the wrong code into a navigational computer.[25] The crew set the on-board computer to direct the plane to a radio beacon called "Romeo" instead of "Rozo." As the plane turned into the mountains, the pilots became confused and failed to revert back to basic radio navigation. An investigation of the accident suggested that the pilots may have been fooled by a discrepancy between standard navigation charts and the navigation computer. Charts used by airlines list a radio beacon designation "R" as "Rozo," but the computer does not recognize "R" as "Rozo." It recognizes "R" as "Romeo." As a result of this tragic accident, pilot training in simulators will place greater emphasis on dealing with navigational errors.

Case Studies

A **case study** is a description about how employees or an organization dealt with a difficult situation. Trainees are required to analyze and critique the actions taken, indicating the appropriate actions and suggesting what might have been done differently.[26] A major assumption of the case study approach is that employees are most likely to recall and use knowledge and skills if they learn through a process of discovery.[27] Cases may be especially appropriate for developing higher-order intellectual skills such as analysis, synthesis, and evaluation. These skills are often required by managers, physicians, and other professional employees. Cases also help trainees develop the willingness to take risks given uncertain outcomes, based on their analysis of the situation. To use cases effectively, the learning environment must give trainees the opportunity to prepare and discuss their case analyses. Also, face-to-face or electronic communication among trainees must be arranged. Because trainee involvement is critical for the effectiveness of the case method, learners must be willing and able to analyze the case and then communicate and defend their positions.

Table 7–4 presents the process used for case development. The first step in the process is to identify a problem or situation. It is important to consider whether the story chosen is related to the instructional objectives, will provoke a discussion, forces decision making, can be told in a reasonable time period, and is generalizable to the situations that trainees may face. Information on the problem or situation must also be readily accessible. The next step is to research documents, interview participants, and obtain data that provide the details of the case. The third step is to outline the story and link the details and exhibits to relevant points in the story. Fourth, the media used to present the case should be determined. Also, at this point in case development, the trainer should consider how the case exercise will be conducted. This may involve determining if trainees will work individually or in teams,

---

TABLE 7–4   Process for Case Development

1. Identify a story.
2. Gather information.
3. Prepare a story outline.
4. Decide on administrative issues.
5. Prepare case materials.

Source: Based on J. Alden and J. K. Kirkhorn, "Case Studies," in *The ASTD Training and Development Handbook,* 4th ed., ed. R. L. Craig (New York: McGraw-Hill, 1996): 497–516.

and how the students will report results of their analysis. Finally, the actual case materials need to be prepared. This includes assembling exhibits (figures, tables, articles, job descriptions, etc.), writing the story, preparing questions to guide trainees' analysis, and writing an interesting, attention-getting case opening that attracts trainees' attention and provides a quick orientation to the case.

There are a number of available sources for preexisting cases. A major advantage of preexisting cases is that they are already developed. A disadvantage is that the case may not actually relate to the work situation or problem that the trainee will encounter. It is especially important to review preexisting cases to determine how meaningful they will be to the trainee. Preexisting cases on a wide variety of problems in business management (e.g., human resource management, operations, marketing, advertising) are available from Harvard Business School, The Darden Business School, University of Virginia, McGraw-Hill publishing company, and various other sources.

One organization that has effectively used case studies is the Central Intelligence Agency (CIA).[28] The cases are historically accurate and use actual data. For example, "The Libyan Attack" is used in management courses to teach leadership qualities. "The Stamp Case" is used to teach new employees about the agency's ethics structure. The CIA uses approximately 100 cases. One-third are focused on management; the rest focus on operations training, counterintelligence, and analysis. The cases are used in the training curriculum where the objectives include teaching students to analyze and resolve complex, ambiguous situations. The CIA found that for the cases used in training programs to be credible and meaningful to trainees, the material had to be as authentic as possible and stimulate students to make decisions similar to those they must make in their work environment. As a result, to ensure case accuracy, the CIA uses retired officers to research and write cases. The CIA has even developed a case writing workshop to prepare instructors to use the case method.

Business Games

Business games require trainees to gather information, analyze it, and make decisions. Business games are primarily used for management skill development. Games stimulate learning because participants are actively involved and they mimic the competitive nature of business. The types of decisions that participants make in games include all aspects of management practice: labor relations (agreement in contract negotiations), marketing (the price to charge for a new product), and finance (financing the purchase of new technology). For example, Market Share, part of a marketing management course at Nynex Corporation, requires participants to use strategic thinking such as competitive analysis to increase market share.[29] The playing board is divided into different segments representing the information industry (e.g., cable, radio). Teams of two or three players compete to gain market share by determining where the team will allocate its efforts and challenge opponents' market share.

Documentation of learning from games is anecdotal.[30] Games may give team members a quick start at developing a framework for information and help develop cohesive groups. For some groups (such as senior executives), games may be more meaningful training activities (because the game is realistic) than presentation techniques such as classroom instruction.

Role Plays

Role plays involve having trainees act out characters assigned to them.[31] Information regarding the situation (e.g., work or interpersonal problem) is provided to the trainees. Role plays differ from simulations on the basis of response choices available to the trainees and the level of detail of the situation given to trainees. Role plays may provide limited information regarding the situation, while the information provided for simulation is usually quite detailed. A simulation focuses on physical responses (e.g., pull a lever, move a dial). Role plays focus on interpersonal responses (e.g., asking for more information, resolving conflict). In a simulation, the outcome of the trainees' response depends on a fairly well-defined model of reality. (If a trainee in a flight simulator decreases the angle of the flaps, that influences the direction of the aircraft.) In a role play, outcomes depend on the emotional (and subjective) reactions of the other trainees.

For role plays to be effective, trainers need to engage in several activities before, during, and after the role play. Before the role play, it is critical to explain the purpose of the activity to the trainees. This increases the chances that they will find the activity meaningful and be motivated to learn. Second, the trainer needs to clearly explain the role play, the characters' roles, and the time allotted for the activity. A short video may also be valuable for quickly showing trainees how the role play works. During the activity, the trainer needs to monitor the time, degree of intensity, and focus of the group's attention. (Is the group playing the roles or discussing other things unrelated to the exercise?) The more meaningful the exercise is to the participants, the less trouble the trainer should have with focus and intensity. At the conclusion of the role play, debriefing is critical. Debriefing involves helping trainees understand the experience and discuss their insights with each other. Trainees should also be able to discuss their feelings, what happened in the exercise, what they learned, and how the experience, their actions, and resulting outcomes relate to incidents in the workplace.

Behavior Modeling

Behavior modeling involves presenting trainees with a model who demonstrates key behaviors to replicate and provides trainees with the opportunity to practice the key behaviors. Behavior modeling is based on the principles of social learning theory (discussed in Chapter 4), which emphasize that learning occurs by (1) observing behaviors demonstrated by a model and (2) seeing the model being reinforced for using those behaviors (a process known as vicarious reinforcement).

Behavior modeling is more appropriate for learning skills and behaviors than factual information. Research suggests that behavior modeling is one of the most effective techniques for teaching interpersonal and computer skills.[32]

Table 7–5 presents the activities in a behavior modeling training session. These activities include an introduction, skill preparation and development, and application planning.[33] Each training session, which typically lasts four hours, focuses on one interpersonal skill such as coaching or communicating ideas. Each session includes a presentation of the rationale behind the key behaviors, a videotape of a model performing the key behaviors, practice opportunities using role playing, evaluation of a model's performance in the videotape, and a planning session devoted to understanding how the key behaviors can be used on the job. In the practice sessions, trainees are provided with feedback regarding how closely their behavior matches the key behaviors demonstrated by the model. The role playing and modeled performance are based on actual incidents in the employment setting in which the trainee needs to demonstrate success.

Developing behavior modeling training programs involves identifying the key behaviors, creating the modeling display, providing opportunities for practice, and facilitating transfer of training.[34] The first step in developing behavior modeling training programs is to determine (1) the tasks that are not being adequately performed due to lack of skill or behavior and (2) the key behaviors that are required to perform the task. A **key behavior** is one of a set of behaviors that are necessary to complete a task. In behavior modeling, key behaviors are typically needed to be performed in a specific order for the task to be completed. Key behaviors are identified through identifying the task, skills, and behavior necessary to complete the task and identifying the skills or behaviors used by employees who are effective in completing the task.

TABLE 7–5   Activities in a Behavior Modeling Training Program

Introduction   (45 mins.)
- Present key behaviors using video.
- Give rationale for skill module.
- Trainees discuss experiences in using skill.

Skill Preparation and Development   (2 hrs., 30 mins.)
- View model.
- Participate in role plays and practice.
- Receive oral and video feedback on performance of key behaviors.

Application Planning   (1 hr.)
- Set improvement goals.
- Identify situations to use key behaviors.
- Identify on-the-job applications of the key behaviors.

Table 7–6 presents key behaviors for a behavior modeling training program on problem analysis. The table specifies behaviors that the trainee needs to engage in to be effective in problem analysis skills. Note that the key behaviors do not specify the exact behaviors needed at every step of solving a problem. Rather, the key behaviors in this skill module specify more general behaviors that are appropriate across a wide range of situations. If a task involves a clearly defined series of specific steps that must be accomplished in a specific order, then the key behaviors that are provided are usually more specific and explained in greater detail. For example, in teaching tennis players how to serve, a detailed sequence of activities must be followed to be effective (e.g., align feet on service line, take the racquet back over the head, toss the ball, bring the racquet over the head, pronate the wrist, and strike the ball). In teaching interpersonal skills, because there is more than one way to complete the task, more general key behaviors should be developed. This helps to promote far transfer (discussed in Chapter 5). That is, trainees are prepared to use the key behaviors in a variety of situations.

Another important consideration in developing behavior modeling programs is the modeling display. The **modeling display** provides the key behaviors that the trainees will practice to develop the same set of behaviors. Videotape is the predominant method used to present modeling displays, although new technology is being used to permit modeling displays to be shown using a computer. (We discuss new technology in Chapter 8.) Effective modeling displays have six characteristics:[35]

1. The display clearly presents the key behaviors. Music and characteristics of the situation shown in the display do not interfere with the trainee seeing and understanding the key behaviors.
2. The model is credible to the trainees'.
3. An overview of the key behaviors is presented.
4. Each key behavior is repeated. The trainee is shown the relationship between the behavior of the model and each key behavior.

TABLE 7–6   Example of Key Behaviors in Problem Analysis

Get all relevant information by
    Rephrasing the question or problem to see if new issues emerge.
    Listing the key problem issues.
    Considering other possible sources of information.
Identify possible causes.
If necessary, obtain additional information.
Evaluate the information to ensure that all essential criteria are met.
Restate the problem considering new information.
Determine what criteria indicate that the problem or issue is resolved.

5. A review of the key behaviors is included.

6. Models engaging in both positive use of key behavior and negative models (ineffective models not using the key behaviors) are presented.

Providing opportunities for practice involves (1) having trainees cognitively rehearse and think about the key behaviors and (2) placing trainees in situations (such as role plays) where they have to use the key behaviors. Trainees may interact with one other person in the role play or in groups of three or more where each trainee can practice the key behaviors. The most effective practice session allows trainees to practice the behaviors multiple times, in a small group of trainees where anxiety or evaluation apprehension is reduced, with other trainees who understand the company and the job.

Practice sessions should include a method for providing trainees with feedback. This feedback should provide reinforcement to the trainee for behaviors performed correctly as well as information needed to improve behaviors. For example, if role plays are used, trainees can receive feedback from the other participants who serve as observers when not playing the role. Practice sessions may also be videotaped and played back to the trainees. The use of video objectively captures the trainees' behavior and provides useful, detailed feedback. Having the trainees view the video shows them specifically how they need to improve their behaviors and identifies behaviors they are successfully replicating.

Behavior modeling helps to ensure that transfer of training occurs by using application planning. **Application planning** involves preparing trainees to use the key behaviors on the job (i.e., enhances transfer of training). Application planning involves having each participant prepare a written document identifying specific situations where they should use the key behaviors. Some training programs actually have trainees complete a "contract" outlining the key behaviors they agree to use on the job. The trainer may follow up with the trainees to see if they are performing according to the contract. Application planning may also involve preparing trainees to deal with situational factors that may inhibit their use of the key behaviors (similar to relapse prevention discussed in Chapter 5). As part of the application planning process, a trainee may be paired with another participant, with the stated expectation that they should periodically communicate with each other to discuss successes and failures of the use of key behaviors.

Group Building Methods

Group building methods refer to training methods designed to improve team or group effectiveness. Training is directed at improving the trainees' skills as well as team effectiveness. Group building methods involve trainees sharing ideas and experiences, building group identity, understanding the dynamics of interpersonal relationships, and getting to know their own strengths and weaknesses and those of their co-workers. Group techniques focus on helping teams increase their skills for effective teamwork. A number of training techniques are available to improve work group or team performance, to establish a new team, or to improve interactions among different teams. All involve examination of feelings, perceptions, and beliefs about the functioning of the team, discussion, and development of plans to apply what was learned in training to the team's performance in the work setting. Group building methods include adventure learning, team training, and action learning.

Adventure Learning

Adventure learning focuses on the development of teamwork and leadership skills using structured outdoor activities.[36] Adventure learning is also known as wilderness training and outdoor training. Adventure learning appears to be best suited for developing skills related to group effectiveness such as self-awareness, problem solving, conflict management, and risk taking. Adventure learning may involve strenuous, challenging physical activities such as dogsledding or mountain climbing. Adventure learning can also use structured individual and group outdoor activities such as wall climbing, rope courses, trust falls, climbing ladders, and traveling from one tower to another using a device attached to a wire that connects the two towers.

For example, "The Beam" requires team members to get over a six-foot-high beam placed between two trees using only help from the team. Trainees can help by shouting advice and encouragement.[37] Rope-based activities may be held 3 to 4 feet or 25 to 30 feet above the ground. The high-ropes course is an individual-based exercise whose purpose is to help the trainee overcome fear. The low-ropes course requires the entire team of trainees to complete the course successfully. The purpose is to develop team identity, cohesiveness, and communication skills.

For another example, a Chili's restaurant manager in adventure learning was required to scale a three-story-high wall.[38] About two-thirds away from the top of the wall the manager became very tired. She successfully reached the top of the wall using the advice and encouragement shouted from team members on the ground below. When asked to consider what she learned from the experience, she reported that the exercise made her realize that reaching personal success depends on other people. At her restaurant, everyone has to work together to make the customers happy.

For adventure learning programs to be successful, exercises should be related to the types of skills that participants are expected to develop. Also, after the exercises a skilled facilitator should lead a discussion about what happened in the exercise, what was learned, how events in the exercise relate to the job situation, and how to set goals and apply what was learned on the job.[39] Trust falls require each trainee to stand on a platform five to six feet above the ground and fall backward into the arms of fellow group members. If trainees are reluctant to fall, this suggests they don't trust the team members. After completing the trust fall, the facilitator may question trainees to identify sources of their anxiety and to relate this anxiety to specific workplace incidents (e.g., a project delegated to a peer was not completed on time, resulting in distrust of the peer).

The physical demands of adventure learning and the requirement that trainees often touch each other in the exercises may increase a company's risk for negligence claims due to personal injury, intentional infliction of emotional distress, and invasion of privacy. Also, the Americans with Disabilities Act raises questions about requiring disabled employees to participate in physically demanding training experiences.[40]

Given the physically demanding nature of adventure learning, it is important to consider when to use it instead of another training method. Adventure learning allows trainees to interact interpersonally in a situation not governed by formal business rules. This type of environment may be important for employees to mold themselves into a cohesive work team. Also, adventure learning exercises allow trainees to share a strong emotional experience. Significant emotional experiences can help trainees break difficult behavior patterns and open up trainees to change their behaviors. One of the most important characteristics of adventure learning is that the exercises can serve as "metaphors" for organizational behavior. That is, trainees will behave in the same way in the exercises that they would when working as a team (e.g., developing a product launch plan). Similar behavior patterns occur in the adventure learning exercise as are seen at work. As a result, by analyzing behaviors that occur during the exercise, trainees gain insight into ineffective behaviors.

Does adventure learning work? Rigorous evaluations of its impact on productivity or performance have not been conducted. However, former participants often report that they gained a greater understanding of themselves and how they interact with co-workers.[41] One key to an adventure learning program's success may be the insistence that whole work groups participate together so that group dynamics that inhibit effectiveness can emerge and be discussed.

Team Training

Team training involves coordinating the performance of individuals who work together to achieve a common goal. Figure 7–2 shows the three components of team performance: knowledge, attitudes, and behavior.[42] The behavioral requirement means that team members must perform actions that allow them to communicate, coordinate, adapt, and complete complex tasks to accomplish their objective. The knowledge component requires team members to have mental models or memory structures that allow them to function effectively in unanticipated or new situations. Team members' beliefs about the task and feelings toward each other relate to the attitude component. Team morale, cohesion, and identity are related to team performance. For example, in the military as well as the private sector (e.g., nuclear power plants, commercial airlines), much work is performed by crews, groups, or teams. Successful performance depends on coordination of individual activities to make decisions, team performance, and readiness to deal with potentially dangerous situations (e.g., an overheating nuclear reactor). Research suggests that teams that are effectively trained develop procedures to identify and resolve errors, coordinate information gathering, and reinforce each other.[43]

FIGURE 7–2

Components of team performance

Source: Based on E. Salas and J. A. Cannon-Bowers, "Strategies for Team Training," in *Training for 21st Century Technology: Applications of Psychological Research,* eds. M. A. Quinones and A. Dutta (Washington, DC: American Psychological Association, 1997): 249–81.

Figure 7–3 illustrates the four main elements of the structure of team training. As we see, several tools help to define and organize the delivery of team training.[44] These tools also provide the environment (e.g., feedback) needed for learning to occur. These tools work in combination with different training methods to help create instructional strategies. These strategies are a combination of methods, tools, and content required to perform effectively.

The strategies include cross-training and coordination training. **Cross-training** involves having team members understand and practice each other's skills so that members are prepared to step in and take another member's place should he temporarily or permanently leave the team. **Coordination training** involves training the team in how to share information and decision making responsibilities to maximize team performance. Coordination training is especially important for commercial aviation and surgical teams who are in charge of monitoring different aspects of equipment and the environment, but must share information to make the most effective decision regarding patient care or aircraft safety and performance. **Team leader training** refers to training that the team manager or facilitator receives. This may involve training the manager how to resolve conflict within the team or help the team coordinate activities or other team skills.

Team training usually involves multiple methods. For example, a lecture or video may be used to disseminate knowledge regarding communication skills to trainees. Role plays or simulations may be used to give trainees the opportunity to put the communication skills emphasized in the lecture into practice. Boeing utilized team training to improve the effectiveness of teams used to design the Boeing 777.[45] At Boeing, 250 teams with 8 to 15 members each worked on the design of the aircraft. Team members included engineers with different specialties (e.g., design engineers, production engineers), reliability specialists, quality experts, and marketing professionals. This type of team is known as a concurrent engineering team because employees from all the business functions needed to design the aircraft work together at the same time. This contrasts with the traditional linear method to build an aircraft in which each business function works

FIGURE 7–3

Main elements of the structure of team training

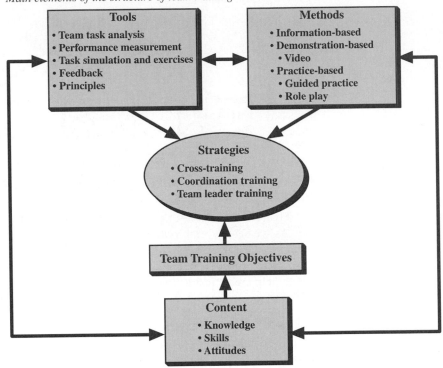

Source: Based on E. Salas and J. A. Cannon-Bowers, "Strategies for Team Training," in *Training for 21st Century Technology: Applications of Psychological Research,* eds. M. A. Quinones and A. Dutta (Washington, DC: American Psychological Association, 1997): 270.

with the product and then passes it along to another function. One advantage of concurrent engineering teams is that design and marketing problems can be addressed earlier in the assembly process (at lower costs) because engineers and marketing employees are working together. For concurrent engineering teams to be successful, team members must understand how the process or product they are working on fits with the finished product. Because each 777 aircraft contains millions of parts, it is important that they fly together!

Boeing's team training approach began with an extensive orientation for team members. The orientation emphasized how team members were supposed to work together. Following orientation, the teams were given their work assignments. Trainers helped the team work through issues and problems on an as-needed basis. That is, trainers were available to help the teams if the teams requested help. Trainers provided training in communication skills, conflict resolution, and leadership.

Action Learning

Action learning involves giving teams or work groups an actual problem, having them work on solving it and committing to an action plan, and then holding them accountable for carrying out the plan.[46] Typically, action learning involves between 6 and 30 employees. It may also include customers and vendors. There are several variations in the composition of the group. One variation is that the group includes a single customer for the problem being dealt with. Sometimes the groups include cross-functional representatives who all have a stake in the problem. Or the group may involve employees from multiple functions who all focus on their own functional problems, each contributing to solving the problems identified.

For example, Whirlpool used action learning to deal with recovering overpaid duty (a type of task) on compressors that the company was importing from Brazil. Members of the procurement group formed a team that dealt with implementing Whirlpool's strategies for cost reduction and inventory control. The team developed a process for recovering the duty, resulting in Whirlpool saving hundreds of thousands of dollars a year.

Action learning—a widespread training practice in Europe—is just starting to be used in the United States. Although action learning has not been formally evaluated, the process appears to maximize learning and transfer of training because it involves real-time problems employees are facing. Also, action learning can be useful for identifying dysfunctional team dynamics that can get in the way of effective problem solving.

Choosing a Training Method

As a trainer or manager you will likely be asked to choose a training method. Given the large number of training methods available to you, this task may seem difficult. One way to choose a training method is to compare methods. Table 7–7 evaluates each training method discussed in this chapter on a number of characteristics. The type of learning outcomes related to each method are identified. Also, for each method, a high, medium, or low rating is provided for each characteristic of the learning environment, transfer of training, cost, and effectiveness.

How might you use this table to choose a training method? The first step in choosing a method is to identify the type of learning outcome that you want training to influence. As we discussed in Chapter 4, these outcomes include verbal information, intellectual skills, cognitive strategies, attitudes, and motor skills. Training methods may influence one or several learning outcomes. Once you have identified a learning method, the next step is to consider the extent to which the method facilitates learning and transfer of training, the costs related to development and use of the method, and its effectiveness.

TABLE 7-7 Comparison of Training Methods

	Presentation		Hands-on								Group-Building		
	Lecture	Video	OJT	Self-Directed Learning	Apprenticeship	Simulation	Case Study	Business Games	Role Play	Behavior Modeling	Adventure Learning	Team Training	Action Learning
Learning Outcome													
Verbal information	Yes	Yes	Yes	Yes	Yes	No	Yes	Yes	No	No	No	No	No
Intellectual skills	Yes	No	No	Yes	Yes	Yes	Yes	Yes	No	No	No	Yes	No
Cognitive strategies	Yes	No	Yes	Yes	No	Yes	Yes	Yes	Yes	Yes	Yes	Yes	Yes
Attitudes	Yes	Yes	No	No	No	No	No	No	Yes	No	Yes	Yes	Yes
Motor skills	No	Yes	Yes	No	Yes	Yes	No	No	No	Yes	No	No	No
Learning Environment													
Clear objective	Medium	Low	High	High	High	High	Medium	High	Medium	High	Medium	High	High
Practice	Low	Low	High	High	High	High	Medium	Medium	Medium	High	Medium	High	Medium
Meaningfulness	Medium	Medium	High	Medium	High	High	Medium	Medium	Medium	Medium	Low	High	High
Feedback	Low	Low	High	Medium	High	High	Medium	High	Medium	High	Medium	Medium	High
Observe and interact with others	Low	Medium	High	Medium	High	High	High	High	High	High	High	High	High
Transfer of Training	Low	Low	High	Medium	High	High	Medium	Medium	Medium	High	Low	High	High
Cost													
Development	Medium	Medium	Medium	High	High	High	Medium	High	Medium	Medium	Medium	Medium	Low
Administrative	Low	Low	Low	Medium	High	Low	Low	Medium	Medium	Medium	Medium	Medium	Medium
Effectiveness	High for verbal information	Medium	High for structured OJT	Medium	High	High	Medium	Medium	Medium	High	Low	Medium	High

As Chapter 4 said, for learning to occur, trainees must understand the objectives of the training program, training content should be meaningful, and trainees should have the opportunity to practice and receive feedback. Also, a powerful way to learn is through observing and interacting with others. As you may recall from Chapter 5, transfer of training refers to the extent to which training will be used on the job. In general, the closer the training content and environment prepare trainees for use of learning outcomes on the job, the greater the likelihood that transfer will occur. As discussed in Chapter 6, two types of costs are important: development costs and administrative costs. Development costs refer to costs related to design of the training program, including costs to buy or create the program. Administrative costs refer to costs incurred each time the training method is used. These include costs related to consultants, instructors, materials, and trainers. The effectiveness rating is based on both academic research and practitioner recommendations.

Several trends in Table 7–7 are worth noting. First, there is considerable overlap between learning outcomes across the training methods. Group building methods are unique because they focus on individual as well as team learning (e.g., improving group processes). Trainers interested in improving the effectiveness of groups or teams should choose one of the group building methods (e.g., action learning, team training, action learning). Second, comparing the presentation methods to the hands-on methods illustrates that most hands-on methods provide a better learning environment and transfer of training than the presentation methods. The presentation methods are also less effective than the hands-on methods. If a trainer is not limited by the amount of money that can be used for development or administration, a hands-on method should be chosen over a presentation method. The training budget for developing training methods can influence the method chosen. Trainers who have limited budgets for developing new training methods can use structured on-the-job training—a relatively inexpensive yet effective hands-on method. Trainers with a larger budget might want to consider hands-on methods that facilitate transfer of training such as simulators.

Summary

In this chapter we discussed presentation, hands-on, and group building training methods. Presentation methods (such as lecture) are effective for efficiently communicating information (knowledge) to a large number of trainees. Presentation methods need to be supplemented with opportunities for the trainees to practice, discuss, and receive feedback to facilitate learning. Hands-on methods get the trainee directly involved in learning. Hands-on methods are ideal for developing skills and behaviors. Hands-on methods include on-the-job training, simulations, self-directed learning, business games, case studies, role plays and behavior modeling. These methods can be expensive to develop but incorporate the conditions needed for learning and transfer of training to occur. Group building methods such as team training, action learning, and adventure learning focus on helping teams increase the skills needed for effective teamwork (e.g., self-awareness, conflict resolution, coordination) and help to build team cohesion and identity. Group building techniques may include the use of presentation methods as well as exercises during which team members interact and communicate with each other. Team training has a long history of success in preparing flight crews and surgical teams, but its effectiveness for developing management teams has not been clearly established.

Key Terms

presentation methods   163
lecture   164
audiovisual instruction   165
hands-on methods   166
on-the-job training (OJT)   166
self-directed learning   168
apprenticeship   169
simulation   172
case study   173
business games   174
role plays   175

behavior modeling   175
key behavior   176
modeling display   177
application planning   178
group building methods   178
adventure learning   179
team training   180
cross-training   181
coordination training   181
team leader training   181
action learning   183

Discussion Questions

1. What are the strengths and weaknesses of the lecture, case study, and behavior modeling?

2. If you had to choose between adventure learning and action learning for developing an effective team, which would you choose? Defend your choice.

3. Discuss the process of behavior modeling training.

4. How can the characteristics of the trainee affect self-directed learning?

5. What are the components of effective team performance? How might training strengthen these components?

6. Table 7–7 compares training methods on a number of characteristics. Explain why simulation and behavior modeling receive high ratings for transfer of training.

7. What are some reasons why on-the-job training can be ineffective? What can be done to ensure its effectiveness?

Application Assignments

1. Choose a job you are familiar with. Develop a self-directed learning module for a skill that is important for that job.

2. Visit the Web site www.trainingsupersite.com developed by Lakewood Publications (which publishes *Training* magazine). Visit the "Research Center" at the Web site. The "Research Center" provides access to articles, research materials, case studies, and surveys on training topics. Using the "Research Site" find an article that deals with a training method. Based on the article write a two-page report including a description of the method and how it was used. Provide an evaluation of the effectiveness of the method.

3. Divide into teams of two students. One student should be designated as a "trainer," the other as a "trainee." The trainer should read the instructions for folding a paper cup. The trainee should briefly leave the room. After the trainers have read the instructions the trainees should return to the room. The trainers should then train the trainees how to fold a paper cup (about 15 minutes). When the instructor calls time the trainer should note the steps he followed to conduct the training. The trainee should record his evaluation of the strengths and weaknesses of the training session (5–10 minutes). If time allows switch roles.

   Be prepared to discuss the training process and your reactions as a trainee. Also, be prepared to discuss the extent to which the training followed the steps for effective on-the-job training.

Endnotes

1. C. Lee, "Who Gets Trained in What?"; A. P. Carnevale, L. J. Gainer, and A. S. Meltzer, *Workplace Basics Training Manual* (San Francisco: Jossey-Bass, 1990).
2. M. Van Wart, N. J. Cayer, and S. Cook, *Handbook of Training and Development for the Public Sector* (San Francisco: Jossey-Bass, 1993); R. S. House, "Classroom Instruction," in *The ASTD Training and Development Handbook,* 4th ed., ed. R. L. Craig (New York: McGraw-Hill, 1996): 437–52.
3. Van Wert, Cayer, and Cook, *Handbook of Training and Development for the Public Sector.*
4. C. Lee, "Who Gets Trained in What?"
5. R. B. Cohn, "How to Choose a Video Producer," *Training* (July 1996): 58–61.
6. A. P. Carnevale, "The Learning Enterprise," *Training and Development Journal* (February 1989): 26–37.
7. B. Filipczak, "Who Owns Your OJT?" *Training* (December 1996): 44–49.
8. Ibid.
9. W. J. Rothwell and H. C. Kazanas, "Planned OJT is Productive OJT," *Training and Development Journal* (October 1996): 53–56.
10. Filipczak, "Who Owns Your OJT?"
11. G. M. Piskurich, *Self-Directed Learning* (San Francisco: Jossey-Bass, 1993).

12. D. B. Youst and L. Lipsett, "New Job Immersion without Drowning," *Training and Development Journal* (February 1989): 73–75.

13. G. M. Piskurich, "Self-Directed Learning," in *The ASTD Training and Development Handbook,* 4th ed.: 453–72; G. M. Piskurich, "Developing Self-Directed Learning," *Training and Development* (March 1994): 31–36.

14. C. M. Solomon, "When Training Doesn't Translate," *Workforce* (March 1997): 40–44.

15. P. Warr and D. Bunce, "Trainee Characteristics and the Outcomes of Open Learning," *Personnel Psychology* 48 (1995): 347–75; T. G. Hatcher, "The Ins and Outs of Self-Directed Learning," *Training and Development* (February 1997): 35–39.

16. R. W. Glover, *Apprenticeship Lessons from Abroad* (Columbus, OH: National Center for Research in Vocational Education, 1986).

17. Commerce Clearing House, Inc., *Orientation-Training* (Chicago: Personnel Practices Communications, Commerce Clearing House, 1981): 501–05.

18. A. H. Howard III, "Apprenticeships," in *The ASTD Training and Development Handbook,* 4th ed.: 803–13.

19. D. Lenhardt, "Minneapolis Shows the Way," *Business Week* (September 1, 1997): 70.

20. *Eldredge* v. *Carpenters JATC* (1981), 27 Fair Employment Practices (Bureau of National Affairs): 479.

21. M. McCain, "Apprenticeship Lessons from Europe," *Training and Development* (November 1994): 38–41.

22. K. L. Miller and K. N. Anhalt, "Without Training, I Can't Start My Real Life," *Business Week* (September 16, 1996): 60.

23. A. F. Cheng, "Hands-on Learning at Motorola," *Training and Development Journal* (October 1990): 34–35.

24. M. W. McCall Jr. and M. M. Lombardo, "Using Simulation for Leadership and Management Research," Management Science 28 (1982): 533–49.

25. S. McCartney, "Colombia Says Pilot Error Was Cause of '95 Crash of American Airlines Plane," *Wall Street Journal* (September 30, 1996): B5.

26. J. Alden and J. Kirkhorn, "Case Studies," in *The ASTD Training and Development Handbook,* 4th ed.: 497–516.

27. H. Kelly, "Case Method Training: What It Is and How It Works," in *Effective Training Delivery,* ed. D. Zielinski (Minneapolis: Lakewood Books, 1989): 95–96.

28. T. W. Shreeve, "On the Case at the CIA," *Training & Development* (March 1997): 53–54.

29. M. Hequet, "Games That Teach," *Training* (July 1995): 53–58.

30. Ibid.

31. S. Thiagarajan, "Instructional Games, Simulations, and Role Plays," in *The ASTD Training and Development Handbook,* 4th ed.: 517–33.

32. S. J. Simon and J. M. Werner, "Computer Training through Behavior Modeling, Self-Paced and Instructional Approaches: A Field Experiment," *Journal of Applied Psychology* 81 (1996): 648–59.

33. W. C. Byham and A. Pescuric, "Behavior Modeling at the Teachable Moment," *Training* (December 1996): 51–56.

34. P. Decker and B. Nathan, *Behavior Modeling Training* (New York: Praeger Scientific, 1985).

35. Ibid.; T. T. Baldwin, "Effects of Alternative Modeling Strategies on Outcomes of Interpersonal-Skills Training," *Journal of Applied Psychology* 77 (1992): 147–54.

36. R. J. Wagner, T. T. Baldwin, and C. C. Rowland, "Outdoor Training: Revolution or Fad?" *Training and Development Journal* (March 1991): 51–57; C. J. Cantoni, "Learning the Ropes of Teamwork," *The Wall Street Journal* (October 2, 1995): A14.

37. C. Steinfeld, "Challenge Courses Can Build Strong Teams," *Training and Development* (April 1997): 12–13.

38. Ibid.

39. G. M. Tarullo, "Making Outdoor Experiential Training Work," *Training* (August 1992): 47–52.

40. C. Clements, R. J. Wagner, and C. C. Roland, "The Ins and Outs of Experiential Training," *Training and Development* (February 1995): 52–56.

41. G. M. McEvoy, "Organizational Change and Outdoor Management Education," *Human Resource Management* 36 (1997): 235–50.

42. E. Salas and J. A. Cannon-Bowers, "Strategies for Team Training," in *Training for 21st Century Technology: Applications for Psychological Research,* eds. M. A. Quinones and A. Dutta (Washington, DC: American Psychological Association, 1997).

43. R. L. Oser, A. McCallum, E. Salas, and B. B. Morgan, Jr., "Toward a Definition of Teamwork: An Analysis of Critical Team Behaviors," Technical Report 89-004 (Orlando, FL: Naval Training Research Center, 1989).

44. E. Salas and J. A. Cannon-Bowers, "Strategies for Team Training."

45. B. Filipczak, "Concurrent Engineering," *Training* (August 1996): 54–59.

46. P. Froiland, "Action Learning," *Training* (January 1994): 27–34.

8 USE OF NEW TECHNOLOGIES IN TRAINING

Objectives

After reading this chapter, you should be able to

1. Explain how new technologies are influencing training.

2. Discuss potential advantages and disadvantages of multimedia training.

3. Evaluate a Web-based training site.

4. Explain how learning and transfer of training are enhanced by using new training technologies.

5. Describe to a manager the different types of distance learning.

6. Discuss the technologies used for training support.

7. Compare and contrast the strengths and weaknesses of traditional training methods with training methods based on new technology.

8. Identify and explain the benefits of new technologies that can be used to improve the efficiency of training administration.

ADVANCING MEDICAL TECHNOLOGY THROUGH TRAINING TECHNOLOGY

Medtronic is a 12,000-employee Minneapolis, Minnesota-based company that specializes in developing and selling medical technology. Medtronic provides about half of the heart pacemakers in the world, and also manufactures heart valves, angioplasty catheters, and blood-pumping devices. As in most companies, sales is a top priority. But sales at Medtronic relates to life and death. Salespeople just don't sell products. They must teach consumers (physicians) how to use the products. It is not uncommon for Medtronic salespeople to be advising physicians in the operating room while they are changing heart valves or installing a pacemaker into a patient!

Multimedia was first used at Medtronic for purely marketing purposes. Salespeople would use a laptop personal computer equipped with a CD player to show physicians the benefits and correct usage of heart valves. When the interactive program was introduced at a national sales meeting, demand for the CD exceeded supply. Salespeople went out and purchased laptop computers so that they could use the CD!

This created a training challenge for Medtronic. The sales staff had to learn to use the laptop PCs and understand how to use the interactive program. Classroom instruction, role playing, and a built-in tutorial were developed to teach salespeople how to use the PC and the CD program.

Medtronic is exploring expanding the use of multimedia for training as well as marketing. Currently, Medtronic extensively uses classroom-based training for salespeople. Although the product CDs are being used as a learning tool by helping to prepare the staff for sales presentations, the CDs are only one step the company is taking toward the goal of enhancing learning. The current manager of sales training is pushing for expanded use of multimedia training because it can cut salespeople's time in the classroom. The manager believes that multimedia training will increase the consistency and efficiency of training and provide salespeople with feedback regarding which dimensions of the product they "know." The current CD-based product programs work best for experienced salespeople who already are familiar with the product. New salespeople need feedback and help screens, both being available from multimedia applications. New salespeople need to be able to interact with the product at their own pace, so that they are comfortable explaining and demonstrating all aspects of the product to physicians. Salespeople's time is also in great demand. Multimedia provides accessibility to training wherever and whenever they can access their laptop computer. Multimedia can also help the entire sales force learn about new products as quickly as possible.

The next step in the process is convincing the marketing department that new multimedia products need to be developed so that they can be used for both marketing and training. ■

Source: W. Webb, "High-Tech in the Heartland," *Training* (May 1997): 51–56.

Introduction

As the chapter opening illustrates, technology is having a major impact on the delivery of training programs. Medtronic is considering using multimedia training for its sales force because of its potential learning and accessibility advantages. We will discuss the advantages and disadvantages of multimedia training in this chapter. Medtronic is not alone in its efforts to use new technologies to deliver training. Several surveys of businesses suggest that although the traditional training methods discussed in Chapter 7 are the most common methods for delivery, many companies are actually using or planning to use new technologies such as multimedia training, distance learning, and electronic support systems.[1] Companies report that approximately 17 percent of training time involves the new technologies discussed in this chapter, compared to 72 percent of training time devoted to traditional trainer-led methods. By the year 2000, however, 35 percent of training time is expected to involve new technologies.[2]

This chapter begins by discussing new technologies' influence on training delivery, support, and administration. Next, the chapter explores emerging multimedia training techniques (computer-based training, CD-ROM, interactive video, the Internet). More sophisticated technologies that are just beginning to be marketed commercially for training delivery (expert systems, virtual reality, intelligent tutoring systems) are introduced. The use of expert systems and groupware exemplify how technology is used to support training through serving as a storage place for intellectual capital (information and learned capabilities), which facilitates access to information and communication of knowledge between employees. The chapter also shows how new technology such as interactive voice responses and imaging is used in training administration. The last section of the chapter compares training methods based on new technology, employing the characteristics used to evaluate the traditional training methods discussed in Chapter 7. As you will see, several training methods discussed in this chapter can replace or substitute for traditional training methods under certain conditions.

How Are New Technologies Influencing Training?

Figure 8–1 illustrates how new technologies are influencing training. Technology has influenced the delivery of training. New technologies allow training to be delivered on a 24-hour basis to geographically dispersed employees. New technology is also being used to streamline training administration. These technologies include imaging, interactive voice response systems, and specialized training

FIGURE 8–1

How new technologies are influencing training

software. These technologies reduce training costs and make it easier to administer training programs. New technologies also provide support for training. Electronic performance support systems and groupware (a special type of software) give employees access to information from experts on an as-needed basis.

Technology is making it possible for[3]

- Employees to gain complete control over when and where they receive training.
- Employees and managers to access knowledge and expert decision rules on an as-needed basis.
- Employees to select the type of media they want to use in a training session.
- Training administration (course enrollment, testing, records) to be conducted electronically.
- Close monitoring of training in progress.

Multimedia Training

Multimedia training combines audiovisual training methods with computer-based training.[4] These programs integrate text, graphics, animation, audio, and video. Because multimedia training is computer-based, the trainee can interact with the content. Interactive video, Internet, or intranets may be used to deliver training.

How prevalent is multimedia training? A survey of 146 training managers of Fortune 1000 companies found that approximately 16 percent of all training hours are now delivered via multimedia.[5] It is estimated that by the year 2001 this figure will double. The survey also found that while managers indicated that multimedia-based training is used most frequently to train employees in software and basic computer skills (42 percent of the managers mentioned these skills), training in management skills and technical training is also occurring (25 percent). Almost all companies that use multimedia training deliver it using CD-ROM, with approximately one-third using the World Wide Web. The high use of CD-ROMs relates to how multimedia training is delivered. Seventy-one percent of the managers reported that multimedia training is delivered via central training centers. That is, to use multimedia-based training, employees have to visit a designated learning center. This may be changing. Currently, the largest barrier to increased use of multimedia training appears to be employees' access to the Internet—only about 25 percent of employees have access. However, most managers reported that employee access to the Internet is expected to double by the year 2001.

Table 8–1 shows the major advantages and disadvantages of multimedia training. Multimedia training motivates trainees to learn, provides immediate feedback and guidance (through on-line help), tests employees' level of mastery, and allows employees to learn at their own pace.[6] A major disadvantage of mul-

---

TABLE 8–1   Advantages and Disadvantages of Multimedia Training

Advantages	**Disadvantages**
Self-paced	Expensive to develop
Interactive	Ineffective for certain training content
Consistency of content	
Consistency of delivery	Trainee anxiety with using technology
Unlimited geographic accessibility	
Immediate feedback	Difficult to quickly update
Built-in guidance system	Lack of agreement on effectiveness
Appeals to multiple senses	
Can test and certify mastery	
Privacy	

Source: Based on S. V. Bainbridge, "The Implications of Technology-Assisted Training," *IHRIM-Link* (December 1996/January 1997): 62–68; M. Hequet, "How Does Multimedia Change Training?" *Training* (February 1997): A20–A22.

timedia training is the cost. Initial development costs for a computerized version can range from $25,000 to $250,000 depending on the complexity of material and media used.[7] These costs can be recovered over time by savings gained from reductions in travel costs and instruction costs if the content does not require frequent updating.[8] Multimedia training may also be difficult to use for training interpersonal skills, especially where the learner needs to recognize and practice subtle behavioral cues or cognitive processes.

Note that few conclusions can be made regarding the effectiveness of multimedia training compared to traditional training methods.[9] For example, a division of PepsiCo used a multimedia training program for meal packers at fast food restaurants. Employees' reactions to the program were positive. However, the multimedia delivery method was discontinued because less costly methods including use of technical manuals and job aids (laminated cards at workstations) resulted in the same level of learning and behavior as the more expensive multimedia program.

Computer-Based Training

Computer-based training (CBT) is an interactive training experience in which the computer provides the learning stimulus, the trainee must respond, and the computer analyzes the responses and provides feedback to the trainee.[10] This includes interactive video, CD-ROM, and other systems when they are computer-driven. The most common CBT programs consist of software on a floppy disk that runs on a personal computer. CBT was one of the first new technologies to be used in training. Computer-based training has become more sophisticated with the development of laser discs and CD-ROMs and increasing use of the Internet. These technologies allow greater use of video and audio than possible by relying solely on the computer.

For example, to teach managers how to complete performance reviews, Vidicon Enterprises, which operates convenience stores in Washington, purchased software called "Performance Now!"[11] Managers learned how to write better performance reviews and to improve their management skills. The program works by asking the manager to identify which of several job dimensions he wants to evaluate. For the dimension "job quality," the manager is asked to rate the employee in various categories such as "Strives to Achieve Goals." The program automatically summarizes the ratings into a paragraph, which the manager can edit. The program taught the managers effective language to use in performance evaluations. If the manager writes something inappropriate (e.g., "the employee is too young for the position"), a box appears on the screen with a warning not to equate age with experience. Also, use of the categories underlying each job dimension has broadened managers' views of employee performance.

CD-ROM and Laser Disc

Using a personal computer, animation, video clips, and graphics can be integrated into a training session. Also, the user can interact with the training material through using a joystick or touch-screen monitor. A **CD-ROM** utilizes a laser to read text, graphics, audio, and video off an aluminum disc. A **laser disc** uses a laser to provide high-quality video and sound. A laser disc can be used alone (as a source of video) or as part of a computer-based instruction delivery system.

For example, at Pilgrim Nuclear Power Plant in Plymouth, Massachusetts, a newly hired security guard learns the layout of the facility by using a computer, television, monitor, joystick, and video disc.[12] The new hire can tour the trash-compactor facility, examine the components on a panel of electrical controls, ride elevators, and listen to colleagues discuss machinery, equipment, and high-radiation areas he should be aware of. With more than 77,000 photos on the laser disc, she can travel at normal walking speed, look upward or downward, quickly change location, and store images for future reference!

Interactive Video

Interactive video combines the advantages of video and computer-based instruction. Instruction is provided one-on-one to trainees via a monitor connected to a keyboard. Trainees use the keyboard or touch the monitor to interact with the program. Interactive video is used to teach technical procedures and interpersonal skills. The training program may be stored on a videodisc or compact disc (CD-ROM).

Apple Computer's and Federal Express's experience with CD-ROMs provides a good example of how a CD-ROM can provide greater accessibility to consistent training as well as facilitate learning. Apple Computer's managers wanted access to training, but their busy schedules made it difficult for them to leave their jobs to attend training sessions.[13] As a result of this need for an alternative to classroom instruction, Apple connected CD-ROM drives to all of its computers. CD-ROM training programs were created for the managers. One CD-ROM-based program covered basics of employment law, offering both narrated text and video. The CD-ROM also allowed the manager to access reference materials included on the CD, such as a list of legal interview questions and demonstrations of violations of law (e.g., sexual harassment).

Federal Express's 25-disc interactive video curriculum includes courses related to customer etiquette, defensive driving, and delivery procedures.[14] As Federal Express discovered, interactive video has many advantages. First, training is individualized. Employees control what aspects of the training program they view. They can skip ahead where they feel competent, or they can review topics. Second, employees receive immediate feedback concerning their performance. Third, training is accessible on a 24-hour basis regardless of employees' work schedules. From the employer's standpoint, the high cost of developing interactive video programs and purchasing the equipment was offset by the reduction in instructor costs and travel costs related to a central training location. At Federal Express, interactive video has made it possible to train 35,000 customer-contact employees in 650 locations nationwide, saving the company millions of dollars. Without interactive video, Federal Express could not deliver consistent high-quality training.

The Internet or Web-Based Training

The **Internet** is a widely used tool for communications, a method for sending and receiving communications quickly and inexpensively, and a way to locate and gather resources, such as software and reports.[15] According to a recent survey, 11 percent of the North American population over age 16 is on the Internet, and 17.6 million people use the World Wide Web![16] To gain access to the Internet you need a personal computer with a direct connection via an existing network or a modem to dial into the Internet. Educational institutions, government agencies, and commercial service providers such as Prodigy, CompuServe, Microsoft, and America Online provide access to the Internet.

Managers can communicate with other managers at their locations or across the globe, leave messages or documents, and get access to "rooms" designated for conversation on certain topics (the Americans with Disabilities Act, for example). Various newsgroups exist, which are bulletin boards dedicated to areas of interests. There you can read, post, and respond to messages and articles. Internet sites can have home pages—mailboxes that identify the person or company, and contain text, images, sounds, or even moving pictures.

The **World Wide Web (WWW)** is a user-friendly service on the Internet.[17] The Web provides browser software (e.g., Mosaic, Netscape) that enables the user to explore the Web. Besides browser software, users also need a search engine (e.g., Yahoo, Infoseek, Alta Vista, Excite, Lycos) to find information on topics of their choice.

Every home page on the Web has an address or "uniform resource locator" or Web address. For example, the Web address for Texaco Corporation's Web site is http://www.texaco.com.

The Internet is a valuable source of information on a wide range of topics. The inside of the front cover of the book and Table 8–2 provide Internet and Web site addresses related to training topics. For example, one manager at Hydro Quebec, a large Canadian utility, used the Internet to research topics related to TQM and business process reengineering. When the company wanted information on diversity and women's issues, the manager logged onto a Cornell University Web site and quickly downloaded two dozen reports on the topic. When the company needed to develop a satisfaction survey, the manager used the Internet to identify similar-sized companies that had conducted comprehensive surveys. Within one day, 30 HR professionals including managers at Federal Express and United Parcel Service responded. The manager has also networked with HR managers at Motorola, IBM, and other companies.[18]

TABLE 8–2 Sample of Internet Resources Related to Training Topics
Addresses and Descriptions

http://itech1.coe.uga.edu./EPSS/EPSS.html	http://stats.bls.gov:80/epthome.htm
Resources for the design and development of an electronic support system	*U.S. Bureau of Labor Statistics reports on training*
http://www.tmreview.org	http://iconode.ca/trdev/
Review of training products	*Training and development issues and topics*
http://www.astd.org	http:www.ccl.com
Home page for American Society for Training and Development	*Home page for Center for Creative Leadership, an organization involved in managerial development, assessment, leadership training, and diversity training*
http://www.clark.net/pub/nractive/wbt.html	
Lakewood Publishing site including training products, research, job bank, and chat rooms	
http://www.trainingsupersite.com	
Example of how the Web is being used to provide training	

Source: Based on B. J. Finch, *The Management Guide to Internet Resources, 1997 Edition* (New York: McGraw-Hill, 1997); K. Wulf, "Training via the Internet," *Training and Development* (May 1996); "Performance Improvement Strategies," *Issues and Trends Report* (Alexandria, VA: American Society for Training and Development, Fall 1996).

Internet-based training refers to training that is delivered on public or private computer networks and displayed by a Web browser.[19] **Intranet-based training** refers to training delivered using the company's own computer network. The training programs are accessible only to the company's employees, not to the general public. Approximately 24 percent of companies report using the Internet to deliver training compared to 10 percent using the company's intranet. Both Internet-based and intranet-based training is stored in a computer and accessed using a computer network. The two types of training use similar technologies. The major difference is that access to the intranet is restricted to a company's employees. For example, Amdahl Corporation (a mainframe computer manufacturer) has set up an intranet.[20] Employees use Netscape to browse the Web along with a company-developed Web browser. Every department at Amdahl has its own Web home page. The home page describes what services the department provides. Many employees also have their own personal home pages. The training department home page includes a list of courses offered by the training department. The manufacturing department gives employees access to technical manuals via the intranet.

Web-based training supports virtual reality, animation, interactions, communications between trainees, and real-time audio and video. As Figure 8–2 shows, there are six levels of Internet-based training. The simplest level facilitates communications between trainers and trainees. More complex uses of the Internet involve actual delivery of training. At the highest level, the Internet (or intranet) is used for both training and storage of intellectual capital. At the highest level, trainees are very actively involved in learning. Sound, automation, and video are used in web-based training. In addition, trainees are linked to other resources on the Web. They are also required to share information with other trainees and to deposit knowledge and their insights gained from the training (such as potential applications of the training content) in a database that is accessible to other company employees.

Internet- or intranet-based training has advantages similar to other multimedia methods. Advantages of Internet-based training include the ability to deliver training to trainees anywhere in the world at any time, cost savings and efficiency in training administration, the use of self-directed, self-paced instruction, the ability to monitor trainees' performance, and controllable access to training.[21] Web-based training has several advantages from learning and cost perspectives. Web-based training allows the trainee to have complete control over

FIGURE 8–2

Levels of Internet-based training

Communications	On-line referencing	Testing assessment	Distribution of computer-based training	Delivery of multimedia	Delivery of multimedia, linking to other resources, sharing knowledge

Level					
1	2	3	4	5	6

Source: Based on K. Kruse, "Five Levels of Internet-Based Training," *Training & Development* (February 1997): 60–61.

the delivery of training, provides links to other resources, and allows the trainee to share information and communicate with other trainees and the trainer or to make "deposits" into databases. This sharing can occur before, during, or after training. Learner control, linking, and sharing facilitate learning and transfer of training because trainees are actively involved in learning and the material is directly related to current issues and problems the employee is facing. Web-based training also allows more than one person to access the training materials at the same time (asynchronous training). For example, at Xerox Management Institute, team members from the United States, Europe, and South America use the Web site (http://www.isim.com) to access study guides, discuss assignments with other students, and interact with the trainer.[22] Homework assignments are posted and addresses of other links that lead to additional information on topics are provided. These links, known as **hyperlinks,** allow a user to easily move from one Web page to another. Owens-Corning's learning resource home page has hyperlinks to all available forms of training information including CD-ROM, Web-based, and trainer-led programs. The site supports on-line registration for courses and allows assessment tools (such as quizzes) to be sent to the trainee, scored, and used to register trainee registration in appropriate courses.[23] At both Xerox and Owens-Corning, employees can access the classes on their own timetables. This has boosted employee participation and lowered training costs. Savings are realized by avoiding travel and lodging costs.

An additional advantage of Internet-based training is ease of updating the training program using authoring language (such as HTML), which continues to become more user-friendly. Trainers can quickly make changes at low cost. These changes take effect as soon as they are made. Ease of changing program content is an advantage that Internet-based training has over CD-ROM. To change a CD-ROM program requires that a new master CD be produced and copies made and distributed to trainees.

Allen Telecom Group's Web site provides a good example of the types of training administration tasks that can be handled by a Web site.[24] The training department can publish training bulletins, schedule classes, prepare class rosters, track attendance, track costs, and store and modify training records. Employees can access the site to review class offerings, access current schedules, register for classes, communicate with trainers, and generate their own personal training records.

Disadvantages include computer networks' inability to handle extensive video and audio (often referred to as the bandwidth problem), the need to control and bill users, and the difficulty of writing or revising training curricula based on a linear learning method (e.g., learn A first, then B, then C) to hypermedia. Hypermedia allow the user to decide the direction and order of learning.

Trainers and managers interested in developing Web-based training need to consider the design rules in Table 8–3. The rules are organized into five categories. Development rules relate to how to build Web-based training. Instructional effectiveness rules relate to features that need to be included to create a positive learning environment. Learner control relates to trainees' control over the pace, delivery, and degree of involvement in the program. Linkages relate to access to other resources. Sharing rules refer to the opportunity to interact with others.

TABLE 8–3   Rules for the Design of Effective Web-Based Training Programs

---

Development

1. Purpose of the program is to enhance performance.

2. Program development is based on an analysis of trainees' needs, skills, knowledge, and work environment.

3. Music, graphics, icons, animation, and video facilitate and do not interfere with learning.

4. Content is relevant to real-world experiences.

5. Training is tested on end-users (managers, potential trainees, experts).

6. Employees and experts are used to provide content example, exercises, and assignments.

Instructional Effectiveness

1. Trainees have opportunities to practice and receive feedback through problems, exercises, assignments, and tests.

2. Assessment of learning outcomes is built into the program.

3. Abstract concepts are presented using real examples.

4. Trainees are urged to identify obstacles to using content in their jobs and ways to overcome obstacles.

5. Multiple examples, exercises, and applications for the learning objectives are presented.

Learner Control

1. A navigator or content map is provided so trainees can move forward or backward through the program and easily access resources and links to other sites as needed.

2. Trainee can compare answers, approaches, and responses to questions to those provided by others.

3. Trainees can begin the program where they want or a starting point can be based on an assessment of their knowledge, skills, or experiences related to the program.

Linkages

1. Follow-up materials and additional resources (e.g. charts, tables, other Web sites) are identified and easily accessible to trainees.

Sharing

1. Opportunities exist for electronically interacting with and sharing with trainers, peers, other trainees, and experts. This may be done through e-mail, chat rooms, or bulletin boards.

Source: Based on "Rules for good WBT Design," World Wide Web site address http://www.clark.net/pub/nractive/f6.html; R. Zemke and J. Armstrong, "Evaluating Multimedia," *Training* (August 1996): 48–52; A. Rossett and J. Barnett, "Designing Under the Influence," *Training* (December 1996): 39–42.

As the rules in the table emphasize, use of the Web, rather than a traditional training method, does not guarantee that training will be effective. Effective Web-based training is based on a thorough needs assessment and complete learning objectives. Also, the site must use a combination of sound, words, and diagrams to ensure that it appeals to the learning preferences of the majority of users. The Web must create a learning environment through providing meaningful material, communicating objectives, and enabling trainees to practice and receive feedback. **Repurposing** refers to directly translating a training program that uses a traditional training method onto the Web. Web-based training that involves merely repurposing an ineffective training program based on lecture or another traditional training method will result in ineffective training! Unfortunately, in their haste to use intranet- or Internet-based training, many companies are repurposing bad training. Effective Web-based training takes advantage of the Web's dynamic nature by including linking, sharing, and learner control in the training program.

Virtual Reality

Virtual reality is a computer-based technology that provides trainees with a three-dimensional learning experience. Using specialized equipment or viewing the virtual model on the computer screen, trainees move through the simulated environment and interact with its components.[25] Technology is used to stimulate multiple senses of the trainee.[26] Devices relay information from the environment to the senses. For example, audio interfaces, gloves that provide a sense of touch, treadmills, or motion platforms are used to create a realistic, artificial environment. Devices also communicate information about the trainee's movements to a computer. These devices allow the trainee to experience **presence** (the perception of actually being in a particular environment). Presence is influenced by the amount of sensory information available to the trainee, control over sensors in the environment, and the trainees' ability to modify the environment.

For example, Motorola's advanced manufacturing courses for employees learning to run the Pager Robotic Assembly facility use virtual reality. Employees are fitted with a head-mount display that allows them to view the virtual world, which includes the actual lab space, robots, tools, and assembly operation. Trainees hear and see the actual sounds and sights as if they were using the real equipment. Also, the equipment responds to the employees' actions (e.g., turning on a switch or dial).

One advantage of virtual reality is that it allows the trainee to practice dangerous tasks without putting herself or others in danger. Research suggests that virtual reality training is likely to have the greatest impact on complex tasks or tasks that involve extensive use of visual cues.[27] The virtual reality environment can be virtually identical to the actual work environment. Another potential advantage relates to the cognitive processing required by the learner. The use of such a realistic environment in training may make more memory available for learning. Memory that was previously used to convert one- or two-dimensional training scenarios into three-dimensional space can now be used for processing information.

Obstacles to developing effective virtual reality training include poor equipment that results in a reduced sense of presence (e.g., poor tactile feedback and inappropriate time lags between sensing and responding to trainees' actions). Poor presence may result in the trainee experiencing vomiting, dizziness, and headaches (simulator sickness) because senses are distorted.

Intelligent Tutoring Systems

Intelligent tutoring systems (ITSs) refer to instructional systems using artificial intelligence.[28] There are three types of ITS: tutoring, coaching, and empowering environments. Tutoring is a structured attempt to increase trainee understanding of a content domain. Coaching provides trainees with the flexibility to practice skills in artificial environments. Empowering refers to the student's ability to freely explore the content of the training program. The five components of ITS are shown in Figure 8–3. As we see, the ITS has information about the content domain as well as expectations about the trainee's level of knowledge.

ITS can be distinguished from other new training technologies in several ways:[29]

- ITS has the ability to match instruction to individual student needs.
- ITS can communicate and respond to the student.
- ITS can model the trainee's learning process.
- ITS can decide, on the basis of a trainee's previous performance, what information to provide to him.
- ITS can make decisions about the trainee's level of understanding.
- ITS can complete a self-assessment resulting in a modification of its teaching process.

FIGURE 8–3

Components of intelligent tutoring systems

Domain expert
- **Provides information about how to perform the task**

Trainee model
- **Provides information about student's knowledge**

User interface
- **Enables trainee to interact with the system**

Training session manager
- **Interprets trainees actions and reports the results or provides coaching**

Trainee scenario generator
- **Determines difficulty and order in which problems are presented to trainee**

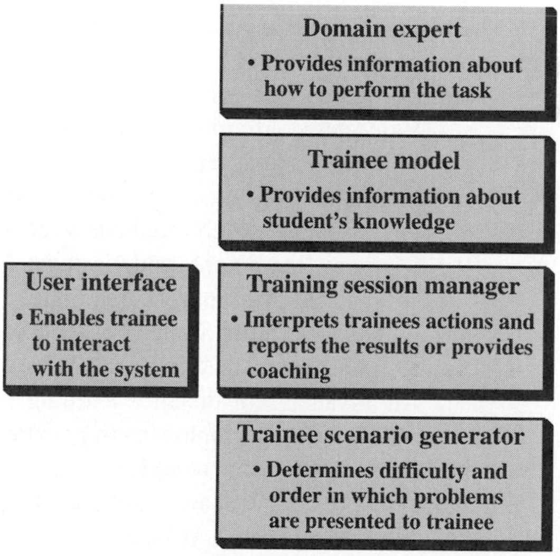

Source: Based on D. Steele-Johnson and B. G. Hyde, "Advanced Technologies in Training: Intelligent Tutoring Systems and Virtual Reality," in *Training for a Rapidly Changing Workplace,* eds. M. A. Quinones and A. Ehrenstein (Washington, DC: American Psychological Association, 1997): 225–48.

ITS has been used by NASA in astronaut training.[30] For example, the Remote Maneuvering System ITS was used to teach astronauts how to use the robotic arm on the space shuttle. Astronauts had to learn to complete tasks and procedures related to grappling a payload. The ITS generated processes matched to individual astronauts. Feedback was matched to their pattern of success and failure in learning the tasks. The system recorded performance data for each astronaut, made decisions regarding the student's level of understanding, and used those decisions to provide appropriate feedback.

Distance Learning

Distance learning is used by geographically dispersed companies to provide information about new products, policies, or procedures, as well as skills training and expert lectures to field locations.[31] Distance learning features two-way communications between people. Distance learning currently involves two types of technology.[32] First, it includes simultaneous learning in which trainees attend training programs in training facilities in which they can communicate with trainers (who are at another location) and other trainees using the telephone or personal computer. This includes audioconferencing, videoconferencing, and docuconferencing (allowing employees to collaborate on a shared document via computers). A second type of distance learning also includes individualized, personal-computer-based training.[33] Employees participate in training anywhere they have access to a personal computer. This type of distance learning may involve multimedia training methods such as Web-based training. Course material and assignments can be distributed using the company's intranet, video, or CD-ROM. Trainers and trainees interact using e-mail, bulletin boards, and conferencing systems.

Video teleconferencing usually includes a telephone link so that trainees viewing the presentation can call in questions and comments to the trainer. Also, satellite networks allow companies to link up with industry-specific and educational courses for which employees receive college credit and job certification. IBM, Digital Equipment, and Eastman Kodak are among the many firms that subscribe to the National Technological University, which broadcasts courses throughout the United States that technical employees need to obtain advanced degrees in engineering.[34]

An advantage of distance learning is that the company can save on travel costs. It also allows employees in geographically dispersed sites to receive training from experts who would not otherwise be available to visit each location. For example, the Research and Development group at 3M found considerable cost savings by using videoconferencing to conduct an eight-week class on imaging technology that involved instructors from Europe and the United States.[35] Without videoconferencing the class would have cost $100,000, making it too expensive. With videoconferencing the course cost $13,000.

The major disadvantage of distance learning is the potential for lack of interaction between the trainer and the audience. A high degree of interaction between trainees and the trainer is a positive learning feature that is missing from distance learning programs that merely use technology to broadcast a lecture to geographically dispersed employees. All that is done in this case is repurposing a traditional lecture (with its limitations for learning and transfer of training) for a new training technology! That's why establishing a communications link between employees and the trainer is important. Also, on-site instructors or facilitators should be available to answer questions and moderate question-and-answer sessions.

Technologies for Training Support

New technologies such as expert systems, groupware, and electronic support systems are being used to support training efforts. Training support means that these technologies are helping to capture training content so that it is available to employees who may not have attended training. Training support also means that these technologies provide information and decision rules to employees on an as-needed basis (i.e., they are job aids). Employees can access these technologies in the work environment.

Table 8–4 shows when training support technologies are most needed. Many conditions shown in the table relate to characteristics of the task or the environment that can inhibit transfer of training. For example, an employee may work some distance away from her manager, her manager may be difficult to contact, or she may have special expertise that the manager lacks. This makes it difficult for the employee to find answers to problems that arise on the job. Training support technologies can help to ensure that transfer of training occurs by helping the employee generalize training content to the work environment and providing new information (not covered in training) to the employee.

Expert Systems

Expert systems refer to technology (usually software) that organizes and applies the knowledge of human experts to specific problems.[36] Expert systems have three elements:

- A knowledge base that contains facts, figures, and rules about a specific subject.
- A decision making capability that, imitating an expert's reasoning ability, draws conclusions from those facts and figures to solve problems and answer questions.
- A user interface that gathers and gives information to the person using the system.

TABLE 8–4   **Conditions When Training Support Technologies Are Most Needed**

1. Performance of task is infrequent.
2. The task is lengthy, difficult, and information-intensive.
3. The consequences of error are damaging.
4. Performance relies on knowledge, procedures, or approaches that frequently change.
5. There is high employee turnover.
6. Little time is available for training or resources for training are few.
7. Employees are expected to take full responsibility for learning and performing tasks.

Source: Based on A. Rossett, "Job Aids and Electronic Performance Support Systems," in *The ASTD Training and Development Handbook,* 4th ed., ed. R. L. Craig (New York: McGraw-Hill, 1996): 554–77.

Expert systems are used as a support tool that employees refer to when they have problems or decisions they feel exceed their current knowledge and skills. For example, a large international food processor uses an expert system called Performer, which is designed to provide training and support to its plant operators. One problem the company was facing was determining why potato chips were being scorched in the fryer operation. A operator solved the problem using Performer. He selected the "troubleshooting" menu, then "product texture/flavor," then "off oil flavor." The program listed probable causes, beginning with high oxidation during frying. The operator chose that cause, and the system recommended adjusting the cooking line's oil flush, providing detailed steps for that procedure. Following those steps resolved the problem.[37]

Although expert systems are discussed as a technology that supports training, expert systems can also be used as a delivery mechanism. Expert systems can be used to train employees in the decision rules of the experts.

Expert systems can both deliver high quality and lower costs. By using the decision processes of experts, the system enables many people to arrive at decisions that reflect experts' knowledge. An expert system helps avoid the errors that can result from fatigue and decision biases. The efficiencies of an expert system can be realized if it can be operated by fewer or less skilled (and likely less costly) employees than the company would otherwise require.

Groupware

Groupware (electronic meeting software) is a special type of software application that enables multiple users to track, share, and organize information, and to work on the same document simultaneously.[38] A groupware system combines such elements as electronic mail, document management, and an electronic bulletin board. The most popular brand of groupware is Lotus Notes.

Companies have been using groupware to improve business processes such as sales and account management, to improve meeting effectiveness, as well as to identify and share knowledge in the organization. (See Chapter 5's discussion of creating a learning organization.) Monsanto uses Lotus Notes to link salespeople, account managers, and competitor-intelligence analysts.[39] The database contains updated news on competitors and customers, information from public news sources, salesperson's reports, an in-house directory of experts, and attendees' notes from conventions and conferences.

As noted earlier in the chapter, many companies are creating their own intranets. Intranets are cheaper and simpler to use than groupware programs but pose potential security problems because of the difficulty of keeping persons out of the network.[40]

Electronic Performance Support Systems

Electronic performance support systems (EPSSs) are computer applications that provide, as requested, skills training, information access or expert advice.[41] In Chapter 5 electronic performance support systems (EPSSs) were discussed as a means to help training transfer. EPSS can also be used as a substitute for training. For example, at Aetna Life and Casualty Company, a performance support tool known as the AMP facilitator was distributed to employees to load on their computers. AMP refers to the company's internal management process. The AMP facilitator helps employees deal with problems by structuring the task, coaching them, providing examples, and allowing them to print out the results in a work plan. Employees do not need to know anything about AMP before using the software. EPSS may also reside on the Web or be based within a program (as is the case for intelligent authoring systems).

To use EPSS as a substitute for training, trainers must determine whether problems and tasks require employees to actually acquire knowledge, skill, or ability (learned capability) and whether periodic assistance through an EPSS is sufficient.

Technologies for Training Administration

New technology is making training administration more efficient and effective. Training administration includes record keeping, employee enrollment in courses, and testing and certification. Interactive voice technology, imaging, and software applications have made it easier to track training information. They also provide easy access to training information for trainers to use in decision making.

Interactive Voice Technology

Interactive voice technology uses a conventional PC to create an automated phone response system. This technology is especially useful for benefits administration. For example, at Hannaford Brothers—a supermarket chain spread through the Northeastern United States—the HR department installed an interactive voice response system that allows employees to get information on their retirement accounts, stock purchases, and benefit plans by using the touch-tone buttons on their phones.[42] Employees can also directly enroll in training programs and speak to an HR representative if they have questions. As a result of the technology, the company was able to reduce its HR staff and more quickly serve employees' benefit needs.

Imaging

Imaging refers to scanning documents, storing them electronically, and retrieving them.[43] Imaging is particularly useful because paper files take a large volume of space and are difficult to access. Training records can be scanned and stored in a database for access at a later date. Some software applications allow the user to scan documents based on key words such as *job history, education,* or *experience.* This is a valuable feature when answering managers' and other customers' questions regarding employees' training and skills. For example, inquiries such as "I need an engineer to take an expatriate assignment in France. Do we have any engineers who speak French?" can be easily and quickly answered by scanning training databases. Imaging can also help a training department better serve its customers by reducing the time needed to locate a file or service a phone inquiry from an employee, providing the ability for employee training records to be shared simultaneously, eliminating the need to refile, and reducing the physical space needed to store training records.

Training Software Applications

Training software applications have primarily been used to track information related to training administration (e.g., course enrollments, tuition reimbursement summaries, and training costs), employee skills, and employees' training activities. Important database elements for training administration include training courses completed, certified skills, and educational experience. Georgia Power uses a database system that tracks internal training classes, available classroom space, instructor availability, costs, and the salaries of training class members.[44] Figure 8–4 illustrates a screen showing training costs for an accounting department. Cost information can be used by managers to determine which departments are exceeding their training budgets. This information can be used to reallocate training dollars during the next budget period. Other databases give access to summaries of journal articles, legal cases, and books to help professional employees such as engineers and lawyers keep up to date.[45]

FIGURE 8–4

Example of a training budget screen

	Budget	Expenditure	Variance
■ **Cost Center: Accounting**			
■ **Total Budget: 4500**			
Course	3500	1000	2500
Accommodation	600	00	600
Meals	300	00	300
Travel	100	00	100
Total	4500	1000	3500

Source: Adapted from Spectrum Human Resource Systems Corporation, "TD/2000: Training and Development System: Sample Screens and Reports" (Denver, CO).

Software applications can be useful for decision making. Managers can use skills inventories to ensure that they get the maximum benefit out of their training budget. Using skill inventories, managers can determine which employees need training and can suggest training programs to them that are appropriate for their job and skill levels. Skill inventories are also useful for identifying employees who are qualified for promotions and transfers. Finally, they can also be useful for helping managers to quickly build employee teams with the necessary skills to respond to customer needs, product changes, international assignments, or work problems.

Choosing New Technology Training Methods

Table 8–5 compares training methods that use new technology on the same characteristics used to compare traditional training programs in Chapter 7. Several trends are apparent in this table. First, these methods require considerable investment in development. Development costs are related to purchasing hardware and software as well as developing programs and transferring programs to new media (e.g., CD-ROM). However, although development costs are high, costs for administering the program are low. As we've said, advantages of these methods include (1) cost savings due to training being accessible to employees at their home or office and (2) reduced costs associated with employees traveling to a central training location (e.g., airfare, food, lodging). Moreover, with the exception of

TABLE 8–5   Comparison of Training Methods Using New Technology

	CBT	CD-ROM	Internet WWW	Intranet	Distance Learning	Intelligent Tutoring	Virtual Reality
Learning Outcome							
Verbal information	Yes	Yes	Yes	Yes	Yes	Yes	Yes
Intellectual skills	Yes	Yes	Yes	Yes	Yes	Yes	Yes
Cognitive strategies	Yes	Yes	Yes	Yes	Yes	Yes	Yes
Attitudes	No	Yes	No	No	No	No	No
Motor skills	No	No	No	No	No	Yes	Yes
Learning Environment							
Clear objective	Medium	High	High	High	Medium	High	High
Practice	Medium	High	Medium	Medium	Low	High	High
Meaningfulness	Medium	High	High	High	Medium	High	High
Feedback	Medium	High	Medium	Medium	Low	High	High
Observe and interact with others	Low	High	Medium	Medium	Low	Low	Low
Transfer of Training	Medium	High	Medium	Medium	Low	High	High
Cost							
Development	High	High	High	High	Medium	High	High
Administrative	Low	Low	Low	Low	Low	Low	Low
Effectiveness	Medium	High	?	?	Medium	?	High

distance learning, most important characteristics needed for learning to occur (practice, feedback, etc.) are built into these methods. Note that limited studies of the effectiveness of several methods (Web-based training, intelligent tutoring) are available because companies are just starting to use these technologies for training. However, their effectiveness is likely to be high if the method including characteristics of a positive learning environment and learner control, sharing, and linking are built into these methods.

How do new technology training methods relate to traditional training methods discussed in Chapter 7? Virtual reality and intelligent tutoring systems are best suited for learning complex processes related to operating machinery, tools, and equipment. These methods are an extension of simulations. CD-ROMs, the Internet, and the intranet are best suited for learning facts, figures, cognitive strategies (e.g., how to hold an effective meeting), and interpersonal skills (e.g., closing a sale). These methods are technological extensions of traditional training methods such as behavior modeling, on-the-job training, and apprenticeship. While traditional training methods can be effective, managers and trainers should consider using new technology training methods under certain conditions:

1. There is sufficient budget provided to develop and use new technology.
2. Trainees are geographically dispersed and travel costs related to training are high.
3. Trainees are comfortable using technology including the Web, personal computers, and CD-ROMs.
4. The increased use of new technology is part of the company's business strategy. New technology is being used or implemented in manufacturing of products or service processes.
5. Employees have a difficult time attending scheduled training programs.
6. Current training methods allow limited time for practice, feedback, and assessment.

Summary

This chapter provided an overview of new technologies' use in training delivery, support, and administration. Many new technologies have features that help to ensure learning and transfer of training (e.g., multimedia training methods such as the Intranet). These features include the ability to appeal to multiple senses, self-pace, receive feedback and reinforcement, and find information from experts on an as-needed basis. New technologies also enable employees to participate in training from home or work on a 24-hour basis. Employees control not only the presentation of training content but also when and where they participate in training! New technologies such as virtual reality also can create a more realistic training environment, which can make the material more meaningful and increase the probability that training will transfer to the job. Expert systems and electronic support systems are tools that employees can access on an as-needed basis to obtain knowledge and information. Groupware and intranets help to capture the knowledge that employees gain from training and facilitate their sharing of information. Interactive voice technologies, imaging, and software applications especially designed for training make it easier to store and record training information such as course enrollments and employee training records. This technology also makes it easier to retrieve training-related information for managerial decision making.

The chapter concludes by showing that most new technology training methods can be superior to traditional methods because a positive learning environment can be built into the method. But development costs of new technology training methods are high. Considerations include monies for development, geographic dispersion of employees, employees' difficulty in attending training, and whether new technologies are part of the company's business strategy.

Key Terms

Discussion Questions

1. Explain how new technologies influence training.
2. What are some advantages and disadvantages of multimedia training?
3. What are the differences between expert systems and electronic performance tools?
4. Are training support technologies always needed? Justify your answer.
5. Discuss how new technologies make it easier to learn. How do they facilitate transfer of training?
6. Is all Internet training the same? Explain.
7. What are some potential problems with using virtual reality technology for training?
8. How can interactive voice technology and imaging help with training administration?
9. Explain learner control, sharing, and linking. How do they contribute to the effectiveness of Web-based training?
10. What is repurposing? How does it affect use of new technologies in training?
11. Distance learning can be used to deliver a lecture to geographically dispersed trainees. How might distance learning be designed and used to avoid some of the learning and transfer of training problems of the traditional lecture method?

Application Assignments

1. Using only the Web, further investigate any new technology discussed in this chapter. Utilizing any browser on the Web (e.g., Yahoo), conduct a search for information about the technology you have chosen. Find

information describing the technology, hints for developing or purchasing the technology, and examples of companies marketing and/or using the technology. Include Web addresses in your summary.

2. The Interactive Patient is a realistic interactive computer simulation of a patient's visit to a physician's office. The Interactive Patient is a Web-based training program used to train medical students at Marshall University and provide continuous education credits to practicing physicians.

Visit and review the Interactive Patient at http://medicus.marshall.edu/medicus.htm.

Evaluate the program according to Table 8–3's rules for the design of effective Web-based training.

a. What are the program's strengths and weaknesses?

b. How would you improve the program?

Endnotes

1. L. J. Bassi, A. L. Gallagher, and E. Schroer, *The ASTD Training Data Book* (Washington, DC: American Society for Training and Development, 1996). See Chapter 5, "Technology Use," pages 59–70. Technology and Training, in "Training Industry Report 1996," *Training* (October 1996): 73–79.

2. "HRD Executives Forecast Tremendous Growth of Learning Technologies," in *National Report of Human Resources,* ed. D. Koehle (Alexandria, VA: American Society of Training and Development, November/December 1997): 3.

3. S. E. O'Connell, "New Technologies Bring New Tools, New Rules," *HR Magazine* (December 1995): 43–48; S. E. O'Connell, "The Virtual Workplace Moves at Warp Speed," *HR Magazine* (March 1996): 51–57.

4. J. J. Howell and L. O. Silvey, "Interactive Multimedia Systems," in *The ASTD Training and Development Handbook,* 4th ed., ed. R. L. Craig (New York: McGraw-Hill, 1996): 534–53.

5. "Multimedia Training in the Fortune 1000," *Training* (September 1996): 53–60.

6. R. Zemke and J. Armstrong, "Evaluating Multimedia," *Training* (August 1996): 48–52.

7. K. Murphy, "Pitfalls vs. Promise in Multimedia Training," *New York CyberTimes* (May 6, 1996), http://www.nytimes.com.

8. Howell and Silvey, "Interactive Multimedia Systems."

9. Murphy, "Pitfalls vs. Promise in Multimedia Training."

10. W. Hannum, *The Application of Emerging Training Technologies* (Alexandria, VA: American Society for Training and Development, 1990).

11. A. Field, "Class Act," *Inc.* (January 1997): 55–57.

12. S. Greengard, "How Technology Is Advancing HR," *Personal Journal* (September 1993): 80–90.

13. L. Keegan and S. Rose, "The Good News about Desktop Learning," *Training and Development* (June 1997): 24–27.

14. F. Filipowski, "How Federal Express Makes Your Package Its Most Important," *Personnel Journal* (February 1992): 40–46.

15. S. Greengard, "Catch the Wave as HR Goes Online," *Personnel Journal* (July 1995): 54–68; M. I. Finney, "It's All in the Knowing How," *HR Magazine* (July 1995): 36–43. "A Survey of the Internet" (special section), *The Economist* (July 1, 1995): 3–18; A. Doran, "The Internet: The New Tool for the HR Professional," *The Review* (August/September 1995): 32–35.

16. J. Sandberg, "On-line Population Reaches 24 Million in North America," *The Wall Street Journal* (October 30, 1995): B2.

17. S. Greengard, "Leverage the Power of the Internet," *Workforce* (March 1997): 76–85.

18. S. Greengard, "Catch the Wave as HR Goes Online."

19. "What is Web-Based Training," World Wide Web site http://www.clark.net/pub/nractive/f1.html.

20. B. Filipczak, "An Internet of Your Very Own," in *Using Technology-Delivered Training,* ed. D. Zielinski (Minneapolis, MN: Lakewood, 1997): 127–28.

21. D. Glener, "The Promise of Internet-Based Training," *Training and Development* (September 1996): 57–58.

22. "The Real World of Intranet-Based Training, *Training with Multimedia* 2 (1996): 1–5.

23. C. Pollack and R. Masters, "Using Internet Technologies to Enhance Training," *Performance Improvement* (February 1997): 28–31.

24. "The Real World of Internet-Based Training."

25. N. Adams, "Lessons from the Virtual World," *Training* (June 1995): 45–48.

26. D. Steele-Johnson and B. G. Hyde, "Advanced Technologies in Training: Intelligence Tutoring Systems and Virtual Reality," in *Training for a Rapidly Changing Workplace,* eds. M. A. Quinones and A. Ehrenstein (Washington, DC: American Psychological Association, 1997): 225–48.

27. Ibid.

28. Ibid.

29. R. J. Seidel, O. C. Park, and R. S. Perez, "Expertise of ICAI: Developmental Requirements," *Computers in Human Behavior* 4 (1988): 235–56.

30. Steele-Johnson and Hyde, "Advanced Technologies in Training: Intelligent Tutoring Systems and Virtual Reality."

31. "Putting the Distance into Distance Learning," *Training* (October 1995): 111–18.

32. D. Picard, "The Future Is Distance Training," *Training* (November 1996): s3–s10.

33. A. F. Maydas, "On-line Networks Build the Savings into Employee Education," *HR Magazine* (October 1997): 31–35.

34. J. M. Rosow and R. Zager, *Training: The Competitive Edge,* (San Francisco: Jossey-Bass, 1988).

35. M. Nadeau, "Reach Out and Touch Someone," *Personnel Journal* (May 1995): 120–24; B. Filipczak, "An Internet of Your Very Own."

36. Hannum, *The Application of Emerging Training Technologies.*

37. P. A. Galagan, "Think Performance: A Conversation with Gloria Gery," *Training and Development* (March 1994): 47–51.

38. J. Clark and R. Koonce, "Meetings Go High-Tech," *Training & Development* (November 1995): 32–38; A. M. Townsend, M. E. Whitman, and A. R. Hendrickson, "Computer Support Adds Power to Group Processes," *HR Magazine* (September 1995): 87–91.

39. T. A. Stewart, "Getting Real about Brainpower," *Fortune* (November 27, 1995): 201–203.

40. B. Ziegler, "Internet Software Poses Big Threat to Notes, IBM's Stake in Lotus," *The Wall Street Journal* (November 7, 1995): A1, A8.

41. S. Caudron, "Your Learning Technology Primer," *Personnel Journal* (June 1996): 120–36.

42. S. Greengard, "How Technology Is Advancing HR."

43. A. L. Lederer, "Emerging Technology and the Buy–Wait Dilemma: Sorting Fact from Fantasy," *The Review* (June/July 1993): 16–19.

44. S. E. Forrer and Z. B. Leibowitz, *Using Computers in Human Resources* (San Francisco: Jossey-Bass, 1991); V. R. Ceriello and C. Freeman, *Human Resource Management Systems* (Lexington, MA: Lexington Books, 1991).

45. L. Granick, A. Y. Dessaint, and G. R. VandenBos, "How Information Systems Can Help Build Professional Competence," in *Maintaining Professional Competence,* eds. S. L. Willis and S. S. Dubin (San Francisco: Jossey-Bass, 1990): 278–305.

9   EMPLOYEE DEVELOPMENT

Objectives

After reading this chapter, you should be able to

1. Discuss current trends in using formal education for development.

2. Relate how assessment of personality type, work behaviors, and job performance can be used for employee development.

3. Describe the benefits that proteges and mentors receive from a mentoring relationship.

4. Explain the characteristics of successful mentoring programs.

5. Tell how job experiences can be used for skill development.

6. Explain how to train managers to coach employees.

7. Describe the steps in the development planning process.

8. Discuss the employee's and company's responsibilities in the development planning process.

JEWEL FOOD STORES' DEVELOPMENT PROGRAM

Jewel Food Stores is headquartered in the Chicago area and has supermarkets in Illinois, Indiana, Iowa, and Wisconsin. Employing approximately 3,000 employees, Jewel has a reputation for attracting employees with the potential for management positions and developing their managerial talent. Jewel believes that the quality of the store managers relates to store performance. High-quality managers are nec-

essary to create working conditions that motivate employees to provide high-quality customer service and a clean, pleasant shopping environment. This results in satisfied customers and employees. For example, some top-level managers of Toys "R" Us, Staples, and Kmart Super Centers have been products of Jewel's development program.

How does Jewel develop managerial talent? Jewel recruits talent from local colleges. In one program, recruits are placed in an accelerated development program that prepares them for a management job within three to five years. In another program, recruits work directly under a senior manager who oversees their training and development to ensure that they get the types of experiences necessary for them to compete for store management positions. Besides relying on talent recruited from outside the company, Jewel identifies current employees who have the potential to take on managerial responsibilities. Jewel provides financial support for these employees to get an education to prepare them for managerial work.

All programs include individual coaching with a psychologist who is available to work with employees and their managers to help improve on-the-job training and development. ■

Source: E. Burton, "Jewel Food Stores: A Profile," in "Corporate Corner," Management and Education Division of the Academy of Management Newsletter 23 (March 1997): 9.

Introduction

As the Jewel Food Stores example illustrates, management development is a key component of a company's employee development efforts. Traditionally, development has focused on management-level employees, while line employees received training designed to improve a specific set of skills needed for their current job. However, with the greater use of work teams and employees' increased involvement in all aspects of business, development is becoming more important for all employees. **Development** refers to formal education, job experiences, relationships, and assessments of personality and abilities that help employees prepare for the future. Because it is future-oriented, it involves learning that is not necessarily related to the employee's current job.[1] Table 9–1 shows the differences between training and development. Traditionally, training is focused on helping improve employees' performance in their current jobs. Development helps prepare them for other positions in the company and increases their ability to move into jobs that may not yet exist.[2] Development also helps employees prepare for changes in their current job that may result from new technology, work designs, customers, or product markets. Because training often focuses on

TABLE 9–1   **Comparison between Training and Development**

	Training	*Development*
Focus	Current	Future
Use of work experiences	Low	High
Goal	Preparation for current job	Preparation for changes
Participation	Required	Voluntary

improving employees performance in their current job, attendance at training programs is required. Development may be mandatory for employees who have been identified to have managerial potential. However, most employees must take the initiative to become involved in development. Chapter 2 emphasized the strategic role of training. Note that as training continues to become more strategic (more related to business goals), the distinction between training and development will blur. Both training and development will be required and focus on current and future personal and company needs.

Why is employee development important? Employee development is a necessary component of a company's efforts to improve quality, to meet the challenges of global competition and social change, and to incorporate technological advances and changes in work design. Increased globalization of product markets compels companies to help their employees understand cultures and customs that affect business practices. For high-involvement companies and work teams to be successful, their employees need strong interpersonal skills. Employees must also be able to perform roles traditionally reserved for managers. Legislation (such as the Civil Rights Act of 1991), labor market forces, and a company's social responsibility dictate that employers provide women and minorities with access to development activities that will prepare them for managerial positions. Companies must help employees overcome stereotypes and attitudes that inhibit the innovative contributions that can come from a work force made up of employees with diverse ethnic, racial, and cultural backgrounds.

This chapter discusses approaches that companies use to develop employees and the development process. The chapter begins by exploring development approaches including formal education, assessment, job experiences, and interpersonal relationships. The chapter emphasizes the types of skills, knowledge, and behaviors that are strengthened by each development method. Developmental approaches are one part of the development planning process. Before one or multiple developmental approaches are used, the employee and the company must have an idea of the employee's development needs and the purpose of development. Identifying needs and purpose of development is part of the development planning process. The chapter provides an overview of the development planning process. This includes a discussion of the roles of the employee and the company in the development process.

Approaches to Employee Development

Four approaches are used to develop employees: formal education, assessment, job experiences, and interpersonal relationships.[3] Many companies use a combination of these approaches. For example, the New York City–based Metropolitan Transportation Authority (MTA) found that it needed a system for developing employees for first-level management positions.[4] As a result, the Future Managers Program (FMP) was created. Its goal was to develop first-level managers who understood the transportation business and operations. Employees selected for FMP survive a rigorous selection process that involves interviews and assessment centers. FMP uses assessment, courses, job experiences, and relationships to develop managers. The program combines classroom instruction with job rotation. Classroom instruction provides a learning foundation while job rotation exposes employees to a wide variety of on-the-job experiences. Classtime is devoted to case study analysis, team building, and developing skills in problem solving, delegation, leadership, and communications. Working in groups, students must complete a project that involves real issues such as creating a customer service brochure in Chinese. Examples of assignments in the job rotations include working at Grand Central Terminal, working with the system road foreman, and working in the operations control center. The purpose of job rotation is to familiarize employees with different aspects of operations so they are prepared to move into a new area when a position becomes available.

Because future managers are often confronted with new situations, mentors are provided to help trainees understand the culture of the agency and help answer questions. Students receive continued feedback on their performance throughout the program based on supervisor and peer evaluations.

Does the program work? Although they are not guaranteed a job after completing the program, the majority of graduates have received jobs they targeted after graduation. The long-term success of the program will be determined by analyzing graduates' career progression in the MTA.

Keep in mind that although the large majority of development activity is targeted at managers, all levels of employees may be involved in one or more development activity. For example, clerks in a grocery store usually receive performance appraisal feedback (a development activity related to assessment). As a result of the appraisal process, they are asked to complete an individual development plan outlining (1) how they plan to change their weaknesses and (2) their future plans (including positions or locations desired and education or experience needed). Next we discuss each type of development activity in greater detail. Specific issues related to developing managers (succession planning, dealing with dysfunctional managers, creating more opportunities for women and minorities to become managers) are discussed in Chapter 10.

Formal Education

Formal education programs include off-site and on-site programs designed specifically for the company's employees, short courses offered by consultants or universities, executive MBA programs, and university programs in which participants actually live at the university while taking classes. These programs may involve lectures by business experts, business games and simulations, adventure learning, and meetings with customers. Many companies (e.g., Motorola, IBM, GE, Metropolitan Financial, Dow) have training and development centers that offer one- or two-day seminars as well as week-long programs. For example, General Electric's Management Development Institute in Crotonville, New York, offers courses in manufacturing and sales, marketing, and advanced management training.[5] Tuition ranges from $800 for a half-week conference to $14,000 for a four-week executive development course. Tuition is paid for by the employee's business unit. The types of development programs used at GE and their target audiences are shown in Figure 9–1. Let's describe several courses to help you understand the techniques used to facilitate development:

- *Corporate entry leadership conferences.* New hires learn about global competition and GE's values and are asked to examine their personal values. Three years after attending this program, the employees return for a program on total business competitiveness. They are given real projects to work on and have to agree to make changes in their business units.
- *New manager development course.* New managers learn how to manage at GE. The program has special emphasis on teaching people skills to be used in hiring, appraising, and building work teams.
- *Senior functional program.* Senior functional managers attend programs on leadership development in their specific functional areas (e.g., marketing, finance). Managers work on real business problems as part of the program.
- *Executive programs.* Executive programs include adventure learning and projects. In one program, the head of a business unit presents an

FIGURE 9–1

Examples of Development Programs at General Electric

Program	Description	Target Audience	Courses
Executive Development Sequence	Courses emphasize strategic thinking, leadership, cross-functional integration, competing globally, customer satisfaction.	Senior professionals and executives identified as high-potential	Manager Development Course Global Business Management Course Executive Development Course
Core Leadership Program	Courses develop functional expertise, business excellence, management of change.	Managers	Corporate Entry Leadership Conference Professional Development Course New Manager Development Course Experienced Manager Course
Professional Development Program	Courses emphasize preparation for specific career path.	New employees	Audit Staff Course Financial Management Program Human Resources Program Technical Leadership Program

Source: Based on World Wide Web site http://www.ge.com/ibcrucl8.htm.

unresolved business problem that teams of managers must solve. The managers interview customers and competitors and collect background information on which they base their recommendations.

- *Officer workshops.* In these workshops, the CEO and the company officers meet to try to solve companywide issues.

These descriptions emphasize that most formal programs actively involve the employees in learning. Separate programs are usually offered for supervisors, middle managers, and executives. Special programs for particular jobs (such as engineer) are also available. (One course at Honeywell is called "Personal Computers in Manufacturing Operations.") Companies may also include personal development courses as part of their education programs. (American Medical Systems, a division of Pfizer, offers courses in stress management and preretirement planning.)

Leadership, implementation of business strategies, and management of organizational change are the most important topics in executive education programs. Programs directed at developing executives' understanding of global business issues are another important part of executive development.[6]

Table 9–2 shows the five largest institutions for executive education. There are several important trends in executive education. Increasingly many companies and universities are using distance learning (which we discussed in Chapter 8) to reach executive audiences.[7] For example, Duke University's Fuqua School of Business is offering an electronic executive MBA program.[8] Using their personal computers, students "attend" CD-ROM video lectures. They can download study aids and additional videos and audio programs. Students discuss lectures and work on team projects using computer bulletin boards, e-mail,

TABLE 9–2   Five Largest Institutions for Executive Education

School	Annual Revenue ($ millions)	Five-Year Growth	Percentage of Customized Programs	Number of Programs
University of Pennsylvania, Wharton School (Philadelphia, Pennsylvania)	$25.0	257%	55%	100
TMD (Lausanne, Switzerland)	23.5	42	39	124
Harvard University Business School (Boston, Massachusetts)	30.1	20	5	28
Center for Creative Leadership (Greensboro, North Carolina)	23.7	57	34	28
University of Michigan (Ann Arbor, Michigan)	21.5	53	10	63

Data Source: J. A. Byrne, "Virtual Business Schools," *Business Week* (October 23, 1995): 68.

and live chat rooms. They use the Internet to research specific companies and class topics. Besides the electronic learning environment, students spend time in traditional face-to-face instruction for several weeks at the beginning and end of the program. They also travel for two weeks to Europe, China, and South America for classes and meetings with local business owners.

Another trend in executive education is for companies and the education provider (business school or other educational institution) to create short, custom courses, with the content designed specifically to meet the needs of the audience. For example, in the Global Leadership Program run by Columbia University's business school, executives work on real problems they face in their jobs. A manager for window maker Pella Corporation left the program with a plan for international sales![9]

The final important trend in executive education is to supplement formal courses from consultants or university faculty with other types of development activities. Avon Products' "Passport Program" is targeted at employees the company thinks can become general managers.[10] To learn Avon's global strategy, they meet for each session in a different country. The program brings a team of employees together for six-week periods spread over 18 months. Participants are provided with a general background of a functional area by university faculty and consultants. Then teams work with senior executives on a country project such as how to penetrate a new market. The team projects are presented to Avon's top managers.

Managers who attend the Center for Creative Leadership development program take psychological tests, receive feedback from managers, peers, and direct reports, participate in group building activities (like adventure learning discussed in Chapter 12), receive counseling, set improvement goals, and write development plans.[11]

Most companies consider the primary purpose of education programs to be providing the employee with job-specific skills.[12] Unfortunately, there has been little research on formal education programs' effectiveness. In a study of Harvard University's Advanced Management Program, participants reported that they had acquired valuable knowledge (e.g., how globalization affects a company's structure) from the program. They said the program broadened their perspective on issues facing their company, increased their self-confidence, and helped them learn new ways of thinking and looking at problems.[13]

Assessment

Assessment involves collecting information and providing feedback to employees about their behavior, communication style, or skills.[14] The employees as well as their peers, managers, and customers may be asked to provide information. Assessment is most frequently used to identify employees with managerial potential and to measure current managers' strengths and weaknesses. Assessment is also used to identify managers with the potential to move into higher-level executive positions, and it can be used with work teams to identify individual team members' strengths and weaknesses as well as the decision processes or communication styles that inhibit the team's productivity.

Companies vary in the methods and sources of information they use in developmental assessment. Many companies provide employees with performance appraisal information. Companies with sophisticated development systems use psychological tests to measure employees' skills, personality types, and communication styles. Self, peer, and manager's ratings of employees' interpersonal styles and behaviors may also be collected. Let's look at several popular assessment tools.

Myers-Briggs Type Indicator®.   Myers-Briggs Type Indicator (MBTI) is the most popular psychological test for employee development. As many as 2 million people take the MBTI in the United States each year. The test consists of more than 100 questions about how the person feels or prefers to behave in different situations (e.g., "Are you usually a good 'mixer' or rather quiet and reserved?"). The MBTI is based on the work of psychologist Carl Jung, who believed that differences in individuals' behavior resulted from decision making, interpersonal communication, and information gathering preferences.

The MBTI identifies individuals' preferences for energy (introversion versus extroversion), information gathering (sensing versus intuition), decision making (thinking versus feeling), and life-style (judging versus perceiving).[15] The energy dimension determines where individuals gain interpersonal strength and vitality. Extroverts (E) gain energy through interpersonal relationships. Introverts (I) gain energy by focusing on personal thoughts and feelings. The information gathering preference relates to the actions individuals take when making decisions. Individuals with a Sensing (S) preference tend to gather facts and details. Intuitives (I) tend to focus less on facts and more on possibilities and relationships between ideas. Decision making style preferences differ based on the amount of consideration the person gives to others' feelings in making a decision. Individuals with a Thinking (T) preference tend to be very objective in making decisions. Individuals with a Feeling (F) preference tend to evaluate the impact of potential decisions on others and be more subjective in making a decision. The life-style preference reflects an individual's tendency to be flexible and adaptable. Individuals with a Judging (J) preference focus on goals, establish deadlines, and prefer to be conclusive. Individuals with a Perceiving (P) preference tend to enjoy surprises, like to change decisions, and dislike deadlines.

Sixteen unique personality types result from the combination of the four MBTI preferences. (See Table 9–3.) Each person has developed strengths and weaknesses as a result of using her preferences. For example, individuals who are Introverted, Sensing, Thinking, and Judging (known as ISTJs) tend to be serious, quiet, practical, orderly, and logical. They can organize tasks, be decisive, and follow through on plans and goals. ISTJs have several weaknesses because they have not used the opposite preferences of Extroversion, Intuition, Feeling, and Perceiving. Potential weaknesses for ISTJs include problems dealing with unexpected opportunities, appearing too task-oriented or impersonal to colleagues, and being overly quick to make decisions.

TABLE 9–3   **The 16 Personality Types Used in the Myers-Briggs Type Inventory**

	Sensing Types (S)		Intuitive Types (N)	
	Thinking (T)	*Feeling (F)*	*Feeling (F)*	*Thinking (T)*
Introverts (I)				
Judging (J)	**ISTJ** Serious, quiet, earn success by concentration and thoroughness. Practical, orderly, matter-of-fact, logical, realistic, and dependable. Take responsibility.	**ISFJ** Quiet, friendly, responsible, and conscientious. Work devotedly to meet obligations. Thorough, painstaking, accurate. Loyal, considerate.	**INFJ** Succeed by perseverance, originality, and desire to do whatever is needed or wanted. Quietly forceful, conscientious, concerned for others. Respected for their firm principles.	**INTJ** Usually have original minds and great drive for their own ideas and purposes. Skeptical, critical, independent, determined, often stubborn.
Perceiving (P)	**ISTP** Cool onlookers— quiet, reserved, and analytical. Usually interested in impersonal principles, how and why mechanical things work. Flashes of original humor.	**ISFP** Retiring, quietly friendly, sensitive, kind, modest about their abilities. Shun disagreements. Loyal followers. Often relaxed about getting things done.	**INFP** Care about learning, ideas, language, and independent projects of their own. Tend to undertake too much, then somehow get it done. Friendly, but often too absorbed.	**INTP** Quiet, reserved, impersonal. Enjoy theoretical or scientific subjects. Usually interested mainly in ideas; little liking for parties or small talk. Sharply defined interests.
Extraverts (E)				
Perceiving (P)	**ESTP** Matter-of-fact, do not worry or hurry, enjoy whatever comes along. May be a bit blunt or insensitive. Best with real things that can be taken apart or put together.	**ESFP** Outgoing, easy-going, accepting, friendly, makes things more fun for others by their enjoyment. Like sports and making things. Find remembering facts easier than mastering theories.	**ENFP** Warmly enthusiastic, high-spirited, ingenious, imaginative. Able to do almost anything that interests them. Quick with a solution and to help with a problem.	**ENTP** Quick, ingenious, good at many things. May argue either side of a question for fun. Resourceful in solving challenging problems, but may neglect routine assignments.
Judging (J)	**ESTJ** Practical, realistic, matter-of-fact, with a natural head for business or mechanics. Not interested in subjects they see no use for. Like to organize and run activities.	**ESFJ** Warm-hearted, talkative, popular, conscientious, born cooperators. Need harmony. Work best with encouragement. Little interest in abstract thinking or technical subjects.	**ENFJ** Responsive and responsible. Generally feel real concern for what others think or want. Sociable, popular. Sensitive to praise and criticism.	**ENTJ** Hearty, frank, decisive, leaders. Usually good in anything that requires reasoning and intelligent talk. May sometimes be more positive than their experience in an area warrants.

The MBTI is used for understanding such things as communication, motivation, teamwork, work styles, and leadership. For example, it can be used by salespeople or executives who want to become more effective at interpersonal communication by learning things about their own personality styles and the way they are perceived by others. The MBTI can help develop teams by matching team members with assignments that allow them to capitalize on their preferences and helping employees understand how the different preferences of team members can lead to useful problem solving.[16] For example, employees with an Intuitive preference can be assigned brainstorming tasks. Employees with a Sensing preference can be given the responsibility of evaluating ideas.

Research on the validity, reliability, and effectiveness of the MBTI is inconclusive.[17] People who take the MBTI find it a positive experience and say it helps them change their behavior. MBTI scores appear to be related to one's occupation. Analysis of managers' MBTI scores in the United States, England, Latin America, and Japan suggests that a large majority of all managers have certain personality types (ISTJ, INTJ, ESTJ, or ENTJ). However, MBTI scores are not necessarily stable or reliable over time. Studies administering the MBTI at two different times found that as few as 24 percent of those who took the test were classified as the same type the second time.

The MBTI is a valuable tool for understanding communication styles and the ways people prefer to interact with others. Because it does not measure how well employees perform their preferred functions, it should not be used to appraise performance or evaluate employees' promotion potential. Furthermore, MBTI types should not be viewed as unchangeable personality patterns.

Assessment Center.   The **assessment center** is a process in which multiple raters or evaluators (also known as assessors) evaluate employees' performance on a number of exercises.[18] An assessment center is usually held at an off-site location such as a conference center. From 6 to 12 employees usually participate at one time. Assessment centers are primarily used to identify if employees have the personality characteristics, administrative skills, and interpersonal skills needed for managerial jobs. They are also increasingly being used to identify if employees have the necessary skills to work in teams.

The types of exercises used in assessment centers include leaderless group discussions, interviews, in-baskets, and role plays.[19] In a **leaderless group discussion,** a team of five to seven employees must work together to solve an assigned problem within a certain time period. The problem may involve buying and selling supplies, nominating a subordinate for an award, or assembling a product. An **in-basket** is a simulation of the administrative tasks of the manager's job. The exercise includes a variety of documents that may appear in the in-basket on a manager's desk. The participant is asked to read the materials and decide how to respond to them. Responses might include delegating tasks, scheduling meetings, writing replies, or completely ignoring the memo!

Role plays refer to the participant taking the part or role of a manager or other employee. For example, an assessment center participant may be asked to take the role of a manager who has to give a negative performance review to a subordinate. The participant is provided with information regarding the subordinate's performance. The participant is asked to prepare for and actually hold a 45-minute meeting with the subordinate to discuss the performance problems. The role of the subordinate is played by a manager or other member of the assessment center design team or the company. The assessment center might also include testing. Interest and aptitude tests may also be used to evaluate employees' vocabulary, general mental ability, and reasoning skills. Personality tests may be used to determine if employees can get along with others, their tolerance for ambiguity, and other traits related to success as a manager.

The exercises in the assessment center are designed to measure employees' administrative and interpersonal skills. Skills that are typically measured include leadership, oral communication, written communication, judgment, organizational ability, and stress tolerance. Table 9–4 shows an example of the skills measured by the assessment center. As we see, each exercise allows participating employees to demonstrate several skills. For example, the exercise requiring scheduling to meet production demands evaluates employees' administrative

TABLE 9–4   Examples of Skills Measured by Assessment Center Exercises

	Exercises				
	In-basket	*Scheduling Exercise*	*Leaderless Group Discussion*	*Personality Test*	*Role Play*
SKILLS					
Leadership (Dominance, coaching, influence, resourcefulness)	X		X	X	X
Problem solving (Judgment)	X	X	X		X
Interpersonal (Sensitivity, conflict resolution, cooperation, oral communication)			X	X	X
Administrative (Organizing, planning, written communications)	X	X	X		
Personal (Stress tolerance, confidence)			X	X	X

X indicates Skill Measured by Exercise

and problem-solving abilities. The leaderless group discussion measures interpersonal skills such as sensitivity toward others, stress tolerance, and oral communications skills.

Managers are usually used as assessors. The managers are trained to look for employees' behaviors that are related to the skills that will be assessed. Typically, each assessor is assigned to observe and record one or two employees' behaviors in each exercise. The assessors review their notes and rate the employee's level of skills. (For example, 5 = high level of leadership skills, 1 = low level of leadership skills.) After all employees have completed the exercises, the assessors meet to discuss their observations of each employee. They compare their ratings and try to agree on each employee's rating for each skill.

Research suggests that assessment center ratings are related to performance, salary level, and career advancement.[20] Assessment centers may also be useful for development purposes because employees who participate in the process receive feedback regarding their attitudes, skill strengths, and weaknesses.[21] In some organizations, such as Eastman Kodak, training courses and development activities related to the skills evaluated in the assessment center are available to employees.

Benchmarks.   **Benchmarks**© is an instrument designed to measure important factors in being a successful manager. Items measured by Benchmarks© are based on research that examines the lessons executives learn at critical events in their careers.[22] This includes items that measure managers' skills in dealing with subordinates, acquiring resources, and creating a productive work climate. Table 9–5 shows the 16 skills and perspectives believed to be important in becoming a successful manager. These skills and perspectives have been shown to relate to performance evaluations, bosses' ratings of promotability, and actual promotions received.[23] To get a complete picture of managers' skills, the managers' supervisors, their peers, and the managers themselves all complete the instrument. A summary report presenting the self-ratings and ratings by others is provided to the manager along with information about how the ratings compare with those of other managers. A development guide with examples of experiences that enhance each of the skills and how successful managers use the skills is also available.

Performance Appraisals and 360-Degree Feedback Systems.   **Performance appraisal** is the process of measuring employees' performance. There are several different approaches for measuring performance. These include ranking employees, rating their work behaviors, rating the extent to which employees have desirable traits believed to be necessary for job success (e.g., leadership), and directly measuring the results of work performance (e.g., productivity).

These approaches can be useful for employee development under certain conditions.[24] The appraisal system must give employees specific information about their performance problems and ways they can improve their performance. This includes providing a clear understanding of the differences between current performance and expected performance, identifying the causes of the performance discrepancy, and developing action plans to improve performance.

TABLE 9–5   Skills Related to Managerial Success

Resourcefulness	Can think strategically, engage in flexible problem-solving behavior, and work effectively with higher management.
Doing whatever it takes	Has perseverance and focus in the face of obstacles.
Being a quick study	Quickly masters new technical and business knowledge.
Building and mending relationships	Knows how to build and maintain working relationships with co-workers and external parties.
Leading subordinates	Delegates to subordinates effectively, broadens their opportunities, and acts with fairness toward them.
Compassion and sensitivity	Shows genuine interest in others and sensitivity to subordinates' needs.
Straightforwardness and composure	Is honorable and steadfast.
Setting a developmental climate	Provides a challenging climate to encourage subordinates' development.
Confronting problem subordinates	Acts decisively and fairly when dealing with problem subordinates.
Team orientation	Accomplishes tasks through managing others.
Balance between personal life and work	Balances work priorities with personal life so that neither is neglected.
Decisiveness	Prefers quick and approximate actions to slow and precise ones in many management situations.
Self-awareness	Has an accurate picture of strengths and weaknesses and is willing to improve.
Hiring talented staff	Hires talented people for his team.
Putting people at ease	Displays warmth and a good sense of humor.
Acting with flexibility	Can behave in ways that are often seen as opposites.

Source: Adapted from C. D. McCauley, M. M. Lombardo, and C. J. Usher, "Diagnosing Management Development Needs: An Instrument Based on How Managers Develop," *Journal of Management* 15 (1989): 389–403.

Managers must be trained in providing performance feedback and must provide that feedback daily. Managers also need to monitor employees' progress in carrying out the action plan.

A recent trend in the use of performance appraisals for management development is the upward feedback and 360-degree feedback process. Dow Chemical, Hallmark, Honeywell, Raychem, and AT&T, for example, use this type of appraisal process. **Upward feedback** refers to the appraisal process involving collecting subordinates' evaluations of managers' behaviors or skills. The **360-degree feedback** process (see Figure 9–2) is a special case of the upward feedback process. In 360-degree feedback systems, employees' behaviors or skills

FIGURE 9–2

360-degree feedback system

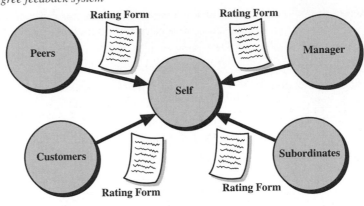

TABLE 9–6   Sample Dimension and Items from a 360-Degree Feedback Instrument

Communicating Information and Ideas

Person makes points effectively to a resistant audience.

Person is skilled at public speaking.

Person is good at disseminating information to others.

Person has good writing skills.

Person writes understandable, easy-to-read memos.

are evaluated not only by subordinates, but by peers, customers, their boss, and themselves. The raters complete a questionnaire asking them to rate the person on a number of different dimensions. Table 9–6 provides an example of the types of skills and items used in a questionnaire designed for a 360-degree feedback system. In this example, "Communicating Information and Ideas" is the dimension of the manager's behavior being evaluated. Each of the five items relates to specific aspects of written and oral communications (e.g., makes point clearly to a resistant audience). Typically, raters are asked to rate the degree to which each particular item is a strength or if development is needed.

The results of a 360-degree feedback system show the manager how he was seen on each item. The results reveal how self-evaluations differ from evaluations from the other raters. Typically, managers are asked to review their results, seek clarification from the raters, and participate in development planning designed to set specific development goals based on the strengths and weaknesses identified.[25]

TABLE 9–7   Activities in Feedback Meeting

1. **Understand strengths and weaknesses.**
   Review ratings for strengths and weaknesses.
   Identify skills or behaviors where self and other's (manager, peer, customer) ratings agree and disagree.

2. **Identify a development goal.**
   Choose a skill or behavior to develop.
   Set a clear, specific goal with a specified outcome.

3. **Identify a process for recognizing goal accomplishment.**

4. **Identify strategies for reaching the development goal.**
   Establish strategies such as reading, job experiences, courses, and relationships.
   Establish strategies for receiving feedback on your progress.
   Establish strategies for receiving reinforcement for new skill or behavior.

Table 9–7 shows the types of activities involved in development planning using the 360-degree feedback process.[26] The first step is to gain an understanding of skill strengths and weaknesses. This includes comparing self-ratings to other ratings (i.e., manager, peers, customers, subordinates) to identify areas of agreement and disagreement. A manager may overrate herself (rate herself too high) in comparison to the other raters. This means that the manager believes she has greater skill than the other raters believe. The manager may also underrate herself (rate herself too low) in comparison to the other raters. This suggests that the manager may lack confidence in her skills. After reviewing strengths and weaknesses, the manager should identify a skill or behavior to develop. Next the manager needs to identify how she will determine her progress toward meeting her development goal. The final step in the process is to provide the manager with strategies for reaching the goal. This includes three components. First, the manager needs to identify specific actions she can take to reach the goal (e.g., job experiences, courses). Next, the manager needs to identify who she will ask to provide feedback about her progress. Third, the manager needs to consider how she will find reinforcement for her progress. Recall from Chapter 5's discussion of transfer of training that it is often difficult to receive reinforcement for using trained skills in the workplace. Similarly, the manager needs to consider self-reinforcement for development progress. This reinforcement could involve buying herself a gift or rewarding herself with a night out on the town.

Benefits of 360-degree feedback include collecting multiple perspectives of managers' performance, allowing employees to compare their own personal evaluation with the views of others, and formalizing communications between employees and their internal and external customers. For example, Robert Allen, a high-level AT&T executive, now more freely airs his opinions in executive committee meetings based on the feedback he received from his subordinates as part of a 360-degree feedback system. Several studies have shown that performance improvement and behavior change occur as a result of participating in upward feedback and 360-degree feedback systems.[27]

Potential limitations of 360-degree feedback systems include the time demands placed on the raters to complete the evaluation, managers seeking to identify and punish raters who provided negative information, the need to have a facilitator to help interpret results, and companies' failure to provide ways that managers can act on the feedback they receive (e.g, development planning, meeting with raters, taking courses).

In developing (or hiring a consultant to develop) a 360-degree feedback system, several factors are necessary for the system to be effective. The system must provide reliable or consistent ratings; feedback must be job-related (valid); the system must be easy to use, understandable, and relevant; and the system must lead to managerial development. Important issues to consider include[28]

- Who will the raters be?
- How will you maintain confidentiality of the raters?
- What behaviors and skills are job-related?
- How will you ensure full participation and complete responses from every employee who is asked to be a rater?
- What will the feedback report include?
- How will you ensure that managers receive and act on the feedback?

New technology has allowed 360-degree questionnaires to be delivered electronically to the raters via their personal computers. This increases the number of completed questionnaires returned, makes it easier to process the information, and makes it quicker to provide feedback reports to managers.

Regardless of the assessment method used, the information must be shared with the employee for development to occur. Along with the assessment information, the employee needs suggestions for correcting skill weaknesses and using skills already learned. These suggestions might be to participate in training courses or develop skills through new job experiences. Based on the assessment information and available development opportunities, employees should develop an action plan to guide their self-improvement efforts.

Job Experiences

Most employee development occurs through job experiences.[29] **Job experiences** refer to relationships, problems, demands, tasks, or other features that employees face in their jobs. A major assumption of using job experiences for employee development is that development is most likely to occur when there is a mismatch between the employee's skills and past experiences and the skills required for the job. To be successful in their jobs, employees must stretch their skills—that is, they must be forced to learn new skills, apply their skills and knowledge in a new way, and master new experiences.[30]

Most of what we know about development through job experiences comes from a series of studies conducted by the Center for Creative Leadership.[31] Executives were asked to identify key events in their careers that made a difference in their managerial styles and the lessons they learned from these experiences. The key events included those involving the job assignment (e.g., fix a failing operation), those involving interpersonal relationships (e.g., getting along with supervisors), and making transitions (e.g., handling situations in which the executive did not have the necessary education or work background). Job demands and what employees can learn from them are shown in Table 9–8. One concern in the use of demanding job experiences for employee development is whether they are viewed as positive or negative stressors. Job experiences that are seen as positive stressors challenge employees to stimulate learning. Job challenges viewed as negative stressors create high levels of harmful stress for employees who are exposed to them. Recent research suggests that all job demands, with the exception of obstacles, are related to learning.[32] Managers reported that obstacles and job demands related to creating change were more likely to lead to negative stress than other job demands. This suggests that companies should carefully weigh the potential negative consequences before placing employees in development assignments involving obstacles or creation of change.

Although research on development through job experiences has focused on executives and managers, line employees can also learn from job experiences. As we noted earlier, for a work team to be successful, its members now need the kinds of skills that only managers were once thought to need (e.g., dealing directly with customers, analyzing data to determine product quality, resolving conflict among team members). Besides the development that occurs when a team is formed, employees can further develop their skills by switching work roles within the team.

Figure 9–3 shows the various ways that job experiences can be used for employee development. These include enlarging the current job, job rotation, transfers, promotions, downward moves and temporary assignments with other organizations.

Enlarging the Current Job.   Job enlargement refers to adding challenges or new responsibilities to an employee's current job. This could include special project assignments, switching roles within a work team, or researching new ways to serve clients and customers. For example, an engineering employee may be asked to join a task force charged with developing new career paths for technical employees. Through this project work, the engineer may be asked to take leadership for certain aspects of career path development (such as reviewing the company's career development process). As a result, the engineer has the opportunity not only to learn about the company's career development system, but also to use leadership and organizational skills to help the task force reach its goals.

TABLE 9–8 Job Demands and the Lessons Employees Learn from Them

Making transitions	*Unfamiliar responsibilities:* The manager must handle responsibilities that are new, very different, or much broader than previous one.
	Proving yourself: The manager has added pressure to show others she can handle the job.
Creating change	*Developing new directions:* The manager is responsible for starting something new in the organization, making strategic changes in the business, carrying out a reorganization, or responding to rapid changes in the business environment.
	Inherited problems: The manager has to fix problems created by a former incumbent or take over problem employees.
	Reduction decisions: Decisions about shutting down operations or staff reductions have to be made.
	Problems with employees: Employees lack adequate experience, are incompetent, or are resistant.
Having high level of responsibility	*High stakes:* Clear deadlines, pressure from senior managers, high visibility, and responsibility for key decisions make success or failure in this job clearly evident.
	Managing business diversity: The scope of the job is large with responsibilities for multiple functions, groups, products, customers, or markets.
	Job overload: The sheer size of the job requires a large investment of time and energy.
	Handling external pressure: External factors that affect the busines (e.g., negotiating with unions or government agencies; working in a foreign culture; coping with serious community problems) must be dealt with.
Being involved in nonauthority relationships	*Influencing without authority:* Getting the job done requires influencing peers, higher management, external parties, or other key people over whom the manager has no direct authority.
Facing obstacles	*Adverse business conditions:* The business unit or product line faces financial problems or difficult economic conditions.
	Lack of top management support: Senior management is reluctant to provide direction, support, or resources for current work or new projects.
	Lack of personal support: The manager is excluded from key networks and gets little support and encouragement from others.
	Difficult boss: The manager's opinions or management styles differs from those of the boss, or the boss has major shortcomings.

Source: C. D. McCauley, L. J. Eastman, and J. Ohlott, "Linking Management Selection and Development through Stretch Assignments," *Human Resource Management* 84 (1995): 93–115. Copyright © 1995 John Wiley and Sons, Inc. Reprinted by permission of John Wiley and Sons, Inc.

FIGURE 9–3

How job experiences are used for employee development

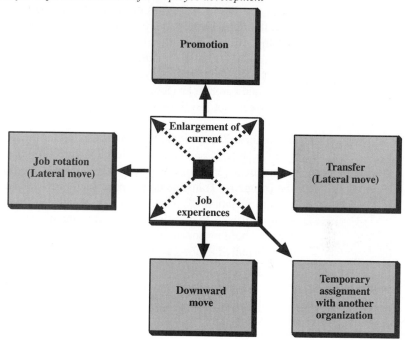

Job Rotation.   **Job rotation** involves providing employees with a series of job assignments in various functional areas of the company or movement among jobs in a single functional area or department. For example, at McDonnell Douglas the job rotation program in finance is within the finance function because employees need to understand all aspects of budgeting. Greyhound Financial Corporation has a job rotation program known as muscle-building for high-potential executive managers.[33] Managers are put in departments where they will have to perform tasks different from those they have performed in the past. They maintain their titles and compensation levels while moving through the assignments, which vary in terms of status. Employees' time spent in each job varies depending on the assignment's purpose. In the Greyhound program, assignments last two years.

Job rotation helps employees gain an overall appreciation of the company's goals, increases their understanding of different company functions, develops a network of contacts, and improves their problem-solving and decision-making skills.[34] Job rotation has also been shown to be related to skill acquisition, salary growth, and promotion rates. There are several potential problems with job rotation from both the employee's and the work unit's points of view. The rotation may create a short-term perspective on problems and solutions in employees being rotated and their peers. Employees' satisfaction and motivation may be adversely affected because they find it difficult to develop functional specialties and they don't spend enough time in one position to receive a challenging assignment. Productivity losses and work load increases may be experienced by both the department gaining a rotating employee and the department losing the employee due to training demands and loss of a resource.

Table 9–9 shows characteristics of effective job rotation systems. As we see, effective job rotation systems are linked to the company's training, development, and career management systems. Also, job rotation is used for all types of employees, not just those with managerial potential.

Transfers, Promotions, and Downward Moves.   Upward, lateral, and downward mobility is available for development purposes in most companies.[35] In a **transfer,** an employee is given a different job assignment in a different area of the company. Transfers do not necessarily involve increased job responsibilities or compensation. They are likely lateral moves (a move to a job with similar responsibilities). **Promotions** are advancements into positions with greater challenges, more responsibility, and more authority than in the previous job. Promotions usually include pay increases.

Transfers may involve relocation within the United States or to another country. They can be stressful for a number of reasons. The employee's work role changes. If the employee has a family, they have to join a new community. Employed spouses may have to find new employment. Transfers disrupt employees' daily lives, interpersonal relationships, and work habits.[36] They have to find new housing, shopping, health care, and leisure facilities, and they may be many miles from the emotional support of friends and family. They also have to learn a new set of work norms and procedures as well as develop interpersonal

---

TABLE 9–9   Characteristics of Effective Job Rotation Systems

1. Job rotation is used to develop skills as well as give employees experience needed for managerial positions.
2. Employees understand specific skills that will be developed by rotation.
3. Job rotation is used for all levels and types of employees.
4. Job rotation is linked with the career management process so employees know the development needs addressed by each job assignment.
5. Benefits of rotation are maximized and costs are minimized through managing timing of rotations to reduce work load costs and help employees understand job rotation's role in their development plans.
6. All employees have equal opportunities for job rotation assignments regardless of their demographic group.

Source: Based on L. Cheraskin and M. Campion, "Study Clarifies Job Rotation Benefits," *Personnel Journal* (November 1996): 31–38.

relationships with their new managers and peers, and they are expected to be as productive in their new jobs as they were in their old jobs even though they may know very little about the products, services, processes, or employees for which they are responsible.

Because transfers can be anxiety provoking, many companies have difficulty getting employees to accept them. Research has identified the employee characteristics associated with a willingness to accept transfers:[37] high career ambitions, a belief that one's future with the company is promising, and a belief that accepting a transfer is necessary for success in the company. Employees who are not married and not active in the community are most willing to accept transfers. Among married employees, the spouse's willingness to move is the most important influence on whether an employee will accept a transfer.

A **downward move** occurs when an employee is given a reduced level of responsibility and authority.[38] This may involve a move to another position at the same level but with less authority and responsibility (lateral demotion), a temporary cross-functional move, or a demotion because of poor performance. Temporary cross-functional moves to lower-level positions, which give employees experience working in different functional areas, are most frequently used for employee development. For example, engineers who want to move into management often take lower-level positions (e.g., shift supervisor) to develop their management skills.

Because of the psychological and tangible rewards of promotions (e.g., an increased feeling of self-worth, high salary, and higher status in the company), employees are more willing to accept promotions than they are to accept lateral or downward moves. Promotions are most readily available when a company is profitable and growing. When a company is restructuring and/or experiencing stable or declining profits, especially if a large number of employees are interested in promotions and the company tends to rely on the external labor market to staff higher-level positions, promotion opportunities may be limited.[39]

Unfortunately, many employees have difficulty associating transfers and downward moves with development. They see them as punishments rather than as opportunities to develop skills that will help them achieve long-term success with the company. Many employees decide to leave a company rather than accept a transfer. Companies need to successfully manage transfers not only because of the costs of replacing employees but because of the costs directly associated with managing them. For example, GTE spends approximately $60 million a year on home purchases and other relocation costs such as temporary housing and relocation allowances.[40] One challenge companies face is learning how to use transfers and downward moves as development opportunities—convincing employees that accepting these opportunities will result in long-term benefits for them.

To ensure that employees accept transfers, promotions, and downward moves as development opportunities, companies can provide[41]

- Information about the content, challenges, and potential benefits of the new job and location.

- Involvement in the transfer decision by sending the employees to preview the new locations and giving them information about the community and other employment opportunities.
- Clear performance objectives and early feedback about their job performance.
- A host at the new location who will help them adjust to the new community and workplace.
- Information about how the job opportunity will affect their income, taxes, mortgage payments, and other expenses.
- Reimbursement and assistance in selling, purchasing, and/or renting a place to live.
- An orientation program for the new location and job.
- A guarantee that the new job experiences will support the employee's career plans.
- Assistance for dependent family members including helping to identify schools as well as child and elder care options.
- Help for the spouse in identifying and marketing his skills and finding employment.

Temporary Assignment with Other Organizations.   Two companies can agree to exchange employees. First Chicago National Bank and Kodak participated in an employee exchange program so that the two companies could better understand each other's business and how to improve the services provided.[42] For example, an employee from First Chicago helped the business imaging division of Kodak identify applications for compact disc technology. The Kodak employee helped First Chicago understand areas within the bank that could benefit from imaging technology.

Interpersonal Relationships

Employees can also develop skills and increase their knowledge about the company and its customers by interacting with a more experienced organizational member. Mentoring and coaching are two types of interpersonal relationships used to develop employees.

Mentoring.   A **mentor** is an experienced, productive senior employee who helps develop a less experienced employee (the protege). Most mentoring relationships develop informally as a result of interests or values shared by mentor and protege. Research suggests that employees with certain personality characteristics (e.g., high needs for power and achievement, emotional stability, ability to adapt their behavior based on the situation) are more likely to seek a mentor and be an attractive protege for a mentor.[43]

Mentoring relationships can also develop as part of a planned company effort to bring together successful senior employees with less experienced employees.

Developing Successful Mentoring Programs.   Although many mentoring relationships develop informally, one major advantage of formalized mentoring programs is that they ensure access to mentors for all employees, regardless of gender or race. An additional advantage is that participants in the mentoring relationship tend to know what is expected of them.[44] One limitation of formal mentoring programs is that mentors may not be able to provide counseling and coaching in a relationship that has been artificially created.[45]

Table 9–10 presents characteristics of a successful formal mentoring program. Mentors should be chosen based on interpersonal and technical skills. They also need to be trained. For example, New York Hospital–Cornell Medical Center developed a mentoring program for housekeeping employees. Each mentor has 5 to 10 proteges who meet on a quarterly basis. To qualify as mentors employees must receive outstanding performance evaluations, demonstrate strong interpersonal skills, and be able to perform basic cleaning tasks and essential duties of all housekeeping positions including safety procedures (such as handling infectious waste).

Mentors undergo a two-day training program that emphasizes communication skills. They are taught how to convey information about the job and give directions effectively without criticizing employees.[46]

TABLE 9–10   Characteristics of Successful Formal Mentoring Programs

1. Mentor and protege participation is voluntary. Relationship can be ended at any time without fear of punishment.

2. Mentor–protege matching process does not limit the ability of informal relationships to develop. For example, a mentor pool can be established to allow proteges to choose from a variety of qualified mentors.

3. Mentors are chosen on the basis of their past record in developing employees, willingness to serve as a mentor, and evidence of positive coaching, communication, and listening skills.

4. The purpose of the program is clearly understood. Projects and activities that the mentor and protege are expected to complete are specified.

5. The length of the program is specified. Mentor and protege are encouraged to pursue the relationship beyond the formal time period.

6. A minimum level of contact between the mentor and protege is specified.

7. Proteges are encouraged to contact one another to discuss problems and share successes.

8. The mentor program is evaluated. Interviews with mentors and proteges are used to obtain immediate feedback regarding specific areas of dissatisfaction. Surveys are used to gather more detailed information regarding benefits received from participating in the program.

9. Employee development is rewarded, which signals managers that mentoring and other development activities are worth their time and effort.

Benefits of Mentoring Relationships.   Both mentors and proteges can benefit from a mentoring relationship. Research suggests that mentors provide career and psychosocial support to their proteges. **Career support** includes coaching, protection, sponsorship, and providing challenging assignments, exposure, and visibility. **Psychosocial support** includes serving as a friend and a role model, providing positive regard and acceptance, and providing an outlet for the protege to talk about anxieties and fears. Additional benefits for proteges include higher rates of promotion, larger salaries, and greater organizational influence.[47]

Mentoring relationships provide opportunities for mentors to develop their interpersonal skills and increase their feelings of self-esteem and worth to the organization. Mentors in the New York Hospital–Cornell program receive a small financial reward (a $1 per hour raise), but they support the program because they are recognized for helping less experienced employees. For individuals in technical fields such as engineering and health services, the protege may help them gain knowledge about important new scientific developments in their field and therefore prevent them from becoming technically obsolete.

Purposes of Mentoring Programs.   Mentor programs are used to socialize new employees and to increase the likelihood of skill transfer from training to the work setting. Mentor programs may also be developed specifically for women and minorities to enable them to gain the experience and skills needed for managerial positions. Consider the New York Hospital–Cornell Medical Center mentoring program just discussed. The program is designed to help new employees more quickly learn housekeeping duties and understand the culture of the hospital. One benefit of the program is that new employees' performance deficiencies are more quickly corrected. Although formal mentoring of new employees lasts only two weeks, mentors are available to provide support many months later.

Steve Croft and Janet Graham have met at least once a month for the past two years to share problems, information, and advice at E. I. du Pont de Nemours and Company corporate headquarters.[48] He is a planning manager in its research division. She is an administrative assistant in the toxicology lab where Steve used to work. Croft and Graham are part of the DuPont Company's eight-year-old mentoring program. Mentees choose from a list of volunteers— mentors (managers and executives) whose skills and experience they want to learn about. Croft, the mentor, has provided Graham, the mentee, with answers to her questions about corporate programs and given her the opportunity to meet scientists and managers in the company. Graham has also learned more about other departments' roles in the company and budgetary priorities. Croft has also benefited from the relationship. He has learned about how management decisions affect employees. For example, when the toxicology lab was forced to begin to charge departments for its services (rather than being supported from the company's general fund), Croft learned about employees' reactions and anxieties from Graham.

Because of the lack of potential mentors, no formal reward system supporting mentoring, and belief that the quality of mentorships developed in a formal program is poorer than informal mentoring relationships, some companies have initiated group mentoring programs. In **group mentoring programs,** a successful senior employee is paired with a group of four to six less experienced proteges. One potential advantage of the mentoring group is that proteges can learn from each other as well as from a more experienced senior employee. The leader helps proteges understand the organization, guides them in analyzing their experiences, and helps them clarify career directions. Each member of the group may have specific assignments to complete or the group may work together on an issue.[49]

Coaching Relationships.   A **coach** is a peer or manager who works with an employee to motivate him, help him develop skills, and provide reinforcement and feedback. There are three roles that a coach can play.[50] Part of coaching may be one-on-one with an employee (e.g., giving feedback). Another role is to help employees to learn for themselves. This involves helping them find experts who can help them with their concerns and teaching them how to obtain feedback from others. Third, coaching may involve providing resources such as mentors, courses, or job experiences that the employee may not be able to gain access to without the coach's help. For example, at National Semiconductor, managers participate in a 360-degree feedback program. Each manager selects another manager as a coach. They both attend a coaching workshop that focuses on skills such as active listening. In the workshop a coaching process is presented that includes creating a contract outlining members' roles and expectations, discussing 360-degree feedback, and identifying specific improvement goals and a plan for achieving them. After each pair works alone for six to eight months, they evaluate their progress.

To develop coaching skills, training programs need to focus on four issues related to managers' reluctance to provide coaching.[51] First, managers may be reluctant to discuss performance issues even with a competent employee because they want to avoid confrontation—especially if the manager is less of an expert than the employee. Second, managers may be better able to identify performance problems than to help employees solve them. Third, managers may feel that the employee might interpret coaching as criticism. Fourth, as companies downsize and operate with fewer employees, managers may feel that there is not enough time for coaching.

The Development Planning Process

The **development planning process** involves identifying development needs, choosing a development goal, identifying the actions that need to be taken by the employee and the company to achieve the goal, determining how progress toward goal attainment will be measured, and establishing a timetable for

TABLE 9–11   Steps and Responsibilities in the Development Planning Process

Employee Responsibility	Company Responsibility
Step	
1 *Opportunity.* How do I need to improve?	Provide assessment information to identify strengths, weaknesses, interests, and values.
2 *Goal identification.* What do I want to develop?	Provide development planning guide. Manager has developmental discussion with employee.
3 *Criteria.* How will I know I am making progress?	Manager provides feedback.
4 *Actions.* What will I do to reach my development goal?	Provide courses, assessment, job experiences, and relationships.
5 *Time.* What is my timetable?	Manager follows up on progress toward development goal and helps employee set a realistic timetable for goal achievement.

development.[52] Table 9–11 shows the development planning process, identifying responsibilities of employees and the company. An emerging trend in development is that the employee must initiate the development planning process.[53] Note that the development approach used is dependent on the needs and developmental goal. To identify development needs, employees must consider what they want to do, what they are interested in doing, what they can do, and what others expect of them. A development need can result from gaps between current capabilities and/or interests and the type of work or position that the employee wants in the future.

How might the development planning process work? Take the example of Robert Brown, a program manager in an information systems department. He needs to increase his knowledge of available project management software. His performance appraisal indicated that only 60 percent of the projects he is working on are being approved due to incomplete information. (Assessment identified his development need.) As a result, Robert and his manager agree that his development goal is to increase his knowledge of available project management software. This software can increase his effectiveness in project management. To boost his knowledge of such software, Robert will read articles (formal education), meet with software vendors, and contact vendors' customers for their evaluations of the project management software they have used (job experiences). His manager will provide the names of customers to contact. Robert and his manager set six months as the target date for completing these activities.

Summary

This chapter emphasized that there are several development methods: formal education, assessment, job experiences, and interpersonal relationships. Most companies use one or more of these approaches to develop employees. Formal education involves enrolling employees in courses or seminars offered by the company or educational institutions. Assessment involves measuring the employees' performance, behavior, skills, and/or personality characteristics. Job experiences include job enlargement, rotating to a new job, promotions, downward moves, temporary assignments and transfers. A more experienced senior employee (a mentor) can help employees understand the company and gain exposure and visibility to key persons in the organization. Part of a manager's job responsibility may be to coach employees. Regardless of the development approaches used, employees need a development plan to identify the type of development needed, development goals, the best approach for development, and a means to determine whether development goals have been reached. For development plans to be effective, both the employee and the company have responsibilities that need to be completed.

Key Terms

development   218
formal education programs   220
assessment   223
Myers-Briggs Type Indicator
  (MBTI)   224
assessment center   226
leaderless group discussion   226
in-basket   226
role plays   227
Benchmarks©   228
performance appraisal   228
upward feedback   229
360-degree feedback   229

job experiences   232
job enlargement   233
job rotation   235
transfer   236
promotions   236
downward move   237
mentor   238
career support   240
psychosocial support   240
group mentoring programs   241
coach   241
development planning process   241

Discussion Questions

1. How could assessment be used to create a productive work team?
2. List and explain the characteristics of effective 360-degree feedback systems.
3. Why do companies develop formal mentoring programs? What are the potential benefits for the mentor and for the protege?

4. Your boss is interested in hiring a consultant to help identify potential managers from current employees of a fast food restaurant. The manager's job is to help wait on customers and prepare food during busy times, oversee all aspects of restaurant operations (including scheduling, maintenance, on-the-job training, and food purchase), and motivate employees to provide high-quality service. The manager is also responsible for resolving disputes between employees. The position involves working under stress and coordinating several activities at one time. She asks you to outline the type of assessment program you believe would best identify employees who could be successful managers. What will you tell her?

5. Many employees are unwilling to relocate geographically because they like their current community, and spouses and children prefer not to move. As a result, it is difficult to develop employees using job experiences that require relocation (eg. transfer to a new location). How could an employee's current job be changed to develop his leadership skills?

6. What is coaching? Is there one type of coaching? Explain.

7. Discuss reasons why many managers are reluctant to coach their employees.

Application Assignments

1. Your manager wants you to develop a one-page form for development planning. Develop the form. Provide a rationale for each category you include on the form.

2. Read the article "A Software Engineer Becomes a Manager with Many Regrets" in *The Wall Street Journal* (May 14, 1997): A1, A14. It describes problems that an engineer faced in trying to manage a software development team. Write a two-page memo outlining a plan for the company to develop engineers to lead a software development team.

Endnotes

1. M. London, *Managing the Training Enterprise* (San Francisco: Jossey-Bass, 1989).

2. R. W. Pace, P. C. Smith, and G. E. Mills, *Human Resource Development* (Englewood Cliffs, NJ: Prentice-Hall, 1991); W. Fitzgerald, "Training versus Development," *Training and Development Journal* (May 1992): 81–84; R. A. Noe, S. L. Wilk, E. J. Mullen, and J. E. Wanek, "Employee Development: Issues in Construct Definition and Investigation of Antecedents," in *Improving Training Effectiveness in Work Organizations,* ed. J. K. Ford (Mahwah, NJ: Lawrence Erlbaum, 1997): 153–89.

3. Campbell, "HR Development Strategies"; in *Developing Human Resources,* ed. K. N. Wexley (Washington, DC: BNA Books. 1991): 5-1–5-34; M. A. Sheppeck and C. A. Rhodes, "Management Development: Revised Thinking in Light of New Events of Strategic Importance," *Human Resource Planning* 11 (1988): 159–72; B. Keys and J. Wolf, "Management Education: Current Issues and Emerging

Trends," *Journal of Management* 14 (1988): 205–29; L. M. Saari, T. R. Johnson, S. D. McLaughlin, and D. Zimmerle, "A Survey of Management Training and Education Practices in U.S. Companies," *Personnel Psychology* 41 (1988): 731–44.

4. K. Walter, "The MTA Travels Far with Its Future Managers Program," *Personnel Journal* (August 1995): 68–72.

5. T. A. Stewart, "GE Keeps Those Ideas Coming," *Fortune* (August 12, 1991): 41–49; N. M. Tichy, "GE's Crotonville: A Staging Ground for a Corporate Revolution," *The Executive* 3 (1989): 99–106.

6. J. Bolt, *Executive Development* (New York: Harper Business, 1989); H. S. Jonas, R. E. Fry, and S. Srivasta, "The Office of the CEO: Understanding the Executive Experience," *Academy of Management Executive* 4 (1990): 36–48; J. Noel and R. Charam, "GE Brings Global Thinking to Light," *Training and Development Journal* (July 1992): 29–33; B. O'Reilly, "How Execs Learn Now," *Fortune* (April 5, 1993); M. A. Hitt, B. B. Tyler, C. Hardee, and D. Park, "Understanding Strategic Intent in the Global Marketplace," *Academy of Management Executive* 9 (1995): 12–19.

7. J. A. Byrne, "Virtual Business Schools," *Business Week* (October 23, 1995): 64–68.

8. T. Bartlett, "The Hottest Campus on the Internet," *Business Week* (October 20, 1997): 77–80.

9. J. Reingold, "Corporate America Goes to School," *Business Week* (October 20, 1997): 66–72.

10. Ibid.

11. L. Bongiorno, "How'm I Doing," *Business Week* (October 23, 1995): 72, 74.

12. T. A. Stewart, "GE Keeps Those Ideas Coming," *Fortune* (August 12, 1991): 41–49.

13. G. P. Hollenbeck, "What Did You Learn in School? Studies of a University Executive Program," *Human Resource Planning* 14 (1991): 247–60.

14. A. Howard and D. W. Bray, *Managerial Lives in Transition: Advancing Age and Changing Times* (New York: Guilford, 1988); Bolt, *Executive Development* J. R. Hinrichs and G. P. Hollenbeck, "Leadership Development," in *Developing Human Resources,* ed. K. N. Wexley (Washington, DC: BNA Books, 1991): 5-221–5-237.

15. S. K. Hirsch, *MBTI Team Member's Guide* (Palo Alto, CA: Consulting Psychologists Press, 1992); A. L. Hammer, *Introduction to Type and Careers* (Palo Alto, CA: Consulting Psychologists Press, 1993).

16. A. Thorne and H. Gough, *Portraits of Type* (Palo Alto, CA: Consulting Psychologists Press, 1991).

17. Druckman and Bjork, *In the Mind's Eye: Enhancing Human Performance* (Washington, DC: National Academy Press, 1991); M. H. McCaulley, "The Myers-Briggs Type Indicator and Leadership," in *Measures of Leadership,* eds. K. E. Clark and M. B. Clark (West Orange, NJ: Leadership Library of America, 1990): 381–418.

18. G. C. Thornton III and W. C. Byham, *Assessment Centers and Managerial Performance* (New York: Academic Press, 1982); L. F. Schoenfeldt and J. A. Steger, "Identification and Development of Management Talent," in *Research in Personnel and Human Resource Management,* vol. 7, eds. K. N. Rowland and G. Ferris (Greenwich, CT: JAI Press, 1989): 151–81.

19. Thornton and Byham, *Assessment Centers and Managerial Performance.*

20. B. B. Gaugler, D. B. Rosenthal, G. C. Thornton, III, and C. Bentson, "Meta-analysis of Assessment Center Validity," *Journal of Applied Psychology* 72 (1987): 493–511; D. W. Bray, R. J. Campbell, and D. L. Grant, *Formative Years in Business: A Long-Term AT&T Study of Managerial Lives* (New York: Wiley, 1974).

21. R. G. Jones and M. D. Whitmore, "Evaluating Developmental Assessment Centers as Interventions," *Personnel Psychology* 48 (1995): 377–88.

22. C. D. McCauley and M. M. Lombardo, "Benchmarks: An Instrument for Diagnosing Managerial Strengths and Weaknesses," in *Measures of Leadership:* 535–45.

23. C. D. McCauley, M. M. Lombardo, and C. J. Usher, "Diagnosing Management Development Needs: An Instrument Based on How Managers Develop," *Journal of Management* 15 (1989): 389–403.

24. S. B. Silverman, "Individual Development through Performance Appraisal," in *Developing Human Resources,* ed. K. N. Wexley (Washington, DC: BNA Books, 1991): 5-120–5-151.

25. J. S. Lublin, "Turning the Tables: Underlings Evaluate Bosses," *The Wall Street Journal* (October 4, 1994): B1, B14; B. O'Reilly, "360 Feedback Can Change Your Life," *Fortune* (October 17, 1994): 93–100; J. F. Milliman, R. A. Zawacki, C. Norman, L. Powell, and J. Kirksey, "Companies Evaluate Employees from All Perspectives," *Personnel Journal* (November 1994): 99–103.

26. Center for Creative Leadership, *Skillscope for Managers: Development Planning Guide* (Greensboro, NC: Center for Creative Leadership, 1992); G. Yukl and R. Lepsinger, "360 Feedback," *Training* (December 1995): 45–50.

27. L. Atwater, P. Roush, and A. Fischthal, "The Influence of Upward Feedback on Self- and Follower Ratings of Leadership," *Personnel Psychology* 48 (1995): 35–59; J. F. Hazucha, S. A. Hezlett, and R. J. Schneider, "The Impact of 360-Degree Feedback on Management Skill Development," *Human Resource Management* 32 (1993): 325–51; J. W. Smither, M. London, N. Vasilopoulos, R. R. Reilly, R. E. Millsap, and N. Salvemini, "An Examination of the Effects of an Upward Feedback Program Over Time," *Personnel Psychology* 48 (1995): 1–34.

28. D. Bracken, "Straight Talk about Multirater Feedback," *Training and Development* (September 1994): 44–51.

29. M. W. McCall, Jr., M. M. Lombardo, and A. M. Morrison, *Lessons of Experience* (Lexington, MA: Lexington Books, 1988).

30. R. S. Snell, "Congenial Ways of Learning: So Near yet So Far," *Journal of Management Development* 9 (1990): 17–23.

31. McCall, Lombardo, and Morrison, *Lessons of Experience;* M. W. McCall, "Developing Executives through Work Experiences," *Human Resource Planning* 11 (1988): 1–11; M. N. Ruderman, P. J. Ohlott, and C. D. McCauley, "Assessing Opportunities for Leadership Development," in *Measures of Leadership:* 547–62; C. D. McCauley, L. J. Estman, and P. J. Ohlott, "Linking Management Selection and Development through Stretch Assignments," *Human Resource Management* 34 (1995): 93–115.

32. C. D. McCauley, M. N. Ruderman, P. J. Ohlott, and J. E. Morrow, "Assessing the Developmental Components of Managerial Jobs," *Journal of Applied Psychology* 79 (1994): 544–60.

33. Management Development Report, Winter 1988/1989 (Alexandria, VA: American Society for Training and Development, 1988/1989); G. B. Northcraft, T. L. Griffith, and C. E. Shalley, "Building Top Management Muscle in a Slow Growth Environment: How Different Is Better at Greyhound Financial Corporation," *The Executive* 6 (1992): 32–41.

34. M. London, *Developing Managers* (San Francisco: Jossey-Bass, 1985); M. A. Campion, L. Cheraskin, and M. J. Stevens, "Career-Related Antecedents and Outcomes of Job Rotation," *Academy of Management Journal* 37 (1994): 1518–42; M. London, *Managing the Training Enterprise* (San Francisco: Jossey-Bass, 1989).

35. D. C. Feldman, *Managing Careers in Organizations* (Glenview, IL: Scott-Foresman, 1988).

36. J. M. Brett, L. K. Stroh, and A. H. Reilly, "Job Transfer," in *International Review of Industrial and Organizational Psychology: 1992,* eds. C. L. Cooper and I. T. Robinson (Chichester, England: John Wiley and Sons, 1992); D. C. Feldman and J. M. Brett, "Coping with New Jobs: A Comparative Study of New Hires and Job Changers," *Academy of Management Journal* 26 (1983): 258–72.

37. R. A. Noe, B. D. Steffy, and A. E. Barber, "An Investigation of the Factors Influencing Employees' Willingness to Accept Mobility Opportunities," *Personnel Psychology* 41 (1988): 559–80; S. Gould and L. E. Penley, "A Study of the Correlates of Willingness to Relocate," *Academy of Management Journal* 28 (1984): 472–78; J. Landau and T. H. Hammer, "Clerical Employees' Perceptions of Intraorganizational Career Opportunities," *Academy of Management Journal* 29 (1986): 385–405; R. P. Duncan and C. C. Perruci, "Dual Occupation Families and Migration," *American Sociological Review* 41 (1976): 252–61; J. M. Brett and A. H. Reilly, "On the Road Again: Predicting the Job Transfer Decision," *Journal of Applied Psychology* 73 (1988): 614–20.

38. D. T. Hall and L. A. Isabella, "Downward Moves and Career Development," *Organizational Dynamics* 14 (1985): 5–23.

39. H. D. Dewirst, "Career Patterns: Mobility, Specialization, and Related Career Issues," in *Contemporary Career Development Issues,* eds. R. F. Morrison and J. Adams (Hillsdale, NJ: Lawrence Erlbaum, 1991): 73–108.

40. N. C. Tompkins, "GTE Managers on the Move," *Personnel Journal* (August 1992): 86–91.

41. *J. M. Brett, "Job Transfer and Well-Being," Journal of Applied Psychology* 67 (1992): 450–63; F. J. Minor, L. A. Slade, and R. A. Myers, "Career Transitions in Changing Times," in *Contemporary Career Development Issues:* 109–120; C. C. Pinder and K. G. Schroeder, "Time to Proficiency Following Job Transfers," *Academy of Management Journal* 30 (1987): 336–53; G. Flynn, "Heck No—We Won't Go!" *Personnel Journal* (March 1996): 37–43.

42. D. Gunsch, "Customer Service Focus Prompts Employee Exchange," *Personnel Journal* (October 1992): 32–38.

43. D. B. Turban and T. W. Dougherty, "Role of Protege Personality in Receipt of Mentoring and Career Success," *Academy of Management Journal* 37 (1994): 688–702; E. A. Fagenson, "Mentoring: Who Needs It? A Comparison of Proteges and Nonproteges Needs for Power, Achievement, Affiliation, and Autonomy," 41 (1992): 48–60.

44. A. H. Geiger, "Measures for Mentors," *Training and Development Journal* (February 1992): 65–67.

45. K. E. Kram, *Mentoring at Work: Developmental Relationships in Organizational Life* (Glenview, IL: Scott-Foresman, 1985); L. L. Phillips-Jones, "Establishing a Formalized Mentoring Program," *Training and Development Journal* 2 (1983): 38–42; K. Kram, "Phases of the Mentoring Relationship," *Academy of Management Journal* 26 (1983): 608–25; G. T. Chao, P. M. Walz, and P. D. Gardner, "Formal and Informal Mentorships: A Comparison of Mentoring Functions and Contrasts with Nonmentored Counterparts," *Personnel Psychology* 45 (1992): 619–36.

46. C. M. Solomon, "Hotel Breathes Life into Hospital's Customer Service," *Personnel Journal* (October 1995): 120.

47. G. F. Dreher and R. A. Ash, "A Comparative Study of Mentoring among Men and Women in Managerial, Professional, and Technical Positions," *Journal of Applied Psychology* 75 (1990): 539–46; J. L. Wilbur, "Does Mentoring Breed Success?" *Training and Development Journal* 41 (1987): 38–41; R. A. Noe, "Mentoring Relationships for Employee Development," in *Applying Psychology in Business: The Handbook for Managers and Human Resource Professionals,* eds. J. W. Jones, B. D. Steffy, and D. W. Bray (Lexington, MA: Lexington Books, 1991): 475–82; M. M. Fagh and K. Ayers, Jr., "Police Mentors," *FBI Law Enforcement Bulletin* (January 1985): 8–13; Kram, "Phases of the Mentor Relationships"; R. A. Noe, "An Investigation of the Determinants of Successful Assigned Mentoring Relationships," *Personnel Psychology* 41 (1988): 457–79; B. J. Tepper, "Upward Maintenance Tactics in Supervisory Mentoring and Nonmentoring Relationships," *Academy of Management Journal* 38 (1995): 1191–1205; B. R. Ragins and T. A. Scandura, "Gender Differences in Expected Outcomes of Mentoring Relationships," *Academy of Management Journal* 37 (1994): 957–71.

48. F. Jossi, "Mentoring in Changing Times," *Training* (August 1997): 50–54.

49. B. Kaye and B. Jackson, "Mentoring: A Group Guide," *Training and Development* (April 1995): 23–27.

50. D. B. Peterson and M. D. Hicks, *Leader as Coach* (Minneapolis, MN: Personnel Decisions, 1996).

51. R. Zemke, "The Corporate Coach," *Training* (December 1996): 24–28.

52. L. Summers, "A Logical Approach to Development Planning," *Training and Development* 48 (1994): 22–31; D. B. Peterson and M. D. Hicks, *Development First* (Minneapolis, MN: Personnel Decisions, 1995).

53. D. T. Jaffe and C. D. Scott, "Career Development for Empowerment in a Changing Work World," in *New Directions in Career Planning and the Workplace,* ed. J. M. Kummerow (Palo Alto, CA: Consulting Psychologists Press, 1991): 33–60.

10 SPECIAL ISSUES IN TRAINING AND EMPLOYEE DEVELOPMENT

Objectives

After reading this chapter, you should be able to

1. Discuss the potential legal issues that relate to training.

2. Develop a program for effectively managing diversity.

3. Design a program for preparing employees for cross-cultural assignments.

4. Discuss the implications of a skill-based pay plan for training.

5. Discuss what a trainer needs to do to ensure that school-to-work and hard-core unemployed training programs are effective.

6. Describe the necessary steps in a program for helping dysfunctional managers.

HELPING "HARD-CORES" HELP THEMSELVES

Marriott International Inc.'s welfare-to-work program has resulted in jobs for 700 people in the past five years. Marriott currently operates the program in several large cities such as New Orleans, Atlanta, and Los Angeles, and plans to expand the program to others including Cleveland, Baltimore, and Richmond, Virginia. Marriott helps find employment for persons who would otherwise be considered to be "hard-core unemployed." Now working for Marriott as hotel employees are persons formerly on welfare because they could not find and retain jobs due to problems ranging from dropping out of high school, drug addiction, and arrest records to emotional scarring from poor marital or family relationships. Marriott's Pathways to Independence program is considered a model of how corporate-sponsored training and employment efforts can move welfare recipients to work. The six-week program consists of classroom training and work sessions in Marriott properties (e.g., hotels).

Marriott's Pathways program was developed not out of goodwill but as a way to attract employees to lower-paying jobs that were difficult to fill. The program costs about $5,000 per trainee and the government funds slightly over half the expenses. It costs approximately $900 to find a new employee to replace an employee who has left. If Marriott can keep the workers it trains two and one-half times longer than the average worker tenure, the training will pay for itself.

To qualify for the program, applicants must have a sixth grade reading level, pass a drug test, and demonstrate a desire to work. Less than 25 percent of the applicants are accepted into the program. Despite the rigorous selection process, program participants need both job skills and life management skills to succeed. Besides providing job skills, trainers have to build trainees' self-confidence and often help the employee deal with personal issues. For example, one Marriott trainer brought a pair of slacks and shoes to work for a trainee. She also made numerous phone calls to arrange child care for other trainees, and spent the afternoon visiting shelters and driving trainees to government agencies. A key problem is how to prepare workers to budget their money and manage their first paycheck. Some participants were spending all of the money they earned on entertainment and not leaving enough to pay rent and buy food. Trainers teach about checking accounts and budgeting.

Once welfare recipients who complete the Pathways program become Marriott "associates" (employees), they are provided with a toll-free phone number where questions dealing with child care, finances, school systems, and domestic and substance abuse can be answered by trained counselors. Marriott has found that the toll-free line was necessary to provide support to program graduates as well as other employees. Marriott created the service as a result of determining that its managers were spending up to 50 percent of their time counseling employees who had personal problems!

Approximately, 45 percent of the 700 Pathways participants remain with the company. Studies have shown that in some areas, such as Washington, D.C., Pathway trainees stay with the company longer than other employees. For example, one employee who had recently overcome an addiction to crack cocaine successfully completed training and received a job offer from a Residence Inn where she now serves as a housekeeper. Another program participant who could not hold down steady employment was promoted from kitchen help to housekeeping in a span of 19 months!

Training evaluation has helped Marriott to modify the program to increase the success rate of Pathway trainees. Analysis revealed that unreliable child care and drug abuse were primary causes of Pathway trainees' failing to complete training or leaving the company. Marriott is planning to use more rigorous criteria for welfare recipients to qualify for the program. Marriott plans to require trainees to have child care, transportation, and housing arrangements. It also plans to run background checks and to require participants to take drug tests before and during training. ■

Source: Based on F. Jossi, "From Welfare to Work," *Training* (April 1997): 45–50; D. Milbank, "Hiring Welfare People, Hotel Chain Finds Is Tough but Rewarding," *The Wall Street Journal* (October 31, 1996): A1, A14; D. Milbank, "Marriott Tightens Job Program Screening," *The Wall Street Journal* (July 15, 1997): A2, A12.

Introduction

The opening vignette illustrates that trainers are often forced to deal with a wide variety of important issues that fall outside of the traditional discussion of the components of instructional system design. Marriott has decided to train hard-core unemployed workers because it can not find (and retain) talented individuals in the labor market. Trainers must be prepared to provide not only adequate skills training but also training in life skills (e.g., keeping a checkbook). This is one example of how the environment (e.g., lack of skills in the labor market) influences training practices.

Other environmental pressures that influence companies include legal issues, globalization, and an increasingly diverse work force. Both trainers and managers who purchase training services must be aware of how legal issues relate to training practices, cross-cultural preparation, diversity training, and school-to-work and hard-core unemployed training programs. These issues are covered in the first part of this chapter.

The second part of the chapter covers issues that result from pressures from the company's internal environment. These pressures include the need to train managerial talent, provide training and development opportunities for all employees (regardless of their personal characteristics), and motivate employees to learn through the company's compensation system. Specifically, the second half of the chapter covers melting the glass ceiling, joint union–management training programs, succession planning programs, training dysfunctional managers, and skill-based pay systems.

Training Issues Resulting from the External Environment

Legal Issues

Table 10–1 shows potential training activities and situations that can make an employer vulnerable to legal actions. Next we describe each situation and potential implications for training.[1]

Employee Injury during a Training Activity.   On-the-job training and simulations often involve the use of work tools and equipment (e.g., welding machinery, printing press) that could cause injury if incorrectly used. Workers' compensation laws in many states make employers responsible for paying employees their salary and/or providing them with a financial settlement for injuries received during any employment-related activity such as training. Managers should ensure that (1) employees are warned of potential dangers from incorrectly using equipment and (2) safety equipment is used.

Employees or Others Injured outside a Training Session.   Managers should ensure that trainees have the necessary level of competence in knowledge, skills, and behaviors before they are allowed to operate equipment or

TABLE 10–1   Training Situations That May Result in Legal Action

- Employee injury during a training activity
- Employees or others injured outside the training session
- Breach of confidentiality or defamation
- Reproducing and using copyrighted material in training classes without permission
- Excluding women, minorities, and older Americans from training programs
- Not ensuring equal treatment while in training
- Requiring employees to attend training programs they find offensive
- Revealing discriminatory information during a training session
- Not accommodating trainees with disabilities

interact with customers. Even if a company pays for training to be conducted by a vendor it is still liable for injuries or damages resulting from the actions of poorly, incorrectly, or incompletely trained employees. A company that contracts out training to a vendor or consultant should ensure that it has liability insurance, be sure that the trainers are competent, and determine if there has been previous litigation against the trainer or the vendor providing the training. Also, trainers should be sure to keep copies of notes, activities, and training manuals that show that training procedures were correct and followed the steps provided by licensing or certification agencies (if appropriate).

Breach of Confidentiality or Defamation.   Managers should ensure that information placed in employees' files regarding performance in training activities is accurate. Also, before discussing an employee's performance in training with other employees or using training performance information for promotion or salary decisions, managers should tell employees that training performance will be used in that manner.

Reproducing and Using Copyrighted Material in Training Classes without Permission.   Copyrights protect the expression of an idea (e.g., a training manual for a software program) but not the ideas that the material contains (e.g., the use of help windows in the software program).[2] Copyrights also prohibit others from creating a product based on the original work and from copying, broadcasting, or publishing the product without permission.

The use of videotapes, learning aids, manuals, and other copyrighted materials in training classes without obtaining permission from the owner of the material is illegal. Managers should ensure that all training materials are purchased from the vendor or consultant who developed them or that permission to reproduce materials has been obtained. For example, Wilson Learning Corporation—

a major developer and distributor of training-related products—holds the copyright to sales training materials. To use the product, clients must pay Wilson Learning a fee and agree to attend a training seminar to familiarize them with the materials.

Excluding Women, Minorities, and Older Employees from Training Programs.   Two pieces of legislation make it illegal for employers to exclude women, minorities, or older persons from training programs. Title VII of the Civil Rights Act of 1964 (amended in 1991) makes it illegal to deny access to employment or deprive a person employment because of the person's race, color, religion, gender, or national origin. The Age Discrimination in Employment Act (ADEA) prohibits discrimination against persons who are over age 40. The Equal Employment Opportunity Commission (EEOC) is responsible for enforcing both the Civil Rights Act and the ADEA.

Although these two pieces of legislation have existed for several years, a study by the U.S. Department of Labor found that training experiences necessary for promotion are not as available or accessible to women and minorities compared to white males.[3] Women, minorities, and older employees can be illegally excluded from training programs by not being made aware of opportunities for training or purposeful exclusion from enrolling in training programs. Managers and trainers must ensure that stereotypes do not influence (1) decisions about who to send to training programs or (2) to whom training opportunities are communicated. For example, stereotypes such as "older workers are resistant to change" and "women are not aggressive enough for managerial positions" may result in excluding qualified women and older workers from training programs.

Not Ensuring Equal Treatment of All Employees while in Training.   Equal treatment of all trainees means that conditions of the learning environment such as opportunities for practice, feedback, and role playing are available for all trainees regardless of their background. Also, trainers should avoid jokes, stories, and props that might create a hostile learning environment.

Requiring Employees to Attend Programs That Might Be Offensive.   For example, Allstate Insurance has been the focus of several religious discrimination lawsuits by insurance agents who found Scientology principles emphasized in agent training programs to be offensive and counter to their religious beliefs (e.g., employees who met their sales goals were not to be questioned no matter how they behaved and persons who failed to meet their sales goals deserved to be harassed and treated poorly).[4]

Revealing Discriminatory Information during a Training Session.   At Lucky Store Foods, a California supermarket chain, notes taken during a diversity training program were used as evidence of discrimination.[5] In the training session supervisors were asked to verbalize their stereotypes. Some comments ("women cry more," "black women are aggressive") were derogatory toward women and minorities. The plaintiff in the case used the notes as evidence that the company conducted the training session to avoid an investigation by the Equal Employment Opportunity Commission. The case was settled out of court.

Not Accommodating Trainees with Disabilities.   The **Americans with Disabilities Act (ADA)** of 1990 prohibits individuals with disabilities from being discriminated against in the workplace. The ADA prohibits discrimination based on disability in employment practices including hiring, firing, compensation, and training. The ADA defines a disability as a physical or mental impairment that substantially limits one or more major life activities, a record of having an impairment, or being regarded as having such an impairment. This includes serious disabilities such as epilepsy, blindness, or paralysis as well as persons who have a history of heart disease, mental illness, or cancer that is currently in remission.

The ADA requires companies to make "reasonable accommodation" to the physical or mental condition of a person with a disability who is otherwise qualified unless it would impose an "undue hardship" on the organization's operations. Determination of undue hardship is made by analyzing the type and cost of the accommodation in relation to the company's financial resources. Even if the undue hardship can be justified, the ADA requires that the person with the disability be provided the option of paying that part of the cost that causes the undue hardship.

In the context of training, **reasonable accommodation** refers to making training facilities readily accessible to and usable by individuals with disabilities. Reasonable accommodation may also include modifying instructional media, adjusting training policies, and providing trainees with readers or interpreters. Employers are not required to make reasonable accommodation if the person does not request them. Employers are also not required to make reasonable accommodation if persons are not qualified to participate in training programs (e.g., they lack the prerequisite certification or educational requirements).

One example of how the ADA might influence training activities involves adventure learning. Adventure learning experiences demand a high level of physical fitness. Employees who have a disability can not be required to attend adventure learning training programs.[6] If it does not cause an undue hardship, employees should be offered an alternative program for developing the learned capabilities emphasized in the adventure learning program.

It is impossible to give specific guidelines regarding the type of accommodations that trainers and managers should make to avoid violating the ADA. It is important to identify if the training is related to "essential" job functions. That is, are the tasks or knowledge, skills, and abilities that are the focus of training fundamental to the position? Task analysis information (discussed in Chapter 3) can be used to identify essential job functions. For example, tasks that are frequently performed and critical for successful job performance would be considered essential job functions. If training relates to a function that may be performed in the job but does not have to be performed by all persons (a marginal job function), then a disability in relation to that function can not be used to exclude that person from training. To the extent that the disability makes it difficult for the person to receive training necessary to complete essential job functions, the trainer must explore whether it is possible to make reasonable accommodations.

Cross-Cultural Preparation

As we mentioned in Chapter 1, companies today are challenged to expand globally. In a recent two-year period, for example, U.S. businesses doubled their annual investment in foreign operations.[7] Such expansion is good business sense, considering the growth potential of foreign markets. China's population is so large and its demand for products and services growing so fast that some observers predict that doing business there will turn regional companies into major global players. Hard Rock Cafe is an example of a U.S. company expanding into Asia. It has restaurants in Bangkok, Kuala Lumpur, Djakarta, Taipei, Bali, and Beijing.[8]

Because of the increase in global operations, employees often work outside their country of origin or work with employees from other countries. Table 10–2 shows the different types of expatriate employees. An **expatriate** works in a country other than his country of origin. For example, Microsoft is headquartered in the United States but has facilities around the world. To be effective, expatriates in the Microsoft Mexico operations in Mexico City must understand the region's business and social culture. Because of a growing pool of talented labor around the world, greater use of host-country nationals is occurring.[9] A key reason is that a host-country national can more easily understand the values and customs of the work force than an expatriate can. Also, training and transporting U.S. employees and their families to a foreign assignment and housing them there tend to be more expensive than hiring a host-country national.

Cross-cultural preparation involves educating employees (expatriates) and their families who are to be sent to a foreign country. To successfully conduct business in the global marketplace, employees must understand the business practices and the cultural norms of different countries. Table 10–3's column "impression shock" shows the typical impressions that a Japanese manager may have of the U.S. culture. The "integration shock" column describes the typical American interpretation of Japanese managers' style. Clearly, for American and Japanese managers to have successful business discussions, they need to be prepared to deal with cultural differences!

TABLE 10–2   **Types of Expatriates**

Parent-country national: Employee whose country of origin is where the company has its headquarters

Host-country national: Employee from the host country

Third-country national: Employee who has a country of origin different from both the parent country and host country where he or she works

TABLE 10–3   Negative Surprises Facing the Newly Arrived Japanese Manager

	Impression Shock— *Japanese Perceptions* *of American Ways*	*Integration Shock—* *American Responses* *to Japanese Ways*
Community Life	Social Diversity	Aloof/clannish community
	Violence and crime	Misunderstood customs
	Poverty and homelessness	Economic takeover
	Education problems	Lingering resentment
	Ignorance of foreign ways	Self-serving conduct
Business Practice	Different operations	Vagueness and delay
	Shortsightedness	Overworked employees
	Lackluster service	Unfair industrial groups
	Hasty dealmaking	Ethical violations
	Legal minefields	Influence peddling
Organizational Dynamics	No spiritual quality	Management inexperience
	Individual careerism	Avoided accountability
	Narrow job focus	Closed inner circle
	Political confrontation	Stifled employees
	Employee disloyalty	Discriminatory practices
Interpersonal Dealings	Assertiveness	Distrust/secrecy
	Frankness	Arrogance/hubris
	Egoism	Withheld sentiments
	Glibness	Cautious intimacy
	Impulsiveness	Excessive sensitivity

Note: The rows and tables are not symmetrical. They merely list the major surprises experienced by visitors.

Source: Richard G. Linowes, "The Japanese Manager's Traumatic Entry into the United States: Understanding the American–Japanese Cultural Divide," *Academy of Management Executive* 7, no. 4 (1993): 26.

Dimensions of Cultural Differences

Before discussing the specific steps in cross-cultural preparation you should understand the cultural characteristics that influence employee behavior. A **culture** refers to the set of assumptions group members share about the world and how it works and the ideals worth striving for.[10] Culture is important because it influences the effectiveness of different behaviors and management styles. A management style that seems friendly to some employees might offend others who would rather maintain distance and respect toward their bosses.

FIGURE 10–1

Cultural dimensions with relative standing of selected countries

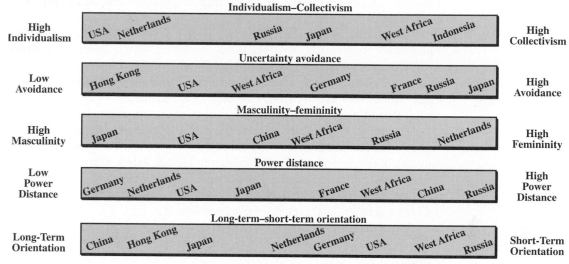

Source: From P. M. Wright and R. A. Noe, *Management of Organizations* (Burr Ridge, IL: Irwin-McGraw Hill, 1996).

Cultures have been described in terms of five dimensions: individualism–collectivism, uncertainty avoidance, masculinity–femininity, power distance, and long-term–short-term orientation.[11] Figure 10–1 shows where research has indicated that selected countries are located on these dimensions. Awareness of these dimensions can help trainers develop cross-cultural preparation programs that include meaningful information regarding the culture the expatriates will find themselves working in. Awareness of these dimensions can also help trainers adapt their training styles to employees in non-U.S. locations. But note that individuals differ within any culture, so these generalizations describe some members of a culture better than others.

The degree to which people act as individuals rather than as members of a group is the cultural dimension known as **individualism–collectivism.** In an individualistic culture like the United States, employees expect to be hired, evaluated, and rewarded based on their personal skills and accomplishments. In a collectivist culture, employees are more likely to have a voice in decisions. As we saw in Table 10–3, Japanese managers, who tend to have a collectivist orientation, can be shocked by the apparent self-interest of their American colleagues!

Upjohn Company of Kalamazoo, Michigan, and Pharmacia AB of Sweden recently experienced a clash of cultures after the companies agreed to merge.[12] Because of the similarities between Swedes and Americans, the companies were not prepared for the cultural differences they encountered. For example, both speak English and enjoy similar life-styles. However, there were significant cultural differences in decision-making styles. Swedes are used to an open system, in which small teams are largely left on their own and executives prefer to get consensus before making a decision. Upjohn was used to more authoritarian, top-down decision making. This caused relationships between the companies to be strained.

Uncertainty avoidance refers to the degree to which people prefer structured rather than unstructured situations. A culture with a strong uncertainty avoidance orientation (e.g., Japan, Russia) favors structured situations. Religion, law, or technology in these countries socialize people to seek security through clear rules on how to act. In a culture with weak uncertainty avoidance (e.g., Jamaica, Hong Kong), employees cope by not worrying too much about the future.

Masculinity–femininity refers to the extent to which the culture values behavior considered traditionally masculine (competitiveness) or feminine (helpfulness). Examples of "masculine" cultures include Japan, Germany, and the United States. Here assertiveness and competitiveness are valued. In contrast, in a culture such as the Netherlands, a higher value is likely placed on quality of life, helping others, and preserving the environment.

Power distance refers to expectations for the unequal distribution of power in a hierarchy. India, Mexico, and Russia, for example, have great power distance. This means that people attempt to maintain differences between various levels of the hierarchy. For example, because complaining about managers is unthinkable in Mexico, a U.S. manager of a steel conveyor plant failed in his effort to establish a system to handle employee complaints. Under the system, employees were to first discuss the problem with their manager. No one ever complained so the managers were caught by surprise when employees staged a plant walkout.[13]

Long-term–short-term orientation refers to the degree to which a culture focuses on the future rather than the past and present. In cultures with a short-term orientation, such as the United States, Russia, and West Africa, the orientation is toward the past and present. These cultures tend to emphasize respect for tradition and social obligations. A culture with a long-term orientation, such as Japan and China, values such traits as thrift and persistence, which pay off in the future rather than the present.

Steps in Cross-Cultural Preparation

To prepare employees for cross-cultural assignments, companies need to provide cross-cultural training. Most U.S. companies send employees overseas without any preparation. As a result, the number of employees who return home before completing their assignments is higher for U.S. companies than for European and Japanese companies.[14] U.S. companies lose more than $2 billion a year as a result of failed overseas assignments.

To be successful in overseas assignments, expatriates (employees on foreign assignments) need to be

1. Competent in their area of expertise.
2. Able to communicate verbally and nonverbally in the host country.

3. Flexible, tolerant of ambiguity, and sensitive to cultural differences.
4. Motivated to succeed, able to enjoy the challenge of working in other countries, and willing to learn about the host country's culture, language, and customs.
5. Supported by their families.[15]

One reason for U.S. expatriates' high failure rate is that companies place more emphasis on developing employees' technical skills than on preparing them to work in other cultures. Research suggests that the comfort of an expatriate's spouse and family is the most important determinant of whether the employee will complete the assignment.[16]

The key to a successful foreign assignment appears to be a combination of training and career management for the employee and his family. Foreign assignments involve three phases: predeparture, on-site, and repatriation (preparing to return home). Training is necessary in all three phases.

Predeparture Phase.   In the predeparture phase, employees need to receive language training and an orientation in the new country's culture and customs. It is critical that the family be included in the orientation programs.[17] Expatriates and their families need information about housing, schools, recreation, shopping, and health care facilities in the area where they will live. An expatriate also must discuss with her manager how the foreign assignment fits into her career plans and what type of position she can expect upon return.

Cross-cultural training methods range from presentational techniques, such as lectures that expatriates and their families attend on the customs and culture of the host country, to actual experiences in the home country in culturally diverse communities.[18] Experiential exercises, such as miniculture experiences, allow expatriates to spend time with a family in the United States from the ethnic group of the host country.

Research suggests that the degree of difference between the United States and the host country (cultural novelty), the amount of interaction with host country citizens and host nationals (interaction), and the familiarity with new job tasks and work environment (job novelty) all influence the "rigor" of the cross-cultural training method used.[19] Figure 10–2 shows the relationship between training rigor and characteristics of the training program. Experiential training methods are most effective (and most needed) in assignments with a high level of cultural and job novelty that require a good deal of interpersonal interaction with host nationals.

On-Site Phase.   On-site training involves continued orientation to the host country and its customs and cultures through formal programs or through a mentoring relationship. Expatriates and their families may be paired with an employee from the host country who helps them understand the new, unfamiliar work environment and community.[20]

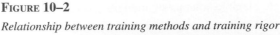

FIGURE 10–2

Relationship between training methods and training rigor

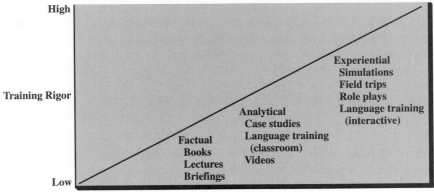

Source: Based on M. Mendenhall, E. Dunbar, and G. Oddou, "Expatriate Selection, Training, and Career-Pathing: A Review and Critique," *Human Resource Management* 26 (1987): 331–45.

Repatriation Phase.   Repatriation prepares expatriates for return to the parent company and country from the foreign assignment. Expatriates and their families are likely to experience high levels of stress and anxiety when they return because of the changes that have occurred since their departure. This shock can be reduced by providing expatriates with company newsletters and community newspapers and by ensuring that they receive personal and work-related mail from the United States while they are on foreign assignment. It is also not uncommon for employees and their families to have to readjust to a lower standard of living in the United States than they had in the foreign country, where they may have enjoyed maid service, a limousine, private schools, and clubs. Salary and other compensation arrangements should be worked out well before employees return from overseas assignments.

Aside from reentry shock, many expatriates decide to leave the company because the assignment they are given upon returning to the United States has less responsibility, challenge, and status than the foreign assignment.[21] As noted earlier, career planning discussions need to be held before the employees leave the United States to ensure that they understand the positions they will be eligible for upon repatriation.

Monsanto has a successful repatriation program. Monsanto is an agricultural, chemical, and pharmaceutical company with 50 expatriates and 35 international employees working in the United States. Preparation for repatriation begins before the employee leaves the United States. Employees and both their sending and receiving manager develop an agreement about their understanding of the assignment and how it fits into the company's business objectives. Expectations regarding the assignment and how the knowledge gained will be used when the employee returns are specified. Monsanto's program involves having expatriates share their experiences with American peers, superiors, and subordinates. The program also provides repatriating employees with a way to work through personal difficulties. After their return, expatriates meet with several colleagues of their choice for a debriefing segment. The debriefing segment includes a trained counselor who discusses all the important aspects of the repatriation and helps the employee understand what he is experiencing. The debriefing not only helps the returning expatriate but also helps educate peers and colleagues to better understand different cultural issues and business environments.[22]

Training Foreign Employees

Table 10–4 presents the implications of each of the cultural dimensions for training. In the United States, interaction between the trainer and the trainees is viewed as a positive characteristic of the learning environment. However in other cultures, this type of learning environment may not be familiar to the trainee or may violate expected norms of good instruction. For example, in China, a culture high on power distance, trainees do not expect to be asked to question the trainer.[23] This means that the instructor must actively seek out their participation. Also, when seeking audience participation in China, the senior member of the group may be invited to speak first; questions from other trainees may be forwarded to this person. This avoids embarrassing a senior executive by having an employee of lower status ask a better question.

Expectations regarding the environment in which training is to occur may also differ from U.S. culture. On-the-job training may be viewed skeptically by Russian employees because historically most workers were expected to have been formally trained by attending lectures at an institute or university.[24] Because Russian culture values family relationships (Russian culture is more "feminine" than American culture), the meaningfulness of training materials is likely to be enhanced by using examples from employees' work and life situations.

Besides cultural dimensions, trainers must consider language differences in preparing training materials. If an interpreter is used, it is important to conduct a

---

TABLE 10–4   Implications of Cultural Dimensions for Training Design

Cultural Dimension	*Implications*
Uncertainty avoidance	Culture high in uncertainty avoidance expects formal instructional environment. Less tolerance for impromptu style.
Individualism	Culture high in individualism expects participation in exercises and questioning to be determined by status in the company or culture.
Power distance	Culture high in power distance expects trainer to be expert. Trainers expected to be authoritarian and controlling of session.
Masculinity	Culture low in masculinity values relationships with fellow trainees. Female trainers less likely to be resisted in low-masculinity cultures.

Source: Based on B. Filipczak, "Think Locally, Act Globally," *Training* (January 1997): 41–48.

practice session with the interpreter to evaluate pacing of the session and whether the amount of topics and material is appropriate. Training materials including videos and exercises need to be translated well in advance of the training session.

The key to success in a foreign training session is preparation! The needs assessment must include an evaluation of cultural dimensions and the characteristics of the audience (such as language ability, trainees' company, and cultural status).

Managing Work Force Diversity

The goals of diversity training are (1) to eliminate values, stereotypes, and managerial practices that inhibit employees' personal development and (2) therefore to allow employees to contribute to organizational goals regardless of their race, sexual orientation, gender, family status, religious orientation, or cultural background.[25] Because of Equal Opportunity Employment laws, companies have been forced to insure that women and minorities were adequately represented in their labor force. That is, companies were focused on insuring equal access to jobs. **Managing diversity** involves creating an environment that allows all employees to contribute to organizational goals and experience personal growth. This includes access to jobs as well as fair and positive treatment of all employees. This requires the company to develop employees so that they are comfortable working with others from a wide variety of ethnic, racial, and religious backgrounds.

Table 10–5 shows how managing diversity can help companies gain a competitive advantage. Management of diversity has been linked to improved productivity and lower employee turnover and other costs related to human resources.[26] Various customer groups appreciate doing business with employees like themselves. Also, diverse employees can contribute insights into customers and product markets. For example, Voice Processing Corporation benefits from having employees with different language skills and cultural orientations.[27] Diversity gives the firm an edge in producing and marketing software that enables computers to process voice commands. Companies also need creativity and innovation to cope with the rapid pace of change. Research supports the view that these traits are more likely to exist in a company whose employees come from a variety of backgrounds.[28]

Capitalizing on diversity also plays a major role in the success of work teams.[29] Diversity goes beyond racial, physical, and ethnic differences to include differences in communication and problem-solving style and professional and functional expertise (e.g., marketing versus engineering). When teams don't capitalize on differences but instead get caught up in identifying differences, distrust and unproductive teams usually result. Many companies (e.g., IBM, Colgate-Palmolive) have used a strategy focusing on awareness of differences and providing skills that team members need to be successful. Teams need to have mission statements that reflect not only what the team is supposed to accomplish but how interpersonal conflict should be handled. Some companies also require forced rotation of responsibilities so each person has a chance to demonstrate her abilities (and show that stereotypes based on race or function are not valid).

TABLE 10–5   How Managing Diversity Can Provide Competitive Advantage

Argument	*Rationale*
Cost	As organizations become more diverse, the cost of a poor job in integrating workers will increase. Those who handle integration well will thus create cost advantages over those who don't.
Resource acquisition	Companies develop reputations on favorability as prospective employers for women and ethnic minorities. Those with the best reputations managing diversity will win the competition for the best personnel. As the labor pool shrinks and changes composition, this edge will become increasingly important.
Marketing	For multinational organizations, the insight and cultural sensitivity that members with roots in other countries bring to the marketing effort should improve these efforts in important ways. The same rationale applies to marketing to subpopulations within domestic operations.
Creativity	Diversity of perspectives and less emphasis on conformity to norms of the past (which characterize the modern approach to management of diversity) should improve the level of creativity.
Problem solving	Heterogeneity in decisions and problem-solving groups potentially produces better decisions through a wider range of perspectives and more through critical analysis of issues.
System flexibility	An implication of the multicultural model for managing diversity is that the system will become less determinant, less standardized, and therefore more fluid. The increased fluidity should create greater flexibility to react to environmental changes (i.e., reactions should be faster and at less cost).

Source: T. H. Cox and S. Blake, "Managing Cultural Diversity: Implications for Organizational Competitiveness," *Academy of Management Executive* 5 (1991): 47. Reprinted with permission.

Managing Diversity through Adherence to Legislation

One approach to managing diversity is through affirmative action policies and by making sure that human resource practices meet standards of equal employment opportunity laws.[30] This approach rarely results in changes in employees' values, stereotypes, and behaviors that inhibit productivity and personal development. Figure 10–3 shows the cycle of disillusionment resulting from managing diversity by relying solely on adherence to employment laws. The cycle begins when the company realizes that it must change policies regarding women and minorities because of legal pressure or a discrepancy between the number or percentage of women and minorities in the company's work force and the number available in the broader labor market. To address these concerns, a greater number of women and minorities are hired by the company. Managers see little need for additional action because women and minority employment

FIGURE 10–3

Cycle of disillusionment resulting from managing diversity through adherence to legislation

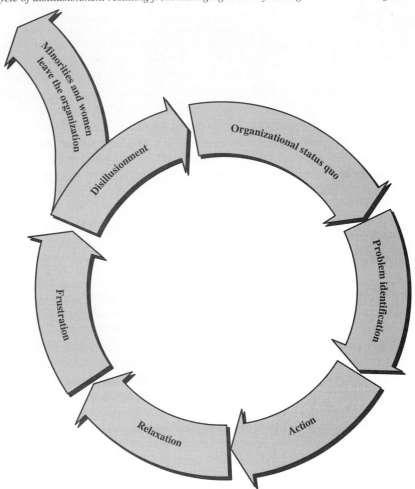

Source: "Capitalizing on Global Diversity" by Cresencio Torres and Mary Bruxelles, *HR Magazine,*
December 1992, pp. 30–33. Reprinted with the permission of *HR Magazine.* Published by the Society for
Human Resource Management, Alexandria, VA.

rates reflect their availability in the labor market. However, as women and minorities gain experience in the company, they likely become frustrated. Managers and co-workers may avoid providing coaching or performance feedback
to women and minorities because they are uncomfortable interacting with individuals from different gender, ethnic, or racial backgrounds. Co-workers may
express beliefs that women and minorities are employed only because they received special treatment (e.g., hiring standards were lowered).[31] As a result of
their frustration, women and minorities may form support groups to voice their
concerns to management. Because of the work atmosphere, women and minorities may fail to fully utilize their skills and leave the company.

Managing Diversity through Diversity Training Programs

The preceding discussion is not to suggest that companies should be reluctant to engage in affirmative action or pursue equal opportunity employment practices. However, affirmative action without additional supporting strategies does not deal with issues of assimilating women and minorities into the work force. To successfully manage a diverse work force, companies need to ensure that

- Employees understand how their values and stereotypes influence their behavior toward others of different gender, ethnic, racial, or religious backgrounds.
- Employees gain an appreciation of cultural differences among themselves.
- Behaviors that isolate or intimidate minority group members improve.

This can be accomplished through diversity training programs. **Diversity training** refers to training designed to change employee attitudes about diversity and/or developing skills needed to work with a diverse work force. Diversity training programs differ according to whether attitude or behavior change is emphasized.[32]

Attitude Awareness and Change Programs.   **Attitude awareness and change programs** focus on increasing employees' awareness of differences in cultural and ethnic backgrounds, physical characteristics (e.g., disabilities), and personal characteristics that influence behavior toward others. The assumption underlying these programs is that, by increasing their awareness of stereotypes and beliefs, employees will be able to avoid negative stereotypes when interacting with employees of different backgrounds. The programs help employees consider the similarities and differences between cultural groups, examine their attitudes toward affirmative action, or analyze their beliefs about why minority employees are successful or unsuccessful in their jobs. Many of these programs use videotapes and experiential exercises to increase employees' awareness of the negative emotional and performance effects of stereotypes, values, and behaviors on minority group members. For example, 3M conducts workshops in which managers are asked to assess their attitudes toward stereotypical statements about race, age, and gender.[33] The participants select two stereotypes they hold and consider how these stereotypes affect their ability to manage. One of the most popular video training packages, Copeland Griggs Productions' "Valuing Diversity Training Program," involves three days of training that focuses on managing differences, diversity in the workplace, and cross-cultural communications.

The attitude awareness and change approach has been criticized for several reasons.[34] First, by focusing on group differences, the program may communicate that certain stereotypes and attitudes are valid. For example, in diversity training a male manager may learn that women employees prefer to work by building consensus rather than by arguing until others agree with their point. He might conclude that the training has validated his stereotype. As a result, he will continue to fail to give women important job responsibilities that involve "heated" negotiations with customers or clients. Second, encouraging employees to share their attitudes, feelings, and stereotypes toward certain groups may cause employees to feel guilty, angry, and less likely to see the similarities among racial, ethnic, or gender groups and the advantages of working together.

Behavior-Based Programs. **Behavior-based programs** focus on changing the organizational policies and individual behaviors that inhibit employees' personal growth and productivity.

One approach of these programs is to identify incidents that discourage employees from working up to their potential. Groups of employees are asked to identify specific promotion opportunities, sponsorship, training opportunities, or performance management practices that they believe were handled unfairly. Their views regarding how well the work environment and management practices value employee differences and provide equal opportunity may also be collected. Specific training programs may be developed to address the issues presented in the focus groups.

Another approach is to teach managers and employees basic rules of behavior in the workplace.[35] For example, managers and employees should learn that it is inappropriate to use statements and engage in behaviors that have negative racial, sexual, or cultural content. Companies that have focused on teaching rules and behavior have found that employees react less negatively to this type of training than to other diversity training approaches.

Characteristics of Successful Diversity Efforts

Is a behavior-based or an attitude awareness and change program most effective? Increasing evidence shows that attitude awareness programs are ineffective and that one-time diversity training programs are unlikely to succeed. For example, R. R. Donnelley & Sons suspended its diversity awareness training program even though the company has spent more than $3 million on it as a result of a racial discrimination lawsuit.[36]

At various training sessions participants were encouraged to voice their concerns. Many said that they were experiencing difficulty in working effectively due to abuse and harassment. The managers attending the training disputed the concerns. Also, after training, an employee who applied for an open position was rejected. She was told that she was rejected because she was too honest in expressing her concerns during the diversity training session. Although R. R. Donnelley held many diversity training sessions, little progress was made in increasing the employment and promotion rates of women and minorities. Because of the low ratio of black employees to white employees, many black employees were asked to attend multiple training sessions to ensure diverse groups, which they resented. The company declined to release data requested by shareholders that it provided to the Equal Employment Opportunity Commission regarding female and minority representation in jobs throughout the company. The firm also failed to act on recommendations made by company-approved employee "diversity councils."

More generally, a survey of diversity training efforts found that

- The most common area addressed through diversity is the pervasiveness of stereotypes, assumptions, and biases.
- Fewer than one-third of the companies do any kind of long-term evaluation or follow-up. The most common indicators of success were reduced grievances and lawsuits, increased diversity in promotions and hiring, increased self-awareness of biases, and increased consultation of HR specialists on diversity-related issues.
- Most programs lasted only one day or less.
- Three-fourths of the survey respondents indicated that they believed the typical employee leaves diversity training with positive attitudes toward diversity. However, over 50 percent reported that the programs have no effect over the long term.[37]

Table 10–6 shows the characteristics associated with the long-term success of diversity programs. It is critical that the diversity program be tied to business objectives. For example, cultural differences affect the type of skin cream consumers believe they need or the fragrance they may be attracted to. Understanding cultural differences is part of understanding the consumer (which is critical to the success of companies such as Avon). Top management support can be demonstrated by creating a structure to support the initiative. For example, Bank of America in San Francisco has a diversity department to handle day-to-day issues. The CEO of the bank created a corporate diversity task force involving 28 executives from different geographical locations and business functions whose goals were to gather employee feedback, review current programs, and

---

TABLE 10–6   Characteristics Associated with Diversity Programs' Long-Term Success

- Top management provides resources, personally intervenes, and publicly advocates diversity.
- The program is structured.
- Capitalizing on a diverse workforce is defined as a business objective.
- Capitalizing on a diverse workforce is seen as necessary to generate revenue and profits.
- The program is evaluated.
- Manager involvement is mandatory.
- The program is seen as a culture change, not a one-shot program.
- Managers and demographic groups are not blamed for problems.
- Behaviors and skills needed to successfully interact with others are taught.
- Managers are rewarded on progress toward meeting diversity goals.

Source: S. Rynes and B. Rosen, "What Makes Diversity Programs Work?" *HR Magazine* (October 1994): 67–73; S. Rynes and B. Rosen, "A Field Survey of Factors Affecting the Adoption and Perceived Success of Diversity Training," *Personnel Psychology* 48 (1995): 247–70; J. Gordon, "Different from What? Diversity as a Performance Issue," *Training* (May 1995): 25–33.

suggest new ways to promote diversity. Diversity business councils were created to formulate strategies to ensure that the diversity effort was related to business needs. Diversity networks are available to assist white males, women, Hispanics, and African Americans in their personal and professional development.[38]

Another important characteristic of diversity programs is that managers are rewarded for progress toward meeting diversity goals.[39] Allstate Insurance Company surveys all 50,000 of its employees four times a year. The survey asks employees to evaluate how well the company is satisfying customers and employees. Several questions are used as a "diversity index." Employees are asked questions about the extent to which manager's racial or gender biases affect development opportunities, promotions, and service to customers. Twenty-five percent of a manager's yearly bonus is determined by how employees evaluate them on the diversity index.

Gannett is a $4 billion information and communication company that publishes *USA Today* plus daily and weekly newspapers in cities and communities throughout the United States and owns many radio and TV stations. Its diversity program incorporates many characteristics shown in Table 10–6.[40] The commitment to diversity starts at the top of the company. The company's operating principles include guaranteeing respect for and fairness in dealing with employees and creating a work environment where opportunity is based on merit. The company's top executives report to the board of directors each year on progress in diversity and the report is shared with the rest of the company. Gannett measures diversity efforts through a survey that measures the work climate for women and minority employees. Managers provide employees with the survey results and then work with them to address issues raised in the survey. Gannett offers many workshops addressing behavior change and awareness of attitudes. For example, a case approach is used in a program called "It Takes All Kinds." In this program, trainees discuss how they would handle situations such as a women who wants to work at home or a minority group member who wants a position he is not qualified for. Gannett also extensively communicates regarding diversity efforts. Weekly and monthly articles about diversity efforts and successes are published in the company newspaper, newsletter, and employees magazine.

Gannett's diversity program has resulted in more women and minorities moving into the managerial level—23 percent of managers are women, 9 percent are minorities. Gannett has received numerous awards for its diversity efforts (e.g., the Catalyst award for corporations with distinguished records in the employment and advancement of women).

As you can see from this discussion, successful diversity programs involve more than just an effective training program. Top management support, diversity policies and practices, training and development, and administrative structures, such as conducting diversity surveys and evaluating managers' progress on diversity goals, are needed.[41]

School-to-Work Transition

Industry and education experts agree that a system is needed for training students who do not attend college directly after high school. **School-to-work transition programs** combine classroom experiences with work experiences to prepare high school graduates for employment. Many school districts have changed their curriculum to include more work experience as part of the traditional classroom-based educational experience. The federal government, recognizing a need for this type of program, has helped to fund local government efforts. The **School-to-Work Opportunities Act** signed by President Clinton in 1994 was designed to assist the states in building school-to-work systems that prepare students for high-skill, high-wage jobs or future education. The act encourages partnerships between educational institutions, employers, and labor unions. The act requires that every school-to-work system include work-based learning, school-based learning, and connecting activities that match students with employers and bring classrooms and workplaces together. For example, a high school in Wisconsin has a program that combines engineering classes at school with paid, on-the-job engineering experience.[42] Wisconsin has one of the most fully developed school-to-work programs. Apprenticeships are offered in 13 fields ranging from tourism to engineering. Committees of employers and educators developed the skill sets to be covered and identified appropriate classroom and work experiences.

Although students are seeking to enroll in the program, less than 1 percent of all high school juniors and seniors in Wisconsin participate. The problem is that employer interest in the program can not support the number of students who are interested. There is a shortage of workplace apprenticeship experiences. One reason for employers' lack of enthusiasm is that they don't understand what school-to-work programs involve. Another is that, although apprenticeships provide the most intense, relevant experience, they are the most time consuming to develop and implement. The key is to identify how the student can benefit the company. The challenge is to make the program practical enough for employers, with a large payoff to educators to create learning opportunities for the students that are interesting and relevant to careers.

Training the Hard-Core Unemployed

The opening vignette showed how Marriott Corporation is attempting to help hard-core unemployed welfare recipients gain full-time employment. As the example illustrates, these training programs must focus on both job and life skills. Because most participants have suffered poor schooling as well as substance, physical, or emotional abuse, they know little about the demands of the workplace. Such things as dependability and reliability must be emphasized. Trainers also may find that hard-core unemployed have a sense of entitlement because of their many years of dependence on a paycheck from the government. They don't understand that it is inappropriate to leave work in the middle of the day without first requesting personal leave time from their manager.

There are two methods for training welfare recipients.[43] The first model involves government agencies referring welfare recipients to a company-sponsored training program subsidized with money and tax credits from the government. An example is Marriott's Pathways to Progress program. The second method is for state and local governments to provide life and skills training directly to welfare recipients. The skills developed are often based on the needs of local employers. For example, in Oregon, the Department of Human Resources JOBS training program has helped 19,000 people find work. Participants attend training sessions on basic work habits and learn to interview, write resumes, and manage their personal lives. The welfare-to-work transition is facilitated by a state law that requires welfare recipients to find work or risk losing their benefits. Another program requires the state to reimburse companies for the wages of welfare recipients for six months, while the employers provide meaningful work experiences and training. In one program for clerical workers, 85 percent of those who stayed in the program for four months were hired by the employers and still had jobs even after the state subsidy ended.

Training Issues Related to Internal Needs of the Company

Basic Skills Training

Chapter 1 highlighted employers' difficulty in finding competent entry-level job candidates—persons with appropriate reading, writing, and arithmetic skills. Chapter 3 emphasized the relationship between cognitive ability, reading skills and training success. Also Chapter 3 discussed how basic skills can be identified during needs assessment. Because employers have not been successful at finding job candidates with appropriate levels of basic skills (a recruiting and selection issue), employers are forced to develop basic skill training programs. Also, as companies move toward high-performance workplace systems, they may find that current employees lack the skills needed to realize these systems' benefits.

As explained in Chapter 3, basic skills programs involve several steps. First, the necessary skill level needs to be identified. That is, what level of basic skills do employees need to be successful in their jobs? Second, employees' current skill levels must be assessed. Based on the gap between current skill level and desired skill level, training programs need to be developed. Training programs need to include an emphasis on basic skills in the context of work problems to increase their meaningfulness to trainees. In 24-hour operations (such as a manufacturing plant) using several shifts of employees, basic skills training needs to be available to employees during their off-shift times. Finally, many employees who lack basic skills do not want their peers to be aware of these deficiencies.

Participation in basic skills training needs to be as private as possible. If privacy can not be guaranteed, those employees who most need basic skills training may not participate.

In Chapter 3 we discussed how Georgia-Pacific identified basic skills deficiencies and contracted with a local community college to offer basic skills training. Other companies are developing on-site learning centers to help employees develop basic skills.

For example, the Brenlin Group, based in Akron, Ohio, developed a literacy program for its employees.[44] The program was created because, as the company moved to adopt Total Quality Management Principles, it discovered that employees were unable to learn new ways of working (e.g., use statistics to analyze processes). The company found that 30 percent of its employees read below a fifth grade level, and two-thirds scored below that level on basic math skills.

Because of these deficiencies, Brenlin decided to establish learning centers at four of its plants. Each learning center contains 8 to 16 personal computers located in private study carrels. The centers offer training in literacy, job skills, and Total Quality Management. An individualized needs assessment is conducted for each employee. The program is tailored based on the employee's needs. The centers are also open to employees' family members. Interactive software is used to help employees work in privacy at their own pace to improve math, reading, and verbal skills. The centers also enable the company to provide a consistent learning environment for all employees. Besides focusing on basic skills, Brenlin is also using the centers to provide non–English-speaking workers with opportunities to study English as a second language and to develop employees' computer skills.

Learning and results evaluations of the program have been positive. The average gain in basic skills was two grade levels after 60 hours of training. One manufacturing facility reported a 21 percent increase in productivity since the training started.

Melting the Glass Ceiling

A major training and development issue facing companies today is how to get women and minorities into upper-level management positions—how to break the **glass ceiling.** The glass ceiling is a barrier to advancement to the higher levels of the organization. This barrier may be due to stereotypes or company systems that adversely affect the development of women or minorities.[45] The glass ceiling is likely caused by lack of access to training programs, appropriate developmental job experiences, and developmental relationships (such as mentoring).[46] Research has found no gender differences in access to job experiences involving transitions or creating change.[47] However, male managers of similar ability and managerial level received significantly more assignments involving high levels of responsibility (high stakes, managing business diversity, handling external pressure) than female managers. Also, female managers reported experiencing more challenge due to lack of personal support (a type of job demand considered to be an obstacle that has been found to relate to harmful stress) than male managers. This suggests that managers making developmental assignments must carefully consider whether gender biases or stereotypes are influencing the types of assignments given to women versus men.

Women and minorities often have trouble finding mentors because of their lack of access to the "old boy network," managers' preference to interact with other managers of similar status rather than with line employees, and intentional exclusion by managers who have negative stereotypes about women's and minorities' abilities, motivation, and job preferences.[48] Potential mentors may view minorities and women as a threat to their job security because they believe affirmative action plans give those groups preferential treatment.

As part of their approach to managing a diverse work force, many companies are using mentoring programs to ensure that women and minorities gain the skills and visibility needed to move into managerial positions. For example, at Pacific Bell, a task force was appointed to study why there were relatively few promotions of minority managers and few structured programs to help managers improve their skills.[49] The task force found that support from an older mentor at some time in a manager's career was necessary for career advancement and skill development. As a result, Pacific Bell devised a development program for minority managers. Besides working with their immediate supervisors to develop career goals, trainees work with executive mentors who are at least two levels above the trainees. The mentors have input into the development plan and meet frequently with the trainees. Pacific Bell received an award from the U.S. Department of Labor for its commitment to equal employment opportunity.

Joint Union–Management Programs

To be more competitive, U.S. industries that have lost considerable market share to foreign competition (e.g., the auto industry) have developed joint union–management training. Both labor and management have been forced to accept new roles. Employees need to become involved in business planning and strategic decision making, and management needs to learn how to share power and allow worker participation in decision making.

The initial goal of these programs was to help displaced employees find new jobs by providing skill training and outplacement assistance. Currently, **joint union–management training programs** provide a wide range of services designed to help employees learn skills that are directly related to their job and also develop skills that are "portable"—that is, valuable to employers in other companies or industries.[50] Both employers and unions contribute money to run the programs and both oversee their operation. Major joint efforts involve the United Auto Workers with Ford and General Motors, the Communication Workers of America with US WEST, and the United Steel Workers with 12 major steel companies.

The United Auto Workers–Ford Education Development and Training Program includes

- A Life/Education Planning Program that helps employees determine their career needs and interests and links them with resources in the community.
- An Education and Training Assistance Plan that assists employees in identifying appropriate courses at colleges and universities and provides tuition reimbursement.
- A Skills Enhancement Program providing counseling and assistance related to adult basic education, high school completion, general education development, and English as a second language.
- A College and University Options Program that makes both degree and nondegree college and technical training more accessible for employees. It provides workshops for employees, on-site course registration, classes at times that are convenient to employees, and credits for college-level knowledge.
- Targeted education, training, or counseling projects related to the specific educational or counseling needs of a specific location or segment of the work force.
- A Successful Retirement Planning Program offering preretirement planning to employees and their spouses.
- A Financial Education Program covering topics such as personal financial planning, investment, and insurance as well as wills and trusts.[51]

Yes, these programs are costly (General Motors has spent $1.6 billion jointly with the UAW since 1984) and employees may get trained in skills that are not directly related to their current jobs. But both labor and management believe that these programs improve the literacy levels of the work force and contribute to productivity. Both parties believe that encouraging lifelong learning is a key aspect of the work force being able to adapt to new technologies and global competition.

Succession Planning

Succession planning refers to the process of identification and tracking of high-potential employees. High-potential employees are those the company believes are capable of being successful in higher-level managerial positions such as general manager of a strategic business unit, functional director (e.g., director of marketing), or chief executive officer (CEO).[52] High-potential employees typically participate in fast-track development programs that involve education, executive mentoring and coaching, and rotation through job assignments.[53] Job assignments are based on the successful career paths of the managers the high-potential employees are being prepared to replace. High-potential employees may also receive special assignments, such as making presentations and serving on committees and task forces. The objectives of fast-track development programs are

- Developing future managers for midmanager to executive positions.
- Providing companies with a competitive advantage in attracting and recruiting talented employees.
- Helping retain managerial talent within the company.[54]

Research suggests that the development of high-potential employees involves three stages.[55] A large pool of employees may initially be identified as high-potential employees, but the numbers are reduced over time because of turnover, poor performance, or a personal choice not to strive for a higher-level position. In stage 1, high-potential employees are selected. Those who have completed elite academic programs (e.g., an MBA at Stanford) or who have been outstanding performers are identified. Psychological tests—such as those done at assessment centers—may also be used.

In stage 2, high-potential employees receive development experiences. Those who succeed are the ones who continue to demonstrate good performance. A willingness to make sacrifices for the company is also necessary (e.g., accepting new assignments or relocating to a new location). Good oral and written communication skills, ease in interpersonal relationships, and talent for leadership are a must. In what is known as a tournament model of job transitions, high-potential employees who meet the expectations of their senior managers in this stage are given the opportunity to advance into the next stage of the process.[56] Employees who do not meet the expectations are ineligible for higher-level managerial positions in the company.

To reach stage 3, high-potential employees usually have to be seen by top management as fitting into the company's culture and having the personality characteristics needed to successfully represent the company. These employees have the potential to occupy the company's top positions. In stage 3, the CEO becomes actively involved in developing the employees, who are exposed to the company's key personnel and are given a greater understanding of the company's culture. Note that the development of high-potential employees is a slow process. Reaching stage 3 may take 15 to 20 years.

At American Greetings Corporation headquartered in Cleveland, Ohio, the succession planning process involves several steps.[57] A four-person team (the senior vice president of human resources, the president, the chief executive officer, and the executive development director) identifies high-potential candidates for the company's top three levels of management. On an ongoing basis, each committee member recommends four or five lower-level managers who show leadership potential. Each recommendation is challenged to demonstrate evidence (performance, experiences, etc.) that the nominees have high potential. The committee reviews each individual's set of competencies and compares them against standards that the company has determined are necessary for its leaders. The committee then identifies developmental tasks for any weaknesses in leadership capabilities. For example, if a high-potential employee lacks overseeing a project that has a major impact on the business, the employee is scheduled to receive an opportunity to become involved in a project of large scope when one becomes available. After completion of the project, the employee is required to brief the development committee on the project's results.

Some companies' succession planning systems identify a small number of potential managers for each position. While this approach allows developed activities to be targeted to a select few highly talented managers, it also limits the company's ability to staff future managerial positions and may cause a "talent drain." That is, high-potential employees who are not on the short list for managerial positions may leave the company. American Greetings' approach to succession planning focuses on identifying and creating a large number of qualified leaders so it increases the likelihood that the company will have qualified leaders even if managerial responsibilities change in the future. This approach helps build commitment among a larger number of high-potential employees. This broad approach to succession planning also makes these high-potential employees more effective in their current positions.

Developing Managers with Dysfunctional Behaviors

A number of studies have identified managerial behaviors that can cause an otherwise competent manager to be ineffective. These behaviors include insensitivity to others, inability to be a team player, arrogance, poor conflict-management skills, inability to meet business objectives, and inability to change or adapt during a transition.[58] For example, a skilled manager who is interpersonally abrasive, aggressive, and an autocratic leader may find it difficult to motivate subordinates, may alienate internal and external customers, and may have trouble getting her ideas accepted by her superiors. These managers are in jeopardy of losing their jobs and have little chance of future advancement because of their dysfunctional behaviors. Typically, a combination of assessment, training, and counseling are used to help managers change dysfunctional behavior.

One example of a program designed specifically to help managers with dysfunctional behavior is the Individual Coaching for Effectiveness (ICE) program.[59] Although the effectiveness of these types of programs needs to be further investigated, research suggests that managers' participation in these programs result in skill improvement and reduced likelihood of termination.[60] The ICE program includes diagnosis, coaching, and support activities. The program is tailored to the manager's needs. Clinical, counseling, or industrial/organizational psychologists are involved in all phases of the ICE program. They conduct the diagnosis, coach and counsel the manager, and develop action plans for implementing new skills on the job.

The first step in the ICE program, diagnosis, involves collecting information about the manager's personality, skills, and interests. Interviews with the manager, his supervisor, and colleagues plus psychological tests are used to collect this information, which is used to determine whether the manager can actually change the dysfunctional behavior. For example, personality traits such as extreme defensiveness may make it difficult for the manager to change his behavior. If it is determined that the manager can benefit from the program, then specific developmental objectives tailored to his needs are set. The manager and his supervisor are typically involved in this process.

The coaching phase of the program first involves presenting the manager with information about the targeted skills or behavior. This may include information about principles of effective communication or teamwork, tolerance of individual differences in the workplace, or conducting effective meetings. The second step is for the manager to participate in behavior-modeling training, which we discussed in Chapter 7. The manager also receives psychological counseling to overcome beliefs that may inhibit learning the desired behavior.

The support phase of the program involves creating conditions to ensure that on the job the manager is able to use the new behaviors and skills acquired in the ICE program. The supervisor is asked to provide feedback to the manager and the psychologist about progress made in using the new skills and behavior. The psychologist and manager identify situations in which the manager may tend to rely on dysfunctional behavior. The coach and manager also develop action plans that outline how the manager should try to use new behavior in daily work activities.

Training and Pay Systems

Compensation refers to pay and benefits that companies give to employees in exchange for performing their jobs. Companies use compensation systems to achieve many objectives including attracting talented employees to join the company, motivating employees, and retaining employees by paying wages and benefits that meet or exceed those the employee might receive from other companies in the labor market (local as well as national or even international companies). As we discussed in Chapter 1, to remain competitive, companies need employees who possess a wide range of skills and are willing and able to learn new skills to meet changing customer service and product requirements.

Training is increasingly linked to employees' compensation through the use of skill-based pay systems. In **skill-based** or **knowledge-based pay systems** employees' pay is based primarily on the knowledge and skills they possess rather than the knowledge or skills necessary to successfully perform their current job.[61] The basic idea is that to motivate employees to learn, pay is based on the skills that employees possess. Why would a company do this? The rationale is that this type of system ensures that employees are learning and gives the company additional flexibility in using employees to provide products and services. Skill-based pay systems are often used to facilitate cross-training. **Cross-training** involves training employees to learn the skills of one or several jobs.

TABLE 10–7   Example of a Skill-Based Pay System

Skill Block	Description	Pay Rate
A	*Molding:* Operates molding machines and performs machine setup	$10 per hour
B	*Finishing:* Operates finishing machine and performs finishing machine setup function	$10.30 per hour
	Inspection: Operates both inspection machines and makes scrap/rework decisions	
	Packaging: Operates packaging equipment and performs inventory and shipping functions	
C	*Quality control:* Performs quality control functions	$11 per hour

Source: Based on R. L. Bunning, "Models for Skill-Based Pay Plans," *HR Magazine* (February 1992): 62–64.

This is especially critical for work teams where employees need to be able to rotate between jobs or substitute for employees who are absent.

The skill-based pay approach contributes to better use of employees' skills and ideas. It also provides the opportunity for leaner staffing levels because employee turnover or absenteeism can be covered by employees who are multiskilled. Multiskilled employees are important where different products require different manufacturing processes or where supply shortages call for adaptive or flexible responses. These are characteristics typical of many so-called advanced manufacturing environments (e.g., flexible manufacturing or just-in-time systems).[62]

Table 10–7 shows a skill-based pay system. In this example, skills are grouped into skill blocks. Employees' compensation increases as they master each skill block. Entry-level employees begin at $10 per hour and can progress to $11 per hour by mastering other skill blocks.

Skill-based pay systems have implications for needs assessment, delivery method, and evaluation of training.[63] Since pay is directly tied to the amount of knowledge or skill employees have obtained, employees will be motivated to attend training programs. This means that the volume of training conducted as well as training costs will increase. Although employee motivation to attend training may be high, it is important to conduct a thorough needs assessment (e.g., using testing) to ensure that employees have the prerequisite skills needed to master the new skills.

Training must also be accessible to all employees. For example, if the company manufactures products and provides services on a 24-hour basis, training must be available for employees working all shifts. Computer-assisted instruction or Intranet-based training are ideal for skill-based pay systems. Training can be easily offered at all hours on an as-needed basis—employees only need access to a computer! Also, computer-based instruction can automatically track an employee's progress in training.

In skill-based pay systems, managers and or peers usually serve as trainers. Training involves a combination of on-the-job training and use of presentation techniques such as lectures or videos. As a result, employees need to be trained to be trainers.

Finally, a key issue in skill-based pay systems is skill perishability—ensuring that employees have not forgotten the skills when it comes time to use them. Skill-based pay systems require periodic evaluation of employees' skills and knowledge using behavior and learning outcomes. Although employees may be certified that they have mastered skills, many skill-based pay programs require them to attend refresher sessions on a periodic basis to remain certified (and receive the higher wage).

Summary

This chapter explored special training and development issues relating to pressures that companies face from the external and internal company environments. External environmental pressures include the need to comply with laws, globalization, an increasingly diverse work force, and lack of skills in the labor market. To prepare you for these environmental pressures, the chapter covered legal issues in training, cross-cultural preparation, diversity training, and school-to-work transition and hard-core unemployed training programs.

Internal issues that companies face relate to preparing the company's current work force for the future, helping dysfunctional managers, and motivating employees to learn. The chapter discussed succession planning systems, basic skills training, joint union–management training programs, and how to ensure that women and minorities can receive training and development opportunities (melting the glass ceiling). Skill-based pay systems directly linking training to employees' wage rates to encourage employees to learn were also discussed.

Note that for many issues discussed in this chapter, training is one part of the solution. For example, trainers and managers can take steps to ensure that women and minorities are not excluded from training programs, but this will not solve the broader issue of discrimination in our society. Similarly, companies like Marriott are using training to provide welfare recipients with employment. However, training can not overcome broader societal ills that have resulted in persons being overly dependent on the welfare system. Only through partnerships between education, private sector training practices, and government legislation can societal problems of discrimination and hard-core unemployment be resolved.

Key Terms

copyrights   252

Americans with Disabilities Act
  (ADA)   254

reasonable accommodation   254

expatriate   255

cross-cultural preparation   255

culture   256

individualism–collectivism   257

uncertainty avoidance   258

masculinity–femininity   258

power distance   258

long-term–short-term
  orientation   258

repatriation   260

managing diversity   262

diversity training   265

attitude awareness and change
  programs   265

behavior-based programs   266

school-to-work transition
  programs   269

School-to-Work Opportunities
  Act   269

glass ceiling   271

joint union–management training
  programs   272

succession planning   273

skill-based pay systems   276

knowledge-based pay systems   276

cross-training   276

Discussion Questions

1. What are some potential legal issues that a trainer should consider before deciding to run an adventure learning program?

2. Discuss the steps in preparing a manager to go overseas.

3. List the five dimensions of culture. How does each of the dimensions affect employee behavior?

4. What does the "rigor" of a cross-cultural training program refer to? What factors influence the level of training rigor needed?

5. What does "managing diversity" mean to you? Assume you were in charge of developing a diversity training program. Who would be involved? What would you include as the content of the program?

6. What are school-to-work transition programs? Why are they needed?

7. What are some potential advantages and disadvantages of attitude-awareness–based diversity training programs?

8. Discuss the implications of a skill-based pay system for training practices.

Application Assignments

1. Texaco Inc. has been accused of discriminating against minorities. The company has taken many steps (including diversity training) to correct this problem. Visit the World Wide Web address http://www.bus.msu.edu/pim/faculty/noe/ray.htm. Find the articles related to Texaco's diversity problems under the heading "What's News." Read the articles related to Texaco's problems with discrimination and diversity efforts. Also, check Texaco's home page (http://www.texaco.com) for the most recent news releases regarding its diversity efforts.

   Based on the information provided, write a brief critique of the company's response. What actions do you believe will be most effective? Least effective? If you had to develop a diversity training program at Texaco, what would you do?

2. You are in charge of preparing a team of three managers from the United States to go to Ciudad Juarez, Mexico, where you have recently acquired an auto assembly plant. The managers will be in charge of reviewing current plant operations and managing the plant for the next three years. You have one month to prepare them to leave on assignment. What will you do? Use the following resources to help develop your plan: M. Gowan, S. Ibarreche, and C. Lackey, "Doing the Right Things in Mexico," *Academy of Management Executive,* 10, no. 1 (1996): 74–81; and M. de Forest, "Thinking of a Plant in Mexico," *Academy of Management Executive* 8, no. 1 (1994): 33–40. Also, the web site www.shrm.org/hrlinks/intl.htm includes resources on foreign labor statistics, cost of living, and country descriptions.

Endnotes

1. J. K. McAfee and L. S. Cote, "Avoid Having Your Day in Court," *Training and Development Journal* (April 1985): 56–60.
2. G. Kimmerling, "A Licensing Primer for Trainers," *Training and Development* (January 1997): 30–35.
3. U.S. Department of Labor, *A Report on the Glass Ceiling Initiative* (Washington, DC: U.S. Government Printing Office, 1991); C. Petrini, "Raising the Ceiling for Women," *Training and Development* (November 1995): 12.
4. R. Sharpe, "In Whose Hands? Allstate and Scientology," *The Wall Street Journal* (March 22, 1995): A1, A4.
5. Bureau of National Affairs, "Female Grocery Store Employees Prevail in Sex-Bias Suit against Lucky Stores," *BNAs Employee Relations Weekly* 10 (1992): 927–38; *Stender* v. *Lucky Store Inc.,* DC Ncalifornia, No. c-88-1467, 8/18/92.
6. J. Sample and R. Hylton, "Falling Off a Log—and Landing in Court," *Training* (May 1996): 67–69.
7. M. J. Mandel, "Business Rolls the Dice," *Business Week* (October 17, 1994): 88–90.
8. "It's Only Rock 'n' Rice," *The Economist* (April 9, 1994): 71.

9. B. Ettorre, "Let's Hear It for Local Talent," *Management Review* (October 1994): 9; S. Franklin, "A New World Order for Business Strategy," *Chicago Tribune* (May 15, 1994): sec. 19, 7–8.

10. V. Sathe, *Culture and Related Corporate Realities* (Homewood, IL: Richard D. Irwin, 1985); M. Rokeach, *Beliefs, Attitudes and Values* (San Francisco: Jossey-Bass, 1968).

11. G. Hofstede, "Dimensions of National Cultures in Fifty Countries and Three Regions," in *Expectations in Cross-Cultural Psychology,* eds. J. Deregowski, S. Dziurawiec, and R. C. Annis (Lisse, Netherlands: Swet and Zeitlinger, 1983); G. Hofstede, "Cultural Constraints in Management Theories," *Academy of Management Executive* 7, no.1 (1993): 81–94.

12. R. Frank and T. M. Burton, "Cross-Border Merger Results in Headaches for a Drug Company," *The Wall Street Journal* (February 4, 1997): A1, A12.

13. M. E. de Forest, "Thinking of a Plant in Mexico?" *Academy of Management Executive* 8, no. 1 (1994): 33–50.

14. R. L. Tung, "Selection and Training of Personnel for Overseas Assignments," *Columbia Journal of World Business* 16 (1981): 18–78.

15. W. A. Arthur, Jr., and W. Bennett, Jr., "The International Assignee: The Relative Importance of Factors Perceived to Contribute to Success," *Personnel Psychology* 48, 99–114; G. M. Spreitzer, M. W. McCall, Jr., and Joan D. Mahoney, "Early Identification of International Executive Potential," *Journal of Applied Psychology* 82 (1997): 6–29.

16. J. S. Black and J. K. Stephens, "The Influence of the Spouse on American Expatriate Adjustment and Intent to Stay in Pacific Rim Overseas Assignments," *Journal of Management* 15 (1989): 529–44.

17. E. Dunbar and A. Katcher, "Preparing Managers for Foreign Assignments," *Training and Development Journal* (September 1990): 45–47.

18. J. S. Black and M. Mendenhall, "A Practical but Theory-Based Framework for Selecting Cross-Cultural Training Methods," in *Readings and Cases in International Human Resource Management,* eds. M. Mendenhall and G. Oddou (Boston: PWS–Kent, 1991): 177–204.

19. S. Ronen, "Training the International Assignee," in *Training and Development in Organizations,* ed. I. L. Goldstein (San Francisco: Jossey-Bass, 1989): 417–53.

20. P. R. Harris and R. T. Moran, *Managing Cultural Differences* (Houston: Gulf Publishing, 1991).

21. Ibid.

22. C. M. Solomon, "Repatriation: Up, Down, or Out?" *Personnel Journal* (January 1995): 28–37; D. R. Briscoe, *International Human Resource Management* (Englewood Cliffs, NJ: Prentice-Hall, 1994).

23. B. Filipczak, "Think Locally, Train Globally," *Training* (January 1997): 41–48.

24. L. Thach, "Training in Russia," *Training and Development,* (July 1996): 34–37.

25. S. E. Jackson and Associates, *Diversity in the Workplace: Human Resource Initiatives* (New York: Guilford Press, 1992).

26. T. C. Cox, *Cultural Diversity in Organizations* (San Francisco: Berrett-Kohler, 1993): 24–27.

27. M. Selz, "Small Company Goes Global with Diverse Workforce," *The Wall Street Journal* (October 12, 1994): B2.

28. R. M. Kanter, "When a Thousand Flowers Bloom: Structural, Collective, and Social Conditions for Innovations in Organizations," in *Research in Organizational*

Behavior, vol. 10, eds. L. L. Cummings and B. M. Staw (Greenwich, CT: JAI Press, 1988): 169–211; W. Watson, Kamalesh Kumar, and L. K. Michaelsen, "Cultural Diversity's Impact on Interaction Process and Performance: Comparing Homogeneous and Diverse Task Groups," *Academy of Management Journal* 36 (1993): 590–602.

29. S. Caudron, "Diversity Ignites Effective Work Teams," *Personnel Journal* (September 1994): 54–63.

30. R. R. Thomas, "Managing Diversity: A Conceptual Framework," in *Diversity in the Workplace* (New York: Guilford Press): 306–18.

31. M. E. Heilman, C. J. Block, and J. A. Lucas, "Presumed Incompetent? Stigmatization and Affirmative Action Efforts," *Journal of Applied Psychology* 77: 536–44.

32. B. Gerber, "Managing Diversity," *Training* (July 1990): 23–30; T. Diamante, C. L. Reid, and L. Ciylo, "Making the Right Training Moves," *HR Magazine* (March 1995): 60–65.

33. C. M. Solomon, "The Corporate Response to Workforce Diversity," *Personnel Journal* (August 1989): 43–53; A. Morrison, *The New Leaders: Guidelines on Leadership Diversity in America* (San Francisco: Jossey-Bass, 1992).

34. S. M. Paskoff, "Ending the Workplace Diversity Wars," *Training* (August 1996): 43–47; H. B. Karp and N. Sutton, "Where Diversity Training Goes Wrong," *Training* (July 1993): 30–34.

35. S. M. Paskoff, "Ending the Workplace Diversity Wars."

36. A. Markels, "Diversity Program Can Prove Divisive," *The Wall Street Journal* (January 30, 1997): B1–B2; "R. R. Donnelley Curtails Diversity Training Moves," *The Wall Street Journal* (February 13, 1997): B3.

37. S. Rynes and B. Rosen, "What Makes Diversity Programs Work?" *HR Magazine* (October 1994): 67–73; S. Rynes and B. Rosen, "A Field Survey of Factors Affecting the Adoption and Perceived Success of Diversity Training," *Personnel Psychology* 48 (1995): 247–70.

38. G. Flynn, "Do You Have the Right Approach to Diversity?" *Personnel Journal* (October 1995): 68–72; M. Galen and A. T. Palmer, "Diversity: Beyond the Numbers Game," *Business Week* (August 14, 1995): 60–61.

39. L. E. Wynter, "Allstate Rates Managers on Handing Diversity," *The Wall Street Journal* (November 1, 1997): B1.

40. Ibid. Also, see Gannett's home page at http://www.gannett.com, "Gannett's Basic Game Plan."

41. C. T. Schreiber, K. F. Price, and A. Morrison, "Workforce Diversity and the Glass Ceiling: Practices, Barriers, Possibilities," *Human Resource Planning* 16 (1994): 51–69.

42. D. Stamps, "Will School-to-Work Transition Work?" *Training* (June 1996): 72–81.

43. F. Jossi, "From Welfare to Work," *Training* (April 1997): 45–50.

44. P. J. O'Connor, "Getting Down to Basics," *Training & Development* (July 1993): 62–64.

45. U.S. Department of Labor, *A Report on the Glass Ceiling Initiative* (Washington, DC: U.S. Government Printing Office, 1991).

46. P. J. Ohlott, M. N. Ruderman, and C. D. McCauley, "Gender Differences in Managers' Developmental Job Experiences," *Academy of Management Journal* 37 (1994): 46–67.

47. L. A. Mainiero, "Getting Anointed for Advancement: The Case of Executive Women," *Academy of Management Executive* 8 (1994): 53–67; J. S. Lublin,

"Women at Top Still Are Distant from CEO Jobs," *The Wall Street Journal* (February 28, 1995): B1, B5; P. Tharenov, S. Latimer, and D. Conroy, "How Do You Make It to the Top? An Examination of Influences on Women's and Men's Managerial Advancement," *Academy of Management Journal* 37 (1994): 899–931.

48. U.S. Department of Labor, *A Report on the Glass Ceiling Initiative* (Washington, DC: U.S. Government Printing Office, 1991); R. A. Noe, "Women and Mentoring: A Review and Research Agenda," *Academy of Management Review* 13 (1988): 65–78; B. R. Ragins and J. L. Cotton, "Easier Said than Done: Gender Differences in Perceived Barriers to Gaining a Mentor," *Academy of Management Journal* 34 (1991): 939–51.

49. L. Roberson and N. C. Gutierrez, "Beyond Good Faith: Commitment to Recruiting Management Diversity at Pacific Bell," in *Diversity in the Workplace:* 65–88.

50. M. Hequet, "The Union Push for Lifelong Learning," *Training,* March (1994): 26–31; S. J. Schurman, M. K. Hugentoble, and H. Stack, "Lessons from the UAW–GM Paid Education Leave Program," in *Joint Training Programs,* eds. L. A. Ferman, M. Hoyman, J. Cutcher-Gershenfeld, and E. J. Savoie (Ithaca, NY: ILR Press, 1991): 71–94.

51. E. S. Tomasko and K. K. Dickinson, "The UAW–Ford Education Development and Training Program," in *Joint Training Programs:* 55–70.

52. C. B. Derr, C. Jones, and E. L. Toomey, "Managing High-Potential Employees: Current Practices in Thirty-three U.S. Corporations," *Human Resource Management* 27 (1988): 273–90.

53. H. S. Feild and S. G. Harris, "Entry-Level, Fast-Track Management Development Programs: Developmental Tactics and Perceived Program Effectiveness," *Human Resource Planning* 14 (1991): 261–73.

54. Ibid.

55. Derr, Jones, and Toomey, "Managing High-Potential Employees"; K. M. Nowack, "The Secrets of Succession," *Training and Development* 48 (1994): 49–54; J. S. Lublin, "An Overseas Stint Can Be a Ticket to the Top," *The Wall Street Journal* (January 29, 1996): B1–B2.

56. Ibid.

57. S. Caudron, "Plan Today for an Unexpected Tomorrow," *Personnel Journal* September (1996): 40–45.

58. M. W. McCall, Jr., and M. M. Lombardo, "Off the Track: Why and How Successful Executives Get Derailed," Technical Report no. 21 (Greensboro, NC: Center for Creative Leadership, 1983); E. V. Veslor and J. B. Leslie, "Why Executives Derail: Perspectives across Time and Cultures," *Academy of Management Executive* 9 (1995): 62–72.

59. L. W. Hellervik, J. F. Hazucha, and R. J. Schneider, "Behavior Change: Models, Methods, and a Review of Evidence," in *Handbook of Industrial and Organizational Psychology,* 2d ed., eds. M. D. Dunnette and L. M. Hough (Palo Alto, CA: Consulting Psychologists Press, 1992), 3: 823–99.

60. D. B. Peterson, "Measuring and Evaluating Change in Executive and Managerial Development." Paper presented at the annual conference of the Society for Industrial and Organizational Psychology, Miami, FL, 1990.

61. G. E. Ledford, "Paying for the Skills, Knowledge, Competencies of Knowledge Workers," *Compensation and Benefits Review* (July–August 1995): 55.

62. E. E. Lawler III, *Strategic Pay* (San Francisco: Jossey-Bass, 1990).

63. D. Feuer, "Paying for Knowledge," *Training* (May 1987): 57–66.

11 CAREERS AND CAREER MANAGEMENT

Objectives

After reading this chapter, you should be able to

1. Identify the reasons why companies should help employees manage their careers.

2. Discuss why and how the concept of a career has changed.

3. Explain the development tasks and activities in the career development process.

4. Design a career management system.

5. Effectively perform the manager's role in career management.

THE END OF THE JOB

He moves from company to company, working on computer problems as a consultant. His earnings vary from month to month depending on demands for his services. His luggage is always packed with a change of clothes and 35 pounds of technical manuals. The battery in his laptop computer is always charged.

This is the life of a consultant. As the gradual trend away from traditional jobs continues due to downsizing, short product life cycles, and increases in project work, consultants are becoming more prevalent. Traditional full-time employees, contract employees, and consultants are combined into teams that break up when the project is completed. The consultants then move on to their next jobs. The consultants may have to stay away from family and friends for months and live with financial insecurity. Although their skills are valued by their clients, when they arrive on the job they often are alienated from full-time employees they have to work with who feel threatened by their presence.

The move toward using consultants is especially prevalent in the information services area. Internal information processing staffs have been downsized as companies have decided that they don't need internal staffs and can find talented employees on an as-needed basis. As a result, many talented technological experts have become consultants. With many corporations trying to move from mainframe computers to personal-computer–based applications, many companies have an overabundance of experienced information systems staff who have spent their careers building,

writing language for, operating, and repairing mainframe computer systems. These experts tend to identify with their employer, while the outside consultants tend to be ambitious, more risk-taking, and loyal primarily to themselves. ■

Source: B. Wysocki, Jr., "High Tech Nomads Write New Program for Future Work," *The Wall Street Journal* (August 19, 1996): A1, A6.

Introduction

As the opening vignette illustrates, new technology and changes in business priorities have resulted in a new kind of career: the project career. For example, many experienced information systems specialists who are now in a consulting role find a large demand for their services related to projects involving fixing computer problems resulting from switching from the year 1999 to the year 2000. The project career is one example of the types of careers that have emerged as a result of competitive challenges that companies are experiencing. (See Chapter 1.) One reason the project career has emerged is the restructuring of organizations and changing work design.[1] Many companies are using teams to produce products and provide services. This gives companies the flexibility to bring talented persons both inside (full-time employees) and outside the company (temporary and contract employees) to work on services and products on an as-needed basis. These changes are creating changes in the career concept and increasing the importance of career management from both the employee's and the company's perspective.

You may wonder why a training book covers career and career management. It is important to recognize that employees' motivation to attend training programs, the outcomes they expect to gain from attendance, their choice of programs, and how and what they need to know has been affected by changes in the concept of a "career." As you will learn in the chapter, changing expectations that employers and employees have for one another (referred to as the psychological contract) have caused more emphasis to be placed on using job experiences and relationships for learning rather than formal training courses and seminars. Also, trainers may be responsible for designing programs to help managers play an effective role in career management systems.

We begin this chapter by discussing why career management is important. The second part of the chapter introduces you to changes in the concept of a career. The implications of these changes for career management are emphasized. Based on the new career concept we present a model of career development that highlights the developmental challenges employees face and how companies can help employees meet these challenges. The chapter concludes by examining the specific components of career management systems. The roles that employees, managers, and companies need to fulfill for career management systems to be successful are discussed.

Why Is Career Management Important?

Career management is the process through which employees

- Become aware of their own interests, values, strengths, and weaknesses.
- Obtain information about job opportunities within the company.
- Identify career goals.
- Establish action plans to achieve career goals.[2]

Career management is important from both the employees' perspective and the company's perspective.[3] From the company's perspective, the failure to motivate employees to plan their careers can result in a shortage of employees to fill open positions, lower employee commitment, and inappropriate use of monies allocated for training and development programs. From the employees' perspective, lack of career management can result in frustration, feelings of not being valued in the company, and being unable to find suitable employment should a job change (internal or with another company) be necessary due to mergers, acquisitions, restructuring, or downsizing.

Companies need to help employees manage their careers to maximize their career motivation. Career motivation has three aspects: career resilience, career insight, and career identity.[4] Career resilience is the extent to which employees are able to cope with problems that affect their work. Career insight involves (1) how much employees know about their interests, and their skill strengths and weaknesses and (2) how these perceptions relate to their career goals. Career identity is the degree to which employees define their personal values according to their work.

Figure 11–1 shows how career motivation can create value for both the company and employees. Career motivation likely has a significant relationship to the extent to which a company is innovative and adaptable to change. Employees who have high career resilience are able to respond to obstacles in the work environment and adapt to unexpected events (such as changes in work processes or customer demands). They are dedicated to continuous learning, are willing to develop new ways to use their skills, take responsibility for career management, and are committed to the company's success.[5] Research suggests that low career motivation may be especially detrimental for older, more experienced employees.[6]

Employees with high career insight set career goals and participate in development activities that help them reach those goals. They tend to take actions that keep their skills from becoming obsolete. Employees with high career identity are committed to the company; they are willing to do whatever it takes

FIGURE 11–1

The value of career motivation

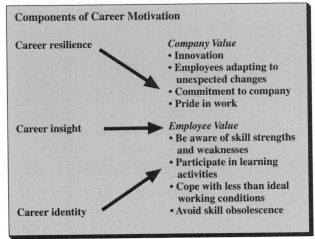

(e.g., work long hours) to complete projects and meet customer demands. They also take pride in working for the company and are active in professional and trade organizations.

Career motivation is positively influenced by how much companies provide opportunities for achievement, encouragement for development, and information about career opportunities. Career management systems help identify these opportunities and provide career information. Sears Credit's experience with career management is a good example of (a) how career management can help a company cope with competitive challenges and (b) the positive outcomes that can result from career management.[7] Sears Credit is responsible for all credit transactions in the retail stores of Sears Merchandise Group. Sears Credit underwent a major reorganization. The company's strategic plan caused nine units to expand, closed 50 small units, offered a major voluntary retirement program, and accepted third-party charge cards in competition with the Sears charge card. As a result of the reorganization, the company lost 3,000 associates (employees), going from 13,000 to 10,000 associates.

The reorganization created a career development nightmare. Virtually all jobs were redefined or newly created. Career paths were obsolete. There was a need to develop succession plans so associates were prepared to fill future positions. As a result, a major career development initiative was launched to align employees' skills and work loads. Senior management decided that it wanted the company to have more open communications about career opportunities and to redefine career success in terms of what was important to the associate rather than in terms of training and developing to preparing for promotion opportunities. Senior management also emphasized the need to have employees take more personal responsibility for managing their career and for managers to accept their role as career coaches.

A key element of the career development process was identifying the competencies needed for success in the restructured jobs. Five major categories of competencies were identified based on surveys of associates and managers: business knowledge and contribution to financial results, leadership, customer focus, individual effectiveness, and associate development. Sears Credit also decided to implement an assessment system involving manager, self, and peer evaluations to help employees identify growth areas. To ensure that associates understood the system, Sears Credit had to develop workshops. All exempt employees were expected to participate in a two-day workshop explaining the self-assessment activities and the development planning process. Managers also participated in a workshop to help them develop career coaching skills and provide advice on how they could manage their own careers. Technology was utilized to make new job descriptions available to all employees on the electronic mail system. Also, a data bank of employees' career goals was developed. The data bank was available to match employees' needs and interests with specific jobs and to assist in planning training activities. Because career development is impacted by a company's incentive system, Sears Credit introduced a new compensation program. The program, known as broadbanding, expanded pay grades and allowed for salary increases for lateral job moves that traditionally were not entitled to increased compensation. The hope was that the broadbanding system would motivate employees to develop a broader range of skills.

Preliminary evaluations of the program have been positive. Most associates report taking responsibility for their own career, developing specific career plans and goals, and being more aware and realistic about their interests, strengths, and development needs. As Tom Cataruzolo, director of HR and training, explains, "The career-development process was the catalyst that changed personal career planning from passive participation of each manager to a very active role in individual career growth. It heightened the awareness of self-assessments, job competencies, and performance. More importantly, it helped foster an environment of openness."

What Is a Career?

Traditionally, careers have been described in several different ways.[8] Careers have been described as a sequence of positions held within an occupation. For example, university faculty members can hold assistant, associate, and full professor positions. A career has also been described in the context of mobility within an organization. For example, an engineer may begin her career as a staff engineer. As her expertise, experience, and performance increase, she may move through advisory engineering, senior engineering, and senior technical positions. Finally, a career has been described as a characteristic of the employee. Each employee's career consists of different jobs, positions, and experiences.

The new concept of the career is often referred to as a protean career.[9] A **protean career** is a career that is frequently changing based on both changes in the person's interests, abilities, and values and changes in the work environment.

Compared to the traditional career, employees take major responsibility for managing their careers. For example, an engineering employee may take a sabbatical from her engineering position to work at the United Way Agency for a year in a management position. The purpose of this assignment is to develop her managerial skills as well as personally evaluate if she likes managerial work more than engineering. Table 11–1 compares the traditional career to the protean career on several dimensions. Changes in the psychological contract between employees and company have influenced the career concept.[10] A **psychological contract** is the expectation that employers and employees have about each other. Traditionally, the psychological contract emphasized that the company would provide continued employment and advancement opportunities if the employee remained with the company and maintained a high level of job performance. Pay increases and status were linked directly to vertical movement in the company (promotions).

However, the psychological contract between employees and employers has changed. Why? One reason is the change in company's organizational structure. Because companies' structures tend to be "flat," i.e. the structure has fewer layers of management, authority is decentralized, and more of employees' responsibilities are organized on a project or customer basis rather on a functional basis. As a result, employees are expected to develop a wide variety of skills (recall the technological, structural, and social competitive challenges discussed in Chapter 1). Another reason is that due to increased domestic and global competition as well as mergers and acquisitions, companies can't offer job security. Instead of job security, companies can help ensure that employees have opportunities to

TABLE 11–1   Comparison of Traditional Career and Protean Career

Dimension	*Traditional Career*	*Protean Career*
Goal	Promotions Salary increase	Psychological success
Psychological contract	Security for commitment	Employability for flexibility
Mobility	Vertical	Lateral
Responsibility for management	Company	Employee
Pattern	Linear and expert	Spiral and transitory
Expertise	Know how	Learn how
Development	Heavy reliance on formal training	Greater reliance on relationships and job experiences

Source: Based on D. T. Hall, "Protean Careers of the 21st Century," *Academy of Management Executive* 10 (1996): 8–16; N. Nicholson, "Career Systems in Crisis: Change and Opportunity in the Information Age," *Academy of Management Executive* 10 (1996): 40–51; K. Brousseau, M. J. Driver, K. Eneroth, and R. Larsson, "Career Pandemonium: Realigning Organizations and Individuals," *Academy of Management Executive* 10 (1996): 52–66.

attend training programs and participate in work experiences that can increase their employability with their current and future employers.

The goal of the new career is psychological success. **Psychological success** is the feeling of pride and accomplishment that comes from achieving life goals that are not limited to achievements at work (e.g., raising a family, good physical health). Psychological success is more under the control of the employee than the traditional career goals, which were not only influenced by employee effort but controlled by the availability of positions in the company. Psychological success is self-determined rather than solely determined through signals the employee receives from the company (e.g., salary increase, promotion). Psychological success appears to be especially prevalent among the new generation of persons entering the work force. Many members of this generation, often referred to as Generation X, are unimpressed with status symbols, want flexibility in doing job tasks, and desire meaning from their work.[11]

Another important difference between the traditional career and the protean career is the need to be motivated and able to learn rather than relying on a static knowledge base. This has resulted from companies' need to be more responsive to customers' service and product demands. The types of knowledge that an employee needs to be successful have changed.[12] In the traditional career, "knowing how"—having the appropriate skills and knowledge to provide a service or produce a product—was critical. Although knowing how remains important, employees need to "know why" and "know whom." Knowing why refers to understanding the company's business and culture so that the employee can develop and apply knowledge and skills that can contribute to the business. Knowing whom refers to relationships that the employee may develop to contribute to company success. These relationships may include networking with vendors, suppliers, community members, customers, or industry experts. To learn to know whom and know why requires more than formal courses and training programs. Learning and development in the protean career are increasingly likely to involve relationships and job experiences rather than formal courses. For example, as we mentioned in Chapter 9, through mentoring relationships employees can gain exposure and visibility to a wide range of persons inside and outside the company. Job experiences involving project assignments and job rotation can provide employees with a better understanding of the business strategy, functions and divisions of the company as well as helping employees developing valuable contacts.

The emphasis on continuous learning and learning beyond knowing how as well as changes in the psychological contract are resulting in changes in direction and frequency of movement within careers (career pattern).[13] Traditional career patterns consisted of a series of steps arranged in a linear hierarchy, with higher steps in the hierarchy related to increased authority, responsibility, and compensation. Expert career patterns involve a life-long commitment to a field or specialization (e.g. law, medicine, management). These types of career patterns will not disappear. Rather, career patterns involving movement across specializations or disciplines (spiral career patterns) will become more prevalent.

Also, as the chapter introduction illustrates, careers in which the person moves from job to job every three to five years (transitory career patterns) are likely to become more common.

The most appropriate view of a career is that it is "boundaryless."[14] It may include movement across several employers or even different occupations. For example, statistics indicate that the average employment tenure for all U.S. workers is only five years.[15] For example, Craig Matison, 33 years old, took a job with Cincinnati Bell Information System, a unit of Cincinnati Bell Corporation that manages billing for phone and cable companies.[16] Although he has been on the job for only six months, he is already looking to make his next career move. He does not want to stay on the technical career path and regularly explores company databases for job postings, looking for sales and marketing opportunities within the company. A career may also involve identifying more with a job or profession than with the present employer. A career can also be considered boundaryless in the sense that career plans or goals are influenced by personal or family demands and values. Finally, boundaryless may refer to the fact that career success may not be tied to promotions. Rather, career success is related to achieving goals that are personally meaningful to the employee, rather than those set by parents, peers, or the company.

As a result, we consider a **career** to be "the pattern of work-related experiences that span the course of a person's life."[17] Work experiences include positions, job experiences, and tasks. Work experiences are influenced by employees' values, needs, and feelings. Employees' career needs vary depending on their stage of career development and their biological age. As a result, managers must understand the career development process and the differences in employees' needs and interests at each stage of development.

A Model of Career Development

Career development is the process by which employees progress through a series of stages, each characterized by a different set of developmental tasks, activities, and relationships.[18] There are several different career development models. Although it is widely accepted that the concept of a career has changed, the research literature does not agree on which career development model is best.[19]

Table 11–2 presents a model that incorporates the important contributions that the life-cycle, organization-based, and directional pattern models make to understanding career development. The **life-cycle models** suggest that employees face certain developmental tasks over the course of their careers and that they move through distinct life or career stages. The **organization-based models** also suggest that careers proceed through a series of stages, but these models suggest that career development involves employees' learning to perform certain activities. Each stage involves changes in activities and relationships with peers and managers. The **directional pattern model** describes the form or shape of careers.[20] As we noted in the discussion of the changing career concept, these

TABLE 11–2   A Model of Career Development

	Career Stage			
	Exploration	*Establishment*	*Maintenance*	*Disengagement*
Developmental tasks	Identify interests, skills, fit between self and work	Advancement, growth, security, develop life-style	Hold on to accomplishments, update skills	Retirement planning, change balance between work and nonwork
Activities	Helping Learning Following directions	Making independent contributions	Training Sponsoring Policy making	Phasing out of work
Relationships to other employees	Apprentice	Colleague	Mentor	Sponsor
Age	Less than 30	30–45	45–60	61+
Years on job	Less than 2 years	2–10 years	More than 10 years	More than 10 years

models suggest that employees make decisions about how quickly they want to progress through the career stages and at what point they want to return to an earlier career stage. For example, some employees plan on staying in a job or occupation their entire lives and have well-thought-out plans for moving within the occupation (this career having a linear shape). Other employees view their careers as having a spiral shape. As the opening vignette illustrated, the spiral career form is increasing as many employees work on projects or in jobs for a specific period of time and then take a different job or project within or outside their current employer. As discussed in Chapter 9, employees may actually accept a job in another functional area (also known as a downward move) that is lower in status than their current job in order to learn the basic skills and get the experiences needed to be successful in this new function.

As Table 11–2 shows, researchers generally recognize four career stages: exploration, establishment, maintenance, and disengagement. Each career stage is characterized by developmental tasks, activities, and relationships. Research suggests that employees' current career stage influences their needs, attitudes, and job behaviors. For example, one study found that salespersons in the exploration career stage tended to change jobs and accept promotions more frequently than salespersons in other career stages.[21] Another study found that the degree to which employees identify with their job is affected more by the job's characteristics (e.g., variety of tasks, responsibility for task completion) in early career stages than in later career stages.[22]

Exploration Stage.   In the **exploration stage,** individuals attempt to identify the type of work that interests them. They consider their interests, values, and work preferences, and they seek information about jobs, careers, and occupations from co-workers, friends, and family members. Once they identify the type of work or occupation that interests them, individuals can begin pursuing the needed education or training. Typically, exploration occurs in the midteens to early-to-late twenties (while the individual is still a student in high school, college, or technical school). Exploration continues when the individual starts a new job. In most cases, employees who are new to a job are not prepared to take on work tasks and roles without help and direction from others. In many jobs, the new employee is considered an apprentice. From the company's perspective, orientation and socialization activities are necessary to help new employees get as comfortable as possible with their new jobs and co-workers so they can begin to contribute to the company's goals.

Establishment Stage.   In the **establishment stage,** individuals find their place in the company, make an independent contribution, achieve more responsibility and financial success, and establish a desirable life-style. Employees at this stage are interested in being viewed as a contributor to the company's success. They learn how the company views their contributions from informal interactions with peers and managers and from formal feedback received through the performance-appraisal system. For employees in this stage, the company needs to develop policies that help balance work and nonwork roles. Also, employees in this stage need to become more actively involved in career-planning activities.

Maintenance Stage.   In the **maintenance stage,** the individual is concerned with keeping skills up to date and being perceived by others as someone who is still contributing to the company. Individuals in the maintenance stage have many years of job experience, much job knowledge, and an in-depth understanding of how the company expects business to be conducted. Employees in the maintenance stage can be valuable trainers or mentors for new employees. They are usually asked to review or develop company policies or goals. Their opinions about work processes, problems, and important issues that the work unit is facing may be solicited. From the company's perspective, a major issue is how to keep employees in the maintenance stage from plateauing. Also, the company needs to ensure that employees' skills do not become obsolete.

Disengagement Stage.   In the **disengagement stage,** individuals prepare for a change in the balance between work and nonwork activities. When we think of disengagement, we typically think of older employees electing to retire and concentrate entirely on nonwork activities such as sports, hobbies, traveling, or volunteer work. However, for many employees, the disengagement stage does not mean a complete reduction in work hours. Rather, many decide to remain with the company but work reduced hours, perhaps serving as a consultant. Also, regardless of age, employees may elect to leave a company to change occupations or jobs. Some may be forced to leave the company because of downsizing or mergers. Others may leave because of their interests, values, or abilities.

Employees who leave the company often recycle back to the exploration stage. They need information about potential new career areas, and they have to reconsider their career interests and skill strengths. From the company's perspective, the major career management activities in the disengagement stage are retirement planning and outplacement.

As Table 11–2 shows, an employee's age and length of time on the job are believed to be good signals of the employee's career stage. However, relying strictly on these two characteristics would lead to erroneous conclusions about the employee's career needs. For example, many changes that older employees make in their careers involve "recycling" back to an earlier career stage.[23] **Recycling** involves changing one's major work activity after having been established in a specific field. Recycling is accompanied by a reexploration of values, skills, interests, and potential employment opportunities.

It is also not uncommon for employees who are considering recycling to conduct informational interviews with managers and other employees who hold jobs in functional areas they believe may be congruent with their interests and abilities. Nancy Handley, a Wal-Mart employee who oversees the men's department, is trying out management work to see if it matches her interests. She is not sure that she is willing to work the longer hours and live with the possibility of having to transfer to an out-of-state store if she takes a managerial position. Regardless, she is handling personnel issues and spends time at the customer service desk one day a week (both managerial responsibilities).[24]

Now that you are familiar with the career stage model and the concept of recycling, let's consider an example. For a large portion of his life, Sam Lifshus was a furrier and auctioneer. But in his early nineties, he became interested in helping care for the sick. As a result, Sam evaluated career options in the health care field and explored where he would get the education he needed to change careers. Sam decided to take classes through a senior-citizen employment program. Sam successfully completed the program. He is now a nursing assistant at Memorial Hospital in Hollywood, California. Sam's career reinforces the idea that a person can disengage from a career regardless of age and recycle back into an earlier career stage (in his case, exploration).[25]

As the previous discussion illustrates, employees bring a range of career development issues to the workplace. We discuss specific career development issues (e.g., orientation, outplacement, work, and family) in Chapter 12. Besides developing policies and programs that will help employees deal with these issues (in order to maximize their level of career motivation), companies need to provide a career planning system to identify employees' career development needs. A **career management system** helps employees, managers, and the company identify career development needs.

Figure 11–2

The career management process

Self-assessment ⟶ Reality check ⟶ Goal setting ⟶ Action planning

Career Management Systems

Companies' career management systems vary in the level of sophistication and the emphasis they place on the different components of the process. However, all career management systems include the components shown in Figure 11–2: self-assessment, reality check, goal setting, and action planning.

Self-Assessment.   **Self-assessment** refers to the use of information by employees to determine their career interests, values, aptitudes, and behavioral tendencies. It often involves psychological tests such as the Strong-Campbell Interest Inventory and the Self-Directed Search. The former helps employees identify their occupational and job interests; the latter identifies employees' preferences for working in different types of environments (e.g., sales, counseling, landscaping). Tests may also help employees identify the relative value they place on work and leisure activities. Self-assessment can also involve exercises such as the one in Table 11–3. This type of exercise helps employees consider where they are now in their careers, identify future plans, and assess how their career fits with their current situation and available resources. Career counselors are often used to assist employees in the self-assessment process and interpret the results of psychological tests.

For example, a man who had served as a branch manager at Wells Fargo Bank for 14 years enjoyed both working with computers and researching program development issues.[26] He was experiencing difficulty in choosing whether to pursue further work experiences with computers or enter a new career in developing software applications. Psychological tests he completed as part of the company's career assessment program confirmed that he had strong interests in research and development. As a result, he began his own software design company.

Reality Check.   **Reality check** refers to the information employees receive about how the company evaluates their skills and knowledge and where they fit into the company's plans (e.g., potential promotion opportunities, lateral moves). Usually, this information is provided by the employee's manager as part of the performance appraisal process. It is not uncommon in well-developed career planning systems for the manager to hold separate performance appraisals and career development discussions. For example, in Coca-Cola USA's career planning system, employees and managers have a separate meeting after the annual performance review to discuss the employee's career interests, strengths, and possible development activities.[27]

TABLE 11–3   Example of a Self-Assessment Exercise

Activity   (Purpose)

Step 1:   *Where Am I?*   (Examine Current Position of Life and Career.)
Think about your life from past and present to the future. Draw a time line to represent important events.

Step 2:   *Who Am I?*   (Examine Different Roles.)
Using 3 × 5 cards, write down one answer per card to the question "Who am I?"

Step 3:   *Where would I like to be and what would I like to happen?*
            (This helps in future goal setting.)
Consider you life from present to future. Write an autobiography answering three questions: What do you want to have accomplished? What milestones do you want to achieve? What do you want to be remembered for?

Step 4:   *An Ideal Year in the Future*   (Identify Resources Needed.)
Consider a one-year period in the future. If you had unlimited resources, what would you do? What would the ideal environment look like? Does the ideal environment match step 3?

Step 5:   *An Ideal Job*   (Create Current Goal.)
In the present, think about an ideal job for you with your available resources. Consider your role, resources, and type of training or education needed.

Step 6:   *Career by Objective Inventory*   (Summarize Current Situation.)
• What gets you excited each day?
• What do you do well? What are you known for?
• What do you need to achieve your goals?
• What could interfere with reaching your goals?
• What should you do now to move toward reaching your goals?
• What is your long-term career objective?

Source: Based on J. E. McMahon and S. K. Merman, "Career Development," in *The ASTD Training and Development Handbook,* 4th ed., ed. R. L. Craig (New York: McGraw-Hill. 1996): 679–97.

Goal Setting.   Goal setting refers to the process of employees developing short- and long-term career objectives. These goals usually relate to desired positions (e.g., to become sales manager within three years), level of skill application (e.g., to use one's budgeting skills to improve the unit's cash flow problems), work setting (e.g., to move to corporate marketing within two years), or skill acquisition (e.g., to learn how to use the company's human resource information system). These goals are usually discussed with the manager and written into a development plan. Figure 11–3 shows a development plan.

FIGURE 11–3

Career development plan

Development Needs—Current Position

Specific knowledge and skills needed to improve or maintain satisfactory performance:

Development Needs—Future Position

Specific knowledge and skills to get ready for next position:

Target Job:

Development Activities

Manager and employee will work together to implement the following actions:

Development Objectives:

Behavior or results demonstrating development needs are being met:

Results

Date:

Employee's Signature:

Manager's Signature:

Action Planning.   **Action planning** involves employees determining how they will achieve their short- and long-term career goals. Action plans may involve enrolling in training courses and seminars, conducting informational interviews, or applying for job openings within the company.

United Parcel Service's (UPS's) career development system illustrates the career planning process and the strategic role it can play in ensuring that staffing needs are met.[28] UPS has 285,000 employees in 185 nations and territories who are responsible for making sure that packages are picked up and delivered in a timely fashion. In 1991 UPS was forced to deal with how to develop its managerial ranks, which included 49,000 people worldwide. The task was to develop a management development system that would ensure that managers' skills were up to date and link the system to selection and training activities. As a result, UPS designed a career management process. The process starts with the manager identifying the skills, knowledge, and experience that the work team needs to meet current and anticipated business needs. Gaps between needs and relevant qualifications of the team are identified. The manager then identifies the development needs of each team member. Next, the team members complete a series of exercises that help them with self-assessment, goal setting, and development planning (self-assessment). The manager and employee work together to create an individual development plan. In the discussion, the manager shares performance appraisal information and her analysis of team needs with the employee (reality check). The plan includes the employees' career goals and development actions that he will pursue during the next year (goal setting and action planning). To ensure that the career management process helps with future staffing decisions, divisionwide career development meetings are held. At these meetings managers report on the development needs and plans as well as capabilities of their work teams. Training and development managers attend to ensure that a realistic training plan is created. The process is repeated at higher levels of management. The ultimate result is a master plan with training activities and development plans that are coordinated among the functional areas.

The UPS system includes all of the steps in the career planning process. The most important feature of the system is the sharing of information about individual employees, districts, and functional development and training needs and capabilities. This use of information at all three levels allows UPS to be better prepared to meet changing staffing needs and customer demands than many companies.

Several important design factors should be considered in the process of developing a career management system, as shown in Table 11–4. Tying development of the system to business objectives and needs, top management support (as in the Sears Credit example), and having managers and employees participate in building the system are especially important to overcome resistance to using the system.

TABLE 11–4   **Design Factors of Effective Career Management Systems**

---

1. System is positioned as a response to a business need.
2. Employees and managers participate in development of the system.
3. Employees are encouraged to take an active role in career management.
4. Evaluation is ongoing and used to improve the system.
5. Business units can customize the system for their own purposes (with some constraints).
6. Employees need access to career information sources (including advisors and positions available).
7. Senior management supports the career system.
8. Career management is linked to other human resource practices such as performance management, training, and recruiting systems.

Source: Based on B. Baumann, J. Duncan, S. E. Former, and Z. Leibowitz, "Amoco Primes the Talent Pump," *Personnel Journal* (February 1996): 79–84.

Roles of Employees, Managers, Human Resource Managers, and Company in Career Management

Employees, their managers, human resource managers, and the company share the responsibility for career planning.[29] Figure 11–4 shows the roles of employees, managers, human resource managers, and the company in career management.

Employee's Role.   As we mentioned earlier in the chapter, the new psychological contract suggests that employees can increase their value to their current employer (and increase their employment opportunities) by taking responsibility for career planning. Companies with effective career management systems (like Sears Credit and UPS) expect employees to take responsibility for their own career management. British Petroleum Exploration's employees are provided with a personal development planning guidebook that leads them through assessment, goal setting, development planning, and action planning.[30] Participation in the program is voluntary. The employees must also approach their manager to initiate career-related discussion as part of the personal development planning process.

Regardless of how sophisticated the company's career planning system is, employees should take several career management actions:[31]

- Take the initiative to ask for feedback from managers and peers regarding their skill strengths and weaknesses.
- Identify their stage of career development and development needs.
- Gain exposure to a range of learning opportunities (e.g., sales assignments, product design assignments, administrative assignments).
- Interact with employees from different work groups inside and outside the company (e.g., professional associations, task forces).

FIGURE 11–4

Shared responsibility: Roles in career management

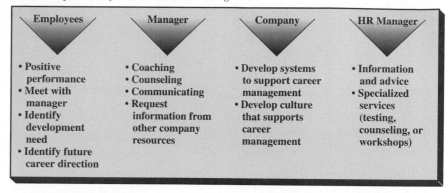

Employees	Manager	Company	HR Manager
• Positive performance • Meet with manager • Identify development need • Identify future career direction	• Coaching • Counseling • Communicating • Request information from other company resources	• Develop systems to support career management • Develop culture that supports career management	• Information and advice • Specialized services (testing, counseling, or workshops)

Manager's Role.   Regardless of the type of formal career planning system in place at the company, managers play a key role in the career management process. In most cases, employees look to their managers for career advice. Why? Because managers typically evaluate employees' readiness for job mobility (e.g., promotions). Also, managers are often the primary source of information about position openings, training courses, and other developmental opportunities. Unfortunately, many managers avoid becoming involved in career planning activities with employees because they do not feel qualified to answer employees' career-related questions, they have limited time for helping employees deal with career issues, and they lack the interpersonal skills needed to fully understand career issues.[32]

To help employees deal with career issues, managers need to be effective in four roles: coach, appraiser, advisor, and referral agent.[33] The responsibilities of each of these roles is shown in Table 11–5. As we see, the manager is responsible for helping the employee manage his career through meeting personal needs as well as company needs. Coaching, appraising, advising, and serving as a referral agent are important roles for managers to play for employees in all stages of their careers. Employees early in their career may need information related to how well their performance is meeting customer expectations. Employees in both establishment and maintenance stages may use the manager as a sounding board for ideas and perspectives on job changes and career paths.

To understand the manager's role in career management, consider the case of José, who works in the oil and chemical industry. José is an industrial hygienist at a chemical plant, where safety is critical. He is unhappy about what he thinks is a lack of career development at the company. As a result, he is considering leaving the company. José has been at a refinery in Texas the past year, but he wants to move back to Utah for family reasons. He was denied a lateral move to a plant in Utah. He made the request at a time when the company was downsizing and seeking voluntary retirements. The company understands that

TABLE 11–5   **Managers' Role in Career Management**

Roles	Responsibilities
Coach	Probe problems. Listen. Clarify concerns. Define concerns.
Appraiser	Give feedback. Clarify company standards. Clarify job responsibilities. Clarify company needs.
Advisor	Generate options. Assist in goal setting. Provide recommendations.
Referral agent	Link to career management resources. Follow up on career management plan.

Source: Based on Z. B. Leibowitz, C. Farren, and B. L. Kaye, *Designing Career Development Systems* (San Francisco: Jossey-Bass, 1986).

José wants to return to Utah, but it does not feel he is ready for another move. José considers his career stunted, and he thinks that the company does not care about him. Although he is unhappy, his performance is acceptable.

How can José's manager help him deal with this career issue to avoid losing a solid performer? José and his manager need to sit down and discuss his career. Table 11–6 presents the type of results that a manager should try to achieve in a career discussion. José's manager needs to clarify José's career concerns (coaching role). The manager also needs to make sure that José understands that although his job performance is acceptable, the company believes he needs to gain more experience at the Texas facility (appraiser role). Third, José's manager needs to discuss with José what can be done now to help him feel better about his job and the company and also help him understand how the company's need for a hygienist with his qualifications at the Texas refinery fits into the larger picture of his career development (advisor role). José and his manager should discuss and agree on a timetable for his next possible move (which could be to a position in Utah). The manager may give José advice concerning the correct timing for requesting a transfer, given the company's financial situation. Finally, José's manager should let him know about career counseling or other career management resources available within the company (role of referral agent).

Human Resource Manager's Role.   The human resource manager should provide information or advice about training and development opportunities.

TABLE 11–6   Characteristics of Successful Career Discussions

Manager gains an awareness of employee's work-related goals and interests.

Manager and employee agree on the next developmental steps.

Employee understands how the manager views his or her performance, developmental needs, and options.

Manager and employee agree on how the employee's needs can be met on the current job.

Manager identifies resources to help the employee accomplish the goals agreed upon in the career discussion.

Source: Adapted from F. L. Otte and P. G. Hutcheson, *Helping Employees Manage Careers* (Englewood Cliffs, NJ: Prentice-Hall, 1992): 57–58.

Also, human resource managers may provide specialized services such as testing to determine employees' values, interests, and skills, help prepare employees for job searches, and often counseling on career-related problems.

Company's Role.   Companies are responsible for providing employees with the resources needed to be successful in career planning. These resources include specific programs as well as processes for career management:

- Career workshops (seminars on such topics as how the career management system works, self-assessment, goal setting, and helping managers understand and perform their roles in career management).
- Information on career and job opportunities (places such as a career center or newsletters, electronic databases, or Web sites where employees can find information about job openings and training programs).
- Career planning workbooks (printed guides that direct employees through a series of exercises, discussions, and guidelines related to career planning).
- Career counseling (advice from a professionally trained counselor who specializes in working with employees seeking assistance with career issues).
- Career paths (planning job sequences, identifying skills needed for advancement within and across job families, such as moving from technical jobs to management jobs).

The company also needs to monitor the career planning system to (1) ensure that managers and employees are using the system as intended and (2) evaluate whether the system is helping the company meet its objectives (e.g., shortening the time it takes to fill positions).

For example, Sun Microsystems offers all of its employees two hours of free counseling each year. Sun encourages employees to think of themselves as self-employed within the organization. Because few managers at Sun Microsystems are specifically trained in counseling and Sun recognizes the time commitment and financial resources that would have to be devoted to developing these skills, Sun contracts with the Career Action Center. The Career Action Center is a not-for-profit organization that counsels employees to help them find their best work within the company or beyond it. Sun also maintains a career library for its employees, which includes books, recordings, and videotapes on career management techniques, occupations, trends, and industries.[34]

At 3M, career management is supported by a network of resources throughout the company.[35] Activities include a performance appraisal and development process designed to facilitate communication between employees and managers, who work together to develop plans for performance and career development. The company also has a career resources center, which provides reference materials, publications, and books regarding career planning issues and development opportunities within the company. Employees can discuss career issues with trained counselors and explore interests, values, and work environment preferences through psychological testing. The Career Resources Department at 3M offers seminars on topics such as self-assessment, interviewing techniques, and managers' roles in career development. The company also provides help in placing employees who have lost their jobs because of transfers, downsizing, health problems, or disabilities. Finally, 3M has two information bases devoted to career issues. The computer-based Job Information System allows employees to nominate themselves for job openings. Through the Internal Search System, managers can use the human resource information system to identify employees who match job requirements. Data regarding employees' job history, location, performance rating, and career interests can be obtained from this system.

Evaluating Career Management Systems

Career management systems need to be evaluated to ensure that they are meeting the needs of employees and the business. The outcomes, methods, and evaluation study designs that we discussed in Chapter 6 relating to training evaluation are relevant for career management system evaluation.

Several types of outcomes can be used to evaluate career management systems. First, the *reactions* of the customers (employees and managers) who use the career management system can be determined through surveys. For example, employees who use the services provided (planning, counseling, etc.) can be asked to evaluate their timeliness, helpfulness, and quality. Managers can provide information regarding how the system affected the time needed to fill open positions in their department as well as the quality of the job candidates and the employees selected for the positions. Second, more objective information related to *results* of the career management system can be tracked such as actual time to fill open positions, employee use of the system (including contact with career counselors, use of career libraries, or inquiries on job postings), or number of employees identified as ready for management positions. If the goals of the system relate to diversity, the number of women and minorities promoted into management positions may be an appropriate measure.

Evaluation of a career management system should be based on its objectives. If improving employee morale is the system's goal, then attitudes should be measured. If the system objectives are more concrete and measurable (such as a system designed to retain employees with high potential for management), then appropriate data (turnover rates) should be collected.

Summary

This chapter focused on understanding the concept of a career and career management. It began by discussing career management's importance for the company and employees. To understand the career management process requires an understanding of the career concept. The changing nature of the career concept was discussed. Today, careers are more flexible and more likely to be evaluated based on psychological success than salary increases or promotions. Based on the new career concept and life-cycle, organizational, and directional pattern perspectives of careers, a career development model was introduced. It suggested that employees face different developmental tasks, depending on their career stage (exploration, establishment, maintenance, disengagement). The actions that companies can take to help employees deal with these developmental tasks were highlighted.

The career management process consists of assessment, reality check, goal setting, and action planning. For career management to be successful, employees, managers, and the company must all be actively involved.

Key Terms

career management   287
protean career   289
psychological contract   290
psychological success   291
career   292
career development   292
life-cycle models   292
organization-based models   292
directional pattern model   292
exploration stage   294

establishment stage   294
maintenance stage   294
disengagement stage   294
recycling   295
career management system   295
self-assessment   296
reality check   296
goal setting   297
action planning   299

Discussion Questions

1. What stage of career development are you in? What career concerns are most important to you? Are these concerns consistent with any one of the development models presented in the chapter?

2. Discuss the implications that the career development model presented in this chapter may have for planning training and development activities.

3. Why should companies be interested in helping employees plan their careers? What benefits can companies gain? What are the risks?

4. What are the three components of career motivation? Which is most important? Which is least important? Why?

5. How does the new career concept differ from the old career concept on the following dimensions: pattern, development sources, goal, responsibility for management?

6. What is a psychological contract? How does the psychological contract influence career management?

7. What are the manager's roles in a career management system? Which role do you think is most difficult for the typical manager? Which is easiest? List the reasons why managers might resist involvement in career management.

Application Assignments

1. The World Wide Web is increasingly being used by companies to list job openings and individuals to find jobs. Using the Web sites listed below (or sites you find yourself by surfing the Web), find two job openings that you may be qualified for. The Web sites include

   http://www.careermosaic.com

   http://www.worldhire.com

   http://www.jobtrak.com

   http://www.espan.com

   http://www.monsterboard.com

   http://www.jobcenter.com

   http://www.careermag.com

   From the company's perspective, what are the advantages of using the Web to recruit new employees? From the "job searchers" perspective?

2. Complete the self-assessment exercise in Table 11–3. What changes would you make in the exercise to improve it?

3. Read the article, "The End of the Job" by W. Bridges in *Fortune,* September 19, 1994, pages 62–74.

   a. Summarize the article in one page.

   b. Discuss the implications of the article for career management systems.

Endnotes

1. A. Howard, ed., *The Changing Nature of Work* (San Francisco: Jossey-Bass, 1995); M. London, ed., *Employees, Careers, and Job Creation* (San Francisco: Jossey-Bass, 1995); "Career Opportunities," management focus column, *The Economist* (July 8, 1995): 59; W. F. Cascio, "Whither Industrial and Organizational Psychology in a Changing World of Work?" *American Psychologist* 50 (1995): 928–39.

2. D. C. Feldman, *Managing Careers in Organizations* (Glenview, IL: Scott-Foresman, 1988).

3. J. E. Russell, "Career Development Interventions in Organizations," *Journal of Vocational Behavior* 38 (1991): 237–87; T. C. Gutteridge, "Organizational Career Development Systems: The State of the Practice," in *Career Development in Organizations,* ed. D. T. Hall & Associates (San Francisco: Jossey-Bass, 1986): 50–94.

4. M. London and E. M. Mane, *Career Management and Survival in the Workplace* (San Francisco: Jossey-Bass, 1987); M. London, "Toward a Theory of Career Motivation," *Academy of Management Review* 8 (1983): 620–30.

5. R. H. Waterman, Jr., J. A. Waterman, and B. A. Collard, "Toward a Career-Resilient Workforce," *Harvard Business Review* (July–August 1994): 87–95.

6. G. Wolf, M. London, J. Casey, and J. Pufahl, "Career Experience and Motivation as Predictors of Training Behaviors and Outcomes for Displaced Engineers," *Journal of Vocational Behavior* 47 (1995): 316–31.

7. P. O'Herron and P. Simonsen, "Career Development Gets a Charge at Sears Credit," *Personnel Journal* (May 1995): 103–6.

8. J. H. Greenhaus and G. A. Callanan, *Career Management,* 2d ed. (Fort Worth, TX: Dryden Press, 1994): .

9. D. T. Hall, "Protean Careers of the 21st Century," *Academy of Management Executive* 10 (1996): 8–16.

10. D. M. Rousseau, "Changing the Deal while Keeping the People," *Academy of Management Executive* 10 (1996): 50–61; D. M. Rousseau and J. M. Parks, "The Contracts of Individuals and Organizations," in *Research in Organizational Behavior* 15, eds. L. L. Cummings and B. M. Staw (Greenwich, CT: JAI Press, 1992): 1–47.

11. P. Sellers, "Don't Call me a Slacker," *Fortune* (December 12, 1994): 181–96.

12. M. B. Arthur, P. H. Claman, and R. J. DeFillippi, "Intelligent Enterprise, Intelligent Careers," *Academy of Management Executive* 9 (1995): 7–20.

13. K. R. Brousseau, M. J. Driver, K. Eneroth, and R. Larsson, "Career Pandemonium: Realigning Organizations and Individuals," *Academy of Management Executive* 10 (1996): 52–66.

14. M. B. Arthur, "The Boundaryless Career: A New Perspective of Organizational Inquiry," *Journal of Organization Behavior* 15 (1994): 295–309; P. H. Mirvis and D. T. Hall, "Psychological Success and the Boundaryless Career," *Journal of Organization Behavior* 15 (1994): 365–80.

15. B. P. Grossman and R. S. Blitzer, "Choreographing Careers," *Training and Development* (January 1992): 67–69.

16. J. S. Lubin and J. B. White. "Throwing Off Angst, Workers are Feeling in Control of Their Careers," *The Wall Street Journal* (1997): A1, A6.

17. Greenhaus and Callanan, *Career Management.*

18. Ibid.

19. D. Brown, L. Brooks & Associates, *Career Choice & Development,* 3d ed. (San Francisco: Jossey-Bass, 1996).

20. D. E. Super, *The Psychology of Careers* (New York: Harper & Row, 1957); G. Dalton, P. Thompson, and R. Price, "The Four Stages of Professional Careers," *Organizational Dynamics* (Summer 1972): 19–42; M. J. Driver, "Career Concepts— A New Approach to Career Research," in *Career Issues in Human Resource Management,* ed. R. Katz (Englewood Cliffs, NJ: Prentice-Hall, 1982): 23–34; D. T. Hall, *Careers in Organizations* (Pacific Palisades, CA: Goodyear, 1976); M. B. Arthur, D. T. Hall, and B. S. Lawrence, *Handbook of Career Theory* (New York: Cambridge University Press, 1989).

21. J. W. Slocum and W. L. Cron, "Job Attitudes and Performance during Three Career Stages," *Journal of Vocational Behavior* 26 (1985): 126–45.

22. S. Rabinowitz and D. T. Hall, "Changing Correlates of Job Involvement," *Journal of Vocational Behavior* 18 (1981): 138–44.

23. F. L. Otte and P. G. Hutcheson, *Helping Employees Manage Careers* (Englewood Cliffs, NJ: Prentice-Hall, 1992).

24. L. Lee, "I'm Proud of What I've Made Myself into—What I've Created," *The Wall Street Journal* (August 28, 1997): B1, B5.

25. D. Lade, "Man Starts New Job at Age 93," *Sun-Sentinel* (Fort Lauderdale, FL), June 13, 1991.

26. Consulting Psychologists Press, "Wells Fargo Helps Employees Change Careers," *Strong Forum* 8, no. 1 (1991): 1.

27. L. Slavenski, "Career Development: A Systems Approach," *Training and Development Journal* (February 1987): 56–60.

28. Z. Leibowitz, C. Schultz, H. D. Lea, and S. E. Forrer, "Shape Up and Ship Out," *Training and Development* (August 1995): 39–42.

29. D. T. Jaffe and C. D. Scott, "Career Development for Empowerment in a Changing Work World," in *New Directions in Career Planning and the Workplace,* ed. J. M. Kumerow (Palo Alto, CA: Consulting Psychologists Press, 1991): 33–59; F. J. Miner, "Computer Applications in Career Development Planning," in *Career Development in Organizations:* 202–35.

30. K. Labich, "Take Control of Your Career," *Fortune* (November 18, 1991): 87–96; R. Tucker and M. Moravec, "Do-It-Yourself Career Development," *Training* (February 1992): 48–52.

31. S. Sherman, "A Brave New Darwinian Workplace," *Fortune* (January 25, 1993): 50–56.

32. B. M. Moses and B. J. Chakins, "The Manager as Career Counselor," *Training and Development Journal* (July 1989): 60–65.

33. Z. B. Leibowitz, C. Farren, and B. L. Kaye, *Designing Career Development Systems* (San Francisco: Jossey-Bass, 1986).

34. N. L. Breuer, "Minimize Distractions for Maximum Output," *Personnel Journal* (May 1995): 70–76.

35. "Personal Career Management." Brochure provided by Susan Runkel, management resource planning specialist, 3M, December 1991.

12　SPECIAL CHALLENGES IN CAREER MANAGEMENT

Objectives

After reading this chapter, you should be able to

1. Design an effective socialization program for employees.

2. Discuss why a dual-career path is necessary for professional and managerial employees.

3. Provide advice on how to help a plateaued employee.

4. Develop policies to help employees and the company avoid technical obsolescence.

5. Develop policies to help employees deal with work-and-life conflict.

6. Select and design outplacement strategies that minimize the negative effects on displaced employees and "survivors."

7. Explain why retirees may be valuable as part-time employees.

REDEFINING SUCCESS FOR MIDDLE-AGE MANAGERS

A 54-year-old manager works out in the gym at 6:45 AM. On the way to the office, he checks his voice mail and contemplates the day's schedule. He will be the first one in the office. The manager has learned that he has to prove himself everyday. Ten years ago, middle-age managers had security. They were seen as a company's memory and mentors to younger employees. Because they were unlikely to advance further in the company—that is, they were plateaued—it was acceptable to spend more time with their families and on work in the community.

Today, for many middle managers the circumstances are similar. They are unlikely to receive promotions. But to avoid being downsized, middle-age managers must keep learning new skills and new technologies. For example, our 54-year-old manager once specialized in marketing production. He has had to learn finance, marketing, and purchasing. He works 12 hours a day doing the same job he did 10 years ago. The salary and status of his job have not changed much. But the knowledge and skills needed and the time demands have increased dramatically. For example, he used to manage people, but now he spends most of his time managing information. He is given fewer resources to accomplish more work. He once had his own secretary to manage his schedule and handle phone calls, but not any more. His phone is constantly ringing, his e-mail box is full with messages.

When he was in his 30s and 40s, he worked long hours because he felt that the hard work would lead to advancement and prosperity. Now, in his mid-50s, he knows the best he can do is hold onto his job. Although he feels he can help younger employees, they don't seek him out as a mentor because of the threat of downsizing. Younger and more experienced employees keep to themselves because they are uncomfortable helping each other when they may end up competing for the same job.

To cope with the stress, our manager meets with a group of middle-age men twice a month. Discussions often revolve around the difficulty of keeping up with new products and the relentless pressure to produce. Many discussions focus on retirement or finding new careers such as consulting or working with the needy. The group's underlying feelings are clear. They feel they have peaked in their careers but not in life. They have been caught unexpectedly by the erosion of the relationship between natural talent, hard work, good morals, job security and stability. ■

Source: Based on J. Kaufman, "A Middle Manager, 54 and Insecure, Struggles to Adapt to the Times," *The Wall Street Journal* (May 5, 1997): A1, A6.

Introduction

As the chapter opening highlights, plateauing is a serious concern for many middle-age managers. In Chapter 11, we discussed the concept of a career and introduced the idea that employees are in different stages of career development. Many middle-age managers might be considered to be in the maintenance stage in which plateauing is a primary concern. This chapter discusses a range of special challenges in career management including potential solutions for helping plateaued employees. Other special challenges discussed include socialization and orientation of new employees, developing dual-career paths, skill obsolescence, balancing work and life, helping employees cope with job loss, and preparing employees for retirement. Although socialization, orientation, and skill obsolescence are included as career management challenges, many companies rely on training programs specifically designed to deal with these challenges.

Socialization and Orientation

Organizational socialization is the process by which new employees are transformed into effective members of the company. As Table 12–1 shows, effective socialization involves being prepared to perform the job effectively, learning

TABLE 12–1   **What Employees Should Learn and Develop Through the Socialization Process**

History	The company's goals, values, traditions, customs, and myths; background of members
Company goals	Rules or principles directing the company
Language	Slang and jargon unique to the company; professional technical language
Politics	How to gain information regarding the formal and informal work relationships and power structures in the company
People	Successful and satisfying work relationships with other employees
Performance proficiency	What needs to be learned; effectiveness in using and acquiring the knowledge, skills, and abilities needed for the job.

Source: Based on G. T. Chao, A. M. O'Leary-Kelly, S. Wolf, H. Klein, and P. D. Gardner, "Organizational Socialization: Its Content and Consequences," *Journal of Applied Psychology* 79 (1994): 730–43.

about the organization, and establishing work relationships. Socialization involves three phases: anticipatory socialization, encounter, and settling in.[1]

Anticipatory Socialization.   Anticipatory socialization occurs before the individual joins the company. Through **anticipatory socialization,** expectations about the company, job, working conditions, and interpersonal relationships are developed. These expectations are developed through interactions with representatives of the company (e.g., recruiters, prospective peers, and managers) during the recruitment and selection process. The expectations are also based on prior work experiences in similar jobs.

Potential employees need to be provided with realistic job information. A **realistic job preview** provides accurate information about the attractive and unattractive aspects of the job, working conditions, company, and location to ensure that employees develop appropriate expectations. This information needs to be provided early in the recruiting and selection process. It is usually given in brochures, in videos, or by the company recruiter during an interview. Although research specifically investigating the influence of realistic job previews on employee turnover is weak and inconsistent, we do know that unmet expectations resulting from the recruitment and selection process have been shown to relate to dissatisfaction and turnover.[2] As we will see, employees' expectations about a job and a company may be formed by interactions with managers, peers, and recruiters rather than from specific messages about the job.

Encounter.   The **encounter phase** occurs when the employee begins a new job. No matter how realistic the information they were provided during interviews and site visits, individuals beginning new jobs will experience shock and surprise.[3] Employees need to become familiar with job tasks, receive appropriate training, and understand company practices and procedures.

Challenging work plus cooperative and helpful managers and peers have been shown to enhance employees' learning a new job.[4] New employees view managers as an important source of information about their job and the company. Research evidence suggests that the nature and quality of the new employee's relationship with the manager has a significant impact on socialization.[5] In fact, the negative effects of unmet expectations can be reduced by the new employee having a high-quality relationship with her manager! Managers can help create a high-quality work relationship by helping the new employee understand her role, providing information about the company, and being understanding regarding the stresses and issues that the new employee is experiencing.

Settling In.   In the settling-in phase, employees begin to feel comfortable with their job demands and social relationships. They begin to work on resolving work conflicts (e.g., too much work to do, conflicting demands of the job) and conflicts between work and nonwork activities. Employees are interested in the company's evaluation of their performance and in learning about potential career opportunities within the company.

Employees need to complete all three phases of the socialization process to fully contribute to the company. For example, employees who do not feel that they have established good working relationships with co-workers will likely spend time and energy worrying about relationships with other employees rather than being concerned with product development or customer service. Employees who experience successful socialization are more motivated, more committed to the company, and more satisfied with their jobs.[6]

Orientation programs play an important role in socializing employees. Orientation involves familiarizing new employees with company rules, policies, and procedures. Table 12–2 shows the content of orientation programs. Typically, a program includes information about the company, department in which the employee will be working, and community.

While the content of orientation programs is important, the process of orientation can not be ignored. Too often, orientation programs consist of completing payroll forms and reviewing personnel policies with managers or human resource representatives. The new employee is a passive recipient of information. New employees have little opportunity to ask questions or interact with peers and their managers.

Effective orientation programs include active involvement of the new employee. Table 12–3 shows the characteristics of effective orientation programs. An important characteristic of effective orientation programs is that peers, managers, and senior co-workers are actively involved in helping new employees adjust to the work group.[7]

Before being assigned to their plant locations, new engineers at Pillsbury, for example, have a one-year headquarters assignment.[8] They are provided with a mentor (a senior engineer), who helps them understand the technical engineering resources available within the company. The mentor also helps them become familiar with the community and deal with relocation issues. New engineers

TABLE 12–2   Content of Orientation Programs

I. Company-Level Information
Company overview (e.g., values, history, mission)
Key policies and procedures
Compensation
Employee benefits and services
Safety and accident prevention
Employee and union relations
Physical facilities
Economic factors
Customer relations

II. Department-Level Information
Department functions and philosophy
Job duties and responsibilities
Policies, procedures, rules, and regulations
Performance expectations
Tour of department
Introduction to department employees

III. Miscellaneous
Community
Housing
Family adjustment

Source: J. L. Schwarz and M. A. Weslowski, "Employee Orientation: What Employers Should Know," *The Journal of Contemporary Business Issues* (Fall 1995): 48.

TABLE 12–3   Characteristics of Effective Orientation Programs

Employees are encouraged to ask questions.
Program includes information on both technical and social aspects of the job.
Orientation is the responsibility of the new employee's manager.
Debasing and embarrassing new employees is avoided.
Formal and informal interactions with managers and peers occur.
Programs involve relocation assistance (e.g., house hunting, information session on the community for employees and their spouses).
Employees are provided the information about the company's products, services, and customers.

attend seminars in which engineers from different divisions (e.g., frozen foods) explain the role of engineering. New employees also have the opportunity to meet key players in engineering management at Pillsbury.

Similarly, new employees and their managers are actively involved in the new orientation program at Corning Glass.[9] Corning Glass was experiencing turnover among its high-potential new employees. Employees were leaving the company because they felt the company had a sink-or-swim attitude toward new hires. As a result, Corning designed a new orientation process including

- *Manager preparation.* Hiring managers are given guidelines and checklists that specify the steps they should take before and after the arrival of new employees.
- *Guided self-learning.* Managers are encouraged to spend the first two weeks orienting new employees to the job and the company rather than focusing on their regular job duties. Each new employee is provided with a workbook that requires him or her to learn about the company's customers, suppliers, objectives, and culture. It is up to the employee to decide how to complete the workbook questions (e.g., interviews, visits to the company resource center). The manager and employee jointly review the answers to the workbook questions. If the employee needs more information, the learning period is extended.
- *Organization acculturation.* During their first three months, employees attend seminars on Corning's philosophy, culture, and values.

Retention data suggest that the orientation program is a success. It has resulted in a 25 to 35 percent increase in retention of new employees in comparison with employees who did not take the new program.

Dual-Career Paths

A **career path** is a sequence of job positions involving similar types of work and skills that employees move through in the company.[10] For companies with professional employees such as engineers and scientists, an important issue is how to ensure that they feel they are valued. Many companies' career paths are structured so that the only way engineers and scientists (individual contributors) can advance and receive certain financial rewards (such as stock options) is by moving into managerial positions. Figure 12–1 shows an example of a traditional career path for scientists and managers. Advancement opportunities within a technical career path are limited. Also, managerial career paths may be more highly compensated than technical career paths. A career path system such as the one in Figure 12–1 can have negative consequences for the company. Scientists may elect to leave the company because of lower status, less salary, and fewer advancement opportunities than managers enjoy. Also, if scientists want to gain status and additional salary, they must choose to become managers.

FIGURE 12–1

Traditional career path for scientists and managers

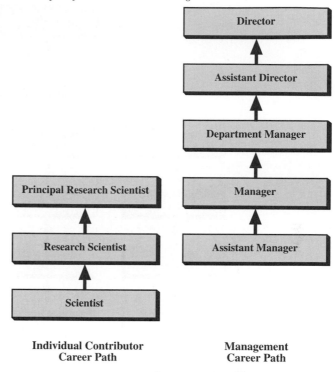

Many companies are developing multiple- or dual-career-path systems to give scientists and other individual contributors additional career opportunities. Developing career paths involves analyzing work and information flows, the types of tasks performed across jobs, similarities and differences in working environments, and the historical movement patterns of employees into and out of jobs (i.e., where in the company employees come from and what positions they take after leaving the job).[11]

A dual-career-path system enables employees to remain in a technical career path or move into a management career path.[12] Figure 12–2 shows a dual-career-path system. Research scientists have the opportunity to move into three different career paths: a scientific path and two management paths. It is assumed that because employees can earn comparable salaries and have similar advancement opportunities in all three paths, they will choose the path that best matches their interests and skills.

Effective career paths have several characteristics:[13]

- Salary, status, and incentives for technical employees compare favorably with those of managers.

FIGURE 12–2

Example of dual-career path system

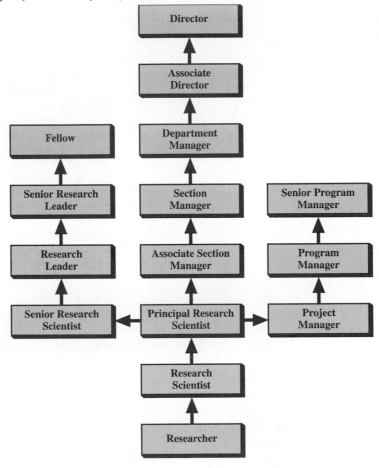

Source: Z. B. Leibowitz, B. L. Kaye, and C. Farren, "Multiple Career Paths," *Training and Development Journal* (October 1992): 31–35.

- Individual contributors' base salary may be lower than managers', but they are given opportunities to increase their total compensation through bonuses (e.g., for patents and developing new products).
- The individual contributor career path is not used to satisfy poor performers who have no managerial potential. The career path is for employees with outstanding technical skills.
- Individual contributors are given the opportunity to choose their career path. The company provides assessment resources (such as psychological tests and developmental feedback, as discussed in Chapters 9 and 11). Assessment information enables employees to see how similar their interests, work values, and skill strengths are to employees in technical and managerial positions.

A good example of the process used to develop an effective dual-career-path system is found at British Petroleum Exploration (BPX).[14] BPX created a dual-career-path system because individual contributors (nonmanagerial employees such as engineers and scientists who are directly involved in the development of a product or service) could not move to higher positions in the company without assuming managerial responsibility. After individual contributors reached the top job in the career path, their choices were to stop progressing upward or leave the company.

BPX decided to develop a dual-career-path system similar to that in Figure 12–2. One path was for managers, the other for individual contributors. The paths were comparable in terms of responsibility, rewards, and influence.

Managers, individual contributors, and human resource staff all contributed to the development of the career path system. The first step in the process was the development of descriptions of skills and performance levels that applied to managerial and individual contributor positions. Skill matrices were developed for the two career paths. Each skill matrix described the skills needed for each position within the career path. The skills needed for each position were also described. The skills matrices were distributed to all employees so that they were aware of the skills they needed in their current jobs and the skills they needed to develop to change jobs. The skill matrices were integrated with other human resource systems including performance management, reward, and training systems. For example, the skills matrices were used as a source of information for BPX's development program. The matrices were used to determine what performance improvement, training, or experience the employee needs to meet current job responsibilities and prepare for their next job experience. Employees can move from the individual contributor to the management career path based on their performance, their qualifications, and business need (e.g., turnover).

BPX believes that innovation is enhanced by providing employees with career paths that reward individual contributors as well as management contributors. Also, BPX believes that it will be easier to recruit and keep talented scientists and engineers because the dual career path demonstrates the company's interests in satisfying employees' career interests.

Skill-based pay systems (discussed in Chapter 10) are also used by companies to reward employees who are unlikely to move into managerial positions. In these systems, part of employees' pay is based on their level of knowledge or skills rather than the requirements of their current job. These systems (1) motivate employees to broaden their skill base and (2) reduce the differential in pay rates between managerial and nonmanagerial positions.

Plateauing

The chapter opening illustrated the feelings and emotions of plateaued managers. **Plateauing** means that the likelihood of the employee receiving future job assignments with increased responsibility is low. As the chapter introduction showed, compared to employees in other career stages, midcareer employees are most likely to plateau. Plateauing is not necessarily bad for the employee or company. A plateaued employee may not desire increased job responsibilities. Job performance may meet the minimum acceptable standards. Plateauing becomes dysfunctional when the employee feels stuck in a job that offers no potential for personal growth. Such frustration results in poor job attitude, increased absenteeism, and poor job performance.[15]

Employees can plateau for several reasons:[16]

- Lack of ability.
- Lack of training.
- Low need for achievement.
- Unfair pay decisions or dissatisfaction with pay raises.
- Confusion about job responsibilities.
- Slow company growth resulting in reduced development opportunities.

Table 12–4 provides several means to help plateaued employees. Employees need to understand why they are plateaued. Being stuck in a position is not necessarily the employee's fault. Plateauing may be due to restructuring of the company that has eliminated many potential positions. (This is known as structural plateauing.) If plateauing is due to a performance problem, employees need to be aware of this so they correct the problem.

Plateaued employees should be encouraged to become involved in developmental opportunities, including training courses, job exchanges, and short-term assignments in which they can use their expertise outside their departments. Participating in developmental opportunities may prepare employees for more challenging assignments in their current job or may qualify them for new positions within the company. Plateaued employees may need career counseling to help them understand why they are plateaued and their options for dealing with the problem. Employees should be encouraged to "reality-test" the solutions they believe will solve their plateauing through discussions with their manager, coworkers, and human resource manager. This is necessary to ensure that their solution is realistic given the resources available in the company. At times it may be in the best interest of the employee and the company if he is encouraged to leave the company.

TABLE 12–4   Possible Remedies for Plateaued Employees

Employee understands the reasons for plateau.
Employee is encouraged to participate in development activities.
Employee is encouraged to seek career counseling.
Employee reality-tests his solutions.

Skills Obsolescence

Obsolescence is a reduction in an employee's competence resulting from a lack of knowledge of new work processes, techniques, and technologies that have developed since the employee completed her education.[17] Avoiding skills obsolescence has traditionally been a concern of employees in technical and professional occupations such as engineering and medicine. However, rapid technological change affects all aspects of business from manufacturing to administration, so all employees are at risk of becoming obsolete. Also, obsolescence needs to be avoided if companies are trying to become learning organizations. If employees' skills become obsolete, both the employee and the company suffer. The company will be unable to provide new products and services to customers, losing its competitive advantage. As we mentioned when discussing plateauing, lack of up-to-date skills is one reason why employees become plateaued. For example, a secretary who fails to keep up with developments in word processing software (e.g., merging text with figures, tables, charts, and pictures) will soon be unable to produce state-of-the-art documents for his internal customer, the advertising manager. The advertising manager's clients may view the company's material as outdated and therefore give their advertising business to a competitor. The secretary will likely be given more mundane and uninteresting work and he will likely be an outplacement candidate.

What can be done to avoid skills obsolescence? Examine Figure 12–3. As we mentioned in Chapter 5, the company culture plays an important role in encouraging employees to develop their skills. Through implementing a climate for continuous learning, many companies combat skills obsolescence by encouraging employees to attend courses, seminars, and programs, and to consider how to do their jobs better on a daily basis. Obsolescence can also be avoided by[18]

FIGURE 12–3

Factors related to updating skills

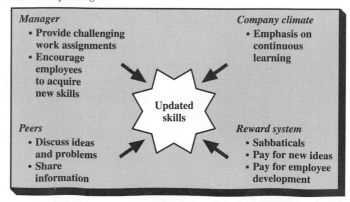

- Providing employees with the opportunity to exchange information and ideas.
- Giving employees challenging job assignments early in their careers.
- Providing job assignments that challenge employees and require them to "stretch" their skills.
- Providing rewards for updating behaviors (such as taking courses), suggestions, and customer service and product innovations.
- Allowing employees to attend professional conferences, subscribe to professional journals and magazines, or enroll in university, technical school, or community center courses at low or no cost.
- Encouraging employees to interact in person or electronically to discuss problems and new ideas.

Sabbaticals are one of companies' methods to help employees avoid obsolescence. A **sabbatical** refers to a leave of absence from the company to renew or develop skills. Employees on sabbatical often receive full pay and benefits. Sabbaticals allow employees to get away from their day-to-day job stresses and acquire new skills and perspectives. Sabbaticals also allow employees more time for personal pursuits such as writing a book or raising young children. Sabbaticals are common in a variety of industries ranging from consulting firms to the fast food industry.[19] For example, McDonald's Corporation offers an eight-week sabbatical to employees with 10 years of service and 16 weeks to those with 20 years of service. How people spend their sabbatical varies from company to company. Some employees work for a nonprofit service agency, some go back to school, while others travel and work on special projects in non-U.S. subsidiaries of the company.

Balancing Work and Life

Families with a working husband, homemaker wife, and two or more children account for only 7 percent of American families. The increasing number of two-career couples and single heads of households creates a challenge for companies. Companies have to carefully consider how to manage employees who are concerned with simultaneously meeting the needs of both work and family. Work and family roles are likely to conflict because employees are forced to take several different roles (e.g., parent, spouse, employee) in a number of different environments (e.g., workplace, home, community). Research suggests that dual-career families, single-parent families, and families with children under age five are likely to experience the most work and family conflict.[20]

Social legislation has been approved to help employees deal with work and family policies. The Family and Medical Leave Act (FMLA) provides for up to 12 weeks of unpaid leave for parents with new infants or newly adopted children. The FMLA also covers employees who must take a leave of absence from work to care for a family member who is ill or to deal with a personal illness. Companies are required to provide the employee with health care benefits during their leave of absence.

Similar types of conflicts are also likely to occur for employees without families or dependents. Many companies are expanding "work–family" policies to "work–life" programs.[21] Flexibility in when and where work is performed, and support services are valuable for helping all employees deal with the stresses and strains related to work and nonwork conflicts. Employees with dependents struggle with child care and elder care. All employees struggle with issues related to participating in nonwork activities that they increasingly have less time for due to work demands.

There are two roles that training can play in balancing work and nonwork. First, trainers and managers may be responsible for developing policies and procedures. Second, trainers may be responsible for developing training programs to teach managers their role in administering and overseeing the use of work–life policies.

Types of Work-Life Conflict

Feelings of frustration are only one outcome of work and nonwork conflict. Work–life conflict has also been found to be related to increased health risks, decreased productivity, tardiness, turnover, and poor mental health.[22] It is also important to recognize that work–family conflict even applies to employees who do not have children or spouses. All employees have nonwork roles and activities that may conflict with work. Three types of work–family conflict have been identified: time-based conflict, strain-based conflict, and behavior-based conflict.[23]

Time-based conflict occurs when the demands of work and nonwork interfere with each other. For example, jobs that demand late evenings at the office, overtime work, or out-of-town travel conflict with family activities and team-sport schedules. **Strain-based conflict** results from the stress of work and nonwork roles. For example, a newborn child deprives parents of sleep; as a result, it is difficult for them to concentrate at work. **Behavior-based conflict** occurs when employees' behavior in work roles is not appropriate for their behavior in nonwork roles. For example, managers' work demands that they be logical, impartial, and authoritarian. At the same time, these same managers are expected to be warm, emotional, and friendly in their relationships with their family members or friends.

Company Policies to Accommodate Work and Nonwork

Besides following the FMLA, many companies are beginning to respond to work and nonwork issues by developing policies designed to reduce the potential for work–life conflict. These policies emphasize the communication of realistic information about the demands of jobs and careers, flexibility in where and when work is performed, and support services such as child care and elder care programs. Research suggests that company policies that help employees manage work and nonwork conflicts enhance employees' job performance, reduce costs associated with disability leave, and reduce turnover and absenteeism.[24]

Communicating Information about Work and Nonwork Policies and Job Demands

Employees need to be made aware of the time demands and the stress related to jobs within the company. This information helps employees choose career opportunities that match the importance they place on work. Employees also need to be aware of the company's work and family practices, such as flexible benefits related to dependent care and leave policies.

Flexibility in Work Arrangements and Work Schedules

A key way to deal with work–life conflicts is to provide employees with more flexibility about when work is performed (work schedules) and where it is performed (work arrangements). Work–family conflict can be reduced by increasing employees' control over work and family demands.[25] One way many companies have provided employees with additional control is through alternative work schedules involving flextime or part-time work. Table 12–5 presents examples of alternative work arrangements and work schedules. These work arrangements provide employees with more control over their work schedule, giving them time to deal with family demands (e.g., paying bills, caring for infants and small children) and avoid the difficulties of commuting. Alternative work arrangements reduce stress and absenteeism. Home-based work is dominated by individuals in educational, professional, business, repair, and social service occupations. The major difficulties posed by alternative work schedules and work arrangements include communication problems (employees may be at different locations and on different work schedules), a lack of necessary supplies and equipment, and family interruptions.[26]

TABLE 12–5   Alternative Work Schedules and Work Arrangements

	Where	*When*
Traditional	Place of employment	5 days, 40 hours per week
Flextime	Place of employment	40 hours per week but have choice of when to start and end work; may require work during certain core hours
Compressed workweek	Place of employment	4 days, 10-hour workdays
Temporary work	Place of employment	On as-needed basis
Job sharing	Place of employment	Split 5-day, 40-hour workweek with another employee
Part-time work	Place of employment	Less than 8 hours a day or 5 days a week
Shift work	Place of employment	Morning, afternoon, or overnight shifts sometimes on a rotating basis
Work at home	Home	Varies, could be 5 days, 40 hours per week

Job sharing might be the most challenging work option. [27] **Job sharing** refers to having two employees divide the hours, the responsibilities, and the benefits of a full-time job. For example, two consulting systems engineers at Bank of America in San Francisco have shared one job for eight years. They are an invaluable source of information for many inexperienced employees. Their experience and expertise are valuable assets that the company could not have received from a series of temporary employees.

For job sharing to be effective,

- The impact of job sharing on clients and customers must be determined. If satisfying client and customer needs is compromised (customers want one consistent contact person, for example), job sharing is likely to be an unattractive option.

- The employee interested in job sharing must find another employee performing the same job who wants reduced work hours.

- The two people sharing the job need to have similar work values and motivations. Otherwise interpersonal conflicts will interfere with completing assignments.

- The manager must actively communicate with the job-sharing employees and accept the fact that they might not be immediately available for consultation.

- Meeting schedules, work assignments, and vacation schedules need to be carefully coordinated. Employees need to plan to overlap some of their time to meet.

- Performance evaluation of job sharers needs to include both an individual and team appraisal.

J&A Corporate Financial has capitalized on the increasing number of corporations seeking outside help with projects and the large number of professionals looking for flexible, part-time work. J&A employs seven consultants who average 10 years experience, all are certified public accountants, and most have MBAs. Six employees are mothers. J&A is a serious rival for larger companies because the staff are paid high wages, which attracts well-qualified candidates, but at the same time they are only paid for the hours they work. Also, because the consultants are independent contractors and work at home, the company does not have to pay Social Security taxes or provide benefits. As a result, they undercut the competition by charging about $100 per hour compared to $250 for larger consulting firms.

Margaret Johnsson, owner of the company, set up a contingency plan to avoid problems with the availability of her work force. For each consulting project, she assigns a primary consultant and a backup. If home obligations (such as having to spend all night in an emergency room with a sick child) force the primary consultant to miss work, the backup takes over. Ms. Johnsson also tries to assign projects based on both skills and schedules. She stresses to clients that even though staff may not be immediately reached, they will return calls within two hours. She insists that staff leave the kids at home and avoid taking excessive breaks to deal with personal problems at clients' offices.[28]

Support Services

Companies need to provide three support services: manager training, child care, and elder care. Many employees are concerned about using flexible work arrangements and schedules because they fear that managers will view them as uninterested in their careers and accuse them of shirking their job responsibilities. They fear that managers may not provide them with development opportunities and will evaluate their performance less favorably. Companies need to train managers to understand that employees' use of work–family policies should not be punished. The more supportive the manager is (e.g., willing to listen to employees' family-related work problems and offer solutions based on the company's program), the less work–family conflict employees will experience.[29]

First Tennessee Bank had been experiencing a turnover problem that influenced customer's perceptions of the bank.[30] Customers wanted to see familiar faces when they walked into the bank's branches. They wanted personal relationships with employees who handled their money. First Tennessee investigated the reasons for the turnover problem, finding that many employees left because of inflexible work schedules. The need for scheduling flexibility was not surprising given that 90 percent of the employees' spouses worked outside the home, 75 percent of employees were women, and half of the employees had dependent children. The lack of flexibility was causing some employees problems in finding child care arrangements. Other employees wanted larger blocks of time off after working long hours at certain times of the month. For example, employees in the accounting department often worked 12-hour days at the beginning of every month to reconcile accounts.

In response to the need for more flexibility, First Tennessee developed more flexible work policies including flextime, flexible hours, and part-time work. To help overcome managers' resistance to the system, First Tennessee trained all 1,000 of its managers. Each training session involved 50 to 100 managers. At each site, the training began by having managers voice their concerns. Each manager discussed a personal or family situation (e.g., a sick child) that had affected work. The training also involved role plays to help the managers deal with employees' requests for flexible scheduling. The program emphasized that the manager needed to work with the employee on scheduling. Discussing scheduling issues with the employee enhanced employees' accepting the managers' decision, even if an employee's scheduling option was denied. The results of the company's work–family strategy have been positive. Turnover rates have dropped and both customers and employees are satisfied.

Almost two-thirds of all women with children younger than 14 are in the work force. Companies can help these employees deal with child care demands in a number of ways. The child care services companies most frequently provide include help in identifying child care resources and flexible benefit plans that allow employees to pay for child care with pretax dollars.

Child care services need to be flexible to meet the needs of a diverse work force. A single parent may need more assistance than an employee with a spouse who works part-time. Employees with infants may want to choose parental leave or work part-time or at home. Unfortunately, only 5 percent of midsize to large companies provide any type of child care assistance.[31] The lack of child care likely has the greatest impact on low-income parents, who cannot afford to pay for child care services. These parents are forced with the difficult decision of working (and leaving children unattended) or not working and staying home with their children.

A growing concern for many employees is elder care—how to care for aging parents. At least 20 percent of all employees currently care for a parent. The care of elderly persons will only increase in importance in the United States because 21 percent of the population will be 65 or over by the year 2000. The stresses of elder care result in problems similar to working parents' difficulties: absenteeism, work interruptions, negative attitudes toward work, and lack of energy.[32] Elder care may be even more demanding than child care if the elder person has a debilitating disease such as Alzheimer's.

Eddie Bauer, the casual–life-style retailer, is assisting employees with elder care in several ways.[33] The company's resource and referral program helps employees deal with housing concerns for elders. Employees can access books, articles, and videos on age-related issues. Counselors are available to provide advice on how to evaluate elder care facilities and how to address specific health problems. They can also help with questions regarding the aging process, intergenerational communications, caregiving at home, managing a long-distance caregiving relationship, and grieving over a parent's death. Companies are also beginning to offer employees insurance programs to defray elder care costs (e.g., nursing home expenses).[34]

Andersen Consulting provides its employees with a unique service to help them balance work and life demands.[35] Recognizing that employees often have difficulty completing personal chores due to work and family demands, Andersen has established an on-site concierge service that gives employees the option of having a service complete errands. The concierge service resulted from an employee survey in which employees complained about not having enough time to take care of their personal lives. Because most Andersen employees are consultants who spend the majority of the workweek on the road, putting in many overtime hours, there is little time left for chores related to daily living. The concierges and errand runners will do any personal or housekeeping errands for employees including house sitting, picking up a car from the repair shop, or helping to arrange a business-related social activity (such as dinner reservations). Although Andersen has yet to formally evaluate the service, the company believes that the service has boosted morale and productivity because employees are spending less time worrying about how they are going to take care of nagging details of living.

Table 12–6 provides recommendations for developing dependent care (elder or child care) assistance programs. The first step is to determine if employees perceive a need for assistance and in what form they need assistance (e.g., on-site child care, referrals for elder care, flexible schedule). Communication of dependent care benefits is critical to ensure that employees are aware of the types of assistance available. As mentioned earlier, managers need to be trained as to the purpose and use of the program. Finally, ongoing evaluation is needed to ensure that the program is satisfying employees' and the company's needs.

TABLE 12–6   **Recommendations for Developing Dependent Care Assistance Programs**

Determine need using surveys and focus groups

Develop a philosophy or rationale related to business objectives

Solicit employees participation in designing and implementing the program

Allocate resources for communicating the program to employees and managers

Request feedback from users to make adjustments to the program

Source: Based on E. E. Kossek, B. J. DeMarr, K. Backman, and M. Kollar, "Assessing employees' emerging eldercare needs and reactions to dependent care benefits," *Public Personnel Management* (Winter 1993): 617–638.

One of the most controversial ideas for alleviating work–family conflict is creating separate career tracks for career-primary and career-family women.[36] Use of this strategy to alleviate work–family conflict would involve identifying, early in a woman's career, whether she is a career-family or career-primary woman (one whose career is the top priority). Career-family women would be provided with high-quality child care and flexible work schedules. As a result of these accommodations, career-family women's pay would be lower than career-primary women's. Career-family women are trading career growth and compensation for fewer job pressures. On the other hand, companies should ensure that talented career-primary women are given the same opportunities for development and advancement as talented men.

These ideas may also apply to men. The basic issue is whether employees' advancement opportunities and compensation should differ depending on the type of trade-offs they are willing to make regarding work and family. Keep in mind that there are several negative outcomes of this strategy. Forcing women (or men) to be permanently tracked or labeled as career-primary or career-family reinforces negative stereotypes concerning the commitment and productivity of employees with families. Permanently tracking or labeling an employee as career-primary or career-family assumes that the degree of work–family conflict remains constant during their career. Forcing employees to remain in a career track that might be unsuitable means that the company is not effectively using employees to gain a competitive advantage. Finally, employees will likely resent having to identify a career track based on their family status, resulting in dissatisfaction and turnover. Providing alternative work arrangements and schedules and support services are a more effective strategy for helping employees cope with work–family conflict than labeling or tracking employees.

Coping with Job Loss

Coping with job loss is an important career development issue because of the increased use of downsizing to deal with excess employees resulting from corporate restructuring, mergers, acquisitions, and takeovers.

Companies that lay off employees can experience lowered job commitment, distrust of management, and difficulties recruiting new employees. Job loss also causes stress and disrupts the personal lives of laid-off employees.[37] Because of the potential damaging effects of downsizing, companies should first seek alternative ways to reduce headcount (the number of employees) and lower labor costs. These alternatives may include asking employees to work fewer hours, offering early retirement plans, delaying wage increases, and deciding not to fill position openings created by turnover and retirements. Job loss may be inevitable due to mergers or acquisitions (which may create redundant positions and excess of employees with similar skills) or downturns in business forcing the company to reduce labor costs by eliminating employees in order to survive.

From a career management standpoint, companies and managers have two major responsibilities. First, they are responsible for helping employees who will lose their jobs. Second, steps must be taken to ensure that the "survivors" of the layoff (the remaining employees) remain productive and committed to the organization.

To prepare employees for layoffs and reduce their potential negative effects, companies need to provide outplacement services. Outplacement services should include[38]

- Advance warning and explanation for a layoff.
- Psychological, financial, and career counseling.
- Assessment of skills and interests.
- Job campaign services such as resume-writing assistance and interview training.
- Job banks where job leads are posted and out-of-town newspapers, phones, and books regarding different occupations and geographic areas are available.
- Electronic delivery of job openings, self-directed career management guides, and values and interest inventories.

Many companies are teaming with the public sector to assist outplaced employees. For example, Boeing Company, the aircraft manufacturer in Washington, is working with the State of Washington and local business and government officials to offer a small business training program to outplaced employees.[39] Selection for the program—which involves classes, reviews of business plans, and consultation—is rigorous. Applicants must have a viable business idea, identify competitors and customers, and indicate how they will support themselves until the business is making a profit. Since the course was first offered in

1994, 61 laid-off workers have started businesses including restaurants, book stores, and accounting offices. Besides helping former employees, the program allows Boeing to hold down its unemployment insurance contributions and improve its image in the community.

Employees in upper-level managerial and professional positions typically receive more personalized outplacement services (e.g., office space, private secretary) than lower-level employees.[40] Outplacement also involves training managers in how to conduct termination meetings with employees. Table 12–7 presents guidelines for such meetings. Providing counseling for laid-off employees is critical because employees first have to deal with the shock of the layoff and their feelings of anger, guilt, disbelief, and blame. Many outplaced employees also experience mood swings, question their self-worth, experience mild depression, and may be indecisive and pessimistic about the future.[41] Trained counselors can help employees work through these concerns so that they can focus full attention on conducting a campaign to find a new job.

Typically companies devote more resources to outplacing employees who have lost their jobs than to employees who remain (the "survivors"). Although losing a job causes grief and denial in employees, once employees have worked through their emotions they are capable of carrying on a campaign to find a new job. Laid-off employees are certain of their future in that they know that they need to seek alternative employment. However, for the **survivors** (employees who remain with the company following a downsizing), uncertainty about their future remains. Survivors feel some sense of gratification because they have kept their jobs. However, they do not know how safe their current job is nor do they know in what direction the company is heading. Also, in many cases, survivors are expected to perform the work of the laid-off employees as well as their own. As a result, survivors experience considerable anxiety, anger toward top-level managers, cynicism toward reorganization and new business plans, resentment, and resignation.[42]

Research suggests that survivors' attitudes and productivity are influenced by their beliefs regarding the fairness of the layoffs and the changes in working conditions.[43] Survivors are more likely to view layoffs as fair if employees are asked to cut costs to avoid layoffs, if the factors used to decide whom to lay off (e.g., performance, seniority) are applied equally to line and staff employees, if advance notice is provided, and if there are clear and adequate explanations for the layoffs. Survivors need to be trained to deal with increased work loads and job responsibilities due to the consolidation and loss of jobs. The company also needs to provide survivors with realistic information about their future with the company.

Dealing with Older Workers

Meeting the Needs of Older Workers

There are several actions that companies can take to meet the needs of older employees.[44] First, flexibility in scheduling allows older employees to take care of sick spouses, go back to school, travel, or work fewer hours. Second, research

---

TABLE 12–7   **Guidelines for Termination Meetings with Employees**

---

1. Planning
- Alert outplacement firm that termination will occur (if appropriate).
- Prepare severance and benefit packages.
- Prepare public statement regarding terminations.
- Prepare statement for employees unaffected by terminations.
- Have telephone numbers available for medical or security emergencies.

2. Timing
- Terminations should not occur on Friday afternoon, very late on any day, or before a holiday.
- Terminate employees early in the week so employees can receive counseling and outplacement assistance.

3. Place
- It usually occurs in employee's office.
- An HR representative may need to be present to explain severance and outplacement package.
- In sensitive cases where severe emotional reaction is expected, a third party is also needed.

4. Length
- Meeting should be short and to the point. Termination should occur within the first two minutes. Remainder of time should be spent on explaining separation benefits and allowing employee to express feelings.

5. Approach
- Provide straightforward explanation, stating reasons for termination.
- Statement should be made that the decision to terminate was made by management and is irreversible.
- Do not discuss your feelings, needs, or problems.

6. Benefits
- Written statement of salary continuation, benefits continuation, outplacement support (e.g., office arrangements, counseling) and other terms and conditions should be provided and discussed with the employee.

Source: Adapted from R. J. Lee, "Outplacement Counseling for the Terminated Manager," in *Applying Psychology in Business,* eds. J. W. Jones, B. D. Steffy, and D. W. Bray (Lexington, MA: Lexington Books, 1991): 489–508.

suggests that the probability of receiving company-sponsored training peaks at age 40 and declines as an employee's age increases.[45] Companies need to ensure that older employees receive the training they need to avoid obsolescence and be prepared to use new technology. Third, older employees need resources and referral help that addresses long-term health care and elder care. Fourth, assessment and counseling is necessary to help older employees to recycle to new jobs or careers, or to transition to less secure positions whose responsibilities are not as clearly outlined. Finally, companies need to ensure that employees do not hold inappropriate stereotypes about older employees (e.g., that they fear new technology or can not learn new skills).

Preretirement Socialization

Preretirement socialization is the process of helping employees prepare for exit from work. It encourages employees to learn about retirement life, plan for adequate financial, housing, and health-care resources, and form accurate expectations about retirement. Employees' satisfaction with life after retirement is influenced by their health, their feelings about their jobs, and their level of optimism. Employees who attend preretirement socialization programs have fewer financial and psychological problems and experience greater satisfaction with retirement compared with employees who do not attend these programs. These programs typically address the following topics:[46]

- Psychological aspects of retirement, such as developing personal interests and activities.
- Housing, including a consideration of transportation, living costs, and proximity to medical care.
- Health during retirement, including nutrition and exercise.
- Financial planning, insurance, and investments.
- Estate planning.
- Collecting benefits from company pension plans and Social Security.

Many companies also use alternative work arrangements to help employees make the transition into retirement while at the same time continuing to utilize their talents. Monsanto Corporation has developed its own in-house temporary employment agency, the Retiree Resource Corporation (RRC), to utilize retirees' talents.[47] Through RRC, retired employees who want to work part-time may do so on a temporary basis. Monsanto's retirees return to work for a number of reasons, but most focus on quality of life. The retirees want time for bridge, golf, and grandchildren, but also to enjoy work.

Monsanto's program is successful because (1) senior management encourages the full use of older workers, (2) more than 2,500 retirees live within commuting distance of company headquarters so there is a large labor pool, (3) detailed information about the program is made available as part of the career management process for employees nearing retirement, and (4) feedback is provided on a retiree's performance on the temporary job.

Monsanto has gained a number of benefits from rehiring its retirees. The benefits include having employees who are dependable and mature, able to handle responsibilities, as well as familiar with how the company operates. This allows returning retirees to get to work on the task faster than inexperienced new employees who are unfamiliar with the company culture and policies.

Although formal preretirement socialization programs are primarily for employees who are considering retirement, financial planning, estate planning and purchasing insurance needs to be done much earlier in their career to ensure that employees will have the financial resources necessary to live comfortably during retirement.

Retirement

Retirement involves leaving a job and work role and making a transition into life without work. For some employees, retirement involves making a transition out of their current job and company and seeking full- or part-time employment elsewhere. This relates to the idea of recycling discussed in Chapter 11.

Research suggests that issues regarding retirement will increase in importance in the near future. By the year 2000, over 22 percent of the U.S. population will be over 65 years of age. Recent changes in the Social Security system and an increase in the mandatory retirement age from 65 to 70 suggest that employees may elect to work longer. However, over half of all employees retire before age 63, and 80 percent leave by the time they are 70. This may be because employees accept companies' offers of early retirement packages, which usually include generous financial benefits. Also, employees may find work less satisfying and be interested in primarily pursuing nonwork activities as a source of satisfaction.

The aging work force and the use of early retirement programs to shrink companies' work forces have three implications. First, companies must meet the needs of older employees. Second, companies must take steps to prepare employees for retirement. Third, companies must be careful that early retirement programs do not unfairly discriminate against older employees.

Early Retirement Programs

Early retirement programs offer employees financial benefits to leave the company. These programs are usually part of the company's strategy to reduce labor costs without having to lay off employees. Financial benefits usually include a lump sum of money and a percentage of salary based on years of service. These benefits can be quite attractive to employees, particularly those with long tenure with the company. Eligibility for early retirement is usually based on age and years of service. For example, GTE Telephone Operations–North Area invites employees to consider retirement when the sum of their age and years of service approaches 76.[48] Early retirement programs have two major problems. First, employees who would be difficult to replace elect to leave the company. Second, older employees may believe that early retirement programs are discriminatory because they feel they are forced to retire. To avoid costly litigation, companies need to make sure that early retirement programs[49]

- Are part of the employee benefit plan.
- Justify age-related distinctions for eligibility for early retirement.
- Allow employees to voluntarily choose early retirement.

Eligibility requirements should not be based on stereotypes about ability and skill decrements that occur with age. Research suggests that age-related declines in specific abilities and skills have little effect on job performance.[50] Employees' decisions are considered voluntary if they can refuse to participate, they are given complete information about the plan, and they receive a reasonable amount of time to make their decisions.

Training plays an important role in early retirement programs. Companies teach employees to understand the financial implications of early retirement. Training programs are also used to help employees understand when and in what forms health benefits and retirement savings can be received. For example, retirement savings can often be distributed to retirees either as a one-time lump-sum of money or payout of a specific amount of money each month, quarterly, or yearly.

Summary

This chapter presented several career management challenges that trainers and managers need to be prepared to deal with. The challenges include new employee orientation and socialization, dual-career paths, plateauing, obsolescence, balancing work and nonwork, coping with job loss, and retirement. Specific practices of companies that have successfully dealt with these issues were presented.

Key Terms

organizational socialization   310
anticipatory socialization   311
realistic job preview   311
encounter phase   311
career path   314
plateauing   317
obsolescence   319
sabbatical   320

time-based conflict   321
strain-based conflict   321
behavior-based conflict   321
job sharing   323
survivors   328
preretirement socialization   330
retirement   331
early retirement programs   331

Discussion Questions

1. Describe the stages of socialization? What are the employees' needs at each stage?
2. Why are content and process important to consider in designing employee orientation programs? What content should an effective orientation program include? What process should be used?

3. What is a dual-career path? What are the characteristics of an effective dual-career path?

4. Why do employees plateau? How could you help a plateaued employee? Discuss the characteristics of a plateaued employee who might resist your help.

5. Why should managers be trained as part of establishing supportive work–life policies?

6. How could you help downsized survivors remain motivated and productive? Rank your recommendations in order of importance. Provide a rationale for your ranking.

7. What advantages and disadvantages might a company gain by rehiring retired employees?

Application Assignments

1. Interview a relative or friend who is currently employed. The interview should
   a. Identify her current career development stage.
   b. Identify a special career management challenge she faces.
   c. Find out how her current employer is helping her deal with the career management challenge.
   d. Evaluate her employer's response to the career management issue.
   e. Suggest how the company might better help her deal with the issue.
   Write a paper summarizing your interview.

2. Visit the Web site http://workfamily.com/ on the World Wide Web. This is a clearinghouse of information about work–life issues and practices. Using this site, find information related to one of the following topics: work and family policies, corporate values, work and family dilemmas, and resources for family support. Summarize what you find in two pages or less. Make sure you include links to other Web sites if they are provided.

3. Visit the Web site http://www.shrm.org/hrmagazine. This is a page from the Web site for the Society for Human Resource Management (SHRM). The page relates to *HR Magazine* which is published monthly by SHRM.
   a. Click on "Articles from previous issues."
   b. Click on the article "Work-life programs reap business benefits" by Michelle Martinez
   c. Read the article
   d. Click on the "Related Resources" icon
   e. Using information from the related resources and the Martinez article, write a one-page paper or send an e-mail to your professor (your professor will let you know if they prefer a paper or e-mail message) identifying specific examples of the types of benefits that companies receive for work-family programs.

4. Visit the Web site http://transition-team.com/. This is the Web site for a company that provides outplacement and other services. Click on the "service" icon. Using information from this site answer the following questions
   a. What are "career transition services"? Define and describe these services.
   b. What does this company do in its retirement seminars?
   c. How do executive, senior manager, and group outplacement services differ? How are they similar?

Endnotes

1. D. C. Feldman, "A Contingency Theory of Socialization," *Administrative Science Quarterly* 21 (1976): 433–52; D. C. Feldman, "A Socialization Process That Helps New Recruits Succeed," *Personnel* 57 (1980): 11–23; J. P. Wanous, A. E. Reichers, and S. D. Malik, "Organizational Socialization and Group Development: Toward an Integrative Perspective," *Academy of Management Review* 9 (1984): 670–83; C. L. Adkins, "Previous Work Experience and Organizational Socialization: A Longitudinal Examination," *Academy of Management Journal* 38 (1995): 839–62; E. W. Morrison, "Longitudinal Study of the Effects of Information Seeking on Newcomer Socialization," *Journal of Applied Psychology* 78 (1993): 173–83.

2. G. M. McEnvoy and W. F. Cascio, "Strategies for Reducing Employee Turnover: A Meta-Analysis," *Journal of Applied Psychology* 70 (1985): 342–53.

3. M. R. Louis, "Surprise and Sense Making: What Newcomers Experience in Entering Unfamiliar Organizational Settings," *Administrative Science Quarterly* 25 (1980): 226–51.

4. R. F. Morrison and T. M. Brantner, "What Enhances or Inhibits Learning a New Job? A Basic Career Issue," *Journal of Applied Psychology* 77 (1992): 926–40.

5. D. A. Major, S. W. J. Kozlowski, G. T. Chao, and P. D. Gardner, " A Longitudinal Investigation of Newcomer Expectations, Early Socialization Outcomes, and the Moderating Effect of Role Development Factors," *Journal of Applied Psychology* 80 (1995): 418–31.

6. D. C. Feldman, *Managing Careers in Organizations* (Glenview, IL: Scott-Foresman, 1988).

7. Ibid; D. Reed-Mendenhall and C. W. Millard, "Orientation: A Training and Development Too," *Personnel Administrator* 25, no. 8 (1980): 42–44; M. R. Louis, B. Z. Posner, and G. H. Powell, "The Availability and Helpfulness of Socialization Practices," *Personnel Psychology* 36 (1983): 857–66; C. Ostroff and S. W. J. Kozlowski, Jr., "Organizational Socialization as a Learning Process: The Role of Information Acquisition," *Personnel Psychology* 45 (1992): 849–74; D. R. France and R. L. Jarvis, "Quick Starts for New Employees," *Training and Development* (October 1996): 47–50.

8. Pillsbury engineering orientation program.

9. D. B. Youst and L. Lipsett, "New Job Immersion without Drowning," *Training and Development* (February 1989): 73–75.

10. Greenhaus, Career Management.

11. R. H. Vaughn and M. C. Wilson, "Career Management Using Job Trees: Charting a Path through the Changing Organization," *Human Resource Planning* 17 (1995): 43–55.

12. H. D. Dewirst, "Career Patterns: Mobility, Specialization, and Related Career Issues," in *Contemporary Career Development Issues* eds. R. F. Morrison and J. Adams (Hillsdale, NJ: Lawrence Erlbaum, 1991): 73–107.

13. Z. B. Leibowitz, B. L. Kaye, and C. Farren, "Multiple Career Paths," *Training and Development Journal* (October 1992): 31–35.

14. M. Moravec and R. Tucker, "Transforming Organizations for Good," *HR Magazine* (October 1991): 74–76; R. Tucker, M. Moravec, and K. Ideus, "Designing a Dual Career Track System," *Training and Development Journal* (June 1991): 55–58.

15. D. C. Feldman and B. A. Weitz, "Career Plateaus Reconsidered," *Journal of Management* 14 (1988): 69–80; Feldman, *Managing Careers in Organizations;* J. P. Near, "A Discriminant Analysis of Plateaued versus Nonplateaued Employees," *Journal of Vocational Behavior* 26 (1985): 177–88; S. K. Stout, J. Slocum, Jr., and W. L. Cron, "Dynamics of the Career Plateauing Process," *Journal of Vocational Behavior* 22 (1988): 74–91.

16. Feldman and Weitz, "Career Plateaus Revisited"; B. Rosen and T. H. Jerdee, "Managing Older Working Careers," in *Research in Personnel and Human Resource Management,* vol. 6, eds. F. R. Ferris and F. M. Rowland (Greenwich, CT: JAI Press, 1988): 37–74.

17. S. S. Dubin, "Maintaining Competence through Updating," in *Maintaining Professional Competence,* eds. S. L. Willis and S. S. Dubin (San Francisco: Jossey-Bass, 1990): 9–43.

18. J. A. Fossum, R. D. Arvey, C. A. Paradise, and N. E. Robbins, "Modeling the Skills Obsolescence Process: A Psychological/Economic Integration," *Academy of Management Review* 11 (1986): 362–74; S. W. J. Kozlowski and B. M. Hults, "An Exploration of Climates for Technical Updating and Performance," *Personnel Psychology* 40 (1988): 539–64.

19. C. J. Bachler, "Workers Take Leave of Job Stress," *Personnel Journal* (January 1995): 38–48.

20. C. Lee, "Balancing Work and Family," *Training* (September 1991): 23–28; D. E. Super, "Life Career Roles: Self-Realization in Work and Leisure," in *Career Development in Organizations,* ed. D. T. Hall (San Francisco: Jossey-Bass, 1986): 95–119; P. Voydanoff, "Work Role Characteristics, Family Structure Demands, and Work/Family Conflict," *Journal of Marriage and the Family* 50 (1988): 749–62; R. F. Kelly and P. Voydanoff, "Work/Family Role Strain among Employed Parents," *Family Relations* 34 (1985): 367–74.

21. J. S. Lublin, "Coopers and Lybrand Tackles Turnover by Letting Workers Have a Life," *The Wall Street Journal* (September 19, 1997): R4; M. Picard, "No Kids? Get Back to Work!" *Training* (September 1977): 33–40.

22. J. H. Greenhaus and N. Beutell, "Sources of Conflict between Work and Family Roles," *Academy of Management Review* 10 (1985): 76–88; J. H. Pleck, *Working Wives/Working Husbands* (Newbury Park, CA: Sage, 1985); Kelly and Voydanoff, "Work Family Role Strain."

23. Greenhaus and Beutell, "Sources of Conflict between Work and Family Roles"; R. G. Netemeyer, J. S. Boles, and R. McMurrian, "Development and Validation of Work–Family Conflict and Family–Work Conflict Scales," *Journal of Applied Psychology* 81 (1996): 401–10.

24. J. H. Greenhaus, "The Intersection of Work and Family Roles: Individual, Interpersonal, and Organizational Issues," in *Work and Family,* ed. E. B. Godsmith (Newbury Park, CA: Sage, 1987): 23–44; Bureau of National Affairs, "Measuring Results: Cost-Benefit Analyses of Work and Family Programs," *Employee Relations Weekly* (Washington, DC: Bureau of National Affairs, 1993); L. T. Thomas and D. C. Ganster, "Impact of Family-Supportive Work Variables on Work–Family Conflict and Strain: A Control Perspective," *Journal of Applied Psychology* 80 (1995): 6–15; New York Times News Service, " Many Americans Shelve Job Success to Be with Family, Study Says," *Chicago Tribune* (Sunday, October 29, 1995): section 1, 17; S. Hand and R. A. Zawacki, "Family Friendly Benefits: More than a Frill," *HR Magazine* (October 1994): 79–84.

25. L. E. Duxbury and C. A. Higgins, "Gender Differences in Work-Family Conflict," *Journal of Applied Psychology* 76 (1991): 60–74.

26. J. L. Pierce, J. W. Newstrom, R. B. Dunham, and P. E. Barber, *Alternative Work Schedules* (Boston: Allyn & Bacon, 1989); F. W. Horvath, "Work at Home: New Findings from the Current Population Survey," *Monthly Labor Review* 109, no. 11 (1986): 31–35; J. R. King, "Working at Home Has Yet to Work Out," *The Wall Street Journal,* (December 22, 1989): B1–B2.

27. C. M. Solomon, "Job Sharing: One Job, Double Headache?" *Personnel Journal* (September 1994): 88–96.

28. B. Marsh, "A Consulting Business Thrives by Hiring Mothers Part-Time," *The Wall Street Journal* (February 24, 1994): .

29. F. S. Rodgers and C. Rodgers, "Business and the Facts of Family Life," *Harvard Business Review* (November–December 1989): 121–29; S. J. Goff, M. K. Mount, and R. L. Jamison, "Employer Support Child Care, Work/Family Conflict, and Absenteeism: A Field Study," *Personnel Psychology* 43 (1990): 793–809.

30. G. Flynn, "Making a Business Case for Balance," *Workforce* (March 1997): 68–74.

31. U.S. Department of Labor, *Childcare: A Workforce Issue* (Washington, DC: U.S. Department of Labor, 1988); M. L. Sher and G. Brown, "What to Do with Jenny," *Personnel Administrator* 34 (1989): 31–41; D. J. Petersen and D. Massengill, "Child Care Programs Benefit Employers Too," *Personnel* 65 (1988): 58–62; E. E. Kossek, "Diversity in Child-Care Assistance Needs: Employee Problems, Preferences, and Work-Related Outcomes," *Personnel Psychology* 43 (1990): 769–91; N. R. Fritz, "Someone to Watch over Them," *Personnel* 65 (1988): 4–5.

32. E. E. Kossek, B. J. DeMarr, K. Backman, and M. Kollar, "Assessing Employees' Emerging Elder Care Needs and Reactions to Dependent Care Benefits," *Public Personnel Management* 22 (1993): 617–37.

33. L. Faught, "At Eddie Bauer You Can Have Work and a Life," *Workforce* (April 1997): 83–90.

34. R. S. Azarnoff and A. E. Scharlach, "Can Employees Carry the Elder-Care Burden?" *Personnel Journal* (September 1988); 60–67; American Association of Retired Persons, *The Aging Workforce* (Washington, DC: American Association of Retired Persons, 1990); J. L. Lefkovich, "Business Responds to Elder-Care Needs," *HR Magazine* (June 1992): 103–8.

35. S. Caudron, "Andersen Is at Employees' Service," *Personnel Journal* (September 1995): 88–96.

36. F. N. Schwartz, "Management Women and the New Facts of Family Life," *Harvard Business Review* (January–February 1989): 65–76.

37. J. Brockner, "The Effects of Work Layoffs on Survivors: Research, Theory, and Practice," in *Research in Organizational Behavior,* vol. 10, eds. B. M. Staw and L. L.

Cummings (Hillsdale, NJ: Lawrence Erlbaum, 1988): 45–95; L. Greenhalgh, A. T. Lawrence, and R. I. Sutton, "Determinants of Workforce Reduction Strategies in Declining Organizations," *Academy of Management Review* 13 (1988): 241–54; J. Nocera, "Living with Layoffs," *Fortune* (April 1, 1996): 69–71; J. Martin, "Where Are They Now?" *Fortune* (April 1, 1996): 100–8.

38. J. C. Latack and J. B. Dozier, "After the Ax Falls: Job Loss as Career Transition," *Academy of Management Review* 11 (1986): 375–92; J. Brockner, "Managing the Effects of Layoffs on Survivors," *California Management Review* (Winter 1992): 9–28; S. L. Guinn, "Outplacement Programs: Separating Myth from Reality," *Training and Development Journal* 42 (1988): 48–49; D. R. Simon, "Outplacement: Matching Needs, Matching Services," *Training and Development Journal* 42 (1988): 52–57; S. Rosen and C. Paul, "Learn the Inner Workings of Outplacement," *The Wall Street Journal* (July 31, 1995): editorial page; S. Spera, E. D. Buhrfeind, and J. P. Pennebaker, "Expressive Writing and Coping with Job Loss," *Academy of Management Journal* 37 (1994): 722–33.

39. J. Cole, "Boeing Teaches Employees How to Run Small Business," *The Wall Street Journal* (November 7, 1995): B1–B2.

40. E. B. Picolino, "Outplacement: The View from HR," *Personnel* (March 1988): 24–27.

41. B. Z. Locker, "Job Loss and Organization Change: Psychological Perspectives," in *Special Challenges in Career Management,* ed. A. J. Pickman (Mahwah, NJ: Lawrence Erlbaum, 1997): 13–24.

42. H. M. O'Neill and D. J. Lenn, "Voices of Survivors: Words That Downsizing CEOs Should Hear," *Academy of Management Executive* 9 (1995): 23–34.

43. Brockner, "Managing the Effects of Layoffs on Survivors"; J. Brockner, M. Konovsky, R. Cooper-Schneider, R. Folger, C. Martin, and R. J. Bies, "Interactive Effects of Procedural Justice and Outcome Negativity on Victims and Survivors of Job Loss," *Academy of Management Journal* 37 (1994): 397–409.

44. L. Thornburg, "The Age Wave Hits," *HR Magazine* (February 1995): 40–45.

45. C.A. Olson, "Who Receives Formal Firm-Sponsored Training in the U.S.?" October 15, 1996, National Center for the Workplace, Institute of Industrial Relations, University of California (Berkeley). Document on server http://violet.lib.berkeley.edu/~iir/.

46. A. L. Kamouri and J. C. Cavanaugh, "The Impact of Preretirement Education Programs on Workers' Preretirement Socialization," *Journal of Occupational Behavior* 7 (1986): 245–56; N. Schmitt and J. T. McCune, "The Relationship between Job Attitudes and the Decision to Retire," *Academy of Management Review* 24 (1981): 795–802; N. Schmitt, B. W. Coyle, J. Rauschenberger, and J. K. White, "Comparison of Early Retirees and Non-retirees," *Personnel Psychology* 32 (1981): 327–40; T. A. Beehr, "The Process of Retirement," *Personnel Psychology* 39 (1986): 31–55; S. M. Comrie, "Teach Employees to Approach Retirement as a New Career," *Personnel Journal* 64, no. 8 (1985): 106–8.

47. L. Phillon and J. Brugger, "Encore! Retirees Give Top Performance as Temporaries," *HR Magazine* (October 1994): 74–77.

48. R. E. Hill and P. C. Dwyer, "Grooming Workers for Early Retirement," *HR Magazine* (September 1990): 59–63.

49. M. L. Colusi, P. B. Rosen, and S. J. Herrin, "Is Your Early Retirement Package Courting Disaster?" *Personnel Journal* (August 1988): 60–67.

50. Rosen and Jerdee, "Managing Older Workers' Careers."

13   THE FUTURE OF TRAINING AND DEVELOPMENT

Objectives

After reading this chapter, you should be able to

1. Identify the future trends that are likely to influence training departments and trainers.

2. Discuss how these future trends may impact training delivery and administration as well as the strategic role of the training department.

3. Describe the components of the change model and how they can be used to introduce a new training method.

4. Benchmark current training practices.

5. Discuss how process reengineering can be used to review and redesign training administration practices (e.g, enrollment in training).

WORKING TOGETHER

LearnShare, formed by a consortium of large, noncompeting manufacturing companies (including Owens Corning, Deere and Company, Motorola, and 3M) and three universities (Ohio State, Farleigh Dickinson, and Arizona State) allows these partners to consolidate their power and use it to their advantage in evaluating and purchasing new multimedia technology. The consortium can also help members by sharing program develop-

ment costs that would be too expensive for any one company's training department to absorb into its budget. The companies involved have huge buying power. They employ 2.2 million employees and have revenues greater than $100 billion!

Besides purchasing power, consortium members hope to share training resources. A survey found that 74 percent of the member companies were addressing the same needs. The consortium is currently developing an electronic library that will let members obtain information they need for training. Some material will be text, other material will be video than can be downloaded via the Internet. LearnShare may also develop "best practices" for a given topic to make available to participating members.

Currently, LearnShare is developing its course offerings. But if the con-

sortium succeeds, it could mean that an employee anywhere in the world could access training based on the best practices (or improvements of the best practices) of some of the world's most successful companies! ■

Source: M. Blumfield, "Learning to Share," *Training* (April 1997): 38–42.

Introduction

LearnShare represents one of the future trends in training and development practices: the formation of partnerships between companies to share training practices and gain leverage with program developers and consultants. The previous 12 chapters discussed training design and delivery as well as employee development and career management. This chapter takes a look toward the future by discussing trends that are likely to influence the future of training and development and your future as a trainer. Table 13–1 presents future trends.

New Technologies Will Increase in Popularity for Training Delivery

The use of multimedia, World Wide Web, and other new technologies will likely increase in the future for several reasons. First, the cost of these technologies will decrease. Also, as the chapter opening illustrates, companies may form partnerships to purchase and use technologies. Second, use of these new technologies can substantially reduce training costs (e.g., travel, food, housing) related to bringing geographically dispersed employees to one central training location. Third, these technologies allow trainers to build into training many of the desirable features of a learning environment (e.g., practice, feedback, reinforcement). Fourth, as companies employ more contingent employees (e.g., part-timers,

TABLE 13–1   Future Trends Affecting Training

1. The use of new technologies for training delivery will increase.
2. Emphasis on storage and use of intellectual capital will rise.
3. Training departments will become "virtual training organizations."
4. Training will become more integrated with other business functions.
5. Training departments will work more with external partners.
6. Training and development will be viewed more from a change model perspective.

consultants) who may not work in a central geographic area, technology will allow training to be delivered to these employees in a timely, effective manner.

New technology also makes it possible to create "smart" products.[1] For example, packages sent by UPS leave an "electronic trail" that can be used to improve shipping and delivery processes. In the future, training products may also leave an electronic trail that will enable trainers and managers to better understand how these products are being used. For example, currently in Web-based training it is possible to track how long it takes a trainee to complete a program. In the future, by incorporating smart technology into Web-based training, trainers can determine which of several available practice exercises trainees choose and if there are any differences in the rate or amount of learning based on the choice of exercise!

Training Departments Will Better Store and Use Intellectual Capital

New technologies such as Lotus Notes and Intranets (a company's own Internet system) as well as an increased emphasis on creating a learning organization (recall Chapter 3's discussion of learning organizations) mean that companies will increasingly seek ways to turn employees' knowledge (intellectual capital) into a shared company asset. Trainers and the training department likely will create functions related to managing knowledge and coordinating organizational learning. For example, Cigna Corporation, a property and casualty insurer, gave its home-office managers the job of building a knowledge base that is contained in the same software that every underwriter uses to process applications. When new information comes in (such as feedback from the claims department or insights from the underwriters) the manager evaluates the information and adds it to the database. Hewlett-Packard has an internal consulting group (Product Process Organization) that provides services to the business units. The Product Process Organization is in charge of collecting case histories, "war stories," and best practices and putting them on the company's Web site. How might the knowledge network be used? Consider a manager who is looking for information regarding outsourcing practices. She can learn how others have done it as well as who has done it. Arthur Andersen, Chicago-based consulting firm, has a two-level approach to capturing knowledge. AA Online is a network onto which information can be posted. Knowledge managers monitor AA Online. When the knowledge manager finds a valuable piece of information they post it on databases designed to store specific types of information (e.g., Performance Measures, Global Best Practices).[2]

The increasing use of new technologies to deliver training and store and communicate knowledge means that trainers must be technologically literate. That is, they must understand the strengths and weaknesses of new technologies and implementation issues such as overcoming users' resistance to change (which we discuss later in this chapter). Also, many companies have created new positions, such as knowledge manager, whose job it is to identify reliable knowledge and make sure it is accessible to employees.

Training Departments Will Become "Virtual Training Organizations"

To contribute to the company's business strategy, training departments will need to better market their services, get customers more involved in program design and delivery as well as provide evidence that training relates to the bottom line. These are characteristics of virtual training organizations discussed in Chapter 2.

The virtual training organization is part of a trend of the training function viewing managers, business units and employees as internal customers. As a result, the training function needs to show how training relates to business, team, and employee performance. For example, a computer-parts maker has the training function assigned to different business units. Each training course has a functional owner and a course owner. Functional owners are training managers for specific business functions who are responsible for all courses. Course owners ensure the quality of courses. If a course does not have a functional owner and course owner it is eliminated.

For traditional training departments, evidence that training relates to the bottom line includes auditing training practices. **Auditing** refers to providing information related to the frequency of training that occurs in the company. This may include counting the number of instructor or training days per year, number of new courses developed, course enrollments, or hours spent in training by different types of employees (e.g., managers, engineers, line employees). While information gained from audits is useful for understanding training activity, it does not show a link between training and performance. Also, as we noted in Chapter 6, current training evaluation focuses more on measuring trainee reactions to programs (e.g., satisfaction with training) than learning or results.

In the future, training departments will need to focus on providing evidence that (1) skills transfer to the workplace and (2) training is related to individual and group performance.[3] As a result, trainers and managers will need to ensure that they can show the relationship between training and (1) specific business goals, and (2) employee and team performance.

Training Will Become More Integrated with Other Business Functions

Because of an increasing focus on contributing to the company's competitive advantage, training departments will have to ensure that they are seen as helping the business functions (e.g., marketing, finance, production) meet their needs. Two ways that training departments will need to be involved include focusing on interventions related to performance improvement and providing support for high-performance work systems.

Training departments' responsibilities will likely include more of a focus on providing systems that employees can use for information (such as expert systems or electronic performance support systems) on an as-needed basis. This need is driven by the use of contingent employees and increased flexibility necessary to adapt products and services to meet customers' needs. For example, companies do not want to spend money to train employees who may be with the company only a few weeks. Instead, through temporary employment agencies, companies can select employees with the exact skill set needed. Training needs to provide mechanisms to support the temporary employees once they are on the job and encounter situations, problems, rules, and policies they are unfamiliar with because they are not yet knowledgeable about the company.

As we discussed in Chapter 1, more companies are striving to create high-performance workplaces because of the productivity gains that can be realized through this type of design. High-performance work requires that employees have interpersonal skills necessary to work in teams. High-performance work systems also require employees to have high levels of technical skills. Employees need to understand statistical process control and the Total Quality Management philosophy. Employees also must understand the entire production and service system so they can better serve both internal and external customers. As more companies move to high-performance work systems, training departments will need to be prepared to provide effective training in interpersonal, quality, and technical skills as well as helping employees to understand all aspects of the customer-service or production system.

Training Departments Will Work More with External Partners

Due to shrinking training staffs resulting from downsizing, the development of specialized new knowledge that employees need to learn, and varying demand for training services, companies are increasing their use of external suppliers of training services. External suppliers may include consultants, academics, graduate students, and companies in the entertainment and mass communications industries. External suppliers can be used as partners or sole providers of training services.

Training departments will increase their partnerships with academic institutions (e.g., community colleges, universities) to provide basic skills training and develop customized programs. For example, in school-to-work transition programs (which we discussed in Chapter 10), companies are actively involved in designing curricula and providing experiences for students to help ensure they are competent to enter the work force. Another use of academic partners is as subject matter experts. The academics evaluate current training practices and modify training programs to increase their effectiveness. Academic partners may also work with training departments to develop specialized programs for employees at all levels in the company. For example, Westcott Communication is working with eight business schools to provide executive education for several companies including Kodak, Disney, and Texas Instruments.[4] Sematech, the semiconductor industry association, is working with community colleges in the Phoenix, Arizona, area to develop a curriculum for training entry-level manufacturing technicians.[5]

The reliance on external suppliers to provide training services is known as **outsourcing.** As the role of external suppliers of training increases, trainers will need to become more savvy in contract negotiations and make-versus-buy analysis.[6] Trainers will need to know how to identify and select training vendors. (As the chapter opening said, this is one potential advantage of partnering with other companies.) Trainers may be called upon to support managers and employees who will actually conduct the training. For example, rather than developing training programs, trainers increasingly are likely to need competency in designing train-the-trainer programs.

Increase in Viewing Training and Development from a Change Model Perspective

Although we usually deal with the concept of change in an organizational behavior course, the reality is that for new training or development practices to be successfully implemented, they must be accepted by the customer (manager, upper management, employees). For managers and employees, change is not easy. Even when we know a practice or program could be better, we have learned to adapt to its inadequacies. Therefore, resistance to new training and development practices is likely. As a result, prior to implementing a new training or development practice you should consider how you can increase the likelihood of its acceptance.

Figure 13–1 provides a model of change. The process of change is based on the interaction among four components of the organization: task, employees, formal organizational arrangements (structures, processes, systems), and informal organization (communications patterns, values, norms).[7] As shown in the Figure, different types of change-related problems occur depending on the organizational component that is influenced by the change. These change-related problems include power imbalance, loss of control, resistance to change, and task redefinition.

For example, introducing new technology for training into a company (such as multimedia training using the Internet) might cause changes in the organization's power structure. Without the new technology managers may have less control over access to training programs than they had with traditional methods of training. As a result, tension related to the power imbalance created by the new system occurs. If these issues are not dealt with, the managers will not accept the new technology or provide support for transfer of training. Four change-related problems need to be considered for any new training practice: **Resistance to change** refers to managers and employees unwillingness to change. Managers and employees may be anxious about change, feel they will be unable to cope, value the current training practice or not understand the value of the new practice. **Control** refers change to managers and employees ability to obtain and distribute valuable resources such as data, information, or money. Changes can cause managers and employees to have less control over resources.

FIGURE 13–1

A change model

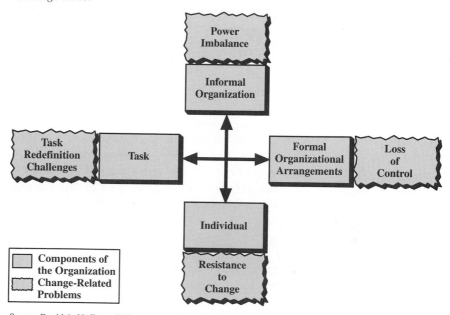

Source: David A. Nadler and Michael L. Tushman, "A Congruence Model for Diagnosing Organizational Behavior," in *Organizational Psychology: A Book of Readings*, eds. D. Rabin and J. McIntyre (Prentice Hall, 1979), as reprinted in David A. Nadler, "Concepts for the Management of Organizational Change," in *Readings in the Management of Innovation*, 2d ed., eds. M. L. Tushman and N. Moore (Ballinger Publishing Co., 1988): 722.

Change can also give managers and employees control over processes that they have not previously been involved in (e.g., choosing which training programs to attend). **Power** refers to the ability to influence others. Managers may lose the ability to influence employees as they gain access to databases and other information, thus getting more autonomy to deliver products and services. Employees may be held accountable for learning in self-directed training. Web-based training methods such as **task redefinition** refers to changes in managers and employees roles and job responsibilities. Employees may be asked not only to participate in training but also to consider how to improve its quality. Managers may be asked to become facilitators and coaches.

Determining if Change Is Necessary: Benchmarking and Process Reengineering

Viewing training from a systems perspective means that companies and trainers need to understand both internal and external environments.[8] Specifically, they need to understand the effectiveness and efficiency of current training practices. They also need to be aware of other companies' practices to ensure that their training practices are the best possible. Benchmarking provides information about other companies' practices. Process reengineering provides information about the effectiveness and efficiency of training systems within the company.

Benchmarking

As we mentioned in Chapter 3, benchmarking is the practice of finding examples of excellent products, services, or systems (i.e., best practices). Benchmarking is an important component of a company's quality strategy. Benchmarking training practices is useful for several reasons.[9] By looking at how excellent companies conduct training, a company can identify how its training practices compare to the best practices. Benchmarking also helps a company learn from others. A company can see what types of training practices work and how they were successfully implemented. Use of this information can increase the chances that new training practices will be accepted and effective. Learning what other successful companies are doing can help managers create a case for changing current training and development practices in the company (i.e., overcoming resistance to change). Benchmarking can also be used to help establish a training strategy and set priorities for training practices.

What does the benchmarking process involve? Xerox's well-known benchmarking process features the 10 steps shown in Table 13–2. Besides collecting its own benchmarking information, a company may want to subscribe to a service that collects data regarding HR practices from several companies. For example, the American Society for Training and Development sponsors a benchmarking forum. The 62 companies that belong to the forum are generally larger companies such as Xerox. They report information regarding training expendi-

---

TABLE 13–2   Xerox's Benchmarking Practices

1. Identify what is to benchmarked.
2. Identify comparable companies.
3. Determine data collection methods and collect data.
4. Determine current performance levels.
5. Project future performance levels.
6. Communicate benchmark results and gain acceptance.
7. Establish functional goals.
8. Develop action plans.
9. Implement action plans and monitor progress.
10. Recalibrate benchmarks.

Source: Based on S. Greengard, "Discover Best Pictures through Benchmarking," *Personnel Journal* (November 1995): 62–73.

tures, structure of training programs, training design, and delivery practices. This information is shared among forum members; a report summarizing the results is sold to other interested parties. Some estimate that as many as 70 percent of Fortune 500 companies use benchmarking on a regular basis.[10]

Trainers need to take several things into account when benchmarking.[11] Trainers must gather information about internal processes to serve as a comparison for best practices. It is important to clearly identify the purpose of benchmarking and the practice to be benchmarked. Upper-level management needs to be committed to the project. Both quantitative (numbers) and qualitative data should be collected. Descriptions of programs and how they operate are as valuable as knowing how best practices contributed to the bottom line. Be careful to gather data from companies both within and outside your industry. Benchmarking may actually limit a company's performance if the goal is only to learn and copy what other companies have done and not consider how to improve upon the process. Be careful not to view HR practices in isolation from each other. For example, examining training practices also requires consideration of the company's staffing strategy (use of internal labor market versus the external labor market to fill positions). Benchmarking will not provide a "right" answer. The information collected needs to be considered in terms of the context of the companies. Finally, benchmarking is one part of an improvement process. As a result, use of the information gathered from benchmarking needs to be considered in the broader framework of organization change, which we discussed above.

Process Reengineering

Trainers need to understand their current training practices and processes and evaluate them to determine what should be changed. **Reengineering** is a complete review of critical processes and redesign of those processes to make them more efficient and able to deliver higher quality. Reengineering is critical to ensuring that the benefits of new training and development programs can be realized. Reengineering is especially important when attempting to deliver training using new technology. Reengineering is also important when trying to streamline administrative processes and improve the services the training department offers to its "customers." This can include course enrollment processes, processes related to receiving tuition reimbursement, and processes related to employees reviewing their training records. Applying new technology (e.g., interactive voice technology) to a course enrollment process burdened with too many steps will not result in improvements in efficiency or effectiveness. What it will result in is increased product or service costs related to the introduction of the new technology.

Reengineering can be used to review the training department functions and processes or it can be used to review a specific training program or development program practice such as a career management system. The reengineering process involves the four steps shown in Figure 13–2: Identify the process to be reengineered, understand the process, redesign the process, and implement the new process.[12]

FIGURE 13–2

The reengineering process

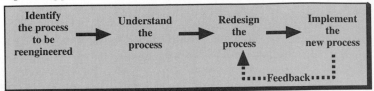

Identify the Process.   Managers and trainers who control the process or are responsible for functions within the process ("process owners") should be identified and asked to participate on the reengineering team. Team members should include employees involved in the process (to provide expertise) and outside the process, as well as internal or external customers who see the outcome of the process.

Understanding the Process.   Several things need to be considered when evaluating a process:

- Can tasks (e.g., course enrollment and pretraining assessment) be combined?
- Can we provide employees with more autonomy? Can we build decision making and control into the process through streamlining it?
- Are all of the steps necessary in the process?
- Are data redundancy or unnecessary checks and controls built into the process?
- How many special cases and exceptions have to be dealt with?
- Are the steps in the process arranged in their natural order?
- What is the desired outcome? Are all of the tasks necessary? What is the value of the process?

A number of techniques are used to understand processes. **Data-flow diagrams** show the flow of data between departments. For example, to investigate why tuition reimbursement checks take too long to reach employees, trainers may want to investigate the relationship between the training department (where tuition reimbursement is approved) and accounting (where checks are issued). **Data-entity relationship diagrams** show the types of data used within a business function and the relationship among the different types of data. These diagrams would be especially useful for investigating the time and people within the training department involved in filling an employee's request for his training records. In **scenario analysis,** simulations of real-world issues are presented to data end-users. The end-users are asked to indicate how a new technology could help address their particular situations and what data should be maintained to deal with those situations. Surveys and focus groups collect information about the data collected, used, and stored in a functional area, as well as information about time and data processing requirements. Users may be asked to evaluate the importance, frequency, and criticality of automating specific tasks within a functional area. (For example, how critical is it to have an employee tracking system that maintains data on employees' fluency in foreign languages?) Cost-benefit analyses compare the costs of completing tasks with and without an automated system or software application. For example, the analysis should include (1) the costs in terms of people, time, materials, and dollars, (2) the anticipated costs of software and hardware, and (3) labor, time, and material expenses.[13]

Redesign the Process.   The team develops models, tests them, chooses a prototype, and determines how to integrate the prototype into the organization.

Implement the Process.   The company tries out the process by testing it in a limited, controlled setting before expanding companywide.

Steps in Implementing a New Training and Development Practice

Change management is the process of ensuring that new interventions such as training practices are accepted and used by employees and managers. The change management process involves four steps: overcoming resistance to change, managing the transition to the new practice, shaping political dynamics, and using training to understand new tasks.

Overcoming Resistance to Change.   This can be done by involving the affected people in planning the change and rewarding them for desired behavior. It is also critical for managers to divide the implementation of the new practice into steps that are understandable and that employees believe they can accomplish. Employees need to understand how new training practices to help them meet their needs.[14] These needs may include better-quality training, faster access to descriptions of training programs, a link between training and compensation, and more meaningful training or access to training programs from their personal computers.

Managing the Transition.   Tactics for managing the transition include communicating a clear picture of the future, and creating organizational arrangements for the transition (e.g., contact person, help line). It might be good to allow an old practice and a new practice to exist simultaneously (run parallel) so that employees can see the benefits and advantages of the new practice. Then any problems that are identified can be worked out. This is commonly done when new technology is introduced in companies.

Shaping Political Dynamics.   Managers need to seek the support of key power groups including formal and informal leaders. For example, as we mentioned in Chapter 10, successful diversity efforts are characterized by active involvement and endorsement by top managers. They not only talk about the need to manage diversity, they actively get involved through mentoring programs, setting up formal committees and positions to promote diversity, and rewarding managers for their diversity efforts.

TABLE 13–3   Managers' Misconceptions about Training

- Training is not valuable.
- Training is an expense, not an investment.
- Anybody can be a trainer.
- The training department is a good place to put poor performers.
- Training is the responsibility of trainers.

Source: Based on R. F. Mager, "Morphing into a . . . 21st Century Trainer," *Training* (June 1996): 47–54.

A key to shaping the political dynamics for managers of support functions such as human resources that are not directly involved in the design, manufacturing, or delivery of a product or service to the marketplace is to become a business partner. Table 13–3 shows several misconceptions that some managers hold about training. These misconceptions are likely due to a lack of understanding of the function and value of the training department.

To counter these misconceptions and gain political alliances with managers in the business functions, trainers need to take several actions. They need to ensure that the training department adds value to the business, builds relationships with functional business managers, and establishes credibility in the company.[15] This is accomplished through helping functional managers deal with training-related problems, evaluating the effectiveness of training practices, and providing excellent service to the function managers (e.g., providing information and finishing projects in a timely manner, committing only to projects that can be realistically delivered).

Using Training to Understand New Tasks.   Because many practices involve changes not only in the way the service or process is going to be provided, but also in employees' and managers' roles, training is critical. Managers and employees need to be trained to deal with new systems whether they involve job redesign (e.g., teams), performance management (e.g., use of 360 degree feedback systems), selection systems (e.g., a structured interview), or new technology (e.g., a new computer-based manufacturing system).

For example, these principles helped with the introduction of a computerized flexible manufacturing system at a manufacturer of diesel engines.[16] The computers were to be used to provide instructions for customized orders and to give the order center updates on production status. The production workers were reluctant to use the computers. Their objections included that they did not know how to type and their jobs made their hands too greasy. To ensure that the production workers would use the new system, the company took several steps. First, an electronic performance support system was placed in the cafeteria to answer employees' questions about the system. Second, the company asked workers for suggestions as they tested prototypes of the system. Third, the touch screen system was modified so that employees could use foot controls, thus alleviating concerns about greasy hands when typing. Twenty months after the process for introducing the new manufacturing system began, the system was in place.

Summary

This chapter discussed future trends that are likely to influence training and development. These trends relate to training delivery and structure of the training function. New technology is likely to have a growing impact on training delivery in the future. Also, new technology allows training departments to store and share intellectual capital throughout the company. Training departments are more likely to develop partnerships with vendors and other companies in the future. The chapter discusses how training is likely to be increasingly viewed from a change perspective. Benchmarking training practices and reengineering training processes are important prerequisites for creating a need for change. For new training practices to be accepted by employees and managers, trainers need to ensure that they overcome resistance to change, manage the transition, shape the political dynamics, and use training to redefine the task.

Key Terms

auditing   342
outsourcing   344
resistance to change   344
control   344
power   345
task redefinition   345

reengineering   347
data-flow diagrams   348
data-entity relationships
  diagrams   348
scenario analysis   348
change management   349

Discussion Questions

1. Discuss how new technologies are likely to impact training in the future.
2. What new skills will trainers need to be successful in the future?
3. What is benchmarking? Explain the process you would use to benchmark a company's safety training programs.
4. What is process reengineering? Why is it relevant to training?
5. Discuss the steps necessary to introduce a new training practice from a change-model perspective.
6. What misconceptions do managers have about training? How could you change those misconceptions?
7. The chapter introduction illustrates how several companies are partners in a consortium, LearnShare. Explain what you believe are the advantages and disadvantages of creating a training consortium or partnership with other companies.

Application Assignments

1. Interview a manager. Ask him to evaluate his company's training department in terms of training delivery, service, expertise, and contribution to the business. Ask him to explain the rationale for his evaluation. Summarize this information. Based on the information you gathered, make recommendations regarding how the training department can be improved.

2. This chapter discussed several trends that we believe will influence the future of training. Based on future social, economic, political, or technological factors, identify one or two additional trends that you think will influence training. Write a two-to-three–page paper summarizing your ideas. Make sure you provide a rationale for your trends. Many organizations are moving from a training perspective to a performance perspective. That is, they are interested in performance improvement, not training just for the sake of training.

3. Go to the Web site http://www.astd.org. This is the Web site for the American Society for Training & Development.

    a. Click on the icon "About the industry."

    b. Click on "Shifting paradigms from training to performance."

    c. Click on the article "New Mindsets." Read the article.

    d. How does the training perspective differ from the performance perspective? What implications does the performance perspective have for how training is conducted in the future?

Endnotes

1. C. E. Plott and J. Humphrey, "Preparing for 2020," *Training and Development* (November 1996): 46–49.
2. T. A. Stewart, "Getting Real about Brainpower," *Fortune* (November 27, 1995): 201–3; P. Stamps, "Managing Corporate Smarts," *Training* (August 1997): 40–46; K. Vander Linde, N. Horney, and R. Koonce, "Seven Ways to Make Your Training Department One of the Best," *Training & Development* (August 1997): 20–28.
3. J. Robinson and D. G. Robinson, "Performance Takes Training to New Heights," *Training and Development* (September 1995).
4. L. J. Bassi, G. Benson, and S. Cheney, "The Top Ten Trends," *Training and Development* (November 1996): 28–42.
5. S. Jackson, "Your Local Campus: Training Ground Zero," *Business Week* (September 30, 1996): 68.
6. C. J. Bachler, "Trainers," *Workforce* (June 1997): 93–105; Bassi, Benson, and Cheney, "The Top Ten Trends."
7. D. A. Nadler, "Concepts for the Management of Organizational Change," in *Readings in the Management of Innovation,*, 2d, ed., eds. M. L. Tushman and N. L. Moore (Cambridge, MA; Ballinger, 1988): 722.

8. A. P. Brache and G. A. Rummler, "Managing an Organization as a System," *Training* (February 1997): 68–74.

9. E. F. Glanz and L. K. Dailey, "Benchmarking," *Human Resource Management,* 31 (1992): 9–20; C. E. Schneier and C. Johnson, "Benchmarking: A Tool for Improving Performance Management and Reward Systems," *American Compensation Association Journal* (Spring/Summer 1993): 14–31.

10. S. Greengard, "Discover Best Practices through Benchmarking," *Personnel Journal* (November 1995): 62–73; J. D. Weatherly. "Dare to Compare for Better Productivity," *HR Magazine* (September 1992): 42–46.

11. C. E. Bogan, and M. J. English, "Benchmarking for Best Practices," in *The ASTD Handbook for Training and Development,* 4th ed., ed. R. L. Craig (New York: McGraw-Hill, 1996): 394–412.

12. T. B. Kinni, "A Reengineering Primer," *Quality Digest* (January 1994): 26–30; "Reengineering is Helping Health of Hospitals and Its Patients," *Total Quality Newsletter* (February 1994): 5; R. Recardo, "Process Reengineering in a Finance Division," *Journal for Quality and Participation* (June 1994): 70–73.

13. S. E. O'Connell, "New Technologies Bring New Tools, New Rules," *HR Magazine* (December 1995): 43–48; S. F. O'Connell, "The Virtual Workplace Works at Warp Speed," *HR Magazine* (March 1996): 51–57.

14. E. Kossek, "The Acceptance of Human Resource Innovation by Multiple Constituencies," *Personnel Psychology* 42 (1989): 263–81.

15. J. J. Laabs, "Put Your Job on the Line," *Personnel Journal* (June 1995): 74–88.

16. M. Samuel, "Managing Change: Safety, Accountability, and Some Discomfort Needed," *Total Quality Newsletter* (September 1994).

360-degree feedback   A special case of the upward feedback system. Here an employee's behaviors or skills are evaluated not only by subordinates but also by peers, customers, her bosses, and herself via a questionnaire rating her on a number of dimensions.

ability   The physical and mental capacity to perform a task.

action learning   Training method that involves giving teams or work groups a problem, having them work on solving it and committing to an action plan, and then holding them accountable for carrying out the plan.

action plan   A written document detailing steps that a trainee and his manager will take to ensure that training transfers to the job.

action planning   An employee's process of determining how he will achieve his short- and long-term career goals.

adventure learning   Training method focusing on developing teamwork and leadership skills using structured outdoor activities.

affective outcomes   Outcomes including attitudes and motivation.

Americans with Disabilities Act (ADA)   A 1990 act prohibiting workplace discrimination against people with disabilities.

andragogy   The theory of adult learning.

anticipatory socialization   Initial phase in organizational socialization involving the development of an employee's expectations about the company, job, working conditions, and interpersonal relationships.

application planning   The preparing of trainees to use key behaviors on the job.

apprenticeship   A work–study training method with both on-the-job and classroom training.

assessment   The collecting of information and providing of feedback to employees about their behavior, communication style, or skills.

assessment center   A process in which multiple raters or evaluators (also known as assessors) evaluate employees' performances on a number of exercises.

attitude   Combination of beliefs and feelings that predispose a person to behave in a certain way.

attitude awareness and change program   Program focusing on increasing employees' awareness of their attitudes toward differences in cultural and ethnic backgrounds, physical characteristics (e.g., disabilities), and personal characteristics that influence behavior towards others.

audiovisual instruction   Media-based training that is both watched and heard.

auditing   As regards training, the providing of information related to the frequency of training within a company.

basic skills   Skills necessary for employees to perform their jobs and learn the content of training programs.

behavior-based conflict   Conflict occurring when an employee's behavior in work roles is not appropriate in nonwork roles.

behavior-based program   Program focusing on changing the organizational policies and individual behaviors that inhibit employees' personal growth and productivity.

behavior modeling   A training method in which trainees are presented with a model who demonstrates key behaviors to replicate and provides them with opportunity to practice those key behaviors.

Benchmarks©   A research instrument designed to measure important factors in being a successful manager.

benefits   What of value the company gains from a training program.

business game   A training method in which trainees gather information, analyze it, and make decisions.

business strategy   A plan that integrates a company's goals, policies, and actions.

career   The pattern of work-related experiences that span the course of a person's life.

career development   The process by which employees progress through a series of stages, each characterized by a different set of developmental tasks, activities, and relationships.

career management   The process through which employees (1) become aware of their own interests, values, strengths, and weaknesses, (2) get information about job opportunities within a company, (3) identify career goals, and (4) establish action plans to achieve career goals.

career management system   System that helps employees, managers, and the company identify career development needs; includes self-assessment, reality check, goal setting, and action planning.

career path   A sequence of job positions involving similar types of work and skills that employees move through in a company.

career support   Coaching, protection, sponsorship, and provision of challenging assignments, exposure, and visibility to an employee.

case study   A description of how employees or an organization dealt with a situation.

CD-ROM   An aluminum disc from which a laser reads text, graphics, audio, and video.

change management   The process of ensuring that new interventions such as training practices are accepted and used by employees and managers.

climate for transfer   Trainees' perceptions about a wide variety of characteristics of the work environment; these perceptions facilitate or inhibit use of trained skills or behavior.

coach   A peer or manager who works with an employee to motivate her, help her develop skills, and provide reinforcement and feedback.

cognitive ability   Verbal comprehension, quantitative ability, and reasoning ability.

cognitive outcomes   Outcomes used to measure what knowledge trainees learned in a training program.

cognitive strategies   Strategies that regulate the learning processes. They relate to the learner's decision regarding what information to attend to, how to remember, and how to solve problems.

cognitive theory of transfer   Theory asserting that the likelihood of transfer depends on the trainee's ability to retrieve learned capabilities.

community of practice   A group of employees who work together, learn from each other, and develop a common understanding of how to get work accomplished.

comparison group   A group of employees who participate in an evaluation study but do not attend a training program.

competency   An area of personal capability that enables an employee to perform his job.

competency model   A model identifying the competencies necessary for each job as well as the knowledge, skills, behavior, and personal characteristics underlying each competency.

competitive advantage   An upper hand over other firms in an industry.

competitiveness   A company's ability to maintain and gain market share in an industry.

computer-based training (CBT)   An interactive training experience in which the computer provides the learning stimulus, the trainee must respond, and the computer analyzes responses and provides feedback to the trainee.

concentration strategy   Business strategy focusing on increasing market share, reducing costs, or creating a market niche for products and services.

consequences   Incentives employees receive for performing well.

contingent work force   Part-time, temporary, and self-employed workers.

continuous learning A learning system in which employees are required to understand the entire work system including the relationships among their jobs, their work units, and the company. Also, employees are expected to acquire new skills and knowledge, apply them on the job, and share this information with fellow workers.

control A manager's or employee's ability to obtain and distribute valuable resources.

coordination training Training a team in how to share information and decision making responsibilities to maximize team performance.

copyright Legal protection for the expression of an idea.

corporate university model A training model in which the client group includes not only company employees and managers but also stakeholders outside the company.

cost–benefit analysis The process of determining the economic benefits of a training program using accounting methods.

course objectives (lesson objectives) The expected behaviors, content, conditions, and standards of a training course or lesson; more specific than program objectives.

course parameters General information about a training program including course title, audience, purpose, goals, location, time, prerequisites, and name of trainer.

criteria relevance The extent to which training outcomes relate to the learned capabilities emphasized in training.

criterion contamination A training program's outcomes measuring inappropriate capabilities or being affected by extraneous conditions.

criterion deficiency The failure to measure training outcomes that were emphasized in training objectives.

cross-cultural preparation The education of employees (expatriates) and their families who are to be sent to a foreign country.

cross-training Training method in which team members understand and practice each other's skills so that members are prepared to step in and take another member's place should he temporarily or permanently leave the team. Also, more simply, training employees to learn the skills of one or several additional jobs.

culture A set of assumptions group members share about the world and how it works as well as ideals worth striving for.

customer model A training model in which a training department is responsible for the training needs of one division or function of the company.

data-entity relationship diagram An illustration of the types of data used within a business function and the relationships among the different types of data.

data-flow diagram An illustration of the flow of data between departments.

detailed lesson plan The translation of the content and sequence of training activities into a guide used by the trainer to help deliver training.

development Formal education, job experiences, relationships, and assessments of personality and abilities that help employees prepare for the future.

development planning process Process of identifying development needs, choosing a development goal, identifying actions the employee and company need to take to achieve the goal, determining how progress toward goal attainment will be measured, and establishing a timetable for development.

direct costs Training costs including salaries and benefits of all employees involved, program supplies, equipment and classroom rental or purchase, and travel costs.

directional pattern model A model describing the form or shape of careers.

discrimination The degree to which trainees' performances on an outcome actually reflect true differences in performance.

disengagement stage Career stage in which an individual prepares for a change in the balance between work and nonwork activities.

disinvestment strategy Business strategy emphasizing liquidation and divestiture of businesses.

distance learning Training method in which geographically dispersed companies provide information about new products, policies, or procedures as well as skills training and expert lectures to field locations.

distributed work Work done outside the traditional office or factory.

diversity training   Training programs designed to change employees' attitudes about diversity and/or to develop skills needed to work with a diverse work force.

downward move   Reduction of an employee's responsibility and authority.

early retirement program   A system of offering employees financial benefits to leave the company.

electronic performance support system (EPSS) Computer application that can provide, as requested, skills training, information access, and expert advice.

empowerment   Giving employees responsibility and authority to make decisions regarding all aspects of product development or customer service.

encounter phase   Middle phase in organizational socialization in which an employee begins a new job.

establishment stage   Career stage in which an individual finds his place in a company, makes an independent contribution, achieves more responsibility and financial success, and establishes a desirable life-style.

evaluation design   Designation of what information to be collected, from whom, when, and how to determine training's effectiveness.

expatriate   A person working in a country other than his nation of origin.

expectancy   Belief about the link between trying to perform a behavior (or effort) and actually performing well; the mental state that the learner brings to the instructional process.

expert systems   Technology (usually software) that organizes and applies human experts' knowledge to specific problems.

exploration stage   Career stage in which individuals attempt to identify the type of work that interests them.

external conditions   Processes in the learning environment that facilitate learning.

external growth strategy   Business strategy emphasizing acquiring vendors and suppliers or buying businesses that allow the company to expand into new markets.

external validity   The generalizability of study results to other groups and situations.

faculty model   A training model that resembles the structure of a college. The training department is headed by director with a staff of experts having specialized knowledge of a particular topic or skill area.

far transfer   Trainees' ability to apply learned capabilities to the work environment even though it is not identical to the training session environment.

feedback   Information employees receive while they are performing concerning how well they are meeting objectives.

formal education program   Off-site or on-site program designed for a company's employees, short course offered by a consultant or school, an executive MBA program, or university program in which students live at the university while taking classes.

formative evaluation   Evaluation conducted to improve the training process. Usually conducted before and during the training process.

generalization   A trainee's ability to apply learned capabilities to on-the-job work problems and situations that are similar but not identical to problems and situations encountered in the learning environment.

generalizing   Adapting learning for use in similar but not identical situations.

glass ceiling   A barrier to advancement to an organization's higher levels.

global challenge   The challenge of expanding into world markets and preparing employees to work in foreign locations.

goal   What a company hopes to achieve in the medium–to–long-term future.

goal setting   An employee's process of developing short- and long-term career objectives.

goal setting theory   A theory assuming that behavior results from a person's conscious goals and intentions.

gratifying   The feedback that a learner receives from using learning content.

group building methods   Training methods designed to improve team or group effectiveness.

group mentoring program   Program in which a successful senior employee is paired with a group of four to six less experienced protégés to help them understand the organization, guide them in analyzing their experiences, and help them clarify career directions.

groupware (electronic meeting software) A special type of software application that enables multiple users to track, share, and organize information, and to work on the same document simultaneously.

hands-on method Training method in which the trainee is actively involved in learning.

high-leverage training Training that uses an instructional design process to ensure that it is effective and that compares or benchmarks the company's training programs against other companies'.

high-performance work system challenge The challenge of integrating new technologies and work design into a work system.

human resource management (HRM) practices Management activities relating to investments in staffing, performance management, training, and compensation and benefits.

human resource planning The identification, analysis, forecasting, and planning of changes needed in a company's human resources area.

hyperlinks Links that allow a user to easily move from one Web page to another.

imaging Scanning documents, storing them electronically, and retrieving them.

in-basket A training exercise involving simulation of the administrative tasks of the manager's job.

indirect costs Costs not related directly to a training program's design, development, or delivery.

individualism–collectivism The cultural dimension reflecting the degree to which people act as individuals rather than members of a group.

input Instructions that tell employees what, how, and when to perform; also, the resources employees are given to help them perform their jobs.

instruction The characteristics of the environment in which learning is to occur.

instructional design process A systematic approach to developing training programs. Its six steps include conducting needs assessment, ensuring employees' readiness for training, creating a learning environment, ensuring transfer of training, selecting training methods, and evaluating training programs.

instrumentality In expectancy theory, a belief that performing a given behavior is associated with a particular outcome.

intellectual capital Cognitive knowledge, advanced skills, system understanding and creativity, and self-motivated creativity.

intellectual skills Mastery of concepts and rules.

intelligent tutoring system (ITS) An instructional system using artificial intelligence.

interactive video Training medium combining video and computer-based instruction, with the trainee interacting with the program.

interactive voice technology Technology using a conventional PC to create a phone-response system.

internal conditions Processes within the learner that must be present for learning to occur.

internal growth strategy Business strategy focusing on new market and product development, innovation, and joint ventures.

internal validity Establishing that the treatment (training) made a difference.

Internet A communications tool for sending and receiving messages quickly and inexpensively; a means of locating and gathering resources.

Internet-based training Training delivered on public or private computer networks and displayed by a Web browser.

intranet-based training Training delivered using a company's own computer network or server.

ISO 9000 A family of standards developed by the International Organization for Standardization that include 20 requirements for dealing with such issues as how to establish quality standards and document work processes.

job A specific position requiring completion of certain tasks.

job enlargement The adding of challenges or new responsibilities to an employee's current job.

job experience The relationships, problems, demands, tasks, and other features that an employee faces on the job.

job rotation Assigning employees a series of jobs in various functional areas of a company or movement among jobs in a single functional area or department.

job sharing   Work situation in which two employees divide the hours, responsibilities, and benefits of a full-time job.

joint union-management training program   Program created, funded, and supported by both union and management to provide a range of services to help employees learn skills that are directly related to their jobs and that are "portable" (valuable to employers in other companies or industries).

key behavior   One of a set of behaviors that is necessary to complete a task. Important part of behavior modeling training.

knowledge   Facts or procedures.

knowledge-based pay system   Pay system based primarily on an employee's knowledge rather than on the knowledge necessary to perform her job (also called skill-based pay system).

lapse   Situation in which a trainee uses previously learned, less effective capabilities instead of trying to apply capabilities emphasized in a training program.

laser disc   A disc that uses a laser to provide video and sound.

leaderless group discussion   A training exercise in which a team of five to seven employees must work together to solve an assigned problem within a certain time period.

learning   A relatively permanent change in human capabilities that does not result from growth processes.

learning organization   A company that has an enhanced capacity to learn, adapt, and change; an organization whose employees continuously attempt to learn new things and then apply what they have learned to improve product or service quality.

lecture   Training method in which the trainer communicates through spoken words what trainees are supposed to learn.

lesson plan overview   A plan matching a training program's major activities to specific times or time intervals.

life-cycle model   A model suggesting that employees face certain developmental tasks over the course of their careers and that they move through distinct life or career stages.

logical verification   Perceiving a relationship between a new task and a task already mastered.

long-term–short-term orientation   The degree to which a culture focuses on the future rather than the past and present.

maintenance   The process of continuing to use newly acquired capabilities over time.

maintenance stage   Career stage in which an individual is concerned about keeping skills up to date and being perceived by others as someone who is still contributing to the company.

Malcolm Baldrige Quality Award   National award created in 1987 to recognize U.S. companies' quality achievements and to publicize quality strategies.

manager support   Trainees' managers (1) emphasizing the importance of attending training programs and (2) stressing the application of training content on the job.

managing diversity   The creation of an environment that allows all employees (regardless of their demographic group) to contribute to organizational goals and experience personal growth.

masculinity–femininity   The cultural dimension reflecting the degree to which a culture values behavior that is considered traditionally masculine (competitiveness) or feminine (helpfulness).

matrix model   A training model in which trainers report to both a manager in the training department and a manager in a particular function.

mentor   An experienced, productive senior employee who helps develop a less experienced employee (a protégé).

mission   A company's long-term reason for existing.

modeling   Having employees who have mastered the desired learning outcomes demonstrate them for trainees.

modeling display   Often done via videotape or computer, a training method in which trainees are shown key behaviors, which they then practice.

motivation to learn   A trainee's desire to learn the content of a training program.

motor skills   Coordination of physical movements.

multimedia training   Training that combines audiovisual training methods with computer-based training.

Myers-Briggs Type Indicator (MBTI) A psychological test for employee development consisting of over 100 questions about how the person feels or prefers to behave in different situations.

near transfer A trainee's ability to apply learned capabilities exactly to the work situation.

need A deficiency that a person is experiencing at any point in time.

needs assessment The process used to determine if training is necessary. The first step in the instructional system design model.

objective The purpose and expected outcome of training activities.

obsolescence A reduction in an employee's competence resulting from a lack of knowledge of new work processes, techniques, and technologies that have developed since s/he completed his or her education.

on-the-job training (OJT) Training in which new or inexperienced employees learn through first observing peers or managers performing the job and then trying to imitate their behavior.

opportunity to perform The chance to use learned capabilities.

organization-based model A model suggesting that careers proceed through a series of stages with each stage involving changes in activities and relationships with peers and managers.

organizational analysis Training analysis involving determining the appropriateness of training, considering the context in which training will occur.

organizational socialization The process of transforming new employees into effective company members. Its phases are anticipatory socialization, encounter, and settling in.

other The conditions under which tasks are performed, e.g. physical condition of the work environment or psychological conditions, such as pressure or stress.

output A job's performance standards.

outsourcing The use of external suppliers to provide training services.

overlearning Employees' continuing to practice even if they have been able to perform the objective several times.

past accomplishments System of allowing employees to build a history of successful accomplishments.

perception The ability to organize a message from the environment so that it can be processed and acted upon.

performance appraisal The process of measuring an employee's performance.

person analysis Training analysis involving (1) determining whether performance deficiencies result from lack of knowledge, skill, or ability or else from a motivational or work-design problem, (2) identifying who needs training, and (3) determining employees' readiness for training.

person characteristics An employee's knowledge, skill, ability, behavior or attitudes.

pilot testing The process of previewing a training program with potential trainees and managers or other customers.

plateauing A workplace situation with little likelihood of the employee receiving future job assignments with increased responsibility.

posttest only An evaluation design in which only posttraining outcomes are collected.

posttraining measure A measure of outcomes taken after training.

power The ability to influence others.

power distance Expectations for the unequal distribution of power in a hierarchy.

practicality The ease with which outcome measures can be collected.

practice An employee's demonstration of a learned capability.

preretirement socialization The process of helping employees prepare for exit from work.

presence In training, the perception of actually being in a particular environment.

presentation methods Training methods in which trainees are passive recipients of information.

pretest/posttest An evaluation design in which both pretraining and posttraining outcomes measures are collected.

pretest/posttest with comparison group   An evaluation design that includes trainees and a comparison group. Both pretraining and posttraining outcome measures are collected.

pretraining measure   A baseline measure of outcomes.

program design   The organization and coordination of the training program.

program objectives   Broad summary statements of a program's purpose.

promotion   An advancement into a position with greater challenges, more responsibility, and more authority than the previous job provided; usually includes a pay increase.

protean career   A career that is frequently changing based on changes in the person's interests, abilities, and values as well as changes in the work environment.

psychological contract   The expectations that employers and employees have about each other, and the employment relationship.

psychological success   A feeling of pride and accomplishment that comes from achieving life goals.

psychosocial support   Serving as a friend and role model to an employee; also includes providing positive regard, acceptance, and an outlet for the protégé to talk about anxieties and fears.

quality challenge   The challenge of meeting customers' service and product needs.

random assignment   The assignment of employees to training or a comparison group on the basis of chance.

reaction outcomes   A trainee's perceptions of a training program, including perceptions of the facilities, trainers, and content.

readability   Written materials' level of difficulty.

readiness for training   The condition of (1) employees having the personal characteristics necessary to learn program content and apply it on the job and (2) the work environment facilitating learning and not interfering with performance.

realistic job preview   Stage in which a prospective employee is provided accurate information about attractive and unattractive aspects of a job, working conditions, company, and location to be sure that he develops appropriate expectations.

reality check   Information an employee receives about how the company values her skills and knowledge as well as where she fits into the company's plans.

reasonable accommodation   In terms of the Americans with Disabilities Act and training, making training facilities readily accessible to and usable by individuals with disabilities; may also include modifying instructional media, adjusting training policies, and providing trainees with readers or interpreters.

recycling   Changing one's major work activity after having been established in a particular field.

reengineering   A complete review and redesign of critical processes to make them more efficient and able to deliver higher quality.

reinforcement theory   Theory emphasizing that people are motivated to perform or avoid certain behaviors because of past outcomes that have resulted from those behaviors.

reliability   The degree to which outcomes can be measured consistently over time.

repatriation   Preparing expatriates for return to the parent company and country from a foreign assignment.

repurposing   Directly translating a training program that uses a traditional training method onto the Web.

request for proposal (RFP)   A document that outlines for potential vendors and consultants the requirements for winning and fulfilling a contract with a company.

resistance to change   Managers' and/or employees' unwillingness to change.

results   Outcomes used to determine a training program's payoff.

retirement   The leaving of a job and work role to make the transition into life without work.

retrieval   The identification of learned material in long-term memory and use of it to influence performance.

return on investment (ROI)   A comparison of a training program's monetary benefits and costs.

role play   A training exercise in which the participant takes the part or role of a manager or some other employee; training method in which trainees are given information about a situation and act out characters assigned to them.

sabbatical   A leave of absence from the company to renew or develop skills.

scenario analysis   Simulation of real-world issues presented to data end-users.

School-to-Work Opportunities Act (1994)   Federal act designed to assist the states in building school-to-work systems that prepare students for high-skill, high-wage jobs or future education.

school-to-work transition program   Program combining classroom experience with work experience to prepare high school students for employment after graduation.

self-assessment   An employee's use of information to determine her career interests, values, aptitudes, and behavioral tendencies.

self-directed learning   Training in which employees take responsibility for all aspects of their learning (e.g., when it occurs, who is involved).

self-efficacy   An employee's belief that she can successfully perform her job or learn the content of a training program.

self-management   person's attempt to control certain aspects of his decision making and behavior.

semantic encoding   The actual coding process of incoming memory.

settling-in phase   Final phase in organizational socialization in which an employee begins to feel comfortable with her job demands and social relationships.

simulation   A training method that represents a real-life situation, with trainees' decisions resulting in outcomes that mirror what would happen if they were on the job.

situational constraints   Work environment characteristics including lack of proper equipment, materials, supplies, budgetary support, and time.

skill   Competency in performing a task.

skill-based outcomes   Outcomes used to assess the level of technical or motor skills or behavior; include skill acquisition or learning and on-the-job use of skills.

skill-based pay system   Pay system based primarily on an employee's skills rather than on the skills necessary to perform his job (also called knowledge-based pay system).

social challenge   The challenge of managing a diverse work force and improving employees' reading, writing, and math skills.

social learning theory   Theory emphasizing that people learn by observing other persons (models) whom they believe are credible and knowledgeable.

social support   Feedback and reinforcement from managers and peers.

Solomon four-group   An evaluation design combining the pretest/posttest comparison group and the posttest-only control group designs.

staffing strategy   A company's decisions regarding where to find employees, how to select them, and the mix of employee skills and statuses.

stakeholders   The parties with an interest in a company's success (include shareholders, employees, customers, and the community).

stimulus generalization approach   The construction of training to emphasize the most important features or general principles.

strain-based conflict   Conflict resulting from the stress of work and nonwork roles.

subject matter expert (SME)   Person who is knowledgeable of (1) training issues, (2) knowledge, skills, and abilities required for task performance, (3) necessary equipment, and (4) conditions under which tasks have to be performed.

succession planning   The process of identifying and tracking high-potential employees for advancement in a company.

summative evaluation   Evaluation of the extent that trainees have changed due to participating in a training program.

support network   A group of two or more trainees who agree to meet and discuss their progress in using learned capabilities on the job.

survivor   An employee remaining with a company after downsizing.

SWOT analysis   An identification of a company's operating environment as well as an internal analysis of its strengths and weaknesses. SWOT is an acronym for strengths, weaknesses, opportunities, and threats.

system-level learning   A company's ability to preserve what is learned over time.

task   A statement of an employee's work activity in a specific job.

task analysis   Training analysis involving identifying the tasks and knowledge, skills, and behaviors that need to be emphasized in training for employees to complete their tasks.

task redefinition   Changes in managers' and/or employees' roles and methods.

team leader training　Training that a team manager or facilitator receives.

team training　Training method that involves coordinating the performances of individuals who work together to achieve a common goal.

theory of identical elements　A theory that transfer of learning occurs when what is learned in training is identical to what the trainee has to perform on the job.

threats to validity　Factors that will lead one to question either (1) study results' believability or (2) the extent to which evaluation results are generalizable to other groups of trainees and situations.

time-based conflict　Situation in which the demands of work and nonwork interfere with each other.

time series　An evaluation design in which training outcomes are collected at periodic intervals pre- and posttraining.

Total Quality Management　A style of doing business that relies on the talents and capabilities of both labor and management to build and provide high quality products and services and continuously improve them.

trainee characteristics　The abilities and motivation that affect learning.

training　A company's planned effort to facilitate employees' learning of job-related competencies.

training administration　Coordination of activities before, during, and after a training program.

training design　Characteristics of the learning environment.

training effectiveness　Benefits that a company and its trainees receive from training.

training evaluation　The process of collecting the outcomes needed to determine if training has been effective.

training outcomes (criteria)　Measures that a company and its trainer use to evaluate training programs.

training site　The place where training is conducted.

transfer　Giving an employee a different job assignment in a different area of the company.

transfer of training　Trainees' applying learned capabilities gained in training to their jobs.

uncertainty avoidance　A preference for structured rather than unstructured situations.

upward feedback　An appraisal process involving collection of subordinates' evaluations of managers' behaviors or skills.

valence　The value that a person places on an outcome.

verbal information　Names or labels, facts, and bodies of knowledge.

verbal persuasion　Offering words of encouragement to convince others that they can learn.

virtual reality　A computer-based technology that provides trainees with a three-dimensional learning experience.

virtual training organization　A training organization operating on four principles: (1) employees, rather than the company, have primary responsibility for learning, (2) training needs to be developed to meet customer needs, (3) the most effective learning occurs on the job, and (4) the manager-employee relationship is critical for training to be translated into improved job performance.

work environment:　On-the-job factors that influence transfer of training.

working storage:　The rehearsal and repetition of information, allowing it to be coded for memory.

World Wide Web:　A user-friendly service on the Internet; provides browser software enabling users to explore the Web.

C O M P A N Y   I N D E X

Page numbers in **bold typeface** represent terms in the glossary.